GROWING OLD
IN AMERICA

ISSN 1538-6686

GROWING OLD IN AMERICA

Barbara Wexler

INFORMATION PLUS® REFERENCE SERIES
Formerly Published by Information Plus, Wylie, Texas

GALE
CENGAGE Learning·

Farmington Hills, Mich • San Francisco • New York • Waterville, Maine
Meriden, Conn • Mason, Ohio • Chicago

Growing Old in America

Barbara Wexler

Kepos Media, Inc.: Steven Long and Janice Jorgensen, Series Editors

Project Editors: Kimberley A. McGrath, Kathleen J. Edgar, Elizabeth Manar

Rights Acquisition and Management: Sheila R. Spencer

Composition: Evi Abou-El-Seoud, Mary Beth Trimper

Manufacturing: Rita Wimberley

Gale
27500 Drake Rd.
Farmington Hills, MI 48331-3535

ISBN-13: 978-0-7876-5103-9 (set)
ISBN-13: 978-1-56995-799-8

ISSN 1538-6686

This title is also available as an e-book.
ISBN-13: 978-1-56995-839-1 (set)
Contact your Gale sales representative for ordering information.

Printed in the United States of America
1 2 3 4 5 6 7 18 17 16 15 14

TABLE OF CONTENTS

PREFACE vii

CHAPTER 1

Older Americans: A Diverse and Growing Population . . . 1

This chapter introduces readers to older Americans of the 21st century. It defines terms that are used when discussing aging and older adults and explains why the U.S. population is growing older. Along with demographic data, this chapter examines attitudes about aging and older adults.

CHAPTER 2

The Economics of Growing Old in the United States . . . 19

This chapter begins with a discussion of some measures that are used to determine economic security, such as net worth and median income. It details income sources for older adults and considers pension funds. Consumer spending trends among older Americans are also documented. Furthermore, an in-depth description of the Social Security program and threats to its continued viability are provided.

CHAPTER 3

Living Arrangements of the Older Population 45

The varied housing arrangements of older Americans, including living with family members, board-and-care facilities, nursing homes, assisted living facilities, shared housing, public housing, and retirement communities are surveyed in this chapter. The challenges of "aging in place" and retrofitting homes to accommodate disabled older adults are described.

CHAPTER 4

Working and Retirement: New Options for Older Adults 63

Older Americans make great contributions to society in both paid and unpaid roles. Discussed in this chapter are changes in lifestyles (from linear to cyclic life paths) and the economy (from agricultural to industrial to service-oriented) that make these contributions possible. Labor participation and volunteerism are reviewed, as are common stereotypes about older workers and age discrimination. Also covered are ways in which older adults are defining and redefining retirement.

CHAPTER 5

Education, Voting, and Political Behavior 81

Greater numbers of older Americans are pursuing continuing education and are active in politics. This chapter outlines the educational attainment of today's older adults and examines trends toward lifetime learning and growing computer literacy. Also explored is the political clout of the older population: their voting conduct and party affiliations and their force as a political bloc.

CHAPTER 6

On the Road: Older Adult Drivers 91

The ability to drive often determines whether an older adult is able to live independently. This chapter investigates driving safety issues, strategies to make driving easier for older adults, and alternative transportation for older Americans who cannot, or choose not to, drive.

CHAPTER 7

The Health and Medical Problems of Older Adults 101

This chapter addresses the epidemiology of aging—the distribution and determinants of health and illness among older adults. It profiles trends in aging and the health of aging Americans; distinctions among healthy aging, disease, and disability; health promotion and prevention as applied to older people; and selected diseases and conditions common in old age.

CHAPTER 8

Mental Health and Mental Illness 131

Changes in mental capabilities are among the most feared aspects of aging. Mental health problems that impair functioning are also among the most common age-related changes. This chapter focuses on how the number of people with mental impairments such as dementia is anticipated to increase as the population ages; why older adults with mental impairment are at risk for institutionalization; and how the financial costs to individuals and to society are expected to escalate.

CHAPTER 9

Caring for Older Adults: Caregivers 145

In the United States most long-term care of older adults continues to be provided by families as opposed to nursing homes, assisted living facilities, social service agencies, and government programs. This chapter explores the continuing commitment to family care of older adults in view of relatively recent changes in the fabric of American society. It also includes descriptions of programs that are aimed at supporting caregivers.

CHAPTER 10

Health Care Use, Expenditures, and Financing 151

Trends in health care use, expenditures, and financing, as well as coverage of the government entitlement programs Medicare and

Medicaid, are presented in this chapter. It also reports on the impact of health care reform legislation on older adults. The challenges of long-term care are highlighted along with in-home services that enable older adults to remain in the community.

also delves into the types of frauds that are perpetrated against the older population, domestic and institutional abuse, and mistreatment.

CHAPTER 11
Crime and Abuse of Older Adults 169
This chapter enumerates the rates and types of crime against older Americans, including characteristics of older crime victims. It

IMPORTANT NAMES AND ADDRESSES. 181

RESOURCES. 185

INDEX 187

PREFACE

Growing Old in America is part of the *Information Plus Reference Series*. The purpose of each volume of the series is to present the latest facts on a topic of pressing concern in modern American life. These topics include the most controversial and studied social issues of the 21st century: abortion, capital punishment, crime, the environment, health care, immigration, national security, social welfare, weight, women, youth, and many more. Although this series is written especially for high school and undergraduate students, it is an excellent resource for anyone in need of factual information on current affairs.

By presenting the facts, it is the intention of Gale, Cengage Learning to provide its readers with everything they need to reach an informed opinion on current issues. To that end, there is a particular emphasis in this series on the presentation of scientific studies, surveys, and statistics. These data are generally presented in the form of tables, charts, and other graphics placed within the text of each book. Every graphic is directly referred to and carefully explained in the text. The source of each graphic is presented within the graphic itself. The data used in these graphics are drawn from the most reputable and reliable sources, such as from the various branches of the U.S. government and from private organizations and associations. Every effort has been made to secure the most recent information available. Readers should bear in mind that many major studies take years to conduct and that additional years often pass before the data from these studies are made available to the public. Therefore, in many cases the most recent information available in 2014 is dated from 2010 or 2011. Older statistics are sometimes presented as well if they are landmark studies or of particular interest and no more-recent data are available.

Although statistics are a major focus of the *Information Plus Reference Series*, they are by no means its only content. Each book also presents the widely held positions and important ideas that shape how the book's subject is discussed in the United States. These positions are explained in detail and, where possible, in the words of their proponents. Some of the other material to be found in these books includes historical background, descriptions of major events related to the subject, relevant laws and court cases, and examples of how these issues play out in American life. Some books also feature primary documents or have pro and con debate sections that provide the words and opinions of prominent Americans on both sides of a controversial topic. All material is presented in an evenhanded and unbiased manner; readers will never be encouraged to accept one view of an issue over another.

HOW TO USE THIS BOOK

The percentage of Americans over the age of 65 years has increased over the past century, and will continue to increase as children born during the mid-20th-century baby boom age. This book explores the current condition of aging in the United States. Included is a general overview on growing old in the United States, the economic status of older people, the Social Security program, Medicare and Medicaid, the living arrangements of older adults, working and retirement, and the education levels and political behavior of older Americans. Physical and mental health problems, drug and alcohol abuse, care for older adults, and crime and victimization of older adults are also covered.

Growing Old in America consists of 11 chapters and three appendixes. Each chapter is devoted to a particular aspect of aging. For a summary of the information that is covered in each chapter, please see the synopses that are provided in the Table of Contents. Chapters generally begin with an overview of the basic facts and background information on the chapter's topic, then proceed to examine subtopics of particular interest. For example, Chapter 2: The Economics of Growing Old in the United States, begins by examining the economic status of older Americans in comparison to other age groups. This is followed by a discussion of the income distribution of older adults, their net worth, and the extent to which they rely on public and private pensions, personal savings, and Social Security in retirement. The chapter concludes with a discussion of the challenges faced by the Social Security program and the ways to ensure its long-term solvency. Readers can find their way through a chapter by looking for the section and subsection headings, which are clearly set off from the text. They can also refer to the book's extensive Index if they already know what they are looking for.

Statistical Information

The tables and figures featured throughout *Growing Old in America* will be of particular use to readers in learning about this issue. These tables and figures represent an extensive collection of the most recent and important statistics on growing old and related issues— for example, graphics cover the living arrangements of older adults, the marital status of older Americans, chronic health conditions, crimes against older Americans, health care costs paid by Medicare and Medicaid, health insurance coverage, and how older adults are redefining retirement. Gale, Cengage Learning believes that making this information available to readers is the most important way to fulfill the goal of this book: to help readers understand the issues and controversies surrounding growing old in the United States and to reach their own conclusions.

Each table or figure has a unique identifier appearing above it for ease of identification and reference. Titles for the tables and figures explain their purpose. At the end of each table or figure, the original source of the data is provided.

To help readers understand these often complicated statistics, all tables and figures are explained in the text. References in the text direct readers to the relevant statistics. Furthermore, the contents of all tables and figures are fully indexed. Please see the opening section of the Index at the back of this volume for a description of how to find tables and figures within it.

Appendixes

Besides the main body text and images, *Growing Old in America* has three appendixes. The first is the Important Names and Addresses directory. Here, readers will find contact information for a number of government and private organizations that can provide further information on growing old. The second appendix is the Resources section, which can also assist readers in conducting their own research. In this section, the author and editors of *Growing Old in America* describe some of the sources that were most useful during the compilation of this book. The final appendix is the detailed Index. It has been greatly expanded from previous editions and should make it even easier to find specific topics in this book.

COMMENTS AND SUGGESTIONS

The editors of the *Information Plus Reference Series* welcome your feedback on *Growing Old in America*. Please direct all correspondence to:

Editors
Information Plus Reference Series
27500 Drake Rd.
Farmington Hills, MI 48331-3535

CHAPTER 1

OLDER AMERICANS: A DIVERSE AND GROWING POPULATION

Old age is the most unexpected of all the things that happen to a man.

—Leon Trotsky

THE UNITED STATES GROWS OLDER

The United States is aging. Throughout the second half of the 20th century and the first two decades of the 21st century the country's older population—adults aged 65 years and older—increased significantly. According to the Administration on Aging (AoA), in *A Profile of Older Americans: 2012* (April 2013, http://www.aoa.gov/ Aging_Statistics/Profile/2012/docs/2012profile.pdf), the number of older adults grew from 35 million in 2000 to 41.4 million in 2011 (the most recent year for which comprehensive data, as opposed to estimates or projections, were available as of July 2013), which represented 13.3% of the total U.S. population. In *The Next Four Decades—The Older Population in the United States: 2010 to 2050* (May 2010, http://www.census.gov/prod/ 2010pubs/p25-1138.pdf), Grayson K. Vincent and Victoria A. Velkoff of the U.S. Census Bureau project that by 2030 one out of five U.S. residents will be aged 65 years and older and that by 2050 the population of people aged 65 years and older will number 88.5 million. Table 1.1 shows projections of the growth in the population of older adults between 2010 and 2050. It also shows how older adults will make up an increasing percentage of the total U.S. population, growing from 13% in 2010 to 20.2% in 2050.

The Census Bureau reports in the press release "Older Americans Month: May 2013" (March 7, 2013, http://www.census.gov/newsroom/releases/archives/facts _for_features_special_editions/cb13-ff07.html) that the percentage of the global population that is aged 65 years and older will rise from 8% in 2013 to 17% in 2050. In 2050 the U.S. population aged 65 years and older will outnumber those aged 15 years and younger. Throughout the world, the growth in the population of older adults will outpace the growth of any other segment of the population. Figure 1.1 compares the percentages of young children (aged five years and younger) and adults aged 65 years and older of the global population between 1950 and 2050; it reveals a steady decline in the percentage of children and a sharp increase in the percentage of older adults between 2000 and 2050. Figure 1.2 shows how the percentage of the oldest older adults (people aged 80 years and older) is expected to increase. For example, in the United States the percentage of older adults aged 80 years and older is projected to increase by six percentage points between 2008 and 2040, from 29.5% to 35.5%. In Japan the percentage of people aged 80 years and older is projected to grow by nearly 12 percentage points during the same period, from 26.4% to 38%.

Fewer children per family and longer life spans have shifted the proportion of older adults in the population. Growth in the population segment of older adults in the United States, often called "the graying of America," is considered to be one of the most significant issues facing the country in the 21st century. The swelling population of people aged 65 years and older affects every aspect of society—challenging policy makers, health care providers, employers, families, and others to meet the needs of older Americans.

Many of the findings and statistics cited in this chapter, as well as a number of the tables and figures presented, are drawn from *Older Americans 2012: Key Indicators of Well-Being* (June 2012, http://www.agingstats.gov/Main _Site/Data/2012_Documents/docs/EntireChartbook.pdf), a report prepared by the Federal Interagency Forum on Aging-Related Statistics. This forum consists of 15 federal entities—the AoA, the Agency for Healthcare Research and Quality, the Centers for Medicare and Medicaid Services, the Census Bureau, the Employee Benefits Security

TABLE 1.1

Projected U.S. population by age, 2010–50

[Number in thousands]

Age	2010	2020	2030	2040	2050
Number					
Total	310,233	341,387	373,504	405,655	439,010
Under 20 years	84,150	90,703	97,682	104,616	112,940
20 to 64 years	185,854	195,880	203,729	219,801	237,523
65 years and over	40,229	54,804	72,092	81,238	88,547
65 to 69 years	12,261	17,861	20,381	18,989	21,543
70 to 74 years	9,202	14,452	18,404	17,906	18,570
75 to 79 years	7,282	9,656	14,390	16,771	15,964
80 to 84 years	5,733	6,239	10,173	13,375	13,429
85 to 89 years	3,650	3,817	5,383	8,450	10,303
90 years and over	2,101	2,780	3,362	5,748	8,738
Percent					
Total	100.0	100.0	100.0	100.0	100.0
Under 20 years	27.1	26.6	26.2	25.8	25.7
20 to 64 years	59.9	57.4	54.5	54.2	54.1
65 years and over	13.0	16.1	19.3	20.0	20.2
65 to 69 years	4.0	5.2	5.5	4.7	4.9
70 to 74 years	3.0	4.2	4.9	4.4	4.2
75 to 79 years	2.3	2.8	3.9	4.1	3.6
80 to 84 years	1.8	1.8	2.7	3.3	3.1
85 to 89 years	1.2	1.1	1.4	2.1	2.3
90 years and over	0.7	0.8	0.9	1.4	2.0

SOURCE: Grayson K. Vincent and Victoria A. Velkoff, "Appendix Table A-1. Projections and Distribution of the Total Population by Age for the United States: 2010 to 2050," in *The Next Four Decades—The Older Population in the United States: 2010 to 2050*, U.S. Census Bureau, May 2010, http://www.census.gov/prod/2010pubs/p25-1138.pdf (accessed May 28, 2013)

FIGURE 1.1

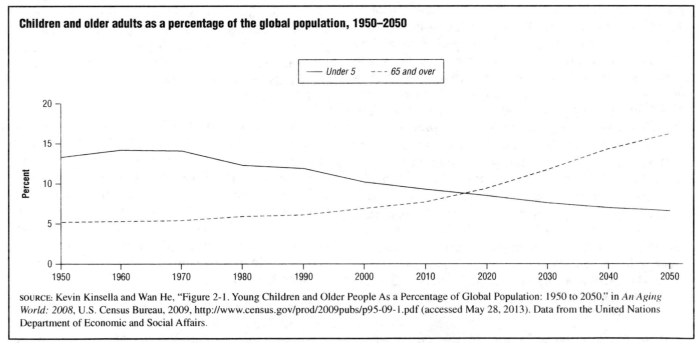

Children and older adults as a percentage of the global population, 1950–2050

SOURCE: Kevin Kinsella and Wan He, "Figure 2-1. Young Children and Older People As a Percentage of Global Population: 1950 to 2050," in *An Aging World: 2008*, U.S. Census Bureau, 2009, http://www.census.gov/prod/2009pubs/p95-09-1.pdf (accessed May 28, 2013). Data from the United Nations Department of Economic and Social Affairs.

Administration, the U.S. Bureau of Labor Statistics, the U.S. Department of Housing and Urban Development, the U.S. Department of Veterans Affairs, the U.S. Environmental Protection Agency, the National Center for Health Statistics (NCHS), the National Institute on Aging, the Office of Statistical and Science Policy, the Office of the Assistant Secretary for Planning and Evaluation (U.S. Department of Health and Human Services), the Office of Research, Evaluation, and Statistics, and the Substance Abuse and Mental Health Services Administration—that

FIGURE 1.2

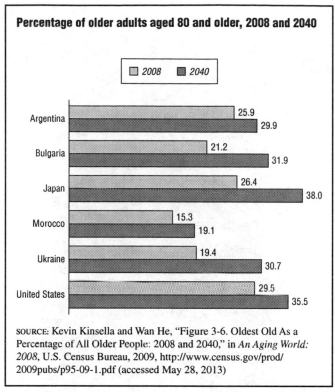

Percentage of older adults aged 80 and older, 2008 and 2040

☐ 2008   ■ 2040

Argentina — 25.9 / 29.9
Bulgaria — 21.2 / 31.9
Japan — 26.4 / 38.0
Morocco — 15.3 / 19.1
Ukraine — 19.4 / 30.7
United States — 29.5 / 35.5

SOURCE: Kevin Kinsella and Wan He, "Figure 3-6. Oldest Old As a Percentage of All Older People: 2008 and 2040," in *An Aging World: 2008*, U.S. Census Bureau, 2009, http://www.census.gov/prod/2009pubs/p95-09-1.pdf (accessed May 28, 2013)

are dedicated to encouraging cooperation and collaboration among federal agencies to improve the quality and utility of data on the aging population. Other data are drawn from the AoA's *Profile of Older Americans.*

To understand the aging of the United States, it is important to not only consider the current population of older adults but also to look at how the older population will fare over time. To anticipate the needs of this growing segment of society, policy makers, planners, and researchers rely on projections and population estimates. Population estimates and projections are made at different times and are based on different assumptions. Therefore, it is not surprising to find considerable variation in the statistics cited by different agencies and investigators. This chapter contains estimates and projections of demographic changes from several different sources, and as a result there is some variability in the data presented.

HOW DO POPULATIONS AGE?

Unlike people, populations can age or become younger. There are key indicators of the age structure of a given population. Populations age or grow younger because of changes in fertility (birth rates expressed as the number of births per 1,000 population per year) and/or mortality (death rates expressed as the number of deaths per 1,000 population per year) or in response to migration—people entering or leaving the population.

The aging of the United States in the early 21st century resulted from changes in fertility and mortality that occurred over the past century. Such shifts in birth and death rates are called demographic transitions. Generally, population aging is primarily a response to long-term declines in fertility, and declining fertility is the basic cause of the aging of the U.S. population. Reduced infant and child mortality, chiefly as a result of public health measures, fueled the decline in the fertility rate; that is, the increased survival of children prompted families to have fewer offspring. The birth of fewer babies resulted in fewer young people.

According to the Central Intelligence Agency (CIA), in *The World Factbook: United States* (July 10, 2013, https://www.cia.gov/library/publications/the-world-factbook/geos/us.html), in 2013 the total fertility rate in the United States was two children born per woman. This rate, which has not changed significantly since the mid-1980s, is sharply lower than the fertility rates between 1946 and 1964, following the end of World War II (1939–1945). Victorious U.S. soldiers returning home after the war were eager to start families, and this was facilitated by the relatively prosperous postwar economy.

Census Bureau statistics indicate that during this period, which came to be known as the baby boom, U.S. fertility rates exploded, at one point approaching four children born per woman. Children born during the baby boom became known as baby boomers, and it is this huge cohort (a group of individuals that shares a common characteristic such as birth years and is studied over time) that is responsible for the tremendous increase projected in the number of people aged 65 years and older, and especially aged 65 to 74 years. The older adult segment of the population is expected to swell until 2030, as the baby boom cohort completes its transition from middle age to old age.

The decline in death rates, especially at the older ages, has also contributed to the increase in the number of older adults. The death rates of older adults began to decrease during the late 1960s and continued to decline through the first decade of the 21st century. Advances in medical care have produced declining death rates for all three of the leading causes of death: heart disease, malignancies (cancer), and cerebrovascular diseases that cause strokes. Arialdi M. Miniño of the NCHS reports in "Death in the United States, 2011" (*NCHS Data Brief*, no. 115, March 2013) that the age-adjusted death rate in the United States reached an all-time low of 740.6 deaths per 100,000 population in 2011, down from 747 deaths per 100,000 population in 2010.

Projections of an increasing proportion of older adults between 2012 and 2030 are based on three assumptions: historic low fertility and the prospect of continuing low fertility until 2030, aging of the baby boom cohort, and continued declines in mortality at older

FIGURE 1.3

Baby boomers' contribution to the U.S. population in 2012, 2035, and 2060

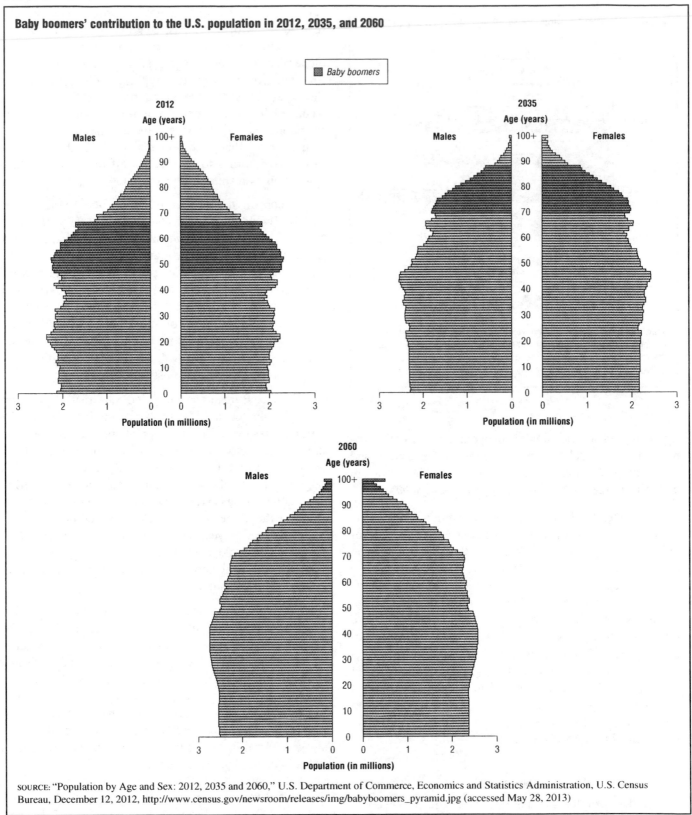

SOURCE: "Population by Age and Sex: 2012, 2035 and 2060," U.S. Department of Commerce, Economics and Statistics Administration, U.S. Census Bureau, December 12, 2012, http://www.census.gov/newsroom/releases/img/babyboomers_pyramid.jpg (accessed May 28, 2013)

ages and low mortality until 2030. Demographers (those who study population statistics) expect that when the entire baby boom generation has attained age 65 (or older) in 2030, the proportion of older people in the U.S. population will stabilize. Figure 1.3 shows how the baby boomers will make a smaller contribution to the population over time, from about 25% of the population in 2012 to 0.6% in 2060.

DEFINING OLD AGE

Forty is the old age of youth; fifty the youth of old age.

—Victor Hugo

When does old age begin? The challenge of defining old age is reflected in the terminology that is used to describe adults aged 50 years and older: for example, middle aged, elder, elderly, older, aged, mature, or senior. The AARP (formerly the American Association of Retired Persons), a national advocacy organization for older adults, invites people to join its ranks at age 50. Many retailers offer senior discounts to people aged 50 or 55 years and older, and federal entitlement programs such as Medicare (a medical insurance program for older adults and people with disabilities) extend benefits to people at age 65, while Social Security (a program that provides retirement income and health care for older adults) benefits may begin as early as age 62. Despite the varying definitions of old age and the age at which one assumes "older adult" status, in this text, unless otherwise specified, the term *older adults* is used to refer to people aged 65 years and older.

Gerontology (the field of study that considers the social, psychological, and biological aspects of aging) distinguishes among three groups of older adults: the young-old are considered to be those aged 65 to 74 years, the middle-old includes those aged 75 to 84 years, and the oldest-old are those aged 85 years and older. Figure 1.4 shows that the oldest segment of older adults, the oldest-old, grew from just over 100,000 in 1900 to 5.5 million in 2010 and is projected to increase to 19 million by 2050.

LIFE EXPECTANCY

Life expectancy (the anticipated average length of life) has increased dramatically since 1900, when the average age of death for men and women combined was 47.3 years. In *Health, United States, 2012* (May 2013, http://www.cdc.gov/nchs/data/hus/hus12.pdf), the NCHS reports that between 2000 and 2010 life expectancy increased by 2.1 years for males and by 1.7 years for females. Most projections see life expectancy continuing to rise; according to the CIA, in *World Factbook: United States*, the life expectancy of a baby born in the United States in 2013 was 76.2 years for males and 81.2 years for females.

However, some researchers caution that the historic trend of increasing longevity has ended, with life expectancy at birth beginning to decline by as much as five years as a direct result of the obesity epidemic in the United States. For example, James A. Greenberg of Brooklyn College estimates in "Obesity and Early Mortality in the United States" (*Obesity*, vol. 21, no. 2, February 2013) that the rise in obesity in the United States may slow or

FIGURE 1.4

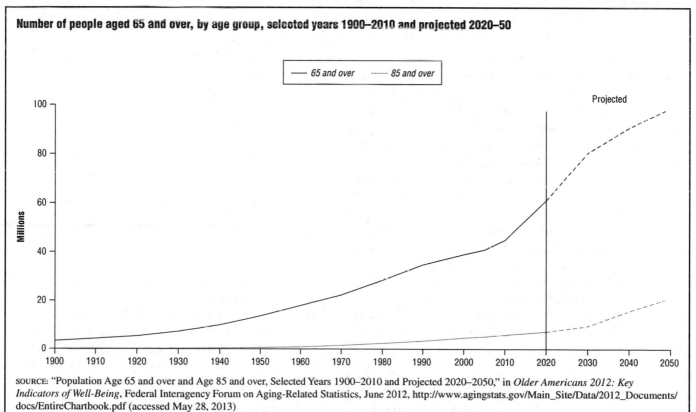

Number of people aged 65 and over, by age group, selected years 1900–2010 and projected 2020–50

SOURCE: "Population Age 65 and over and Age 85 and over, Selected Years 1900–2010 and Projected 2020–2050," in *Older Americans 2012: Key Indicators of Well-Being*, Federal Interagency Forum on Aging-Related Statistics, June 2012, http://www.agingstats.gov/Main_Site/Data/2012_Documents/docs/EntireChartbook.pdf (accessed May 28, 2013)

even reverse the long-term trend of increasing life expectancy. Greenberg bases his projections on an analysis of the body mass index (a number that shows body weight adjusted for height) and finds that obesity currently reduces life expectancy by 9.4 years.

Obesity has an impact not only on life expectancy but also on the health of older adults because obese older adults are more likely than their healthy-weight peers to experience obesity-related conditions such as heart disease, diabetes, arthritis, and some cancers. Furthermore, in "Effect of Obesity on Falls, Injury, and Disability" (*Journal of the American Geriatric Society*, vol. 60, no. 1, January 2012), Christine L. Himes and Sandra L. Reynolds find that obesity is associated with a greater risk of falling in older adults and with a higher risk of disability after a fall.

Global Life Expectancy

The more developed regions of the world have lower death rates than the less developed regions and, as such, have higher life expectancies. In *World Factbook*, the CIA observes that some nations more than doubled their life expectancy during the 20th century. In 2013 the projected life expectancy at birth in Monaco was 89.6 years, and it was at least 79 years in many developed countries. (See Table 1.2.) Many less developed countries have also seen a steady increase in life expectancy, except for countries in Africa that have been hard hit by the human immunodeficiency virus (HIV)/acquired immunodeficiency syndrome (AIDS) epidemic. Table 1.2 shows ranks of the top-51 countries in terms of life expectancy in 2013—the United States is number 51.

Although the United Nations' Department of Economic and Social Affairs predicts in *World Population Prospects: The 2012 Revision—Key Findings and Advance Tables* (2013, http://esa.un.org/wpp/Documentation/pdf/WPP2012_%20KEY%20FINDINGS.pdf) that the gap in life expectancy will narrow during the first half of the 21st century, the developed world will still be far ahead. Table 1.3 reveals this gap and the ranks of the 30 countries with the lowest estimates of life expectancy in 2013. South Africa and Chad had the lowest life expectancy at 49.5 and 49.1 years, respectively. Ahmad Reza Hosseinpoor et al. explain in "International Shortfall Inequality in Life Expectancy in Women and in Men, 1950–2010" (*Bulletin of the World Health Organization*, vol. 90, no. 8, August 2012) that many factors contribute to lower life expectancy in developing countries—chief among them are poverty, inadequate medical care, alcohol and tobacco use, and the HIV/AIDS epidemic.

OLDER ADULTS IN THE UNITED STATES

According to U.S. Census estimates, in 2015 there will be an estimated 47.7 million people aged 65 years

TABLE 1.2

Estimated life expectancy at birth by country, 2013

Rank	Country	(Years)	Date of information
1	Monaco	89.63	2013 est.
2	Macau	84.46	2013 est.
3	Japan	84.19	2013 est.
4	Singapore	84.07	2013 est.
5	San Marino	83.12	2013 est.
6	Andorra	82.58	2013 est.
7	Guernsey	82.32	2013 est.
8	Switzerland	82.28	2013 est.
9	Hong Kong	82.20	2013 est.
10	Australia	81.98	2013 est.
11	Italy	81.95	2013 est.
12	Liechtenstein	81.59	2013 est.
13	Canada	81.57	2013 est.
14	Jersey	81.57	2013 est.
15	France	81.56	2013 est.
16	Spain	81.37	2013 est.
17	Sweden	81.28	2013 est.
18	Israel	81.17	2013 est.
19	Iceland	81.11	2013 est.
20	Anguilla	81.09	2013 est.
21	Netherlands	81.01	2013 est.
22	Bermuda	80.93	2013 est.
23	Cayman Islands	80.91	2013 est.
24	Isle of Man	80.87	2013 est.
25	New Zealand	80.82	2013 est.
26	Ireland	80.44	2013 est.
27	Norway	80.44	2013 est.
28	Germany	80.32	2013 est.
29	Jordan	80.30	2013 est.
30	United Kingdom	80.29	2013 est.
31	Greece	80.18	2013 est.
32	Saint Pierre and Miquelon	80.13	2013 est.
33	Austria	80.04	2013 est.
34	Malta	79.98	2013 est.
35	Faroe Islands	79.98	2013 est.
36	European Union	79.90	2013 est.
37	Luxembourg	79.88	2013 est.
38	Belgium	79.78	2013 est.
39	Taiwan	79.71	2013 est.
40	Virgin Islands	79.61	2013 est.
41	Finland	79.55	2013 est.
42	Korea, South	79.55	2013 est.
43	Turks and Caicos Islands	79.40	2013 est.
44	Wallis and Futuna	79.27	2013 est.
45	Puerto Rico	79.07	2013 est.
46	Saint Helena, Ascension, and Tristan da Cunha	79.06	2013 est.
47	Gibraltar	78.98	2013 est.
48	Denmark	78.94	2013 est.
49	Portugal	78.85	2013 est.
50	Guam	78.66	2013 est.
51	United States	78.62	2013 est.

SOURCE: Adapted from "Country Comparison: Life Expectancy at Birth," in *The World Factbook*, Central Intelligence Agency, 2013, https://www.cia.gov/library/publications/the-world-factbook/rankorder/2102rank.html (accessed May 28, 2013)

and older living in the United States. (See Table 1.4.) The young-old bracket (aged 65 to 74 years) will account for 58% (27.5 million) of the 65 and older population. Twenty-nine percent (13.9 million) of the older adult population will be in the middle-old bracket (aged 75 to 84 years), and 13% (6.3 million) will make up the oldest-old bracket (aged 85 years and older).

By 2020 the number of young-old is projected to rise to 32.8 million, the middle-old will be nearing 16.5 million,

TABLE 1.3

Countries with lowest estimated life expectancy at birth, 2013

Rank	Country	(Years)	Date of information
194	Burundi	59.69	2013 est.
195	Guinea	59.11	2013 est.
196	Rwanda	58.85	2013 est.
197	Liberia	57.81	2013 est.
198	Côte d'Ivoire	57.66	2013 est.
199	Sierra Leone	56.98	2013 est.
200	Congo, Democratic Republic of the	56.14	2013 est.
201	Congo, Republic of the	55.60	2013 est.
202	Cameroon	55.02	2013 est.
203	Angola	54.95	2013 est.
204	Mali	54.55	2013 est.
205	Botswana	54.47	2013 est.
206	Burkina Faso	54.43	2013 est.
207	Niger	54.34	2013 est.
208	Uganda	53.98	2013 est.
209	Zimbabwe	53.86	2013 est.
210	Malawi	52.78	2013 est.
211	Nigeria	52.46	2013 est.
212	Lesotho	52.30	2013 est.
213	Mozambique	52.29	2013 est.
214	Gabon	52.15	2013 est.
215	Namibia	52.03	2013 est.
216	Zambia	51.51	2013 est.
217	Somalia	51.19	2013 est.
218	Central African Republic	50.90	2013 est.
219	Afghanistan	50.11	2013 est.
220	Swaziland	50.01	2013 est.
221	Guinea-Bissau	49.50	2013 est.
222	South Africa	49.48	2013 est.
223	Chad	49.07	2013 est.

SOURCE: Adapted from "Country Comparison: Life Expectancy at Birth," in *The World Factbook*, Central Intelligence Agency, 2013, https://www.cia.gov/library/publications/the-world-factbook/rankorder/2102rank.html (accessed May 28, 2013)

and the oldest-old will be 6.7 million. (See Table 1.4.) Older women are expected to outnumber men in all three age brackets. Longer female life expectancy, combined with the fact that men often marry younger women, contributes to a higher proportion of older women living alone—widowed or unmarried.

The Oldest-Old

The AoA states in *Profile of Older Americans* that in 2011 adults who reached "age 65 had an average life expectancy of an additional 19.2 years (20.4 years for females and 17.8 years for males)." The 85 and older population will grow from 5.7 million in 2010 to 6.6 million in 2020, an increase of 15% for that decade.

In *Older Americans 2012*, the Federal Interagency Forum on Aging-Related Statistics notes that some researchers believe death rates at older ages will decline more rapidly than is reflected in Census Bureau projections, which will result in even faster growth of this population segment. The Census Bureau reports that among the oldest-old, women dramatically outnumber men—in 2015 there will be nearly twice as many women aged 85 years and older than men. (See Table 1.4.) Because it is anticipated that women will

continue to live longer into the middle of the 21st century, they will make up an even larger proportion of the older population and the overall U.S. population in the future.

THE WORLD'S 80-PLUS POPULATION. According to the World Health Organization, in "Are You Ready? What You Need to Know about Ageing" (2013, http://www.who.int/world-health-day/2012/toolkit/background/en/index.html), between 2000 and 2050 the number of people aged 80 years and older is estimated to quadruple to 395 million. Furthermore, people aged 80 years and older will make up the fastest-growing population segment in the world. In *The Demography of Population Aging* (2001, http://www.un.org/esa/population/publications/bulletin42_43/weinbergermirkin.pdf), Barry Mirkin and Mary Beth Weinberger of the United Nations indicate that the 80 and older population will grow from just 1% of the world's population in 2000 to 4% in 2050. In developed countries, one out of 11 people will be aged 80 years or older in 2050. The U.S. population aged 80 years and older is estimated to reach 12.1 million by 2015. (See Table 1.4.)

Centenarians

During the first half of the 21st century the United States will experience a centenarian boom. Living to age 100 and older is no longer a rarity. The chances of living to age 100 have increased by 40% since 1900. The centenarian population more than doubled during the 1980s, and the Census Bureau estimates in "Older Americans Month: May 2013" that in 2010 the country had 53,364 centenarians. By 2050 the number of centenarians will increase more than eightfold to 442,000. (See Table 1.4.)

As the numbers and percentages of all older adults increase, the shape of the U.S. population pyramid (also called the age-sex pyramid and the age structure diagram), which graphically displays the projected population by age, will change. Figure 1.5 shows how the projected population distribution in 2030 and 2050 differs from the distribution in 2010. By 2050 all age groups are projected to be larger than they were in 2010.

According to the Guinness World Records (2013, http://www.guinnessworldrecords.com/records-5000/oldest-person/), the oldest verified age attained by a human is 122 years and 164 days. The Guinness World Records relies on the Gerontology Research Group (GRG; http://www.grg.org/calment.html), which tracks supercentenarians (people aged 110 years and older). The GRG reports that as of June 2013, it had validated 60 living supercentenarians: 55 women and 5 men.

On April 19, 2013, Jiroemon Kimura, the oldest person in the world, celebrated his 116th birthday. In

TABLE 1.4

Projections of the population by age and sex, 2015–60

[Resident population as of July 1. Numbers in thousands.]

Sex and age	2015	2020	2025	2030	2035	2040	2045	2050	2055	2060
Both sexes	321,363	333,896	346,407	358,471	369,662	380,016	389,934	399,803	409,873	420,268
Under 5 years	21,051	21,808	22,115	22,252	22,516	23,004	23,591	24,115	24,479	24,748
5 to 9 years	20,422	21,307	22,104	22,451	22,611	22,886	23,387	23,983	24,516	24,887
10 to 14 years	20,508	20,616	21,534	22,365	22,728	22,893	23,175	23,682	24,284	24,821
15 to 19 years	20,940	20,806	20,972	21,946	22,801	23,174	23,350	23,642	24,158	24,765
20 to 24 years	22,580	21,651	21,646	21,940	22,979	23,863	24,263	24,463	24,775	25,305
25 to 29 years	22,352	23,366	22,579	22,712	23,081	24,151	25,065	25,493	25,717	26,048
30 to 34 years	21,589	22,906	24,019	23,340	23,532	23,924	25,015	25,949	26,395	26,634
35 to 39 years	20,277	21,869	23,247	24,423	23,788	24,002	24,411	25,513	26,456	26,911
40 to 44 years	20,109	20,361	21,988	23,403	24,611	24,000	24,234	24,655	25,763	26,710
45 to 49 years	20,752	20,008	20,293	21,935	23,368	24,595	24,011	24,262	24,692	25,804
50 to 54 years	22,266	20,467	19,769	20,083	21,731	23,176	24,419	23,866	24,137	24,579
55 to 59 years	21,771	21,747	20,039	19,393	19,737	21,384	22,839	24,094	23,581	23,874
60 to 64 years	19,050	21,017	21,052	19,454	18,864	19,242	20,888	22,348	23,610	23,147
65 to 69 years	16,036	18,052	19,980	20,077	18,611	18,090	18,512	20,144	21,602	22,863
70 to 74 years	11,459	14,744	16,666	18,516	18,669	17,374	16,941	17,410	19,002	20,437
75 to 79 years	8,102	10,010	12,955	14,722	16,431	16,640	15,569	15,243	15,754	17,260
80 to 84 years	5,792	6,470	8,061	10,513	12,025	13,501	13,753	12,963	12,751	13,285
85 to 89 years	3,870	3,934	4,453	5,616	7,404	8,555	9,693	9,958	9,485	9,391
90 to 94 years	1,860	2,008	2,079	2,402	3,083	4,138	4,865	5,594	5,819	5,635
95 to 99 years	498	645	714	760	903	1,191	1,644	1,985	2,331	2,471
100 years and over	78	106	143	168	188	230	310	442	564	690
Median age (years)	37.7	38.3	38.9	39.6	40.2	40.4	40.6	40.6	40.8	41.1
Male	158,362	164,812	171,196	177,323	183,013	188,335	193,525	198,770	204,147	209,663
Under 5 years	10,763	11,150	11,307	11,377	11,512	11,761	12,061	12,329	12,515	12,652
5 to 9 years	10,434	10,896	11,304	11,482	11,565	11,705	11,961	12,266	12,538	12,728
10 to 14 years	10,475	10,538	11,017	11,443	11,630	11,715	11,860	12,119	12,427	12,701
15 to 19 years	10,722	10,640	10,736	11,247	11,686	11,879	11,970	12,120	12,384	12,695
20 to 24 years	11,603	11,109	11,103	11,274	11,822	12,278	12,485	12,590	12,751	13,022
25 to 29 years	11,392	11,994	11,580	11,650	11,860	12,423	12,894	13,115	13,232	13,402
30 to 34 years	10,870	11,653	12,307	11,951	12,051	12,270	12,842	13,322	13,552	13,675
35 to 39 years	10,140	10,991	11,805	12,491	12,158	12,267	12,493	13,069	13,553	13,788
40 to 44 years	9,987	10,158	11,026	11,858	12,559	12,237	12,355	12,586	13,165	13,651
45 to 49 years	10,293	9,907	10,095	10,970	11,807	12,517	12,211	12,337	12,573	13,154
50 to 54 years	10,938	10,103	9,745	9,950	10,825	11,665	12,382	12,095	12,232	12,475
55 to 59 years	10,586	10,599	9,818	9,490	9,711	10,583	11,424	12,145	11,883	12,033
60 to 64 years	9,118	10,103	10,148	9,431	9,137	9,377	10,243	11,081	11,803	11,571
65 to 69 years	7,585	8,515	9,471	9,549	8,906	8,654	8,915	9,767	10,595	11,310
70 to 74 years	5,287	6,839	7,713	8,618	8,723	8,174	7,971	8,253	9,073	9,877
75 to 79 years	3,600	4,487	5,844	6,630	7,447	7,576	7,144	6,998	7,294	8,055
80 to 84 years	2,406	2,748	3,459	4,545	5,195	5,875	6,017	5,723	5,636	5,930
85 to 89 years	1,439	1,520	1,763	2,251	2,992	3,457	3,951	4,085	3,933	3,900
90 to 94 years	585	667	719	853	1,109	1,501	1,766	2,051	2,148	2,105
95 to 99 years	125	173	202	224	273	364	506	611	724	772
100 years and over	14	22	31	38	44	56	76	108	137	167
Median age (years)	36.4	37.0	37.6	38.3	38.9	39.1	39.3	39.4	39.7	40.1
Female	163,001	169,084	175,211	181,148	186,649	191,681	196,409	201,034	205,725	210,605
Under 5 years	10,288	10,658	10,807	10,875	11,004	11,243	11,530	11,786	11,964	12,096
5 to 9 years	9,988	10,411	10,799	10,968	11,046	11,181	11,426	11,717	11,978	12,159
10 to 14 years	10,033	10,078	10,516	10,921	11,097	11,178	11,315	11,563	11,857	12,120
15 to 19 years	10,218	10,166	10,236	10,699	11,115	11,295	11,380	11,522	11,774	12,071
20 to 24 years	10,977	10,541	10,543	10,666	11,157	11,585	11,777	11,873	12,024	12,283
25 to 29 years	10,960	11,372	10,999	11,063	11,221	11,728	12,171	12,377	12,485	12,646
30 to 34 years	10,719	11,253	11,712	11,389	11,482	11,654	12,173	12,627	12,843	12,958
35 to 39 years	10,137	10,877	11,442	11,931	11,630	11,736	11,918	12,444	12,903	13,124
40 to 44 years	10,122	10,203	10,962	11,546	12,052	11,763	11,879	12,069	12,598	13,059
45 to 49 years	10,459	10,101	10,198	10,965	11,561	12,078	11,800	11,925	12,119	12,650
50 to 54 years	11,328	10,363	10,024	10,133	10,906	11,511	12,037	11,772	11,905	12,104
55 to 59 years	11,186	11,148	10,221	9,903	10,026	10,801	11,415	11,949	11,698	11,840
60 to 64 years	9,932	10,914	10,903	10,023	9,727	9,866	10,645	11,267	11,808	11,577
65 to 69 years	8,451	9,538	10,509	10,528	9,705	9,437	9,598	10,378	11,007	11,553
70 to 74 years	6,172	7,905	8,953	9,898	9,946	9,200	8,970	9,157	9,929	10,561
75 to 79 years	4,502	5,523	7,112	8,092	8,983	9,063	8,425	8,244	8,460	9,206
80 to 84 years	3,386	3,722	4,602	5,968	6,831	7,626	7,736	7,240	7,115	7,355
85 to 89 years	2,430	2,414	2,690	3,365	4,412	5,098	5,742	5,873	5,553	5,491

"That's a Lot of Candles! World's Oldest Person Celebrates His 116th Birthday and Becomes Longest Living Man EVER" (DailyMail.co.uk, April 19, 2013), Kerry McDermott and Emily Davies recount Kimura's advice about how to live a long life: "Eat light and live long." He died on June 12, 2013.

TABLE 1.4

Projections of the population by age and sex, 2015–60 [CONTINUED]

[Resident population as of July 1. Numbers in thousands.]

Sex and age	2015	2020	2025	2030	2035	2040	2045	2050	2055	2060
90 to 94 years	1,275	1,340	1,359	1,549	1,974	2,637	3,099	3,543	3,672	3,530
95 to 99 years	373	472	512	536	630	827	1,138	1,374	1,607	1,700
100 years and over	64	85	112	130	143	174	235	334	428	523
Median age (years)	39.1	39.6	40.2	40.8	41.5	41.8	41.9	41.9	42.0	42.2

SOURCE: "Table 12. Projections of the Population by Age and Sex for the United States: 2015 to 2060," in *2012 National Population Projections Summary Tables*, U.S. Census Bureau, Population Division, May 2013, http://www.census.gov/population/projections/data/national/2012/summarytables.html (accessed May 28, 2013)

Racial and Ethnic Diversity

The older population is becoming more ethnically and racially diverse, although at a slower pace than the overall population of the United States. In 2010 the older population was made up by approximately 80% of non-Hispanic whites, 9% of African Americans, 7% of Hispanics, and 3% of Asian Americans. (See Figure 1.6.) By 2050 the composition of the older population is projected to be more racially and ethnically diverse: 58% will be non-Hispanic white, 20% Hispanic, 12% African American, and 9% Asian American. Although the older population will increase among African Americans, Asian Americans, and Hispanics, the older Hispanic population will grow the most dramatically, from 2.8 million (6.9%) in 2010 to 17.5 million (19.8%) in 2050. (See Table 1.5.) During this same period non-Hispanic whites will decline from 80% to 58.5%.

The same trend is apparent among the oldest-old adults; however, the rate of change is less dramatic. The population of people aged 85 years and older will be increasingly diverse in 2030 and 2050. (See Table 1.6.) For example, 10.4% will be African American and 6% will be Asian American in 2050.

Marital Status

As in previous years, in 2010 older men were much more likely than older women to be married. Nearly eight out of 10 (78%) men aged 65 to 74 years were married, compared with 56% of women in the same age group. (See Figure 1.7.) The proportion married decreases with advancing age. In 2010, 38% of women aged 75 to 84 and 18% of women aged 85 years and older were married. Among men the proportion that were married decreased with advancing age but not as sharply. Even among the oldest-old, most men (58%) were married.

As older women outnumber older men in all age groups, it is not surprising that there are more widows than widowers. In 2010 four times as many women as men aged 65 to 74 years were widowed—24% of women, compared with 6% of men. (See Figure 1.7.) Although the gap narrows in the older age groups, there were twice as many women as men aged 85 years and older who were widowed—73% of women as opposed to 35% of men. A fairly small proportion of older adults were divorced, whereas an even smaller proportion had never married.

Foreign-Born Older Adults

Elizabeth M. Grieco et al. of the Census Bureau report in *The Foreign-Born Population in the United States: 2010* (May 2012, http://www.census.gov/prod/2012pubs/acs-19.pdf) that in 2010 the nation's foreign-born population numbered nearly 40 million, accounting for an estimated 12.9% of the total U.S. population. Compared with people born in the United States, the proportion of people aged 65 years and older was highest among those born in Europe. Figure 1.8 shows the percent distribution by age of the native and foreign-born population. The foreign-born population from Europe had the highest median age (the middle value; half of all people are younger and half are older) at 51.7, whereas people born in Africa had the lowest median age at 38.

WHERE OLDER AMERICANS LIVE

In *Profile of Older Americans*, the AoA reports that in 2011 adults aged 65 years and older accounted for 15% or more of the population in 11 states. The proportion of the population aged 65 years and older varied by state. In Florida the older adult population was 17.6%, followed by Maine with 16.3%; West Virginia with 16.2%; Pennsylvania with 15.6%; and Montana with 15.2%. The older adult population accounted for 15% of the population in Arkansas, Delaware, Hawaii, Iowa, Rhode Island, and Vermont. (See Figure 1.9.) In 13 states—Alaska (58%), Nevada (53%), Arizona (37%), Colorado (37%), Georgia (37%), Idaho (37%), South Carolina (35%), Utah (35%), New Mexico (33%), North Carolina (32%), Delaware (31%), Texas (30%), and Washington (30%)—the 65 and older population grew by 30% or more between 2000 and 2011. Figure 1.10 shows growth in the older population by state between 2000 and 2011.

FIGURE 1.5

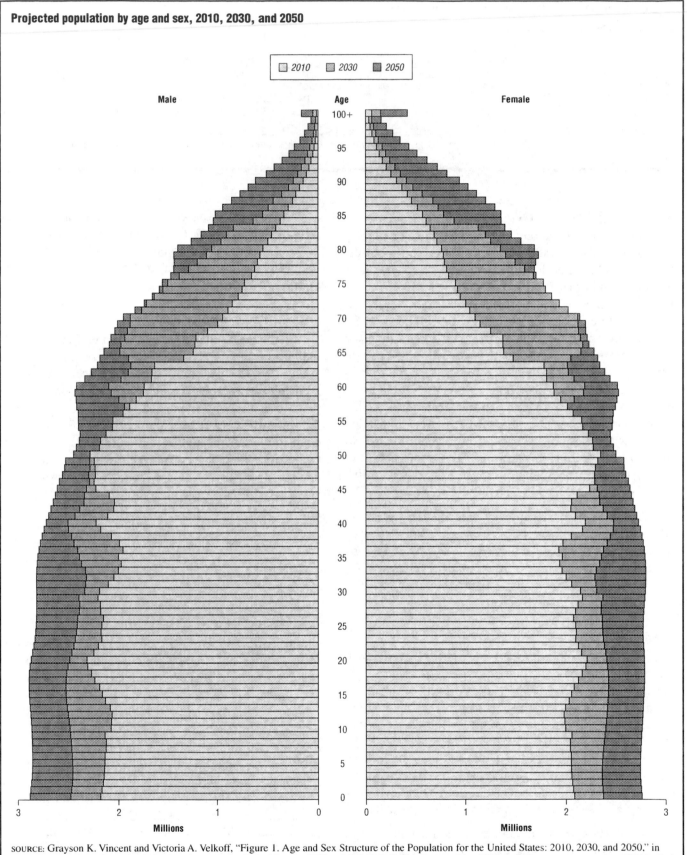

Projected population by age and sex, 2010, 2030, and 2050

◻ 2010   ▨ 2030   ▦ 2050

Male   Age   Female

Millions   Millions

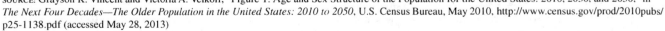

SOURCE: Grayson K. Vincent and Victoria A. Velkoff, "Figure 1. Age and Sex Structure of the Population for the United States: 2010, 2030, and 2050," in *The Next Four Decades—The Older Population in the United States: 2010 to 2050*, U.S. Census Bureau, May 2010, http://www.census.gov/prod/2010pubs/ p25-1138.pdf (accessed May 28, 2013)

FIGURE 1.6

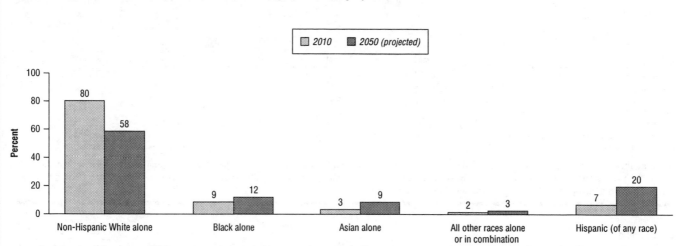

Population aged 65 and over, by race and Hispanic origin, 2010 and projected 2050

SOURCE: "Population Age 65 and over, by Race and Hispanic Origin, 2010 and Projected 2050," in *Older Americans 2012: Key Indicators of Well-Being*, Federal Interagency Forum on Aging-Related Statistics, June 2012, http://www.agingstats.gov/Main_Site/Data/2012_Documents/docs/EntireChartbook .pdf (accessed May 28, 2013)

TABLE 1.5

Population aged 65 and over, by race and Hispanic origin, 2010 and projected 2050

Race and Hispanic origin	2010 census		2050 projections	
	Number (in thousands)	Percent	Number (in thousands)	Percent
Total	40,268	100.0	88,547	100.0
Non-Hispanic white alone	32,209	80.0	51,772	58.5
Black alone	3,438	8.5	10,553	11.9
Asian alone	1,387	3.4	7,541	8.5
All other races alone or in combination	638	1.6	2,397	2.7
Hispanic (of any race)	2,782	6.9	17,515	19.8

SOURCE: "Table 2. Population Age 65 and over, by Race and Hispanic Origin, 2010 and Projected 2050," in *Older Americans 2012: Key Indicators of Well-Being*, Federal Interagency Forum on Aging-Related Statistics, June 2012, http://www.agingstats.gov/Main_Site/Data/2012_Documents/docs/EntireChartbook.pdf (accessed May 28, 2013)

The AoA indicates that in 2011, 81% of older adults lived in metropolitan areas. About two-thirds (66%) of these lived outside of cities and one-third (34%) were city dwellers. Approximately 19% of older adults lived in nonmetropolitan areas. Older adults relocate less often than any other age group. Of the scant 3% of older adults who changed residence between 2011 and 2012, just 16% moved out of state; the vast majority (83%) remained in the same state and just over six out of 10 (61%) stayed in the same county.

Older Americans Are More Religious

The Pew Forum on Religion and Public Life indicates in *Religion among the Millennials* (February 2010, http://pewforum.org/Age/Religion-Among-the-Millennials .aspx) that older Americans tend to be more religious than younger Americans. Consistent with this observation is the fact that older adults are also more likely to say they believe in God. Survey data from the latter half of the first decade of the 21st century reveal that 71% of older adults (born before 1928) and 68% of those born between 1928 and 1945 said they believe in God, compared with 65% of boomers (born between 1946 and 1964), 61% of Generation X (born between 1965 and 1980), and 53% of Millennials (born between 1981 and 2000).

In *Seven in 10 Americans Are Very or Moderately Religious* (December 4, 2012, http://www.gallup.com/poll/159050/seven-americans-moderately-religious.aspx), Frank Newport of the Gallup Organization concurs with the Pew findings. He reports that Gallup poll data reveal that religiousness increases with advancing age and observes that "Americans are least religious at age 23 and most religious at age 80."

TABLE 1.6

Distribution of population aged 85 and older by race, 2010, 2030, and 2050

[Numbers in thousands]

Race	2010		2030		2050	
	Number	Percent	Number	Percent	Number	Percent
85 years and over	**5,751**	**100.0**	**8,745**	**100.0**	**19,041**	**100.0**
White alone	5,189	90.2	7,542	86.2	15,491	81.4
Black alone	397	6.9	701	8.0	1,982	10.4
American Indian and Alaska Native alone	20	0.4	62	0.7	180	0.9
Asian alone	113	2.0	356	4.1	1,145	6.0
Native Hawaiian and other Pacific Islander alone	3	0.1	11	0.1	35	0.2
Two or more races	29	0.5	74	0.8	208	1.1

SOURCE: Grayson K. Vincent and Victoria A. Velkoff, "Table 1. Projections and Distribution of the Population Aged 85 and over by Race for the United States: 2010, 2030, and 2050," in *The Next Four Decades—The Older Population in the United States: 2010 to 2050*, U.S. Census Bureau, May 2010, http://www.census.gov/prod/2010pubs/p25-1138.pdf (accessed May 28, 2013)

FIGURE 1.7

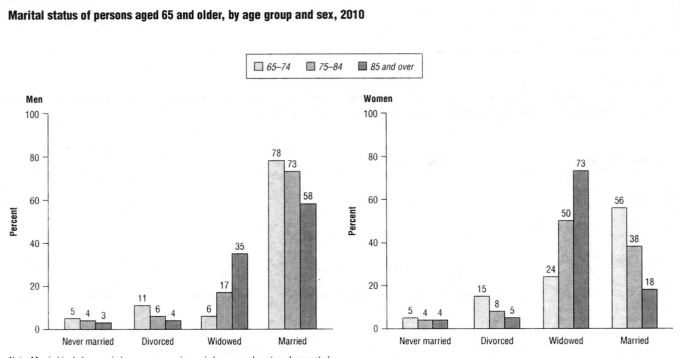

Marital status of persons aged 65 and older, by age group and sex, 2010

Note: Married includes married, spouse present; married, spouse absent; and separated.

SOURCE: "Marital Status of the Population Age 65 and over, by Age Group and Sex, 2010," in *Older Americans 2012: Key Indicators of Well-Being*, Federal Interagency Forum on Aging-Related Statistics, June 2012, http://www.agingstats.gov/Main_Site/Data/2012_Documents/docs/EntireChartbook.pdf (accessed May 28, 2013)

ENJOYMENT OF OLDER AGE

Getting old isn't nearly as bad as people think it will be. Nor is it quite as good.

—Pew Research Center, "Growing Old in America: Expectations vs. Reality" (June 29, 2009)

In view of the myriad difficulties and challenges facing older adults, including ill health, inadequate financial resources, and the loss of friends and loved ones, it seems natural to assume that advancing age will be associated with less overall happiness and more worry.

However, several studies refute this premise. Researchers find less worry among older adults than anticipated and a remarkable ability of older adults to adapt to their changing life conditions.

In "Growing Old in America: Expectations vs. Reality" (June 29, 2009, http://pewresearch.org/pubs/1269/aging-survey-expectations-versus-reality), the Pew Research Center reports the results of a survey of 2,969 young, middle-aged, and older adults about a range of experiences, positive and negative, that are associated

FIGURE 1.8

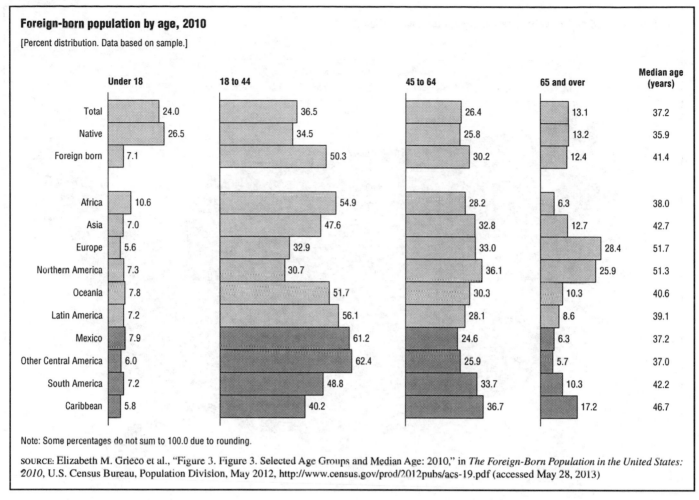

Foreign-born population by age, 2010

[Percent distribution. Data based on sample.]

	Under 18	18 to 44	45 to 64	65 and over	Median age (years)
Total	24.0	36.5	26.4	13.1	37.2
Native	26.5	34.5	25.8	13.2	35.9
Foreign born	7.1	50.3	30.2	12.4	41.4
Africa	10.6	54.9	28.2	6.3	38.0
Asia	7.0	47.6	32.8	12.7	42.7
Europe	5.6	32.9	33.0	28.4	51.7
Northern America	7.3	30.7	36.1	25.9	51.3
Oceania	7.8	51.7	30.3	10.3	40.6
Latin America	7.2	56.1	28.1	8.6	39.1
Mexico	7.9	61.2	24.6	6.3	37.2
Other Central America	6.0	62.4	25.9	5.7	37.0
South America	7.2	48.8	33.7	10.3	42.2
Caribbean	5.8	40.2	36.7	17.2	46.7

Note: Some percentages do not sum to 100.0 due to rounding.

SOURCE: Elizabeth M. Grieco et al., "Figure 3. Figure 3. Selected Age Groups and Median Age: 2010," in *The Foreign-Born Population in the United States: 2010*, U.S. Census Bureau, Population Division, May 2012, http://www.census.gov/prod/2012pubs/acs-19.pdf (accessed May 28, 2013)

with aging. Pew finds that younger adults associated aging with health and financial problems, memory loss, loneliness, and depression far more than older adults. By contrast, older adults reported fewer of the benefits that are associated with aging, such as more time to spend with family, traveling, and on hobbies than the younger adults anticipated. Furthermore, older adults said they have greater financial security than they did when they were younger.

Although reports of happiness decline with advancing age, the Pew Research Center notes that older adults still report considerable happiness. Among survey respondents aged 65 to 74 years, 32% described themselves as "very happy" and an additional 44% said they are "pretty happy." The percentages decline slightly among respondents aged 75 years and older—28% said they are "very happy" and 43% are "pretty happy." Six out of 10 said they feel younger than their age and feel less stress than they felt earlier in their life. The youngest survey respondents, aged 18 to 29 years, report the highest levels of happiness—37% said they are "very happy" and 53% are "pretty happy," but said they feel about their chronological age. In contrast, about half of the respondents aged 50 years and older report feeling at

least 10 years younger than their age. Of the older adult respondents, those aged 65 to 74 years, one-third said they feel 10 to 19 years younger than their age, and one out of six feels at least 20 years younger than their chronological age.

In "The Effect of Birth Cohort on Well-Being: The Legacy of Economic Hard Times" (*Psychological Science*, vol. 24, no. 3, March 1, 2013), Angelina R. Sutin et al. looked at whether differences in happiness reported by people who were middle aged compared with older adults were related to age or broader life circumstances, such as economic depression or prosperity, when they were born and growing up. The researchers find that people born during more difficult times, such as those who lived through the Great Depression (1929–1939), were not as happy as people who were born during periods that were more prosperous. However, when Sutin et al. take into account when people were born, they discover that, overall, people maintain and even increase their happiness and well-being as they age. According to Maia Szalavitz, in "With Age Comes Happiness" (*Time*, February 18, 2013), Sutin explained that "with age, people tend to become more emotional and experience both sadness and happiness."

FIGURE 1.9

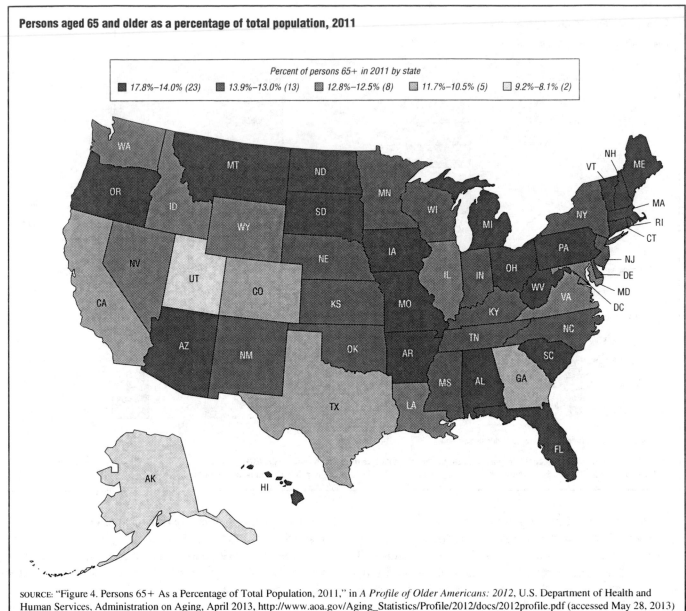

Persons aged 65 and older as a percentage of total population, 2011

Percent of persons 65+ in 2011 by state

■ 17.8%–14.0% (23) ■ 13.9%–13.0% (13) ■ 12.8%–12.5% (8) ■ 11.7%–10.5% (5) □ 9.2%–8.1% (2)

SOURCE: "Figure 4. Persons 65+ As a Percentage of Total Population, 2011," in *A Profile of Older Americans: 2012*, U.S. Department of Health and Human Services, Administration on Aging, April 2013, http://www.aoa.gov/Aging_Statistics/Profile/2012/docs/2012profile.pdf (accessed May 28, 2013)

Heather L. Urry and James J. Gross suggest in "Emotion Regulation in Older Age" (*Current Directions in Psychological Science*, vol. 19, no. 6, December 2010) that older people may seem happier than younger people because they are better able to regulate their emotions. They may also pay more attention to positive as opposed to negative news and may be better able to predict how specific situations will make them feel. As a result, older people may be better able to seek out pleasurable experiences and avoid unpleasant situations.

Positive Perceptions of Aging Influence Longevity and Happiness

Becca R. Levy et al. report in the landmark study "Longevity Increased by Positive Self-Perceptions of Aging" (*Journal of Personality and Social Psychology*, vol. 83, no. 2, August 2002) that older people with more positive self-perceptions of aging lived 7.5 years longer than those with less positive self-perceptions of aging, even after taking into account other factors, including age, gender, socioeconomic status, loneliness, and overall health. Analyzing data from the 660 participants aged 50 years and older in the Ohio Longitudinal Study of Aging and Retirement, the researchers compared mortality rates with responses made 23 years earlier by the participants (338 men and 322 women). The responses included agreeing or disagreeing with statements such as "As you get older, you are less useful."

Levy et al. assert, "The effect of more positive self-perceptions of aging on survival is greater than the physio-

FIGURE 1.10

Percentage increase in population aged 65 and older, 2000–11

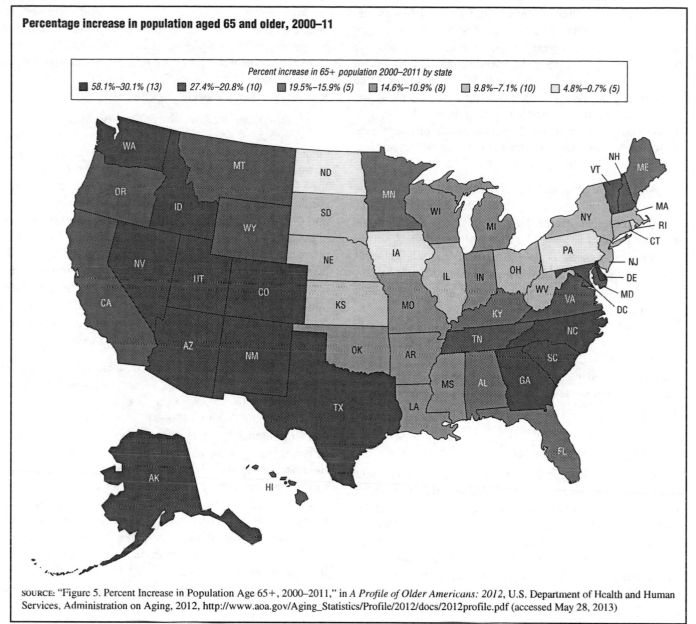

Percent increase in 65+ population 2000–2011 by state

■ *58.1%–30.1% (13)*   ■ *27.4%–20.8% (10)*   ■ *19.5%–15.9% (5)*   ■ *14.6%–10.9% (8)*   ▨ *9.8%–7.1% (10)*   □ *4.8%–0.7% (5)*

SOURCE: "Figure 5. Percent Increase in Population Age 65+, 2000–2011," in *A Profile of Older Americans: 2012*, U.S. Department of Health and Human Services, Administration on Aging, 2012, http://www.aoa.gov/Aging_Statistics/Profile/2012/docs/2012profile.pdf (accessed May 28, 2013)

logical measures of low systolic blood pressure and cholesterol, each of which is associated with a longer life span of 4 years or less.... [It] is also greater than the independent contribution of lower body mass index, no history of smoking, and a tendency to exercise; each of these factors has been found to contribute between 1 and 3 years of added life." They conclude that negative self-perceptions can diminish life expectancy, whereas positive self-perceptions can prolong it.

According to Jennifer Reichstadt et al., in "Building Blocks of Successful Aging: A Focus Group Study of Older Adults' Perceived Contributors to Successful Aging" (*American Journal of Geriatric Psychiatry*, vol. 15, no. 3, March 2007), older adults themselves believe that a positive attitude about life and aging and having

the ability to adapt to change are associated with successful aging and a long, happy life. The researchers interviewed 72 older adults living in the community (as opposed to people living in institutions) and identified the factors that older adults feel contribute to successful aging. The interviewees named psychosocial factors such as a sense of engagement, pursuit of continued stimulation, learning, feeling a sense of purpose in life, and being useful to others and to society as more important for successful aging than factors such as freedom from illness and disability.

In "The Power of Positive Emotions: It's a Matter of Life or Death—Subjective Well-Being and Longevity over 28 Years in a General Population" (*Health Psychology*, vol. 29, no. 1, January 2010), Jingping Xu and Robert

E. Roberts analyze 28 years of data from 6,856 subjects to determine whether happiness and life satisfaction are related to longevity. The researchers find that the subjective assessment of well-being, which includes positive feelings and life satisfaction, predicted a lower risk of mortality in the population. Xu and Roberts explain that "positive emotions broaden our attention and action span, down-regulate ('undo') what negative feelings do to us, and build enduring psychological, physical, and social resources that we can draw upon when needed, thus promote health and longevity."

Andrew Steptoe and Jane Wardle of the University College London report in "Positive Affect Measured Using Ecological Momentary Assessment and Survival in Older Men and Women" (*Proceedings of the National Academy of Sciences*, vol. 108, no. 45, November 8, 2011), a study of over 3,800 people aged 52 to 79 years, that those who said they were happiest had a 35% chance of living longer than those who said they felt least happy. The researchers conclude that their findings "provide further reason to target the positive well-being of older people. In addition to addressing the health status and material circumstances of older people, efforts to improve affective states may have beneficial health consequences."

ATTITUDES ABOUT AGING

People of all ages hold beliefs and attitudes about aging and older adults. Even young children can distinguish age differences, and they display attitudes that appear to be characteristic of their generation. Because attitudes strongly influence behavior and because more Americans reach older ages than ever before, interaction with older people and deeply held beliefs about growing old are likely influenced by cultural and societal attitudes about aging and older adults. The availability, accessibility, adequacy, and acceptability of health care and other services intended to meet the needs of older people are similarly influenced by the attitudes of younger people. The prevailing attitudes and opinions of political leaders, decision makers, health and human services personnel, and taxpayers are particularly important in shaping policies, programs, services, and public sentiment.

In nonindustrialized countries older people are often held in high esteem. Older adults are respected because they have endured and persevered in harsh living conditions and because they have accumulated wisdom and knowledge that younger generations need to survive and carry on the traditions of their culture. In many industrialized societies, including the United States, a person's worth may be measured in terms of income (the flow of money earned through employment, interest on investments, and other sources) and the amount of accumulated wealth. When older adults retire from full-time employment, they may lose status because they are no longer working, earning money, and "contributing" to society. When an individual's sense of self-worth and identity is closely bound to employment or occupation, retirement from the workforce can make him or her feel worthless.

Stereotypes Fuel Worries of Older Adults

Although people of all ages worry about the future, for older adults aging may signify a future threat to their health and well-being, diminished social status, a loss of power, and the possibility of a loss of control over their life. Researchers posit that social stereotypes, such as media portrayals of older adults as weak and helpless and of old age as a time of hardship, loss, and pain, have a powerful influence on attitudes and may be another source of worry for older adults. They contend that the image of a tragic old age can create worries about having a tragic old age. Worse still, the negative image of old age can become a self-fulfilling prophecy, thereby confirming negative stereotypes and promoting ageism (discrimination or unfair treatment based on age).

For example, in "Expectations about Memory Change across the Life Span Are Impacted by Aging Stereotypes" (*Psychology and Aging*, vol. 24, no. 1, March 2009), Tara T. Lineweaver, Andrea K. Berger, and Christopher Hertzog interviewed 373 people, in three different age groups, to find out what they thought about memory throughout the adult life span. They were asked to rate the memory of different older adults, who were described as having positive or negative personality traits. Consistent with previous research, the study subjects believed that memory declines with advancing age. Furthermore, they rated adults described as having positive personality traits with having better memory ability and less age-related memory loss than those described as having negative personality traits. Another important finding was that the older subjects were more strongly influenced by the personality descriptions than the younger subjects.

Gabriel A. Radvansky, Nicholas A. Lynchard, and William von Hippel confirm in "Aging and Stereotype Suppression" (*Aging, Neuropsychology, and Cognition*, vol. 16, no. 1, January 2009) that older adults are more likely than younger adults to believe and use stereotypic information, even when they do not intend to judge people based on stereotypes. Furthermore, older adults have trouble changing or modifying their interpretation of a situation, even when it becomes apparent that their initial interpretation was incorrect. The researchers aver that although older adults may be more susceptible to the influence of stereotypes, this effect can be prevented, or minimized, by providing them with clear information that contradicts stereotypical information.

In "Association between Positive Age Stereotypes and Recovery from Disability in Older Persons" (*Journal of the American Medical Association*, vol. 308, no. 19, November 21, 2012), Becca R. Levy et al. note that older adults who hold positive views of aging such as wisdom, accomplishment, and satisfaction are 44% more likely to fully recover from potentially disabling illnesses then those who hold negative stereotypes of aging. The researchers also find that older adults who view growing old as becoming helpless, useless, or unappreciated are less likely to seek preventive medical care and more likely to suffer from physical problems and memory loss.

Baby Boomers Challenge Stereotypes

Since their inception, baby boomers have left their mark on every U.S. institution. As teenagers and young adults, they created and championed a unique blend of music, pop culture, and political activism. They have witnessed remarkable technological and medical advancements during their lifetime and have come to expect, and even loudly demand, solutions to health and social problems.

As the baby boomers join the ranks of older Americans, they are fomenting a cultural revolution. The almost 80 million boomers approaching age 65 are not content to be regarded as "old." Accustomed to freedom and independence, they want to be recognized and treated as individuals rather than as stereotypes. Overall, the aging boomers are healthier, better educated, and wealthier than any other older adult cohort in history. They are living longer, and many are redefining old age by reinventing retirement, continuing to pursue health, and challenging the public's perception of what it is to be old.

Although baby boomers are living longer than previous generations, they are not necessarily healthier in their 60s. Dana E. King et al. report in "The Status of Baby Boomers' Health in the United States: The Healthiest Generation?" (*Journal of the American Medical Association Internal Medicine*, vol. 173, no. 5, March 11, 2013) that boomers suffer from more chronic diseases than past generations. They are more likely to be obese and to suffer from high blood pressure and high cholesterol—factors that are associated with increased risk of disease. Compared with their predecessors, they are more likely to be disabled, exercise less frequently, and consume more alcohol. According to King et al., one positive aspect is that fewer boomers have smoked cigarettes and, therefore, fewer suffer from smoking-related illnesses such as emphysema. Still, fewer describe themselves as in "excellent" health—just 13.2% compared with 32% of the previous generation.

Along with the image of baby boomers as being healthy and fit, other stereotypes persist. For example, in "Aging America and the Boomer Wars" (*Gerontologist*, vol. 48, no. 6, December 2008), Harry R. Moody, the director of the Office of Academic Affairs for the AARP, describes the polarizing stereotypes of the baby boomers. On one side are people who characterize boomers as selfish, materialistic, whining, and greedy—people who will consume all available resources with no thought to future generations. On the other side are those who view boomers as idealistic advocates of social activism and community service. Moody cautions that these opposing stereotypes should be avoided to prevent "over-simplified polarities and to appreciate the power that public discourse and media images can have in shaping our thinking about generational change in an aging society."

CHAPTER 2
THE ECONOMICS OF GROWING OLD IN THE UNITED STATES

Security was attained in the earlier days through the interdependence of members of families upon each other and of the families within a small community upon each other. The complexities of great communities and of organized industry make less real these simple means of security. Therefore, we are compelled to employ the active interest of the Nation as a whole through government in order to encourage a greater security for each individual who composes it.... This seeking for a greater measure of welfare and happiness does not indicate a change in values. It is rather a return to values lost in the course of our economic development and expansion.

—Franklin D. Roosevelt, Message of the President to Congress, June 8, 1934

The economic status of older Americans is more varied than that of any other age group. Although a few older adults are well off, most have limited resources. As a whole, the older U.S. population has a lower economic status than the overall adult population. During retirement most people rely on Social Security and are supplemented by pensions and assets. Some must also depend on Supplemental Security Income (SSI), a federal assistance program administered by the U.S. Social Security Administration (SSA) that guarantees a minimum level of income for needy older, blind, and/or disabled individuals. It acts as a safety net for individuals who have little or no Social Security or other income and limited resources.

With fixed incomes and sharply limited potential to improve their incomes through employment, many older people become vulnerable to circumstances such as the loss of a spouse, prolonged illness, or even economic variations such as inflation or recession that further compromise their financial well-being, sometimes plunging them into poverty. One common scenario is a couple that has planned well for retirement but then runs through all their assets to pay the health care costs of a long-term illness. When the ill partner dies, the surviving spouse is left impoverished. Another example is retirees who

discover, as many people did during the latter half of the first decade of the 21st century, that their retirement accounts have lost more than half of their value.

The so-called Great Recession, which lasted from late 2007 to mid-2009, had far-reaching effects for older adults. In "Retirement Plan Assets" (April 2013, http://www.urban.org/UploadedPDF/412622-Retirement-Plan-Assets.pdf), Barbara A. Butrica of the Urban Institute reports that individual retirement accounts (IRAs) have been growing since 2009. In fact, from the last quarter of 2012 to the first quarter of 2013 favorable stock market conditions increased retirement account balances by 5%. In contrast, defined benefit pensions (plans that pay guaranteed benefits based on years of service and final salary from retirement until death) have not recovered. In early 2013 their value, when adjusted for inflation, remained 17% below their 2007 value.

Some older adults may want to return to work, but their prospects may be grim. The recession resulted in historically high rates of unemployment across all age groups. Those rates declined after 2009, but because economic uncertainty continued to plague the U.S. economy well into 2013, they were still higher than pre-recession rates. For example, the U.S. Bureau of Labor Statistics (BLS; July 17, 2013, http://www.bls.gov/webapps/legacy/cpsatab10.htm) reports that the unemployment rate for older workers aged 55 years and older increased from 3% in June 2006 to 7% in June 2009. Thereafter, the rate slowly declined to 5.3% in June 2013. Likewise, Carole Fleck observes in "Older Workers See Gains in Jobs Report" (May 3, 2013, http://blog.aarp.org/2013/05/03/older-workers-gain-in-april-jobs-report-labor-statistics-jobless/) that the overall unemployment rate has slowly but steadily declined, from 9% in April 2011, to 8.1% in April 2012, to 7.5% in April 2013. Despite these gains, Fleck notes that half of unemployed older workers had been out of work for six months in April 2013. The duration of unemployment for older workers increased from 49.2 weeks in March 2013 to 50.2 weeks in April 2013. By contrast, the duration of unemployment for workers less than age 55 rose from 35.6 weeks to 36.9 during the same period. Table 2.1 shows that the percentage of workers unemployed for 27 weeks or longer was relatively unchanged through 2012 and declined slightly between February and April 2013.

THE ECONOMIC WELL-BEING OF OLDER ADULTS

There are two important measures of an individual's or household's economic well-being. One is income (the flow of money earned through employment, interest on investments, and other sources) and the other is asset accumulation or wealth (the economic resources—property or other material possessions—owned by an individual or household).

Income Distribution

According to the Federal Interagency Forum on Aging-Related Statistics, in *Older Americans 2012: Key Indicators of Well-Being* (June 2012, http://www.aging stats.gov/Main_Site/Data/2012_Documents/docs/Entire Chartbook.pdf), the trend in median household income (the middle value; half of all households earn less and half earn more) of the older population has been positive, and fewer older adults are living in poverty. Between 2005 and 2010 the proportion of older adults living in poverty declined. (See Figure 2.1.) In 2010, 9% of the older population lived below the poverty threshold, compared with 10.1% in 2005. (See Figure 2.1.) The proportion of the older population in the low-income bracket also fell, from 34.6% in 1974 to 25.6% in 2010. (See Figure 2.2.)

According to the Administration on Aging (AoA), in *A Profile of Older Americans: 2012* (April 2013, http://www.aoa.gov/Aging_Statistics/Profile/2012/docs/2012profile.pdf), the median reported income for all older adults in 2011 was $27,707 for males and $15,362 for females. Figure 2.3 shows the distribution of income among older adults. Households headed by people aged 65 years and older had a median income of $48,538 in 2011, whereas the individual median income for older adults was $19,939. Nearly half (49%) of households headed by an older adult had incomes of $50,000 or more, and 5% had incomes less than $15,000. The median household income for older adults was highest for Asian Americans ($50,971), followed by non-Hispanic whites ($50,658), African Americans ($39,533), and Hispanics ($33,809).

Sources of Income

Unlike younger adults, who derive most of their income from employment, older adults rely on a variety of sources of income to meet their expenses. Since the 1960s Social Security has provided the largest share of income for older Americans. In 2010 Social Security benefits were a major source of income—providing at least 50% of total income—reported for 53% of older couples and 74% of unmarried older adult beneficiaries. (See Figure 2.4.) For 46% of unmarried Americans and 23% of couples over the age of 65 years in 2010, Social Security accounted for 90% of total income.

The AoA explains in *Profile of Older Americans* that the income for most older adults comes from four sources. In 2010 Social Security accounted for 37%, earnings provided 30%, pensions contributed 18%, and asset income accounted for 11% of the older population's income. (See Figure 2.5.)

For older Americans in the lowest fifth of the income distribution in 2010, Social Security accounted for 84% of their aggregate income (total income from all sources), public assistance for 7%, pensions for 3%, earned income for 2%, and asset income for 2%. (See Figure 2.6.) By contrast, the aggregate income for older adults in the highest quintile was 45% from earned income, 19% from pensions, 17% from Social Security, 16% from asset income, and less than 1% from public assistance. Among people aged 80 years and older, their aggregate income largely consisted of Social Security and asset income, with earnings contributing a much smaller proportion, compared with the youngest population of older adults, those aged 65 to 69 years. (See Table 2.2.)

Pension Funds

Many large employers, along with most local and state governments and the federal government, offer pension plans for retirement. In the United States American Express established the first private pension plan (an employer-run retirement program) in 1875. General Motors Corporation provided the first modern plan during the 1940s.

Employers are not required to provide pensions, and pension plans do not have to include all workers; they may exclude certain jobs and/or individuals. Before 1976 pension plans could require an employee to work a lifetime for one company before becoming eligible for pension benefits. As required by the Employee Retirement Income Security Act (ERISA) of 1974, starting in 1976 an employee became eligible after 10 years of service. By 2000 most plans required five years of work before an employee became vested (eligible for benefits). In companies that offer pension plans, employees are eligible to begin receiving benefits when they retire or leave the company if they have worked for the requisite number of years and/or have reached the specified eligibility age.

TABLE 2.1

Duration of unemployment, 2012 and January–April 2013

[Numbers in thousands]

Duration	2012									2013			
	Apr.	May	June	July	Aug.	Sept.	Oct.	Nov.	Dec.	Jan.	Feb.	Mar.	Apr.
Number of unemployed													
Less than 5 weeks	2,567	2,602	2,825	2,697	2,865	2,535	2,633	2,596	2,676	2,766	2,667	2,464	2,474
5 to 14 weeks	2,841	3,007	2,826	3,102	2,848	2,825	2,847	2,757	2,838	3,028	2,782	2,838	2,848
15 weeks and over	7,023	7,088	7,149	6,623	6,846	6,736	6,829	6,604	6,661	6,566	6,493	6,348	6,320
15 to 26 weeks	1,984	1,703	1,813	1,756	1,823	1,866	1,813	1,820	1,895	1,858	1,695	1,737	1,967
27 weeks and over	5,040	5,385	5,336	5,167	5,023	4,871	5,017	4,784	4,766	4,708	4,797	4,611	4,353
Average (mean) duration, in weeks	39.1	39.6	39.7	38.8	39.3	39.6	39.9	39.7	38.1	35.3	36.9	37.1	36.5
Median duration, in weeks	19.3	20.1	19.4	16.8	18.2	18.7	19.6	18.9	18.0	16.0	17.8	18.1	17.5
Percent distribution													
Total unemployed	100.0	100.0	100.0	100.0	100.0	100.0	100.0	100.0	100.0	100.0	100.0	100.0	100.0
Less than 5 weeks	20.6	20.5	22.1	21.2	22.8	21.0	21.4	21.7	22.0	22.4	22.3	21.1	21.3
5 to 14 weeks	22.9	23.7	22.1	24.4	22.7	23.4	23.1	23.1	23.3	24.5	23.3	24.4	24.5
15 weeks and over	56.5	55.8	55.8	54.4	54.5	55.7	55.5	55.2	54.7	53.1	54.4	54.5	54.3
15 to 26 weeks	16.0	13.4	14.2	13.8	14.5	15.4	14.7	15.2	15.6	15.0	14.2	14.9	16.9
27 weeks and over	40.5	42.4	41.7	40.6	40.0	40.3	40.8	40.0	39.1	38.1	40.2	39.6	37.4

Note: Updated population controls are introduced annually with the release of January data.

SOURCE: "A-12. Unemployed Persons by Duration of Unemployment, Seasonally Adjusted," in *Labor Force Statistics from the Current Population Survey*, U.S. Bureau of Labor Statistics, Division of Labor Force Statistics, February 6, 2013, http://www.bls.gov/cps/tables.htm (accessed May 29, 2013)

FIGURE 2.1

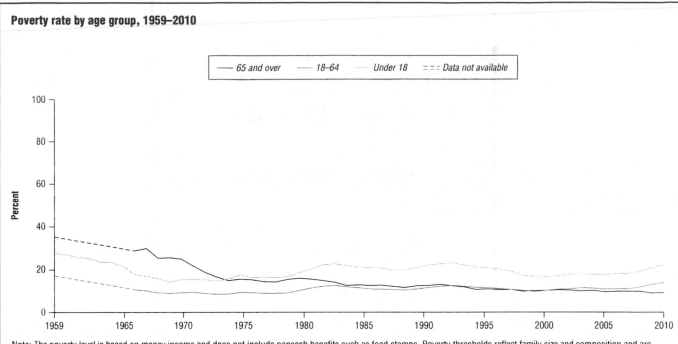

Poverty rate by age group, 1959–2010

| — 65 and over | ···· 18–64 | ···· Under 18 | = = = Data not available |

Note: The poverty level is based on money income and does not include noncash benefits such as food stamps. Poverty thresholds reflect family size and composition and are adjusted each year using the annual average consumer price index.

SOURCE: "Poverty Rate of the Population Living in Poverty, by Age Group, 1959–2010," in *Older Americans 2012: Key Indicators of Well-Being*, Federal Interagency Forum on Aging-Related Statistics, June 2012, http://www.agingstats.gov/Main_Site/Data/2012_Documents/docs/EntireChartbook.pdf (accessed May 28, 2013)

FIGURE 2.2

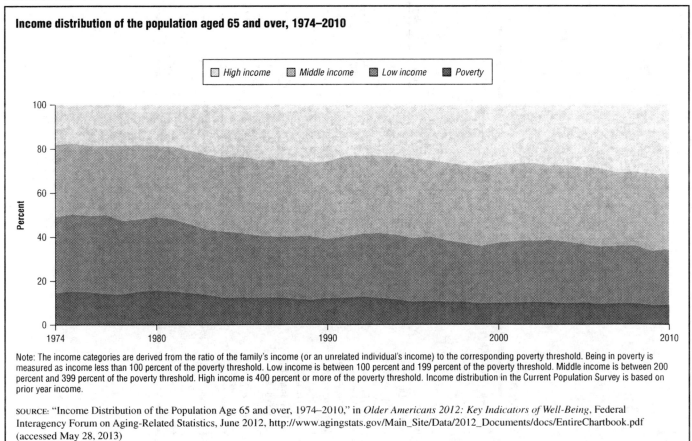

Income distribution of the population aged 65 and over, 1974–2010

| ▢ High income | ▨ Middle income | ▨ Low income | ■ Poverty |

Note: The income categories are derived from the ratio of the family's income (or an unrelated individual's income) to the corresponding poverty threshold. Being in poverty is measured as income less than 100 percent of the poverty threshold. Low income is between 100 percent and 199 percent of the poverty threshold. Middle income is between 200 percent and 399 percent of the poverty threshold. High income is 400 percent or more of the poverty threshold. Income distribution in the Current Population Survey is based on prior year income.

SOURCE: "Income Distribution of the Population Age 65 and over, 1974–2010," in *Older Americans 2012: Key Indicators of Well-Being*, Federal Interagency Forum on Aging-Related Statistics, June 2012, http://www.agingstats.gov/Main_Site/Data/2012_Documents/docs/EntireChartbook.pdf (accessed May 28, 2013)

FIGURE 2.3

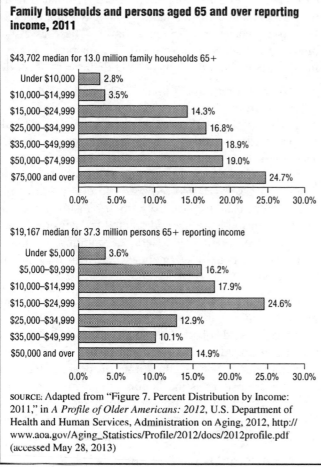

Family households and persons aged 65 and over reporting income, 2011

$43,702 median for 13.0 million family households 65+

Income	Percent
Under $10,000	2.8%
$10,000–$14,999	3.5%
$15,000–$24,999	14.3%
$25,000–$34,999	16.8%
$35,000–$49,999	18.9%
$50,000–$74,999	19.0%
$75,000 and over	24.7%

0.0%   5.0%   10.0%   15.0%   20.0%   25.0%   30.0%

$19,167 median for 37.3 million persons 65+ reporting income

Income	Percent
Under $5,000	3.6%
$5,000–$9,999	16.2%
$10,000–$14,999	17.9%
$15,000–$24,999	24.6%
$25,000–$34,999	12.9%
$35,000–$49,999	10.1%
$50,000 and over	14.9%

0.0%   5.0%   10.0%   15.0%   20.0%   25.0%   30.0%

SOURCE: Adapted from "Figure 7. Percent Distribution by Income: 2011," in *A Profile of Older Americans: 2012*, U.S. Department of Health and Human Services, Administration on Aging, 2012, http://www.aoa.gov/Aging_Statistics/Profile/2012/docs/2012profile.pdf (accessed May 28, 2013)

FIGURE 2.4

Percentage of older adults receiving Social Security benefits, by relative importance of benefits to total income, 2010

Legend:
- All beneficiary units
- Beneficiary married couples
- Nonmarried beneficiaries

Percent (y-axis: 0 to 80)

50% or more of income: 65, 53, 74
90% or more of income: 36, 23, 46

Note: An aged unit is a married couple living together or a nonmarried person, which also includes persons who are separated or married but not living together.

SOURCE: "Percentage of Aged Units Receiving Social Security Benefits, by Relative Importance of Benefits to Total Income," in *Fast Facts and Figures about Social Security, 2012*, U.S. Social Security Administration, Office of Retirement and Disability Policy, August 2012, http://www.ssa.gov/policy/docs/chartbooks/fast_facts/2012/fast_facts12.pdf (accessed May 29, 2013)

DEFINED BENEFIT PLANS AND DEFINED CONTRIBUTION PLANS. There are two principal types of pension plans: defined benefit plans and defined contribution plans. As described earlier, defined benefit plans promise employees a specified monthly benefit at retirement. A defined benefit plan may stipulate the promised benefit as an exact dollar amount, such as $100 per month at retirement. More often, however, benefits are calculated using a plan formula that considers both salary and service—for example, 1% of the average salary for the last five years of employment multiplied by years of service with the employer.

A defined contribution plan does not promise employees a specific amount of benefits at retirement. Instead, the employee and/or employer contribute to a plan account, sometimes at a set rate, such as 5% of earnings annually. Generally, these contributions are invested on the employee's behalf, and the amount of future benefits varies depending on investment earnings.

An example of a defined contribution plan is the 401(k) plan. This plan allows employees to defer receiving a portion of their salary, which is contributed on their behalf to the plan. Income taxes are deferred until the money is withdrawn at retirement. In some instances employers match employee contributions. Created in 1978, these plans were named for section 401(k) of the Internal Revenue Code.

According to Butrica, in 2012 one-fifth of U.S. private-sector workers had a pension plan that provides a defined benefit, whereas half had a defined contribution plan that grows in response to employer and worker contributions. Participation in defined benefit plans has declined, from 42% in 1989 to 20% in 2012, whereas participation in defined contribution plans has increased. The BLS notes in "Who Has Benefits in Private Industry in 2012?" (*Beyond the Numbers*, vol. 1, no. 13, September 2012) that 48% of full-time workers in the private sector participated in defined benefit or defined contribution plans in 2012. (See Table 2.3.) Since the mid-1990s many employers have converted their defined benefit plans to hybrid plans that incorporate elements of both defined benefit and defined contribution plans. For example, cash balance plans are based on defined contributions of pay credits (based on an employee's compensation rate) and interest credits that are deposited annually by the employer into an account, the balance of which serves as the defined benefit.

FIGURE 2.5

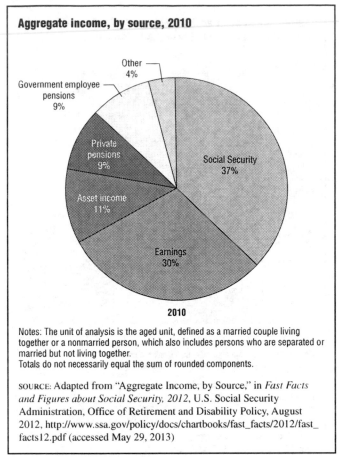

Aggregate income, by source, 2010

Other
4%

Government employee
pensions
9%

Private
pensions
9%

Social Security
37%

Asset income
11%

Earnings
30%

2010

Notes: The unit of analysis is the aged unit, defined as a married couple living together or a nonmarried person, which also includes persons who are separated or married but not living together.
Totals do not necessarily equal the sum of rounded components.

SOURCE: Adapted from "Aggregate Income, by Source," in *Fast Facts and Figures about Social Security, 2012*, U.S. Social Security Administration, Office of Retirement and Disability Policy, August 2012, http://www.ssa.gov/policy/docs/chartbooks/fast_facts/2012/fast_facts12.pdf (accessed May 29, 2013)

the fund; bad investments result in losses. During the early 1970s several major plans were terminated before they accumulated sufficient assets to pay employees and their beneficiaries retirement benefits. These asset-poor plans were unable to make good on their promises, leaving retirees without benefits despite their years of service.

To protect retirement plan participants and their beneficiaries from these catastrophic losses, ERISA was passed in 1974. ERISA established a new set of rules for participation, added mandatory and quicker vesting schedules, fixed minimum funding standards, and set standards of conduct for administering plans and handling plan assets. It also required the disclosure of plan information, established a system for insuring the payment of pension benefits, and created the Pension Benefit Guaranty Corporation, a federal corporation, to provide uninterrupted benefit payments when pension plans are terminated.

The Retirement Equity Act of 1984 requires pension plans to pay a survivor's benefit to the spouse of a deceased vested plan participant. Before 1984 some spouses received no benefits unless the employee was near retirement age at the time of death. Under the 1984 law, pension vesting begins at age 21, or after five years of being on the job, and employees who have a break in employment for reasons such as maternity leave do not lose any time already accumulated.

PENSION FUNDS DECLINE. Because both private and public pension funds are invested in the stock market, many suffered serious losses in response to the Great Recession and its aftereffects, which extended into 2013. According to John W. Ehrhardt, Zorast Wadia, and Alan Perry, in *De-risking Efforts by Plan Sponsors Reduce Pension Obligations, but Continued Discount Rate Declines Produce Record-High Pension Plan Deficits in 2012* (March 2013, http://www.milliman.com/expertise/employee-benefits/products-tools/pension-funding-study/pdfs/2013-pension-funding-study.pdf), the 100-largest corporate (defined benefit) pension plans suffered a record $388.8 billion loss of funded status in 2012, which was a $61.1 billion increase over the 2011 year-end deficit.

The losses in funding sustained during and after the recession, along with the funding requirements by the Pension Protection Act (PPA) of 2006, which provides significant tax incentives to enhance and protect retirement savings for millions of Americans, combined to create a growing pension fund deficit. Ehrhardt, Wadia, and Perry note that the act increased employer contributions to $61.5 billion in 2012. Many companies were expected to make increased contributions in 2013 to avoid benefit restrictions of the PPA. Ehrhardt, Wadia, and Perry predict that contributions of more than $65 billion in 2013 will set a new record.

PRIVATE AND PUBLIC PENSIONS. The SSA reports in *Fast Facts and Figures about Social Security, 2012* (August 2012, http://www.ssa.gov/policy/docs/chartbooks/fast_facts/2012/fast_facts12.pdf) that the proportion of older adults' income from pensions has grown rapidly since the 1960s, with private pensions more than tripling by 2010. (See Figure 2.7.) During the same period the proportion of people receiving government employee pensions increased from 9% in 1962 to 15% in 2010. The proportion of older adults with income from assets—the second-most-common source of income after Social Security—in 2010 (52%) was comparable to 1962 (54%). In contrast, the proportion of older adults with earned income declined from 36% in 1962 to 26% in 2010.

Unlike Social Security and many public plans, most private pension plans do not provide automatic cost-of-living adjustments. Without these adjustments many retirees' incomes and purchasing power erode. Military, government, and Railroad Retirement pensioners are more likely to receive cost-of-living increases than are pensioners in the private sector.

FEDERAL PENSION LAWS. Pension plan funds are often invested in stocks and bonds, much as banks invest their depositors' money. When the investment choice is a good one, the company makes a profit on the money in

FIGURE 2.6

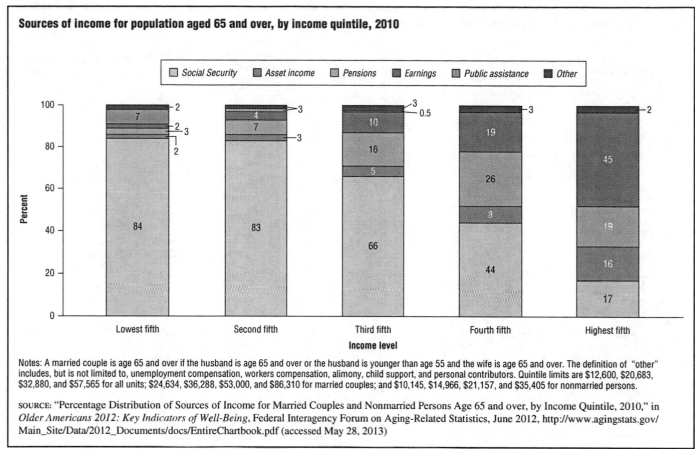

Sources of income for population aged 65 and over, by income quintile, 2010

Legend: Social Security · Asset income · Pensions · Earnings · Public assistance · Other

Notes: A married couple is age 65 and over if the husband is age 65 and over or the husband is younger than age 55 and the wife is age 65 and over. The definition of "other" includes, but is not limited to, unemployment compensation, workers compensation, alimony, child support, and personal contributors. Quintile limits are $12,600, $20,683, $32,880, and $57,565 for all units; $24,634, $36,288, $53,000, and $86,310 for married couples; and $10,145, $14,966, $21,157, and $35,405 for nonmarried persons.

SOURCE: "Percentage Distribution of Sources of Income for Married Couples and Nonmarried Persons Age 65 and over, by Income Quintile, 2010," in *Older Americans 2012: Key Indicators of Well-Being*, Federal Interagency Forum on Aging-Related Statistics, June 2012, http://www.agingstats.gov/Main_Site/Data/2012_Documents/docs/EntireChartbook.pdf (accessed May 28, 2013)

There have also been several instances of alleged pension fraud. For example, in 2013 federal regulators accused the state of Illinois of misleading investors about the health of its public pension fund. In "Illinois Is Accused of Fraud by S.E.C." (NYTimes.com, March 11, 2013), Mary Williams Walsh describes the U.S. Securities and Exchange Commission's settlement of this case. Just two years prior, Mary Williams Walsh and Louise Story reported in "U.S. Inquiry Said to Focus on California Pension Fund" (NYTimes.com, January 7, 2011) that the California Public Employees' Retirement System—the nation's largest public pension fund—not only lost 27% of its value in 2008 but also may have misled investors about the risk in its pension fund. There were two issues that concerned investigators: one was whether conflicts of interest occurred when specific investments were made and the other involved transparency and questions whether the fund should have disclosed the risk profile of its investments.

Other instances of pension fraud include an investigator in the Warren County, New York, district attorney's office, and a New Jersey investment adviser who admitted defrauding investors, including a union pension plan. The Warren County case involved an individual who defrauded the pension fund by collecting a pension while he was still employed, an illegal practice that is called "double dipping." The New Jersey case involved an investment adviser who admitted to defrauding many investors, including the United Marine Division, International Longshoreman's Association, a union for tugboat and ferry workers in the New York and New Jersey waterways.

Personal Savings

One of the most effective ways to prepare for retirement is to save for it. In the issue brief *The 2013 Retirement Confidence Survey: Perceived Savings Needs Outpace Reality for Many* (March 2013, http://www.ebri.org/pdf/surveys/rcs/2013/EBRI_IB_03-13.No384.RCS.pdf), Ruth Helman et al. report on the results of the 2013 Retirement Confidence Survey (RCS). They note that a record low number of Americans—just 13%—said they are confident of having enough money to live comfortably in retirement. This loss of confidence is largely attributable to Americans' more immediate needs such as cost-of-living and day-to-day expenses, as well as job losses, pay cuts, loss of retirement savings, and increased debt.

The 2013 RCS finds that U.S. workers have saved very little for retirement. Helman et al. indicate that in 2013, 57% of workers reported having total savings and investments, excluding the value of their homes, of less

TABLE 2.2

Percentage of persons with income from specified sources, by age group, 2010

Source of family income	Age 55–61	Age 62–64	Age 65 and over Total	65–69	70–74	75–79	80 and over
Earnings	84.3	72.6	38.2	56.2	40.1	30.2	21.4
Wages and salaries	81.0	68.5	35.2	52.2	36.8	27.9	19.3
Self-employment	11.7	10.5	6.4	9.5	6.8	4.7	3.6
Retirement benefits	31.5	61.3	90.9	84.8	92.7	93.8	94.3
Social Security	20.8	51.5	88.0	80.4	90.3	91.4	92.5
Benefits other than Social Security	17.6	32.1	43.0	40.2	43.7	45.9	43.5
Other public pensions	8.5	13.7	17.1	17.5	17.2	18.4	15.9
Railroad Retirement	0.2	0.5	0.7	0.7	0.8	0.9	0.6
Government employee pensions	8.3	13.3	16.5	16.8	16.6	17.6	15.4
Military	1.7	1.9	2.3	2.1	1.9	2.5	2.8
Federal	1.8	3.3	4.5	4.2	4.4	5.2	4.7
State or local	5.0	8.4	10.6	11.7	11.1	11.0	8.6
Private pensions or annuities	9.9	20.1	28.9	25.3	30.2	30.9	30.6
Income from assets	56.2	57.6	56.9	58.5	55.6	56.4	56.5
Interest	53.3	55.5	53.8	55.2	52.6	53.9	53.2
Other income from assets	27.3	27.5	27.1	29.5	27.7	26.3	24.5
Dividends	23.2	23.5	22.0	24.1	22.8	20.7	19.7
Rent or royalties	8.1	8.5	9.1	9.9	8.9	9.6	8.1
Estates or trusts	0.3	0.3	0.4	0.5	0.3	0.2	0.4
Veterans' benefits	3.4	5.1	4.2	3.8	3.5	4.4	5.1
Unemployment compensation	10.8	9.0	3.9	5.4	4.1	3.0	2.6
Workers' compensation	1.4	1.2	0.6	0.8	0.6	0.4	0.6
Cash public assistance and noncash benefits	12.1	11.5	12.2	11.2	11.8	13.8	12.5
Cash public assistance	6.2	5.5	4.6	4.8	4.3	5.1	4.3
Supplemental Security Income	5.6	4.8	4.1	4.4	3.8	4.6	3.8
Other	0.9	0.8	0.6	0.6	0.6	0.5	0.5
Noncash benefits	9.5	8.8	10.0	9.0	9.8	11.5	10.3
Food	7.4	6.6	6.3	6.1	6.3	7.1	5.8
Energy	2.9	2.5	3.3	3.1	3.3	3.6	3.2
Housing	2.5	2.4	3.8	3.0	3.7	4.6	4.1
Personal contributions	2.2	1.8	1.4	1.5	1.1	1.3	1.5
Number (in thousands)	26,829	10,155	39,179	12,160	9,254	7,088	10,676

SOURCE: "Table 9c. Percentage of People Age 55 and over with Family Income from Specified sources, by Age Group, 2010," in *Older Americans 2012: Key Indicators of Well-Being*, Federal Interagency Forum on Aging-Related Statistics, June 2012, http://www.agingstats.gov/Main_Site/Data/2012_Documents/docs/EntireChartbook.pdf (accessed May 28, 2013)

than $25,000, and 28% said they have saved less than $1,000 for retirement. Because this level of savings will render them woefully unprepared for retirement, 22% of workers plan to postpone retirement and 69% of workers are planning to supplement their income by working for pay in retirement.

One popular way to save for retirement is to contribute to individual retirement plans. Individuals fund these retirement plans themselves. The money that they contribute can be tax deductible, the plans' earnings are not taxed, and contributors determine how the money is invested. Since 1974 one of the major types of individual retirement plans has been the IRA. IRAs fall into several different categories, but the two most common types are traditional IRAs (deductible and nondeductible) and Roth IRAs; a variety of factors determine which kind of IRA best serves an individual's needs. Profit-sharing plans for the self-employed (formerly called Keogh plans) are another type of individual retirement plan.

The 2013 RCS finds that workers believe their retirement income will come from a variety of sources. According to Helman et al., 42% of Americans said their

retirement income will primarily come from an employer-sponsored retirement savings plan, 33% said Social Security will be a major source of retirement income, 31% will receive a traditional pension, 27% will rely heavily on their IRAs, 25% will rely on personal savings and investments, and 21% said employment will be their major source of retirement income.

NET WORTH

Because the economic well-being of households depends on income and wealth, assessment of income alone is not the best measure of older adults' financial health. To draw a more complete economic profile of the older population, it is necessary to evaluate older households in terms of measures of wealth, such as home equity, savings, and other assets and liabilities. For example, a household may be in the top one-fifth of the income distribution but be saddled with a large amount of debt.

Net worth is a measure of economic valuation and an indicator of financial security that is obtained by subtracting total liabilities from total assets. Greater net

TABLE 2.3

Percentage of private sector workers with retirement plan benefits, 2012

Retirement and medical care benefits, access, participation, and take-up rates, private industry, in percent, March 2012

Characteristic	Retirement			Medical care		
	Access	Participation	Take-up rate	Access	Participation	Take-up rate
All workers	**65**	**48**	**75**	**70**	**51**	**72**
Worker characteristic						
Management, professional, and related	79	68	86	87	67	76
Service	40	21	51	41	25	62
Sales and office	69	51	74	72	50	70
Natural resources, construction, and maintenance	65	51	78	77	57	75
Production, transportation, and material moving	66	50	76	75	57	76
Full time	74	59	80	86	64	74
Part time	38	19	50	24	13	54
Union	92	85	92	94	78	83
Nonunion	62	45	72	67	48	71
Low-wage workers (lowest 25 percent)	38	17	45	34	19	57
High-wage workers (highest 25 percent)	85	75	89	92	73	79
Establishment characteristic						
1 to 99 workers	50	34	68	57	41	71
100 to 499 workers	79	58	74	82	59	72
500 workers or more	86	76	88	89	68	76

Note: All private industry workers = 100 percent.

SOURCE: "Table 1. Retirement and Medical Care Benefits, Access, Participation, and Take-Up Rates, Private Industry, in Percent, March 2012," in "Who Has Benefits in Private Industry in 2012?" *Beyond the Numbers*, vol. 1, no. 13, September 2012, http://www.bls.gov/opub/btn/volume-1/pdf/ who-has-benefits-in-private-industry-in-2012.pdf (accessed May 29, 2013)

FIGURE 2.7

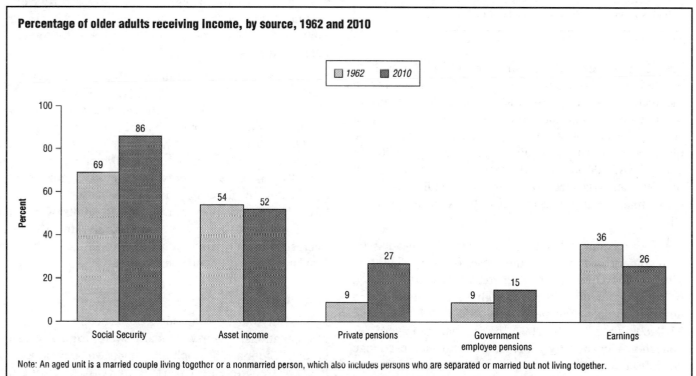

Percentage of older adults receiving income, by source, 1962 and 2010

Note: An aged unit is a married couple living together or a nonmarried person, which also includes persons who are separated or married but not living together.

SOURCE: "Percentage of Aged Units Receiving Income, by Source," in *Fast Facts and Figures about Social Security, 2012*, U.S. Social Security Administration, Office of Retirement and Disability Policy, August 2012, http://www.ssa.gov/policy/docs/chartbooks/fast_facts/2012/fast_facts12.pdf (accessed May 29, 2013)

worth enables individuals and households to weather financial challenges such as illness, disability, job loss, divorce, widowhood, or general economic downturns.

In *Older Americans 2012*, the Federal Interagency Forum on Aging-Related Statistics states that the median net worth of households headed by older white adults

FIGURE 2.8

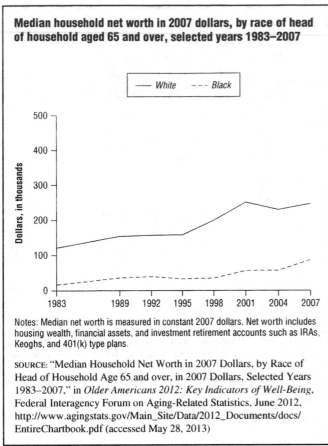

Median household net worth in 2007 dollars, by race of head of household aged 65 and over, selected years 1983–2007

Notes: Median net worth is measured in constant 2007 dollars. Net worth includes housing wealth, financial assets, and investment retirement accounts such as IRAs, Keoghs, and 401(k) type plans.

SOURCE: "Median Household Net Worth in 2007 Dollars, by Race of Head of Household Age 65 and over, in 2007 Dollars, Selected Years 1983–2007," in *Older Americans 2012: Key Indicators of Well-Being*, Federal Interagency Forum on Aging-Related Statistics, June 2012, http://www.agingstats.gov/Main_Site/Data/2012_Documents/docs/EntireChartbook.pdf (accessed May 28, 2013)

aged 65 years and older doubled, from $122,320 in 1983 to $284,300 in 2007. (See Figure 2.8.) During this period the increase in net worth was substantially greater for older white adults than for older African American adults. The median net worth of households headed by older African American adults grew from $17,960 in 1983 to $87,800 in 2007. In 2007 the median net worth of households headed by older white adults was over three times greater than that of older African American adults.

The median net worth of households headed by college-educated older adults rose from $283,200 in 1983 to $510,570 in 2007, whereas households headed by an older adult without a high school diploma did not even double their net worth—$58,030 in 1984 and $101,800 in 2007. In 2007 the median net worth of households headed by older adults with some college education was five times greater than that of households headed by older adults without a high school diploma.

It is important to observe that the net worth of many older Americans declined significantly between 2008 and 2009, at least in part because home equity, which is a primary source of wealth for older Americans, declined sharply. Christopher S. Rugaber indicates in "Average US Household Far from Regaining Its Wealth" (Associ-

ated Press, May 30, 2013) that U.S. household wealth dropped $16 trillion between late 2007 and early 2009. At the close of 2012, U.S. households had regained just $14.7 billion. However, Rugaber explains that "once those figures are adjusted for inflation and averaged across the U.S. population, the picture doesn't look so bright: The average household has recovered only 45 percent of its wealth." Older adults are at a disadvantage compared with other age groups because unlike younger workers, they do not have the time to recoup their losses.

Older Adults Are Hard Hit by the Mortgage Crisis and Low Interest Rates

According to Lori A. Trawinski of the AARP Public Policy Institute, in *Nightmare on Main Street: Older Americans and the Mortgage Market Crisis* (July 2012, http://www.aarp.org/content/dam/aarp/research/public_policy_institute/cons_prot/2012/nightmare-on-main-street-AARP-ppi-cons-prot.pdf), at the close of 2011 about 3.5 million loans to people aged 50 years and older were underwater (the loans were larger than the value of the homes), 600,000 people over the age of 50 years were in foreclosure, and an additional 625,000 people were delinquent in their mortgage payments. The rate of foreclosures for older adults was just 0.1% in 2007. By 2011 it was 23 times higher—2.3% as property values continued to decline in many parts of the country, limiting the ability of older homeowners to refinance their mortgages.

In "3 Ways Low Interest Rates Hurt Seniors" (USNews.com, March 19, 2012), Philip Moeller observes that low interest rates intended to avert economic disaster and spur economic recovery following the Great Recession have hurt retirees counting on the interest income from their savings. Moeller reports that virtually nonexistent interest rates on savings accounts, certificates of deposit, and U.S. Treasury securities have disproportionally harmed older adults who tend to rely in these relatively low-risk investments. Low interest rates may also reduce pension funds, which in turn may reduce payouts for retirees.

POVERTY

Poverty rates are measures of the economic viability of populations. Poverty standards were originally based on the "economy food plan," which was developed by the U.S. Department of Agriculture (USDA) during the 1960s. The plan calculated the cost of a minimally adequate household food budget for different types of households by age of householder. Because USDA surveys showed that the average family spent one-third of its income on food, it was decided that a household with an income three times the amount needed for food was living fairly comfortably. In 1963 the poverty level was calculated by simply multiplying the cost of

TABLE 2.4

People in poverty, by selected characteristics, 2010 and 2011

[Numbers in thousands. People as of March of the following year.]

Characteristic	2010[a] Total	Below poverty Number	Below poverty Percent	2011 Total	Below poverty Number	Below poverty Percent	Change in poverty (2011 less 2010)[b] Number	Change in poverty (2011 less 2010)[b] Percent
People								
Total	306,130	46,343	15.1	308,456	46,247	15.0	−96	−0.1
Family status								
In families	250,200	33,120	13.2	252,316	33,126	13.1	6	−0.1
Householder	79,559	9,400	11.8	80,529	9,497	11.8	96	—
Related children under 18	72,581	15,598	21.5	72,568	15,539	21.4	−59	−0.1
Related children under 6	23,892	6,037	25.3	23,860	5,844	24.5	−193	−0.8
In unrelated subfamilies	1,680	774	46.1	1,623	705	43.4	−69	−2.6
Reference person	654	283	43.2	671	272	40.6	−10	−2.6
Children under 18	933	469	50.2	846	409	48.4	−60	−1.9
Unrelated individuals	54,250	12,449	22.9	54,517	12,416	22.8	−33	−0.2
Race[c] and Hispanic origin								
White	239,982	31,083	13.0	241,334	30,849	12.8	−234	−0.2
White, not Hispanic	194,783	19,251	9.9	194,960	19,171	9.8	−80	—
Black	39,283	10,746	27.4	39,609	10,929	27.6	183	0.2
Asian	15,611	1,899	12.2	16,086	1,973	12.3	74	0.1
Hispanic (any race)	50,971	13,522	26.5	52,279	13,244	25.3	−278	−1.2
Sex								
Male	149,737	20,893	14.0	150,990	20,501	13.6	−391	−0.4
Female	156,394	25,451	16.3	157,466	25,746	16.3	295	0.1
Age								
Under 18 years	73,873	16,286	22.0	73,737	16,134	21.9	−152	−0.2
18 to 64 years	192,481	26,499	13.8	193,213	26,492	13.7	−6	−0.1
65 years and older	39,777	3,558	8.9	41,507	3,620	8.7	62	−0.2
Nativity								
Native born	266,723	38,485	14.4	268,490	38,661	14.4	176	—
Foreign born	39,407	7,858	19.9	39,966	7,586	19.0	−272	−1.0
Naturalized citizen	17,344	1,954	11.3	17,934	2,233	12.5	279	1.2
Not a citizen	22,063	5,904	26.8	22,032	5,353	24.3	−551	−2.5
Region								
Northeast	54,710	7,038	12.9	54,977	7,208	13.1	170	0.2
Midwest	66,038	9,216	14.0	66,023	9,221	14.0	5	—
South	113,681	19,123	16.8	114,936	18,380	16.0	−743	−0.8
West	71,701	10,966	15.3	72,520	11,437	15.8	471	0.5
Residence								
Inside metropolitan statistical areas	258,366	38,466	14.9	261,155	38,202	14.6	−264	−0.3
Inside principal cities	98,816	19,532	19.8	100,183	20,007	20.0	475	0.2
Outside principal cities	159,550	18,933	11.9	160,973	18,195	11.3	−739	−0.6
Outside metropolitan statistical areas[d]	47,764	7,877	16.5	47,301	8,045	17.0	168	0.5
Work experience								
Total, 18 to 64 years	192,481	26,499	13.8	193,213	26,492	13.7	−6	−0.1
All workers	143,687	10,462	7.3	144,163	10,345	7.2	−117	−0.1
Worked full-time, year-round	95,697	2,600	2.7	97,443	2,732	2.8	132	0.1
Less than full-time, year-round	47,991	7,862	16.4	46,720	7,614	10.3	−248	−0.1
Did not work at least 1 week	48,793	16,037	32.9	49,049	16,147	32.9	110	0.1
Disability status[e]								
Total, 18 to 64 years	192,481	26,499	13.8	193,213	26,492	13.7	−6	−0.1
With a disability	14,974	4,196	28.0	14,968	4,313	28.8	117	0.8
With no disability	176,592	22,227	12.6	177,309	22,105	12.5	−122	−0.1

a minimally adequate food budget by three. Later, the U.S. Census Bureau began comparing family income before taxes with a set of poverty thresholds that vary based on family size and composition and are adjusted annually for inflation using the Consumer Price Index (CPI; a measure of the average change in consumer prices over time in a fixed market basket of goods and services).

According to Table 2.4, the poverty rate of adults aged 65 years and older (8.7%) in 2011 was slightly lower than the previous year (8.9%) and represented 3.6 million older adults living in poverty. The rates recorded in 2011 for 18- to 64-year-olds (13.7%) and children under the age of 18 years (21.9%) both exceeded that of older adults. Census Bureau data reveal that in 1959 the poverty rate for people aged 65 years and older was 35%,

TABLE 2.4

People in poverty, by selected characteristics, 2010 and 2011 [CONTINUED]

[Numbers in thousands. People as of March of the following year.]

—Represents or rounds to zero.
[a]Consistent with 2011 data through implementation of Census 2010-based population controls.
[b]Details may not sum to totals because of rounding.
[c]Federal surveys now give respondents the option of reporting more than one race. Therefore, two basic ways of defining a race group are possible. A group such as Asian may be defined as those who reported Asian and no other race (the race-alone or single-race concept) or as those who reported Asian regardless of whether they also reported another race (the race-alone-or-in-combination concept). This table shows data using the first approach (race alone). The use of the single-race population does not imply that it is the preferred method of presenting or analyzing data. The Census Bureau uses a variety of approaches. Information on people who reported more than one race, such as white and American Indian and Alaska Native or Asian and black or African American, is available from Census 2010 through American FactFinder. About 2.9 percent of people reported more than one race in Census 2010. Data for American Indians and Alaska Natives, Native Hawaiians and other Pacific Islanders, and those reporting two or more races are not shown separately.
[d]The "Outside metropolitan statistical areas" category includes both micropolitan statistical areas and territory outside of metropolitan and micropolitan statistical areas.
[e]The sum of those with and without a disability does not equal the total because disability status is not defined for individuals in the armed forces.

SOURCE: Carmen DeNavas-Walt, Bernadette D. Proctor, and Jessica C. Smith, "Table 3. People in Poverty by Selected Characteristics: 2010 and 2011," in *Income, Poverty and Health Insurance Coverage in the United States: 2009*, U.S.Census Bureau, September 2012, https://www.census.gov/hhes/www/poverty/data/incpovhlth/2011/table3.pdf (accessed May 28, 2013)

FIGURE 2.9

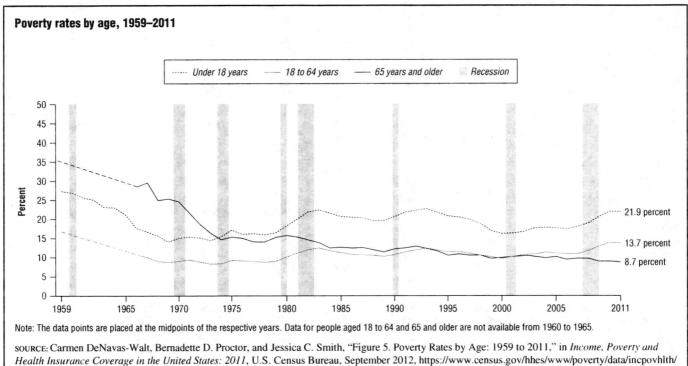

Poverty rates by age, 1959–2011

Note: The data points are placed at the midpoints of the respective years. Data for people aged 18 to 64 and 65 and older are not available from 1960 to 1965.

SOURCE: Carmen DeNavas-Walt, Bernadette D. Proctor, and Jessica C. Smith, "Figure 5. Poverty Rates by Age: 1959 to 2011," in *Income, Poverty and Health Insurance Coverage in the United States: 2011*, U.S. Census Bureau, September 2012, https://www.census.gov/hhes/www/poverty/data/incpovhlth/2011/figure5.pdf (accessed May 28, 2013)

well above the rates for the other age groups. (See Figure 2.9.) The lowest level of poverty in the older population occurred in 2011, when the rate fell to 8.7%.

Poverty Thresholds Are Lower for Older Adults

The Census Bureau measures need for assistance using poverty thresholds (specific dollar amounts that determine poverty status). Each individual or family is assigned one of 48 possible poverty thresholds. Thresholds vary according to family size and the ages of the members. The thresholds do not vary geographically, and they are updated annually for inflation using the CPI.

One assumption used to determine poverty thresholds is that healthy older adults have lower nutritional require-

ments than younger people, so they require less money for food. This assumption has resulted in different poverty thresholds for both the young and old. For example, in 2012 the poverty threshold for a single person under the age of 65 years was $11,945, as opposed to $11,011 for a person aged 65 years or older. (See Table 2.5.) The 2012 poverty threshold for two people including a householder under the age of 65 years was $15,347, compared with $13,878 for two people including a householder aged 65 years or older.

This method of defining poverty fails to take into account the special financial and health challenges that older adults may face. For example, no household costs other than food are counted, although older adults spend

TABLE 2.5

Poverty thresholds, by size of family and number of related children under 18, 2012

Size of family unit	None	One	Two	Three	Four	Five	Six	Seven	Eight or more
One person (unrelated individual)									
Under 65 years	11,945								
65 years and over	11,011								
Two people									
Householder under 65 years	15,374	15,825							
Householder 65 years and over	13,878	15,765							
Three people	17,959	18,480	18,498						
Four people	23,681	24,069	23,283	23,364					
Five people	28,558	28,974	28,087	27,400	26,981				
Six people	32,847	32,978	32,298	31,647	30,678	30,104			
Seven people	37,795	38,031	37,217	36,651	35,594	34,362	33,009		
Eight people	42,271	42,644	41,876	41,204	40,249	39,038	37,777	37,457	
Nine people or more	50,849	51,095	50,416	49,845	48,908	47,620	46,454	46,165	44,387

SOURCE: "Poverty Thresholds for 2012 by Size of Family and Number of Related Children under 18 Years," in *Poverty Thresholds*, U.S. Census Bureau, 2012, http://www.neded.org/files/research/threshold.pdf (accessed May 29, 2013)

a much greater percentage of their income on health care than younger people do. Also, the dollars allocated for food only consider the nutritional needs of healthy older adults; many are in poor health and may require more costly special diets or nutritional supplements.

WELL-OFF OLDER ADULTS

More older Americans live comfortably in the 21st century than at any other time in history. Many of those in their mid-70s to 80s were born during the Great Depression (1929–1939). The enforced Depression-era frugality taught their families to economize and save. During the 1950s and 1960s, their peak earning years, they enjoyed a period of unprecedented economic expansion. Since then, many have raised their children, paid off their home mortgages, invested wisely, and become eligible to receive Social Security payments that are larger than ever.

Although these factors have contributed to a more favorable economic status for this cohort (a group of individuals that shares a common characteristic such as birth years and is studied over time) of older adults than they would have otherwise enjoyed, most older people are not wealthy. Figure 2.3 shows that in 2011, 29% of households headed by older adults had total incomes of $75,000 or more and 20% of households headed by older adults reported incomes ranging from $50,000 to $74,999.

It should also be noted that even well-off older adults were affected by the recession. Mauricio Soto of the Urban Institute explains in the fact sheet "How Is the Financial Crisis Affecting Retirement Savings?" (March 9, 2009, http://www.urban.org/UploadedPDF/411847_update-3-09-2009-pr.pdf) that between September 2007 and March 2009 the stock market lost an estimated $13 trillion. This loss devastated the retirement savings of many Americans, and although older adults typically

have fewer funds invested in stocks than younger adults, many endured substantial losses. However, by 2013 many of these losses had been reversed.

Older adults' responses to economic uncertainty vary. In *Assessing the Impact of Severe Economic Recession on the Elderly: Summary of a Workshop* (2011), Malay Majmundar observes that older adults who reduced their consumption and spending in response to the recession, especially those who vividly remember the toll of the Great Depression, may remain fearful even when the economy recovers and may continue to limit their spending.

CONSUMER EXPENSES

On average, older households spend less than younger households because they generally have less money to spend, fewer dependents to support, and different needs and values. The BLS notes that in 2011 the annual per capita expenditure for people aged 65 to 74 years was $44,646, whereas those aged 75 years and older spent just $32,688. (See Table 2.6.) Those under the age of 25 years were the only group with a smaller expenditure, spending $29,912 per capita annually. The greatest amounts were spent on housing (including utilities), food, transportation, and health care. Not surprisingly, older adults spent more on health care than any other age group, both in actual dollars and as a percentage of expenditures. Older adults spent less on tobacco and smoking products, alcoholic beverages, apparel, and food away from home than other age groups.

Smaller Households Are More Expensive to Run

Most older adult households contain fewer people than younger households. Although larger households, in general, cost more to feed, operate, and maintain, they are less expensive on a per capita basis.

TABLE 2.6

Average annual expenditures and characteristics, by age, 2011

Item	All consumer units	Under 25 years	25–34 years	35–44 years	45–54 years	55–64 years	65 years and older	65–74 years	75 years and older
Number of consumer units (in thousands)	122,287	7,743	20,463	21,699	24,821	21,688	25,873	14,079	11,794
Consumer unit characteristics:									
Income before taxes	$63,685	$27,514	$58,179	$77,376	$78,519	$75,517	$43,232	$52,521	$32,144
Income after taxes	61,673	27,495	56,851	75,537	75,234	72,115	42,326	51,161	31,779
Age of reference person	49.7	21.7	29.5	39.6	49.6	59.2	74.8	68.9	81.8
Average number in consumer unit:									
Persons	2.5	2.1	2.9	3.3	2.8	2.1	1.7	1.9	1.6
Children under 18	0.6	0.5	1.1	1.4	0.7	0.2	0.1	0.1	a
Persons 65 and older	0.3	a	a	a	0.1	0.1	1.4	1.4	1.3
Earners	1.3	1.3	1.5	1.6	1.7	1.3	0.5	0.6	0.3
Vehicles	1.9	1.1	1.7	2.0	2.3	2.1	1.6	1.9	1.3
Percent distribution:									
Sex of reference person:									
Male	47	47	48	48	46	49	43	46	39
Female	53	53	52	52	54	51	57	54	61
Housing tenure:									
Homeowner	65	15	43	62	72	79	81	83	79
With mortgage	40	10	38	53	54	46	22	31	12
Without mortgage	25	5	5	9	18	32	59	52	67
Renter	35	85	57	38	28	21	19	17	21
Race of reference person:									
Black or African-American	12	13	14	14	13	12	9	11	7
White, Asian, and all other races	88	87	86	86	87	88	91	89	93
Hispanic or Latino origin of reference person:									
Hispanic or Latino	12	17	18	18	13	7	6	7	5
Not Hispanic or Latino	88	83	82	82	87	93	94	93	95
Education of reference person:									
Elementary (1–8)	5	2	3	4	4	4	9	6	12
High school (9–12)	34	34	28	30	34	33	42	37	47
College	62	65	69	66	62	63	49	56	41
Never attended and other	b	b	b	b	b	b	b	b	b
At least one vehicle owned or leased	88	66	89	90	91	91	85	90	80
Average annual expenditures	**$49,705**	**$29,912**	**$48,097**	**$57,271**	**$58,050**	**$53,616**	**$39,173**	**$44,646**	**$32,688**
Food	6,458	4,354	6,211	7,765	7,424	6,520	5,158	5,804	4,408
Food at home	3,838	2,382	3,447	4,594	4,421	3,908	3,309	3,594	2,980
Cereals and bakery products	531	336	479	644	610	515	469	479	458
Cereals and cereal products	175	114	175	218	201	161	142	144	139
Bakery products	356	222	303	426	409	354	328	335	319
Meats, poultry, fish, and eggs	832	527	733	1,006	965	894	671	759	569
Beef	223	137	188	264	267	235	186	218	149
Pork	162	96	133	200	178	183	138	162	110
Other meats	123	63	110	155	157	120	92	102	80
Poultry	154	122	154	190	182	152	108	119	95
Fish and seafood	121	69	103	139	125	152	103	111	94
Eggs	50	38	45	59	55	50	45	49	41
Dairy products	407	244	379	481	475	394	359	387	326
Fresh milk and cream	150	97	144	188	172	137	126	132	120
Other dairy products	257	148	234	293	303	256	233	256	207
Fruits and vegetables	715	424	627	841	803	734	663	713	605
Fresh fruits	247	132	210	291	273	262	237	254	217
Fresh vegetables	224	130	195	254	258	239	206	220	189
Processed fruits	116	80	107	143	128	107	105	111	99
Processed vegetables	128	83	115	154	144	125	115	128	100
Other food at home	1,353	850	1,230	1,622	1,567	1,372	1,147	1,255	1,021
Sugar and other sweets	144	78	112	179	163	152	136	144	128
Fats and oils	110	61	95	126	125	111	106	112	99
Miscellaneous foods	690	454	671	834	779	677	577	626	521
Nonalcoholic beverages	361	236	319	434	442	368	284	310	253
Food prepared by consumer unit on out-of-town trips	48	20	33	48	58	64	43	62	21
Food away from home	2,620	1,973	2,764	3,171	3,003	2,611	1,849	2,210	1,429
Alcoholic beverages	456	418	513	497	494	468	338	422	241
Housing	16,803	10,282	17,026	19,979	18,782	17,173	13,706	15,105	12,046
Shelter	9,825	6,732	10,480	12,068	11,111	9,755	7,178	7,966	6,237
Owned dwellings	6,148	1,277	4,826	7,844	7,774	7,002	4,953	5,802	3,939
Mortgage interest and charges	3,184	740	3,207	4,873	4,236	3,244	1,419	2,008	716
Property taxes	1,845	306	1,072	1,930	2,300	2,301	2,025	2,243	1,765
Maintenance, repairs, insurance, other expenses	1,120	231	547	1,041	1,238	1,456	1,509	1,551	1,459

Item	All consumer units	Under 25 years	25–34 years	35–44 years	45–54 years	55–64 years	65 years and older	65–74 years	75 years and older
Rented dwellings	$3,029	$5,111	$5,338	$3,714	$2,582	$1,784	$1,480	$1,234	$1,772
Other lodging	648	345	316	510	756	969	745	929	525
Utilities, fuels, and public services	3,727	1,918	3,296	4,065	4,318	4,053	3,485	3,782	3,131
Natural gas	420	172	341	458	481	461	430	434	426
Electricity	1,423	757	1,256	1,555	1,601	1,555	1,362	1,498	1,199
Fuel oil and other fuels	157	19	77	114	175	197	247	229	267
Telephone services	1,226	777	1,219	1,394	1,502	1,275	921	1,060	756
Water and other public services	501	193	402	544	559	565	525	560	483
Household operations	1,122	505	1,359	1,494	969	958	1,093	952	1,261
Personal services	398	174	804	783	188	69	300	110	525
Other household expenses	724	331	555	710	781	889	793	841	736
Housekeeping supplies	615	268	420	702	691	722	636	695	568
Laundry and cleaning supplies	145	82	117	170	167	151	140	148	130
Other household products	340	141	232	407	368	402	348	379	312
Postage and stationery	130	46	72	125	157	169	148	168	126
Household furnishings and equipment	1,514	858	1,471	1,650	1,693	1,685	1,314	1,711	849
Household textiles	109	37	96	130	107	106	129	183	66
Furniture	358	260	454	404	350	419	229	314	127
Floor coverings	20	5	11	24	21	28	20	31	8
Major appliances	194	82	160	219	209	246	175	214	129
Small appliances, miscellaneous housewares	89	77	77	93	98	89	92	124	55
Miscellaneous household equipment	744	397	674	781	907	797	668	844	464
Apparel and services	1,740	1,448	1,818	2,227	1,978	1,719	1,129	1,195	1,052
Men and boys	404	335	435	559	431	436	210	242	173
Men, 16 and over	324	309	335	375	353	393	187	213	156
Boys, 2 to 15	80	25	100	184	78	43	23	29	16
Women and girls	721	498	694	842	881	727	545	545	545
Women, 16 and over	604	468	569	604	733	653	503	477	533
Girls, 2 to 15	117	29	125	238	148	74	42	68	11
Children under 2	68	129	146	103	45	29	13	17	8
Footwear	321	298	306	449	393	288	189	176	203
Other apparel products and services	226	189	237	274	228	239	173	214	124
Transportation	8,293	5,474	8,860	9,700	9,505	8,991	5,751	6,962	4,309
Vehicle purchases (net outlay)	2,669	2,068	3,203	3,434	2,624	2,953	1,588	1,858	1,267
Cars and trucks, new	1,265	610	1,243	1,629	1,119	1,671	975	1,190	718
Cars and trucks, used	1,339	1,431	1,855	1,715	1,451	1,212	587	622	545
Other vehicles	64	328	104	90	55	70	26	45	3
Gasoline and motor oil	2,655	1,840	2,726	3,188	3,270	2,713	1,755	2,218	1,201
Other vehicle expenses	2,454	1,265	2,402	2,565	2,985	2,746	1,994	2,343	1,581
Vehicle finance charges	233	128	302	328	269	224	100	144	49
Maintenance and repairs	805	456	718	856	977	950	650	820	449
Vehicle insurance	983	505	957	920	1,201	1,089	894	950	829
Vehicle rental, leases, licenses, and other charges	433	176	425	460	538	483	350	429	256
Public and other transportation	516	300	529	513	626	579	414	543	260
Health care	3,313	841	2,094	2,762	3,411	4,048	4,769	5,038	4,449
Health insurance	1,922	456	1,237	1,581	1,801	2,196	3,076	3,154	2,982
Medical services	768	254	546	694	942	1,013	786	894	656
Drugs	489	93	229	377	515	690	714	791	623
Medical supplies	134	38	82	110	153	149	193	199	188
Entertainment	2,572	1,345	2,423	2,926	3,169	2,769	2,009	2,493	1,437
Fees and admissions	594	264	501	810	808	571	400	548	224
Audio and visual equipment and services	977	608	948	1,101	1,111	1,055	808	902	697
Pets, toys, hobbies, and playground equipment	631	333	599	643	744	759	512	626	380
Other entertainment supplies, equipment, and services	370	140	375	372	506	385	289	418	136
Personal care products and services	634	324	570	736	709	695	567	609	517
Reading	115	45	74	100	113	149	157	163	148
Education	1,051	2,253	1,049	818	1,879	866	247	262	229
Tobacco products and smoking supplies	351	256	378	343	465	401	212	289	120
Miscellaneous	775	285	606	781	947	931	753	821	674
Cash contributions	1,721	367	1,130	1,570	1,722	2,112	2,392	2,526	2,231
Personal insurance and pensions	5,424	2,220	5,346	7,068	7,453	6,775	1,985	2,957	825
Life and other personal insurance	317	67	138	308	401	534	280	361	183
Pensions and Social Security	5,106	2,154	5,207	6,760	7,052	6,242	1,706	2,596	643

Home maintenance, such as replacing a roof or major appliance, costs the same for any household, but in larger households the per capita cost is lower. Purchasing small quantities of food for one or two people may be almost as costly as buying in bulk for a larger household. Because older adults often have limited transportation and mobility, they may be forced to buy food and other necessities at small neighborhood stores that generally charge more than supermarkets and warehouse stores. Larger households may also benefit from multiple incomes.

TABLE 2.6

Average annual expenditures and characteristics, by age, 2011 [CONTINUED]

Item	All consumer units	Under 25 years	25–34 years	35–44 years	45–54 years	55–64 years	65 years and older	65–74 years	75 years and older
Sources of income and personal taxes:									
Money income before taxes	$63,685	$27,514	$58,179	$77,376	$78,519	$75,517	$43,232	$52,521	$32,144
Wages and salaries	49,805	23,818	53,600	70,471	70,076	55,381	13,130	19,670	5,321
Self-employment income	3,269	764	1,938	3,386	3,013	7,102	2,005	3,165	620
Social Security, private and government retirement	7,648	294	364	1,079	2,636	9,305	24,539	25,828	23,002
Interest, dividends, rental income, other property income	1,281	127	256	597	960	2,042	2,681	2,789	2,552
Unemployment and workers' compensation, veterans' benefits	579	289	705	642	733	755	218	290	131
Public assistance, supplemental security income, food stamps	520	609	561	573	565	596	310	328	289
Regular contributions for support	364	1,016	455	413	322	204	231	311	136
Other income	218	596	300	215	214	131	118	138	94
Personal taxed (missing values not inputed)	2,012	19	1,328	1,839	3,284	3,402	907	1,360	365
Federal income taxes	1,370	−123	779	1,166	2,407	2,404	595	952	169
State and local income taxes	505	130	477	560	747	786	126	177	65
Other taxes	136	12	72	113	130	211	186	231	131
Income after taxes	61,673	27,495	56,851	75,537	75,234	72,115	42,326	51,161	31,779
Addenda:									
Net change in total assets and liabilities	−$1,826	−$1,701	−$5,006	−$6,157	−$4,130	−$5,009	$9,162	$17,760	−$1,103
Net change in total assets	6,836	4,455	7,135	7,466	4,115	3,594	12,109	22,556	−361
Net change in total liabilities	8,662	6,157	12,141	13,624	8,245	8,603	2,947	4,795	742
Otherfinancial information:									
Other money receipts	729	259	347	260	1,264	1,244	621	464	809
Mortgage principal paid on owned property	−2,008	−249	−1,266	−2,491	−2,800	−2,757	−1,329	−1,893	−656
Estimated market value of owned home	151,165	23,429	78,434	141,991	183,645	196,892	185,117	202,364	164,529
Estimated monthly rental value of owned home	849	168	520	858	998	1,068	980	1,048	898
Gifts of goods and services	1,037	378	496	711	1,553	1,535	1,025	1,269	736
Food	84	14	32	61	132	155	60	72	46
Alcoholic beverages	17	7	14	9	30	9	21	36	5
Housing	194	58	107	152	252	273	220	310	114
Housekeeping supplies	25	7	14	27	28	33	26	31	20
Household textiles	11	1	9	5	12	16	14	22	5
Appliances and miscellaneous housewares	18	3	7	10	19	32	25	41	6
Major appliances	7	c	1	4	8	17	6	11	b
Small appliances and miscellaneous housewares	11	3	6	6	11	14	19	30	6
Miscellaneous household equipment	45	23	23	36	47	65	56	78	32
Other housing	96	23	54	73	146	127	98	137	51
Apparel and services	205	169	148	209	205	263	209	224	192
Males, 2 and over	53	39	48	44	48	68	61	63	58
Females, 2 and over	77	43	35	62	83	119	94	110	76
Children under 2	22	35	24	21	27	24	12	16	6
Other apparel products and services	52	51	41	81	47	53	42	34	51
Jewelry and watches	18	17	12	27	15	22	15	17	12
All other apparel products and services	34	34	29	54	32	31	27	17	39
Transportation	90	17	57	56	142	117	96	144	38
Health care	30	b	5	15	39	39	57	52	62
Entertainment	93	48	68	80	95	162	74	103	41
Toys, games, arts and crafts, and tricycles	26	6	28	32	20	41	19	28	9
Other entertainment	67	42	41	48	76	122	55	75	32
Personal care products and services	15	10	9	11	13	26	14	22	5
Reading	2	1	2	1	3	3	2	2	1
Education	216	46	12	75	548	333	130	101	163
All other gifts	91	7	42	42	94	154	142	203	68

aValue is less than or equal to 0.05.
bValue is less than or equal to 0.5.
cNo data reported.

SOURCE: "Table 3. Age of Reference Person: Average Annual Expenditures and Characteristics, Consumer Expenditure Survey, 2011," in *Consumer Expenditures in 2011*, U.S. Department of Labor, U.S. Bureau of Labor Statistics, September 25, 2012, http://www.bls.gov/cex/2011/Standard/age.pdf (accessed May 30, 2013)

High energy costs also cause older adults physical and financial hardship, prompting some to suffer extreme heat and cold in their home. Programs such as the Low Income Home Energy Assistance Program (LIHEAP; 2013, http://www.acf.hhs.gov/programs/ocs/liheap/), which is operated by the U.S. Department of Health and Human Services' Administration for Children and Families, attempt to prevent older adults from suffering from a lack of heat in their home. LIHEAP assists eligible households to meet their home energy needs.

AGING CONSUMERS: A GROWING MARKET

Older adults have proven to be a lucrative market for many products. Many older adults are working beyond retirement, and these older workers may prove to be an untapped market for advertisers, affecting a number of consumer sectors. Older adults are redefining aging—only a minority of Americans expects to retire as their parents did. Older adults are now more likely to continue working, and working out, rather than retiring to the shuffleboard court or the rocking chair on the front porch. As a result, they are considered an important market for an expanding array of products, such as specialty foods, drinks, anti-aging cosmetics, and over-the-counter and prescription drugs, as well as products that are traditionally marketed to older adults, such as health and life insurance plans and burial plots.

One example of marketing that is targeted to active older adults is the 2013 launch of Amazon.com's "50+ Active and Healthy Living Store." In "Amazon Goes after Older Adults & Seniors with New Store" (Tech-crunch.com, April 15, 2013), Sarah Perez explains that Amazon's new website caters to older adults by offering "nutritional products, wellness, exercise, fitness, medical, personal care, beauty and entertainment items and more." The site also offers subscription-based ordering, which enables consumers to schedule automatic deliveries of frequently used items. Subscribers earn a discount—as much as 15%—on their purchases.

Baby Boomers: The Emerging "Silver" Market

The aging baby boomers (people born between 1946 and 1964) have been dubbed "zoomers" to reflect the generation's active lifestyle. Market researchers believe the sheer size of the soon-to-be silver-haired boomer cohort and its history of self-indulgence, coupled with considerable purchasing power, ensure that this group will contain the most voracious older consumers ever.

The information in this section was drawn from the Boomer Report, a quarterly survey of 1,400 consumers by the Boomer Project/Survey Sampling International that aims to determine how this generation thinks, feels, and responds to marketing and advertising messages, and from "Report Card on the Boomers" (January 3, 2013, http://www.boomerproject.com/documents/viva/RTD-Op-Ed-20130103.pdf) by John W. Martin. Included among the many insights that the Boomer Project research reveals are the following:

- Boomers at age 50 perceive themselves as 12 years younger, and they expect to live 35 more years. They consider themselves to be in early "middle age" and view 72 as the onset of old age. Boomers have created the "longevity climate"—by delaying retirement they have more money to spend during their longer lives.

- Boomers reject any and all age-related labels to describe themselves. They do not want to be called "seniors," "aged," or even "boomers," and they do not want to be compared with their parents' generation or any previous cohort of older adults.

- Boomers over the age of 50 do not want to reverse or stop the signs of aging, they simply want to postpone or slow the process. They are intent on seeking health rather than youth—feeling younger is as important as looking younger for boomers eager to age "on their own terms." Boomers are frequenting the growing number of health clubs, fitness centers, and wellness programs that opened in 2012.

- Boomers want more time, which means that services that offer them free time to pursue work and leisure activities are likely to be in great demand. Examples of these include cleaning, home maintenance, and gardening services.

- Boomers are becoming less interested in material possessions and more interested in gaining a variety of experiences. Rather than embracing the premise that "he who has the most toys wins," boomers believe "he who chalks up the most experiences wins."

- Once dubbed the "me generation," boomers operate on the premise that they are entitled to special treatment, not because they have earned it by virtue of age, but simply because they deserve it. They want products and services that are relevant to them personally. Boomers also lead the "age of responsible consumerism" and are budget conscious, purchasing smaller homes and limiting holiday spending. They remain motivated to fulfill their own needs, whether these needs are for community, adventure, or a spiritual life.

- Boomers are life-long learners and a "wired" generation—learning, connecting, and communicating online and via social networks. Continuing education classes and opportunities to learn and enrich their lives through travel are important to this generation.

- Boomers are still interested in promoting social change. The generation known for protesting the Vietnam War (1954–1975) and questioning authority and traditional American social mores continues to support global and local humanitarian and environmental action.

- Boomers do not want to relocate to traditional retirement enclaves and communities; instead, they prefer to age in place (remaining in their own home rather than relocating to assisted living facilities or other supportive housing). Having witnessed the institutionalization of their parents in nursing homes and in other assisted living facilities, boomers are intent on remaining in their home, and in the community, for as long as they can.

In *Marketing to Baby Boomers—US—December 2012* (2012), Mintel International Group Ltd. indicates that demographic factors influencing boomers' purchasing behaviors include the rise in multigenerational households headed by boomers, their interest in preventive medicine, self-care and their desire to remain young and vital, and older boomers' optimism about the economy.

Kern Lewis reports in "Pick Baby Boomers as Your Target Market for the Holidays" (Forbes.com, November 9, 2012) that boomers have about 70% of disposable income in the United States and are the leading consumers in 119 out of 123 categories of consumer-packaged goods. Lewis notes that boomers spend more money on electronics, health care, and pharmaceuticals than do younger people, purchase nearly two-thirds of new cars and over three-quarters of all luxury travel, and spend a staggering $7 billion per year online.

SOCIAL SECURITY

We can never insure one hundred percent of the population against one hundred percent of the hazards and vicissitudes of life, but we have tried to frame a law which will give some measure of protection to the average citizen and to his family against the loss of a job and against poverty-ridden old age.

—President Franklin D. Roosevelt, on signing the Social Security Act, August 14, 1935

Social Security is a social insurance program that is funded through a dedicated payroll tax. It is also known as Old-Age, Survivors, and Disability Insurance (OASDI), which describes its three major classes of beneficiaries.

During the Great Depression poverty among the older population escalated. In 1934 more than half of older adults lacked sufficient income. Although 30 states had some form of an old-age pension program in place, by 1935 these programs were unable to meet the growing need. Just 3% of the older population received benefits under these state plans, and the average benefit amount was about 65 cents per day.

As advocated by President Franklin D. Roosevelt (1882–1945), social insurance would solve the problem of economic security for older adults by creating a work-related, contributory system in which workers would provide for their own future economic security through taxes paid while employed. By the time the Social Security Act was signed into law by President Roosevelt in August 1935, 34 nations were already operating some form of a social insurance program (government-sponsored efforts to provide for the economic well-being of a nation's citizens).

According to the SSA, in "Social Security Basic Facts" (June 19, 2013, http://www.ssa.gov/pressoffice/basicfact.htm), in 2012 more than nine out of 10 people aged 65 years and older received OASDI. Retired workers and their dependents accounted for more than two-thirds (70%) of total benefits paid, whereas survivors of deceased workers accounted for 11% of the total, and disabled workers and their dependents rounded out the total with 19% of benefits paid. An estimated 94% (161 million) of the U.S. workforce was covered by Social Security.

Although Social Security was not initially intended as a full pension, 23% of married older adults and 46% of unmarried older adults relied almost exclusively (for 90% or more of their income) on the program in 2010. (See Figure 2.4.) In *Time Trends in Poverty for Older Americans between 2001–2009* (April 2012, http://www.ebri.org/pdf/notespdf/EBRI_Notes_04_Apr-12.EldPovty.pdf), Sudipto Banerjee of the Employee Benefit Research Institute (EBRI) observes that programs such as Social Security were created to reduce the probability that Americans would fall into poverty during old age. A recent EBRI study of poverty among Americans aged 50 years and older finds that between 2005 and 2009 the rate of poverty among older adults increased as did the number of older adults now considered to be living in poverty.

Social Security benefits are funded through the Federal Insurance Contributions Act (FICA), which provides that a mandatory tax be withheld from workers' earnings and be matched by their employers. (Self-employed workers pay both the employer and employee shares of FICA taxes.) When covered workers retire (or are disabled), they draw benefits that are based on the amount they contributed to the fund. The amount of the benefit is directly related to the duration of employment and earnings—people who have worked longer and earned higher wages receive larger benefits.

Workers can retire as early as age 62 and receive reduced Social Security benefits, or they can wait until full retirement age and receive full benefits. Until 2003 the full retirement age was 65, but beginning that year it began to increase gradually, such that for people born in 1960 or later, retirement age will be 67. A special credit is given to people who delay retirement beyond their full retirement age. This credit, which is a percentage added to the Social Security benefit, varies depending on the retiree's date of birth. Workers who reached full retirement age in 2008 or later can receive a credit of 8% per year.

Table 2.7 shows the relationship between earnings and Social Security benefits. It shows the average indexed monthly earnings (AIME; this is an amount that summarizes a worker's earnings) and the corresponding benefit amounts. Delaying retirement to age 70 yields the highest ration of retirement benefits to the AIME.

TABLE 2.7

Benefit amount for worker with maximum-taxable earnings, 2013

Retirement in Jan.	Retirement at age 62[a]			Retirement at age 65[b]			Retirement at age 70[c]		
		Monthly benefits			Monthly benefits			Monthly benefits	
	AIME	At age 62	In 2013	AIME	At age 65	In 2013	AIME	At age 70	In 2013
1987	$2,205	$666	$1,390	$2,009	$789	$1,646	$1,725	$1,056	$2,204
1988	2,311	691	1,384	2,139	838	1,678	1,859	1,080	2,162
1989	2,490	739	1,422	2,287	899	1,731	2,000	1,063	2,047
1990	2,648	780	1,434	2,417	975	1,792	2,154	1,085	1,995
1991	2,792	815	1,422	2,531	1,022	1,784	2,332	1,163	2,030
1992	2,978	860	1,447	2,716	1,088	1,831	2,470	1,231	2,072
1993	3,154	899	1,469	2,878	1,128	1,843	2,605	1,289	2,105
1994	3,384	954	1,519	3,024	1,147	1,826	2,758	1,358	2,162
1995	3,493	972	1,506	3,219	1,199	1,857	2,896	1,474	2,283
1996	3,657	1,006	1,519	3,402	1,248	1,885	3,012	1,501	2,266
1997	3,877	1,056	1,550	3,634	1,326	1,946	3,189	1,609	2,362
1998	4,144	1,117	1,605	3,750	1,342	1,929	3,348	1,648	2,368
1999	4,463	1,191	1,690	3,926	1,373	1,947	3,496	1,684	2,389
2000	4,775	1,248	1,727	4,161	1,435	1,986	3,707	1,752	2,426
2001	5,126	1,314	1,757	4,440	1,538	2,057	3,912	1,879	2,513
2002	5,499	1,382	1,802	4,770	1,660	2,164	4,165	1,988	2,591
2003	5,729	1,412	1,815	5,099	1,721	2,213	4,321	2,045	2,629
2004	5,892	1,422	1,791	5,457	1,784	2,247	4,532	2,111	2,658
2005	6,137	1,452	1,781	5,827	1,874	2,298	4,786	2,252	2,761
2006	6,515	1,530	1,803	6,058	1,961	2,310	5,072	2,420	2,851
2007	6,852	1,598	1,822	6,229	1,998	2,279	5,406	2,672	3,047
2008	7,260	1,682	1,874	6,479	2,030	2,263	5,733	2,794	3,114
2009	7,685	1,769	1,864	6,861	2,172	2,288	6,090	3,054	3,218
2010	7,949	1,820	1,917	7,189	2,191	2,309	6,450	3,119	3,286
2011	7,928	1,803	1,900	7,579	2,249	2,370	6,683	3,193	3,364
2012	8,199	1,855	1,887	7,973	2,310	2,349	6,852	3,266	3,321
2013	8,539	1,923	1,923	8,230	2,414	2,414	7,095	3,350	3,350

[a]Retirement at age 62 is assumed here to be at exact age 62 and 1 month. Such early retirement results in a reduced monthly benefit.
[b]Retirement at age 65 is assumed to be at exact age 65 and 0 months. For retirement in 2003 and later, the monthly benefit is reduced for early retirement. (For people born before 1938, age 65 is the normal retirement age. Normal retirement age will gradually increase to age 67.)
[c]Retirement at age 70 maximizes the effect of delayed retirement credits.
AIME = Average Indexed Monthly Earnings.
Note: Initial monthly benefits paid at ages 65 and 70 in 2000–2001 were slightly lower than the amounts shown above because such initial benefits were partially based on a cost-of-living adjustment (COLA) for December 1999 that was originally determined as 2.4 percent based on Consumer Price Indices published by the Bureau of Labor Statistics. Pursuant to Public Law 106-554, however, this COLA is effectively now 2.5 percent, and the above figures reflect the benefit change required by this legislation.

SOURCE: "Worker with Steady Earnings at the Maximum Level since Age 22," in *Workers with Maximum-Taxable Earnings*, U.S. Social Security Administration, Office of the Chief Actuary, October 18, 2012, http://www.socialsecurity.gov/OACT/COLA/examplemax.html (accessed May 30, 2013)

Benefits and Beneficiaries

The SSA indicates in "Social Security Basic Facts" that in 2013 the program paid benefits to nearly 58 million people. The majority were older adults—39.9 million retired workers and their dependents—along with 6.3 million survivors of deceased workers and 10.9 million disabled workers and their dependents. According to the SSA, in *Annual Statistical Supplement to the Social Security Bulletin, 2012* (February 2013, http://www.ssa.gov/policy/docs/statcomps/supplement/2012/supplement12.pdf), 158 million people with earnings covered by Social Security paid payroll taxes in 2011. Social Security income in 2010 was an estimated $564 billion from workers and employers and an additional $103 billion from the general fund of the U.S. Department of the Treasury to the OASDI trust funds to compensate for the lower payroll tax rate in effect for 2011. Table 2.8 shows the number of beneficiaries of all the OASDI programs as well as the average monthly benefits that were paid in December 2011, the most recent month for which data were available as of July 2013.

Social Security Amendments of 1977

Ever since 1940, the year that Americans began receiving Social Security checks, monthly retirement benefits have steadily increased, but during the 1970s they soared. Legislation enacted in 1973 provided for automatic cost-of-living adjustments (COLAs) that were intended to prevent inflation from eroding Social Security benefits. The average benefit was indexed (annually adjusted) to keep pace with inflation as reflected by the CPI. COLAs were 9.9% in 1979 and peaked at 14.3% the following year. (See Table 2.9.) These increases threatened the continued financial viability of the entire system and prompted policy makers to reconsider the COLA formula.

Some legislators felt that indexing vastly overcompensated for inflation, causing relative benefit levels to rise higher than at any previous time in the history of the program. In an attempt to prevent future Social Security benefits from rising to what many considered excessive levels, Congress passed the Social Security

TABLE 2.8

Number and average monthly benefit, by type of benefit and sex, December 2011

Type of benefit	All Number	All Average monthly benefit (dollars)	Male Number	Male Average monthly benefit (dollars)	Female Number	Female Average monthly benefit (dollars)
Total, OASDI	55,404,480	1,122.89	24,985,054	1,276.33	30,419,426	996.87
OASI	44,791,146	1,161.45	19,517,799	1,332.60	25,273,347	1,029.27
Retirement benefits	38,485,716	1,181.92	18,421,242	1,364.63	20,064,474	1,014.17
Retired workers	35,599,569	1,228.57	18,043,009	1,381.38	17,556,560	1,071.53
Spouses of retired workers	2,291,792	607.43	63,232	397.90	2,228,560	613.37
Children of retired workers	594,355	602.65	315,001	599.64	279,354	606.05
Survivor benefits	6,305,430	1,036.50	1,096,557	794.39	5,208,873	1,087.47
Children of deceased workers	1,907,336	783.14	999,186	781.97	908,150	784.43
Widowed mothers and fathers	157,516	883.54	12,318	756.13	145,198	894.35
Nondisabled widow(er)s	3,988,067	1,184.67	71,302	1,027.72	3,916,765	1,187.53
Disabled widow(er)s	251,011	703.54	13,562	515.31	237,449	714.29
Parents of deceased workers	1,500	1,044.74	189	968.42	1,311	1,055.75
DI	10,613,334	960.19	5,467,255	1,075.45	5,146,079	837.74
Disabled workers	8,575,544	1,110.50	4,493,811	1,236.72	4,081,733	971.54
Spouses of disabled workers	164,030	298.54	7,306	257.27	156,724	300.46
Children of disabled workers	1,873,760	330.18	966,138	331.52	907,622	328.76

DI = Disability Insurance. OASDI = Old-Age, Survivors, and Disability Insurance. OASI = Old-Age and Survivors Insurance.

SOURCE: "Table 5.A1. Number and Average Monthly Benefit, by Type of Benefit and Sex, December 2011," in *Annual Statistical Supplement to the Social Security Bulletin, 2012*, U.S. Social Security Administration, February 2013, http://www.ssa.gov/policy/docs/statcomps/supplement/2012/supplement12.pdf (accessed May 30, 2013)

Amendments of 1977 to restructure the benefit plan and design more realistic formulas for benefits. Along with redefining COLAs, the 1977 amendments raised the payroll tax slightly, increased the wage base, and reduced benefits.

There were no COLAs in 2010 and 2011; however, in 2012 the COLA was 3.6%, and in 2013 it was 1.7%. Table 2.9 shows how this COLA increase translated into SSI payments between 1975 and 2013.

The Earnings Test

Legislation enacted on January 1, 2000, changed the way in which the amount that beneficiaries could earn while also receiving retirement or survivors benefits was determined. The retirement earnings test applies only to people younger than normal retirement age, which ranges from age 65 to 67, depending on year of birth. Social Security withholds benefits if annual retirement earnings exceed a certain level, called a retirement earnings test exempt amount, for people who have not yet attained normal retirement age. These exempt amounts generally increase annually with increases in the national average wage index.

Table 2.10 shows the exempt amounts between 2000 and 2013. One dollar in Social Security benefits is withheld for every $2 of earnings more than the lower exempt amount. Similarly, $1 in benefits is withheld for every $3 of earnings more than the higher exempt amount.

SUPPLEMENTAL SECURITY INCOME

SSI is designed to provide monthly cash payments to older, blind, and/or disabled people who have low incomes. Although SSI is administered by the SSA, unlike Social Security benefits, SSI benefits are not based on prior work, and the funds come from general tax revenues rather than from Social Security taxes.

In 1972 Congress passed the legislation establishing SSI to replace several state-administered programs and to provide a uniform federal benefit based on uniform eligibility standards. Although SSI is a federal program, some states provide a supplement to the federal benefit.

In "SSI Federally Administered Payments" (March 2013, http://www.ssa.gov/policy/docs/statcomps/ssi_monthly/2013-02/table02.pdf), the SSA reports that of the 8.3 million people receiving SSI benefits in February 2013, nearly 2.1 million were aged 65 years and older. (See Table 2.11.) Although payments vary by age group, the average monthly benefit received by older adults in February 2013 was $421.70. (See Table 2.12.)

WHAT LIES AHEAD FOR SOCIAL SECURITY?

The Social Security program faces long-range financing challenges that, if unresolved, threaten its solvency (the ability to meet financial obligations on time) in the coming decades. Since the 1980s the program has been collecting more money than it has had to pay out and will continue to do so until 2015. The surplus is not, however, cash that is set aside. Rather,

TABLE 2.9

TABLE 2.10

Social Security income federal payment amounts, 1975–2013

Year	COLA[a]	Eligible individual	Eligible couple
1975	8.0%	$157.70	$236.60
1976	6.4%	167.80	251.80
1977	5.9%	177.80	266.70
1978	6.5%	189.40	284.10
1979	9.9%	208.20	312.30
1980	14.3%	238.00	357.00
1981	11.2%	264.70	397.00
1982	7.4%	284.30	426.40
1983	7.0%[b]	304.30	456.40
1984	3.5%	314.00	472.00
1985	3.5%	325.00	488.00
1986	3.1%	336.00	504.00
1987	1.3%	340.00	510.00
1988	4.2%	354.00	532.00
1989	4.0%	368.00	553.00
1990	4.7%	386.00	579.00
1991	5.4%	407.00	610.00
1992	3.7%	422.00	633.00
1993	3.0%	434.00	652.00
1994	2.6%	446.00	669.00
1995	2.8%	458.00	687.00
1996	2.6%	470.00	705.00
1997	2.9%	484.00	726.00
1998	2.1%	494.00	741.00
1999	1.3%	500.00	751.00
2000	2.5%[c]	513.00	769.00
2001	3.5%	531.00	796.00
2002	2.6%	545.00	817.00
2003	1.4%	552.00	829.00
2004	2.1%	564.00	846.00
2005	2.7%	579.00	869.00
2006	4.1%	603.00	904.00
2007	3.3%	623.00	934.00
2008	2.3%	637.00	956.00
2009	5.8%	674.00	1,011.00
2010	0.0%	674.00	1,011.00
2011	0.0%	674.00	1,011.00
2012	3.6%	698.00	1,048.00
2013	1.7%	710.00	1,066.00

[a]COLA = Cost-of-Living Adjustment.
[b]The increase effective for July 1983 was a legislated increase.
[c]Originally determined as 2.4 percent based on consumer price indices published by the Bureau of Labor Statistics. Pursuant to Public Law 106-554, however, the COLA is effectively now 2.5 percent.

SOURCE: "SSI Monthly Payment Amounts, 1975–2013," in *SSI Federal Payment Amounts*, U.S. Social Security Administration, Office of the Chief Actuary, October 16, 2012, http://www.socialsecurity.gov/OACT/COLA/SSIamts.html (accessed May 30, 2013)

Annual retirement earnings test exempt amounts, 2000–13

Year	Lower amount[a]	Higher amount[b]
2000	$10,080	$17,000
2001	10,680	25,000
2002	11,280	30,000
2003	11,520	30,720
2004	11,640	31,080
2005	12,000	31,800
2006	12,480	33,240
2007	12,960	34,440
2008	13,560	36,120
2009	14,160	37,680
2010	14,160	37,680
2011	14,160	37,680
2012	14,640	38,880
2013	15,120	40,080

[a]Applies in years before the year of attaining the normal retirement age.
[b]Applies in the year of attaining the normal retirement age, for months prior to such attainment.

SOURCE: "Annual Retirement Earnings Test Exempt Amounts," in *Exempt Amounts under the Earnings Test*, U.S. Social Security Administration, Office of the Chief Actuary, March 13, 2013, http://www.ssa.gov/OACT/COLA/rtea.html (accessed May 30, 2013)

pay scheduled benefits in full to older adult retirees and their beneficiaries. The trustees urge immediate action, observing that solvency of the combined OASDI trust funds for the next 75 years could be restored if policy makers increase the combined payroll tax rate from 12.4% (its current level) to an immediate and permanent 15.1% and reduce scheduled benefits in a manner equivalent to an immediate and permanent reduction of 16.5%.

To a large extent, demographic changes precipitated this crisis. Social Security is a "pay-as-you-go" program, with the contributions of present workers paying the retirement benefits of those currently retired. The program is solvent at this time because the number of employees contributing to the system is sufficient. The earliest wave of baby boomers is still in the workforce and at its peak earning years. The large cohort of boomers is funding the smaller cohort of retirees born during the low birth rate cycle of the Great Depression. As a result, there are still fewer retirees depleting funds than there are workers contributing. The trustees note that when monthly Social Security benefits began in 1940, a man aged 65 could expect to live an average of about 12.7 additional years; by 2015 a typical 65-year-old man is likely to live on average another 19 years. (See Table 2.13.)

Saving Social Security

There are three basic ways to resolve Social Security's financial problems: raise taxes, cut benefits, or make Social Security taxes earn more by investing the money. It is most likely that restoring Social Security's long-term financial balance will require a combination of increased revenues and reduced expenditures. The ways to increase revenues include:

it is loaned to the Department of the Treasury, which places it in the general revenue pool and is spent as the government sees fit.

According to the Board of Trustees of the Federal Old-Age and Survivors Insurance and Federal Disability Insurance Trust Funds, in *The 2013 Annual Report of the Board of Trustees of the Federal Old-Age and Survivors Insurance and Federal Disability Insurance Trust Funds* (May 31, 2013, http://www.socialsecurity.gov/oact/tr/2013/tr2013.pdf), without changes to the system, the amount of benefits owed will exceed taxes collected in 2016, and Social Security will have to tap into trust funds to pay benefits. The trustees estimate that the trust funds will be depleted in 2035, leaving Social Security unable to

TABLE 2.11

Supplemental Security Income recipients by eligibility category and age, February 2012–February 2013

Month	Total	Eligibility category		Age		
		Aged	Blind and disabled	Under 18	18–64	65 or older
2012						
February	8,163,730	1,182,828	6,980,902	1,293,648	4,806,424	2,063,658
March	8,161,601	1,158,789	7,002,812	1,288,548	4,807,814	2,065,239
April	8,185,900	1,156,343	7,029,557	1,301,753	4,821,992	2,062,155
May	8,179,285	1,154,369	7,024,916	1,298,404	4,819,531	2,061,350
June	8,183,565	1,154,725	7,028,840	1,296,051	4,823,143	2,064,371
July	8,225,892	1,157,218	7,068,674	1,305,457	4,849,980	2,070,455
August	8,216,619	1,157,345	7,059,274	1,295,417	4,848,470	2,072,732
September	8,246,916	1,159,205	7,087,711	1,306,587	4,862,627	2,077,702
October	8,277,694	1,161,532	7,116,162	1,309,773	4,884,345	2,083,576
November	8,241,018	1,160,126	7,080,892	1,298,560	4,859,516	2,082,942
December	8,262,877	1,156,188	7,106,689	1,311,861	4,869,484	2,081,532
2013						
January	8,291,772	1,160,197	7,131,575	1,312,233	4,890,028	2,089,511
February	8,295,013	1,157,912	7,137,101	1,316,813	4,890,685	2,087,515

Note: Data are for the end of the specified month.

SOURCE: "Table 2. Recipients, by Eligibility Category and Age, February 2012–February 2013," in *SSI Monthly Statistics, February 2013*, U.S. Social Security Administration, Office of the Chief Actuary, March 2013, http://www.ssa.gov/policy/docs/statcomps/ssi_monthly/2013-02/ table02.pdf (accessed May 30, 2013)

- Increasing Social Security payroll taxes

- Investing trust funds in securities with potentially higher yields than the government bonds in which they are currently invested

- Increasing income taxes on Social Security benefits

   The ways to reduce expenditures include:

- Reducing initial benefits to retirees

- Raising the retirement age (already slated to rise from 65 to 67 by 2027)

- Lowering COLAs

- Limiting benefits based on beneficiaries' other income and assets

Ensuring the Long-Term Solvency of Social Security Is a Priority

Although protecting Social Security is vitally important to the nation's retirees and aging baby boomers who will soon retire, some observers believe that actions to secure it may be deferred in favor of other economic priorities, including job creation and reducing the federal deficit. In "Budget Negotiating Chip Has Big Downside for Old and Poor" (NYTimes.com, April 19, 2013), Tara Siegel Bernard reports that in an effort to achieve bipartisan agreement on the federal budget deficit, President Barack Obama (1961–) proposed in early 2013 slowing the rate at which benefits increase over time. Workers retiring at age 65 would receive 3.7% less in benefits after 10 years than they would under the present system; after 20 years, 6.5% less; and after 30 years, 9.2% less.

Siegel Bernard asserts that this proposal is unpopular and cites the results of an ABC News/*Washington Post* poll—51% of respondents opposed benefits increasing at a slower rate, 37% supported the proposal, and 11% had no opinion. Not surprisingly, opposition was strong among older adults—nearly two-thirds (64%) of respondents aged 65 years and older disapproved of the change.

Other possible ways to reform Social Security include means testing, which would reduce benefits to workers if their wealth exceeded a predetermined threshold, permitting the federal government to invest a portion of the funds that enter the Social Security system in an effort to grow these funds, and helping people to save money in other ways such that they do not rely as heavily on Social Security in retirement.

AMERICANS ARE CONCERNED ABOUT CHANGES TO SOCIAL SECURITY. Americans are not completely confident that they will receive Social Security benefits when they retire. Nonetheless, Table 2.14 shows that in 2013 nearly half (47%) of workers aged 60 years and older said they expect Social Security to be a major source of their retirement funds. By contrast, just 19% of people aged 18 to 29 years and 26% of people aged 30 to 49 expect to rely heavily on Social Security benefits in retirement.

Workers' expectations of the role that Social Security will play in their retirement varies with income. Just 17% of people earning $75,000 or more per year say Social Security will be a major source of their retirement funds, whereas 33% of people earning between $30,000 and less than $75,000 and 42% of people earning less than $30,000 expect to rely heavily on Social Security. (See Table 2.15.)

TABLE 2.12

Average monthly SSI (Supplemental Security Income) payment, by eligibility category, age, and source of payment, February 2012–February 2013

[In dollars]

| Month | Total | Eligibility category | | Age | | |
		Aged	Blind and disabled	Under 18	18–64	65 or older
2012			*All sources*			
February	515.60	408.10	533.80	613.60	532.60	414.60
March	518.60	407.90	536.90	624.90	534.40	415.70
April	517.20	406.90	535.40	621.90	533.00	414.60
May	516.00	407.10	534.00	615.90	532.60	414.70
June	517.80	407.30	535.90	623.70	533.40	414.90
July	516.90	407.20	534.90	619.70	532.80	414.80
August	517.10	407.40	535.20	619.80	533.50	415.00
September	517.70	407.60	535.80	621.30	533.80	415.20
October	516.40	407.50	534.20	614.70	533.30	415.20
November	518.80	407.90	537.00	624.60	534.90	415.60
December	519.43	409.31	537.36	620.77	536.06	416.80
2013						
January	525.84	414.13	544.02	627.01	542.99	422.17
February	526.41	413.41	544.74	631.02	542.93	421.70
2012			*Federal payments*			
February	495.40	368.90	515.90	604.40	513.90	378.80
March	498.40	369.00	519.00	615.70	515.70	379.90
April	498.10	369.10	518.50	613.70	515.20	380.00
May	496.80	369.10	517.00	607.70	514.80	380.10
June	498.60	369.30	519.00	615.60	515.70	380.30
July	497.70	369.10	517.90	611.50	515.10	380.10
August	497.90	369.20	518.20	611.70	515.80	380.30
September	498.50	369.40	518.80	613.20	516.10	380.50
October	497.10	369.20	517.20	606.60	515.50	380.40
November	499.60	369.60	520.10	616.50	517.20	380.80
December	500.29	371.17	520.48	612.68	518.39	382.15
2013						
January	506.75	375.99	527.20	618.83	525.45	387.56
February	507.36	375.16	527.97	622.86	525.43	387.03
2012			*State supplementation*			
February	118.30	127.90	115.20	50.20	124.00	129.70
March	118.40	129.30	115.10	50.20	124.10	129.80
April	121.90	130.40	119.10	49.00	129.80	131.30
May	121.80	130.40	119.10	49.00	129.70	131.30
June	121.80	130.40	119.10	49.00	129.70	131.30
July	121.70	130.40	119.00	48.90	129.60	131.30
August	121.80	130.30	119.00	48.90	129.60	131.30
September	121.70	130.40	118.90	48.70	129.50	131.30
October	121.70	130.40	118.90	48.70	129.50	131.40
November	121.80	130.40	119.00	48.70	129.60	131.40
December	121.79	130.66	118.95	48.01	129.58	131.56
2013						
January	121.58	130.43	118.75	48.59	129.30	131.00
February	121.47	130.39	118.63	48.48	129.19	131.35

Note: Data are for the end of the specified month and exclude retroactive payments.

SOURCE: "Table 7. Average Monthly Payment, by Eligibility Category, Age, and Source of Payment, February 2012–February 2013," in *SSI Monthly Statistics, February 2013*, U.S. Social Security Administration, Office of Policy, March 2013, http://www.ssa.gov/policy/docs/statcomps/ssi_monthly/2013-02/table07.pdf (accessed May 30, 2013)

TABLE 2.13

Life expectancy at birth and at age 65, selected years 1940–2090

| | Intermediate | | | | Low-cost | | | | High-cost | | | |
| | At birth[a] | | At age 65[b] | | At birth[a] | | At age 65[b] | | At birth[a] | | At age 65[b] | |
Calendar year	Male	Female	Male	Female	Male	Female	Male	Female	Male	Female	Male	Female
1940	70.4	76.3	12.7	14.7	70.1	76.0	12.7	14.7	70.7	76.6	12.7	14.7
1945	72.2	77.9	13.0	15.4	71.8	77.5	13.0	15.4	72.7	78.4	13.0	15.4
1950	73.5	79.2	13.1	16.2	72.9	78.6	13.1	16.2	74.2	79.9	13.1	16.2
1955	74.2	79.8	13.1	16.7	73.4	79.1	13.1	16.7	75.1	80.7	13.1	16.7
1960	74.9	80.3	13.2	17.4	73.9	79.3	13.2	17.4	76.0	81.4	13.2	17.4
1965	75.7	80.8	13.5	18.0	74.6	79.7	13.5	18.0	77.1	82.1	13.5	18.0
1970	76.9	81.6	13.8	18.5	75.5	80.3	13.8	18.5	78.5	83.1	13.8	18.5
1975	77.8	82.3	14.2	18.7	76.2	80.8	14.2	18.7	79.6	84.0	14.2	18.7
1980	78.7	83.0	14.7	18.8	76.8	81.3	14.7	18.8	80.8	84.9	14.7	18.8
1985	79.3	83.5	15.4	19.0	77.3	81.7	15.4	19.0	81.6	85.6	15.4	19.0
1990	79.9	84.0	16.0	19.3	77.7	82.0	16.0	19.2	82.5	86.3	16.1	19.3
1995	80.6	84.6	16.7	19.6	78.2	82.4	16.6	19.4	83.3	87.0	16.8	19.7
1996	80.7	84.7	16.9	19.6	78.3	82.5	16.8	19.5	83.5	87.1	17.0	19.8
1997	80.8	84.8	17.0	19.7	78.3	82.5	16.9	19.5	83.6	87.3	17.2	19.9
1998	80.9	84.8	17.2	19.8	78.4	82.6	17.0	19.6	83.8	87.4	17.3	20.0
1999	81.0	84.9	17.3	19.8	78.4	82.6	17.2	19.6	83.9	87.5	17.5	20.1
2000	81.1	85.0	17.5	19.9	78.5	82.7	17.3	19.7	84.1	87.6	17.7	20.2
2001	81.2	85.1	17.6	20.0	78.6	82.7	17.4	19.7	84.2	87.7	17.8	20.3
2002	81.3	85.2	17.7	20.1	78.6	82.8	17.5	19.8	84.3	87.8	18.0	20.4
2003	81.4	85.2	17.9	20.2	78.7	82.8	17.6	19.9	84.4	87.9	18.2	20.5
2004	81.5	85.3	18.0	20.2	78.7	82.9	17.7	19.9	84.6	88.0	18.3	20.6
2005	81.6	85.4	18.1	20.3	78.8	82.9	17.8	20.0	84.7	88.1	18.5	20.7
2006	81.7	85.5	18.2	20.4	78.9	83.0	17.8	20.0	84.8	88.2	18.7	20.8
2007	81.8	85.5	18.3	20.5	78.9	83.0	17.9	20.0	84.9	88.3	18.8	21.0
2008	81.9	85.6	18.4	20.5	79.0	83.1	18.0	20.1	85.1	88.4	19.0	21.1
2009	82.0	85.7	18.5	20.6	79.0	83.1	18.0	20.1	85.2	88.5	19.1	21.2
2010	82.1	85.8	18.6	20.7	79.1	83.2	18.1	20.2	85.3	88.6	19.3	21.3
2011	82.2	85.8	18.7	20.7	79.1	83.2	18.1	20.2	85.5	88.7	19.4	21.4
2015	82.5	86.1	19.0	21.0	79.4	83.4	18.3	20.3	86.0	89.1	19.9	21.8
2020	83.0	86.5	19.4	21.3	79.6	83.6	18.5	20.5	86.6	89.6	20.5	22.3
2025	83.4	86.9	19.7	21.6	79.9	83.8	18.7	20.6	87.1	90.1	21.0	22.8
2030	83.8	87.2	20.0	21.9	80.2	84.0	18.8	20.8	87.7	90.6	21.4	23.2
2035	84.2	87.5	20.3	22.2	80.4	84.2	19.0	20.9	88.2	91.0	21.9	23.6
2040	84.6	87.8	20.6	22.4	80.7	84.4	19.2	21.1	88.7	91.4	22.3	24.0
2045	85.0	88.2	20.9	22.7	80.9	84.6	19.3	21.2	89.2	91.8	22.7	24.4
2050	85.4	88.5	21.2	23.0	81.1	84.8	19.5	21.4	89.7	92.2	23.1	24.8
2055	85.7	88.7	21.5	23.2	81.4	85.0	19.6	21.5	90.1	92.5	23.5	25.1
2060	86.1	89.0	21.7	23.4	81.6	85.2	19.8	21.7	90.5	92.9	23.9	25.5
2065	86.4	89.3	22.0	23.7	81.8	85.4	19.9	21.8	91.0	93.2	24.2	25.8
2070	86.7	89.6	22.2	23.9	82.1	85.6	20.1	21.9	91.4	93.6	24.6	26.1
2075	87.1	89.8	22.5	24.1	82.3	85.8	20.2	22.1	91.7	93.9	24.9	26.5
2080	87.4	90.1	22.7	24.3	82.5	86.0	20.4	22.2	92.1	94.2	25.3	26.8
2085	87.7	90.3	22.9	24.6	82.7	86.1	20.5	22.3	92.5	94.5	25.6	27.1
2090	87.9	90.6	23.2	24.8	82.9	86.3	20.7	22.5	92.8	94.8	25.9	27.4

[a]Cohort life expectancy at birth for those born in the calendar year is based on a combination of actual and estimated death rates for birth years 1940 through 2007. For birth years after 2007, these values depend on estimated death rates.
[b]Age 65 cohort life expectancy for those attaining age 65 in calendar years 1940 though 2007 depends on actual death rates or on a combination of actual and estimated death rates. After 2007, these values depend on estimated death rates.
Note: The cohort life expectancy at a given age for a given year is the average number of years of life remaining if a group of persons at that exact age, born on January 1, were to experience the mortality rates for the series of years in which they reach each succeeding age.

SOURCE: "Table V.A4. Cohort Life Expectancy," in *The 2012 Annual Report of the Board of Trustees of the Federal Old-Age and Survivors Insurance and Federal Disability Insurance Trust Funds*, U.S. Social Security Administration, Office of the Chief Actuary, April 2012, http://www.ssa.gov/oact/tr/2012/tr2012 .pdf (accessed May 30, 2013)

TABLE 2.14

Percentage of workers expecting Social Security to be a major source of retirement funds, by age, 2013

	18 to 29 years	30 to 49 years	50 to 59 years	60+ years
	%	%	%	%
401(k), IRA or other retirement savings account	53	46	44	32
Social Security	19	26	42	47
Savings account or CDs	49	21	12	12
Work-sponsored pension plan	20	25	25	26
Part-time work	24	23	17	17
Home equity	19	18	23	23
Individual stock or mutual funds	17	19	18	15
Annuities or insurance plan	15	8	5	6
Inheritance	14	8	3	5
Rent and royalties	7	8	2	4

April 4–14, 2013

SOURCE: Jeffrey M. Jones, "Percentage of Nonretirees Expecting Each Item to Be 'Major Source' of Retirement Funds, by Age," in *Income, Age Key Factors in Retirement Funding Expectations*, The Gallup Organization, May 20, 2013, http://www.gallup.com/poll/162605/income-age-key-factors-retirement-funding-expectations.aspx (accessed May 30, 2013). Copyright © 2013 Gallup, Inc. All rights reserved. The content is used with permission; however, Gallup retains all rights of republication.

TABLE 2.15

Percentage of workers expecting Social Security to be a major source of retirement funds, by income, 2013

	All nonretirees	$75,000 or more	$30,000 to <$75,000	Less than $30,000
	%	%	%	%
401(k), IRA or other retirement savings account	46	65	44	26
Social Security	30	17	33	42
Savings account or CDs	25	25	24	27
Work-sponsored pension plan	24	34	22	15
Part-time work	21	11	26	27
Home equity	20	23	18	17
Individual stock or mutual funds	18	27	16	9
Annuities or insurance plans	9	7	11	9
Inheritance	8	7	10	7
Rent and royalties	6	5	6	7

Notes: IRA = Individual retirement account. CD = Certificate of deposit.

SOURCE: Jeffrey M. Jones, "Percentage of Nonretirees Expecting Each Item to Be 'Major Source' of Retirement Funds, by Annual household Income," in *Income, Age Key Factors in Retirement Funding Expectations*, The Gallup Organization, May 20, 2013, http://www.gallup.com/poll/162605/income-age-key-factors-retirement-funding-expectations.aspx (accessed May 30, 2013). Copyright © 2013 Gallup, Inc. All rights reserved. The content is used with permission; however, Gallup retains all rights of republication.

CHAPTER 3
LIVING ARRANGEMENTS OF THE OLDER POPULATION

The vast majority of older Americans live independently in the community—they are not institutionalized in facilities such as nursing homes or retirement homes. According to the Administration on Aging (AoA), in *Justification of Estimates for Appropriations Committees: Fiscal Year 2013* (February 2012, http://acl.gov/About _ACL/Budget/docs/FY_2013_AoA_CJ_Feb_2012.pdf), approximately 1.7 million of the 39 million people aged 65 years and older in the United States lived in nursing homes in 2012. An additional 5% lived in some type of senior housing, which frequently offered supportive services for residents. The AoA notes in *A Profile of Older Americans: 2012* (April 2013, http://www.aoa.gov/ Aging_Statistics/Profile/2012/docs/2012profile.pdf) that although the overall number of older Americans living in nursing homes was small—nearly 1.5 million (3.6%) people who were 65 years and older in 2011—the percentage of older adults in nursing homes increased dramatically with advancing age, from 1% of 65- to 74-year-olds, to 3% of 75- to 84-year-olds, and to 11% of those aged 85 years and older.

The living arrangements of older adults are important because they are closely associated with their health, well-being, and economic status. For example, older adults who live alone are more likely to live in poverty than those who live with their spouse or other family members. Older adults living alone may also be socially isolated, and their health may suffer because there are no family members or others nearby to serve as caregivers.

LIVING WITH A SPOUSE, OTHER RELATIVES, OR ALONE

Table 3.1 shows that 25.3 million (21.5%) out of 117.5 million households were headed by a person aged 65 years or older in 2010. It also shows a consistent increase in the number of households headed by people aged 75 years and older, from 8.4 million in 1990 to 12.1 million in 2010.

According to the AoA, in *Profile of Older Americans*, more than half (57%) of community-dwelling, civilian (noninstitutionalized—people who are not in the U.S. military, school, jail, or mental health facilities) older adults lived with their spouse in 2011. Significantly more older men than women—72% (13.2 million) of older men, compared with 46% (10.3 million) of older women—lived with their spouse. (See Figure 3.1.) This disparity occurs because women usually live longer than men, are generally younger than the men they marry, and are far less likely to remarry after the death of a spouse, largely because there are relatively few available older men. Among adults aged 75 years and older, about one-third (32%) of women were living with their spouse in 2012.

In addition, the proportion of older adults living with their spouse decreased with age. U.S. Census Bureau data reveal that in 2010, 13.3 million (63.7%) adults aged 65 to 74 years lived with their spouse, compared with 7.9 million (45%) adults aged 75 years and older. (See Table 3.2.)

The AoA reports that in 2012, 11.8 million (28%) community-dwelling older adults lived alone—8.4 million (36%) women and 3.5 million (19%) men. The percentage of older adults who live alone rises with age. Less than half (46%) of women aged 75 years and older lived alone in 2012. Table 3.3 shows that the percentage of women aged 75 years and older living alone rose from 37% in 1970 to 54% in 1990 but decreased to 47.4% in 2010. During this same period the percentage of older men aged 75 years and older living alone remained relatively stable and was 22.6% in 2010.

TABLE 3.1

Households by age of householder and size of household, selected years 1990–2010

[In millions (93.3 represents 93,300,000). As of March. Based on Current Population Survey.]

Age of householder and size of household	1990	2000	2005	2010 Total[a]	White[b]	Black[b]	Asian[b]	Hispanic[c]	Non-Hispanic White
Total	93.3	104.7	113.3	117.5	95.5	14.7	4.7	13.3	83.2
Age of householder									
15 to 24 years old	5.1	5.9	6.7	6.2	4.7	1.0	0.3	1.2	3.7
25 to 29 years old	9.4	8.5	9.2	9.4	7.4	1.3	0.4	1.5	6.0
30 to 34 years old	11.0	10.1	10.1	9.8	7.5	1.4	0.6	1.6	6.0
35 to 44 years old	20.6	24.0	23.2	21.5	16.8	3.0	1.1	3.3	13.7
45 to 54 years old	14.5	20.9	23.4	24.9	20.1	3.2	1.0	2.6	17.7
55 to 64 years old	12.5	13.6	17.5	20.4	16.9	2.4	0.7	1.6	15.5
65 to 74 years old	11.7	11.3	11.5	13.2	11.2	1.3	0.4	0.9	10.4
75 years old and over	8.4	10.4	11.6	12.1	10.7	1.0	0.3	0.6	10.2
One person	23.0	26.7	30.1	31.4	25.2	4.7	0.9	2.1	23.3
Male	9.0	11.2	12.8	14.0	11.2	2.0	0.4	1.1	10.3
Female	14.0	15.5	17.3	17.4	14.0	2.7	0.4	1.0	13.1
Two persons	30.1	34.7	37.4	39.5	33.4	4.0	1.3	3.0	30.6
Three persons	16.1	17.2	18.3	18.6	14.7	2.5	0.9	2.5	12.3
Four persons	14.5	15.3	16.4	16.1	12.9	1.9	1.0	2.6	10.5
Five persons	6.2	7.0	7.2	7.4	5.8	0.9	0.4	1.6	4.3
Six persons	2.1	2.4	2.5	2.8	2.1	0.4	0.2	0.8	1.4
Seven persons or more	1.3	1.4	1.4	1.7	1.2	0.3	0.1	0.6	0.7

[a]Includes other races, not shown separately.
[b]Beginning with the 2003 Current Population Survey (CPS), respondents could choose more than one race. 2005 and 2010 data represent persons who selected this race group only and exclude persons reporting more than one race. The CPS in prior years only allowed respondents to report one race group.
[c]Hispanic persons may be any race.

SOURCE: "Table 62. Households by Age of Householder and Size of Household: 1990 to 2010," in *Statistical Abstract of the United States: 2012*, U.S. Census Bureau, June 27, 2012, http://www.census.gov/compendia/statab/2012/tables/12s0062.pdf (accessed June 1, 2013)

Race and ethnicity play a role in the living arrangements of older adults. In 2010 older African American and non-Hispanic white adults were more likely to live alone than older Hispanic and Asian American adults—1.2 million (35%) older African American and 9.2 million (30.1%) older non-Hispanic white adults, compared with 560,000 (19.9%) older Hispanic and 232,000 (17.2%) older Asian American adults. (See Table 3.2.)

Among the racial and ethnic groups, in 2010 older Hispanic, African American, and Asian American women were the most likely to live with relatives other than a spouse (36%, 35%, and 33%, respectively). (See Figure 3.2.) The living arrangements of older men broke down somewhat differently along racial and ethnic lines than did those of older women. Older African American men were twice as likely to live alone than were older Asian American men (28% versus 12%). Older Hispanic men were the most likely of any group of older men to live with relatives other than a spouse (17%).

Multigenerational Households

The Census Bureau reports in the press release "Grandparents Day 2012: Sept. 9" (July 31, 2012, http://www.census.gov/newsroom/releases/archives/facts_for_features_special_editions/cb12-ff17.html) that in 2010 approximately 2.7 million grandparents were responsible for most of the basic needs of their grandchildren. These grandparents represented 36% of all grandparents whose grandchildren lived with them. The 2009 American Community Survey finds that 6.7 million grandparents were living in the same household with their grandchildren under the age of 18 years in 2009 and that 2.7 million (40%) of these grandparents were responsible for their grandchildren. (See Table 3.4.) In "3 Generations under One Roof" (*AARP Bulletin*, April 2013), Sally Abrahms reports that about 51 million Americans live in a home with at least two adult generations, or a grandparent and at least one other generation, and that nearly one-third (32%) of adults expect to share their home with their parents. Until recently, multigenerational living often occurred when older adults exhausted their resources. However, the so-called Great Recession (which lasted from late 2007 to mid-2009), job losses, and foreclosures have prompted younger adults to move back in with parents and/or grandparents.

While much of the rise in multigenerational households may be attributable to the growing older population and economic considerations, some family members simply want to be closer to one another. According to Abrahms, a 2011 survey of multigenerational households found that 82% of people in these households said the living arrangement brought them closer together, 75% gained care benefits, and 72% experienced improved finances. The visibility and acceptability of

FIGURE 3.1

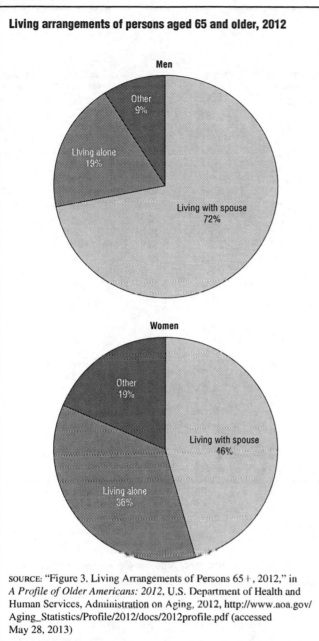

Living arrangements of persons aged 65 and older, 2012

Men

Other 9%

Living alone 19%

Living with spouse 72%

Women

Other 19%

Living alone 36%

Living with spouse 46%

SOURCE: "Figure 3. Living Arrangements of Persons 65+, 2012," in *A Profile of Older Americans: 2012*, U.S. Department of Health and Human Services, Administration on Aging, 2012, http://www.aoa.gov/Aging_Statistics/Profile/2012/docs/2012profile.pdf (accessed May 28, 2013)

multigenerational families rose when 71-year-old Marian Robinson (1937–) moved into the White House with her daughter, Michelle Obama (1964–), her granddaughters, Malia (1998–) and Sasha (2001–), and her son-in-law, President Barack Obama (1961–).

HOMELESSNESS

The U.S. Department of Housing and Urban Development's Office of Community Planning and Development notes in *The 2011 Annual Homeless Assessment Report to Congress* (November 2012, https://www.onecpd.info/resources/documents/2011AHAR_FinalReport.pdf) that between 2007 and 2009 there was a slight increase in the percentage of homeless people over the age of 50

years. Table 3.5 shows that in 2011 homeless individuals in cities, suburban areas, and rural areas were much more likely to be less than age 62 (age 62 is the federal housing program's beginning point for defining "elderly"). Older Americans may be less likely than younger Americans to be homeless because social programs such as Social Security, Supplemental Security Income (SSI), Medicare (a medical insurance program for older adults and people with disabilities), and senior housing act to prevent homelessness. Figure 3.3 shows that between 2007 and 2011 there was a small increase in sheltered people aged 51 to 61 years from 18.9% to 23.4%.

Among the concerns about homelessness are the inherent health-related issues. The relationship between homelessness, health, and illness is complex. Some health problems precede homelessness and contribute to it, whereas others are consequences of homelessness; in addition, homelessness often complicates access and adherence to treatment. For example, mental illness or substance abuse (dependency on alcohol or drugs) may limit a person's ability to work, leading to poverty and homelessness. Without protection from the cold, rain, and snow, exposure to weather may result in illnesses such as bronchitis or pneumonia. Homelessness also increases exposure to crime and violence, which could lead to trauma and injuries.

There are many reasons that homeless people experience difficulties gaining access to health care services and receiving needed medical care. Lacking essentials such as transportation to medical facilities, money to pay for care, and knowledge about how to qualify for health insurance and where to obtain health care services makes seeking treatment complicated and frustrating. Psychological distress or mental illness may prevent homeless people from attempting to obtain needed care, and finding food and shelter may take precedence over seeking treatment. Even when the homeless do gain access to medical care, following a treatment plan, filling prescriptions, and scheduling follow-up appointments often present insurmountable challenges to those who do not have a telephone number, address, or safe place to store medications. Furthermore, because chronic (long-term) homelessness can cause or worsen a variety of health problems, homeless people may not live to old age with the same frequency as their age peers who are not homeless.

LONG-TERM CARE, SUPPORTIVE HOUSING, AND OTHER RESIDENTIAL ALTERNATIVES

Spouses and other relatives are still the major caretakers of older, dependent members of American society. However, the number of people aged 65 years and older living in long-term care facilities such as nursing homes is rising because the older population is increasing rapidly. Although many older adults now live longer,

TABLE 3.2

Living arrangements by age and selected characteristics, 2010

[In thousands (242,047 represents 242,047,000). As of March.]

Living arrangement	Total	15 to 19 years old	20 to 24 years old	25 to 34 years old	35 to 44 years old	45 to 54 years old	55 to 64 years old	65 to 74 years old	75 years old and over
Total[a]	**242,047**	**21,079**	**21,142**	**41,068**	**40,435**	**44,373**	**35,381**	**20,938**	**17,631**
Alone	31,399	95	1,272	3,917	3,453	5,480	5,865	4,709	6,608
With spouse	120,768	178	2,655	18,689	25,729	28,619	23,621	13,340	7,937
With other persons	89,880	20,806	17,215	18,462	11,253	10,274	5,895	2,889	3,086
White	**195,468**	**16,085**	**16,388**	**31,936**	**31,972**	**36,134**	**29,583**	**17,965**	**15,407**
Alone	25,202	71	969	2,895	2,544	4,201	4,739	3,924	5,858
With spouse	103,102	156	2,332	15,455	21,300	24,339	20,465	11,894	7,160
With other persons	67,164	15,858	13,087	13,586	8,128	7,594	4,379	2,147	2,389
Black	**29,350**	**3,314**	**3,082**	**5,515**	**5,086**	**5,333**	**3,703**	**1,908**	**1,411**
Alone	4,705	18	237	689	670	1,015	913	606	557
With spouse	8,834	9	165	1,462	2,092	2,244	1,674	799	388
With other persons	15,811	3,287	2,680	3,364	2,324	2,074	1,116	503	466
Asian	**11,201**	**821**	**918**	**2,353**	**2,364**	**1,948**	**1,447**	**743**	**607**
Alone	850	2	37	214	151	115	98	104	128
With spouse	6,573	1	94	1,302	1,777	1,489	1,114	484	309
With other persons	3,778	818	787	837	436	344	235	155	170
Hispanic origin[b]	**34,272**	**4,041**	**3,866**	**8,085**	**7,068**	**5,292**	**3,109**	**1,687**	**1,124**
Alone	2,054	10	133	354	279	368	349	318	242
With spouse	14,622	61	660	3,449	4,094	3,179	1,811	907	461
With other persons	17,596	3,970	3,073	4,282	2,695	1,745	949	462	421
Non-Hispanic white	**163,727**	**12,429**	**12,892**	**24,486**	**25,324**	**31,263**	**26,637**	**16,344**	**14,353**
Alone	23,299	62	852	2,575	2,287	3,870	4,408	3,616	5,631
With spouse	89,315	97	1,720	12,240	17,399	21,385	18,740	11,012	6,722
With other persons	51,113	12,270	10,320	9,671	5,638	6,008	3,489	1,716	2,000

[a]Includes other races and non-Hispanic groups, not shown separately.
[b]Persons of Hispanic origin may be any race.

SOURCE: "Table 58. Living Arrangements of Persons 15 Years Old and over by Selected Characteristics: 2010," in *Statistical Abstract of the United States: 2012*, U.S. Census Bureau, June 27, 2012, http://www.census.gov/compendia/statab/2012/tables/12s0058.pdf (accessed June 1, 2013)

TABLE 3.3

Population aged 65 and over living alone, by age group and sex, selected years 1970–2010

	Men		Women	
Year	65–74	75 and over	65–74	75 and over
		Percent		
1970	11.3	19.1	31.7	37.0
1980	11.6	21.6	35.6	49.4
1990	13.0	20.9	33.2	54.0
2000	13.8	21.4	30.6	49.5
2003	15.6	22.9	29.6	49.8
2004	15.5	23.2	29.4	49.9
2005	16.1	23.2	28.9	47.8
2006	16.9	22.7	28.5	48.0
2007	16.7	22.0	28.0	48.8
2008	16.3	21.5	29.1	50.1
2009	—	—	—	—
2010	16.4	22.6	27.7	47.4

— Not available.

SOURCE: "Table 5b. Population Age 65 and over Living Alone, by Sex and Age Group, Selected Years 1970–2010," in *Older Americans 2012: Key Indicators of Well-Being*, Federal Interagency Forum on Aging-Related Statistics, June 2012, http://www.agingstats.gov/Main_Site/Data/2012_Documents/docs/EntireChartbook.pdf (accessed May 28, 2013)

healthier lives, the increase in overall length of life has amplified the need for long-term care facilities and supportive housing.

Growth of the home health care industry during the early 1990s only slightly slowed the increase in the numbers of Americans entering nursing homes. Supportive housing (assisted living, congregate housing, and continuing care retirement communities) offers alternatives to nursing home care. The overarching goal of supportive housing is to enable older adults to receive needed assistance while retaining as much independence as possible.

There are three broad classes of supportive housing for older adults. The smallest and most affordable options usually house 10 or fewer older adults and are often in homes in residential neighborhoods. Residents share bathrooms, bedrooms, and living areas. These largely unregulated facilities are alternately known as board-and-care facilities, domiciliary care, personal care homes, adult foster care, senior group homes, and sheltered housing.

FIGURE 3.2

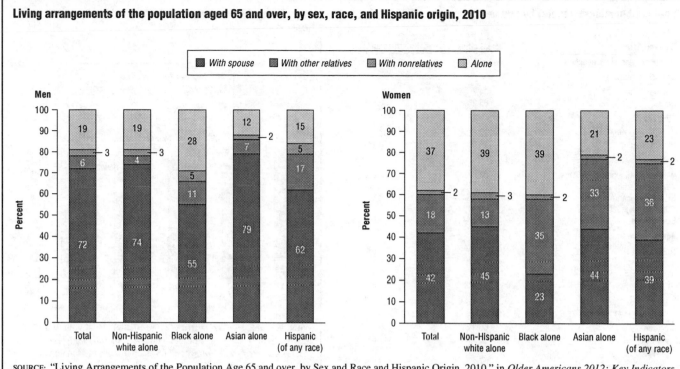

Living arrangements of the population aged 65 and over, by sex, race, and Hispanic origin, 2010

SOURCE: "Living Arrangements of the Population Age 65 and over, by Sex and Race and Hispanic Origin, 2010," in *Older Americans 2012: Key Indicators of Well-Being*, Federal Interagency Forum on Aging-Related Statistics, June 2012, http://www.agingstats.gov/Main_Site/Data/2012_Documents/docs/EntireChartbook.pdf (accessed May 28, 2013)

TABLE 3.4

Grandparents living with grandchildren, by race and sex, 2009

[In thousands (6,687 represents 6,687,000) except percent. Covers both grandparents living in own home with grandchildren present and grandparents living in grandchildren's home. The American Community Survey universe includes the household population and the population living in institutions, college dormitories, and other group quarters.]

Race, Hispanic origin, and sex	Grandparents living with own grandchildren, total	Grandparents responsible for grandchildren		
		Total	30 to 59 years old	60 years old and over
Grandparents living with own grandchildren under 18 years old (1,000)	6,687	2,696	1,815	881
Percent distribution				
Total	100.0	100.0	100.0	100.0
White alone	62.2	63.3	62.7	64.6
Black or African American alone	18.8	23.2	23.7	22.0
American Indian and Alaska Native alone	1.4	2.0	2.0	2.0
Asian alone	7.3	2.9	2.0	4.6
Native Hawaiian and other Pacific Islander alone	0.3	0.3	0.3	0.3
Some other race alone	8.0	6.4	7.3	4.6
Two or more races	1.8	1.9	2.0	1.9
Hispanic origin*	24.7	20.1	22.0	16.2
White alone, not Hispanic	46.8	50.8	49.2	54.1
Male	35.9	37.1	34.7	42.1
Female	64.1	62.9	65.3	57.9

*Persons of Hispanic origin may be any race.

SOURCE: "Table 70. Grandparents Living with Grandchildren by Race and Sex, 2009," in *Statistical Abstract of the United States: 2012*, U.S. Census Bureau, June 27, 2012, http://www.census.gov/compendia/statab/2012/tables/12s0070.pdf (accessed June 1, 2013)

Residential care facilities, assisted living residences, and adult congregate living facilities tend to be larger, more expensive, and offer more independence and pri-vacy than board-and-care facilities. Most offer private rooms or apartments as well as large common areas for activities and meals.

TABLE 3.5

Sheltered homeless people, by age and geography, 2011

Characteristic	Principal cities	Suburban and rural
Number of homeless people	1,041,863	458,652
Gender of adults		
Female	34.7%	43.3%
Male	65.2%	56.7%
Ethnicity		
Non-Hispanic/non-Latino	82.0%	90.0%
Hispanic/Latino	18.0%	10.1%
Race		
White, non-Hispanic/non-Latino	33.6%	52.8%
White, Hispanic/Latino	9.9%	6.6%
Black or African American	42.1%	29.3%
Other one race	6.0%	4.5%
Several races	8.4%	6.8%
Age		
Under age 18	20.6%	25.5%
18 to 30	23.1%	25.3%
31 to 50	36.8%	33.4%
51 to 61	16.3%	13.5%
62 and older	3.2%	2.3%
People by household size		
1 person	66.3%	56.9%
2 people	9.5%	10.8%
3 people	9.5%	13.5%
4 people	7.2%	9.0%
5 or more people	7.5%	9.8%
Disabled (adults only)		
Yes	37.0%	39.5%
No	63.0%	60.5%

SOURCE: "Table 17. Characteristics of All Sheltered Homeless People by Geography, 2011," in *The 2011 Annual Homeless Assessment Report to Congress*, U.S. Department of Housing and Urban Development, Office of Community Planning and Development, November 2012, https://www.onecpd.info/resources/documents/2011AHAR_FinalReport.pdf (accessed June 1, 2013)

FIGURE 3.3

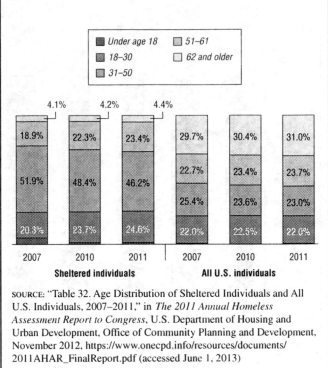

Age distribution of sheltered people and U.S. population, 2007–11

SOURCE: "Table 32. Age Distribution of Sheltered Individuals and All U.S. Individuals, 2007–2011," in *The 2011 Annual Homeless Assessment Report to Congress*, U.S. Department of Housing and Urban Development, Office of Community Planning and Development, November 2012, https://www.onecpd.info/resources/documents/2011AHAR_FinalReport.pdf (accessed June 1, 2013)

Continuing care retirement communities and life care communities are usually large complexes that offer a comprehensive range of services from independent living to skilled nursing home care. These facilities are specifically designed to provide nearly all needed care, except hospital care, within one community. Facilities in this group tend to be the most costly.

Nursing Homes

Nursing homes fall into three categories: residential care facilities, intermediate care facilities, and skilled nursing facilities. Each provides a different range and intensity of services:

- A residential care facility (RCF) provides meals and housekeeping for its residents, plus some basic medical monitoring, such as administering medications. This type of home is for people who are fairly independent and do not need constant medical attention but need help with tasks such as laundry and cleaning. Many RCFs also provide social activities and recreational programs for their residents.

- An intermediate care facility (ICF) offers room and board and nursing care as necessary for people who can no longer live independently. Much like RCFs, ICFs provide exercise and social programs, and some offer physical therapy and rehabilitation programs.

- A skilled nursing facility (SNF) provides around-the-clock nursing care, plus on-call physician coverage. SNFs are for patients who need intensive nursing care, as well as services such as occupational, physical, or respiratory therapies.

NURSING HOME RESIDENTS. The National Center for Health Statistics (NCHS) reports in *Health, United States, 2012* (May 2013, http://www.cdc.gov/nchs/data/hus/hus12.pdf) that there were 15,702 certified nursing homes in 2011. (See Table 3.6.) These facilities had an occupancy rate of 81.6% and housed nearly 1.4 million residents. The highest occupancy rates were in Alaska (91.7%), Rhode Island (91.6%), Minnesota (90.2%), and Maine (89.7%). The lowest occupancy rates were in Oregon (61.3%), Utah (65%), Oklahoma (67%), and Missouri (68.1%).

The number of nursing homes has increased dramatically since 1980. Table 3.7 shows that the number of SNFs certified by Medicare grew from 5,052 in 1980 to 15,084 in 2010. In "Best Nursing Homes 2012: Behind the Rankings" (USNews.com, February 7, 2012), Avery Comarow

TABLE 3.6

Residents and occupancy rates of nursing homes, by state, selected years 1995–2011

[Data are based on a census of certified nursing facilities]

State	Residents				Occupancy rate*			
	1995	2000	2010	2011	1995	2000	2010	2011
				Number				
United States	1,479,550	1,480,076	1,396,473	1,389,241	84.5	82.4	82.0	81.6
Alabama	21,691	23,089	22,968	22,855	92.9	91.4	86.2	85.6
Alaska	634	595	641	607	77.9	72.5	94.0	91.7
Arizona	12,382	13,253	11,878	11,472	76.6	75.9	72.2	69.9
Arkansas	20,823	19,317	17,864	18,071	69.5	75.1	72.8	73.5
California	109,805	106,460	102,591	102,377	78.3	80.8	84.7	84.7
Colorado	17,055	17,045	16,302	16,099	85.7	84.2	80.5	80.0
Connecticut	29,948	29,657	25,972	25,748	91.2	91.4	88.8	88.6
Delaware	3,819	3,900	4,145	4,195	80.6	79.5	83.1	84.1
District of Columbia	2,576	2,858	2,595	2,610	80.3	92.9	93.5	94.2
Florida	61,845	69,050	71,907	72,068	85.1	82.8	87.5	87.3
Georgia	35,933	36,559	34,704	34,272	94.3	91.8	86.8	86.0
Hawaii	2,413	3,558	3,880	3,800	96.0	88.8	90.2	88.1
Idaho	4,697	4,640	4,388	4,315	81.7	75.1	71.3	70.4
Illinois	83,696	83,604	75,224	74,580	81.1	75.5	74.4	74.3
Indiana	44,328	42,328	39,167	38,994	74.5	74.6	67.9	66.3
Iowa	27,506	29,204	25,463	25,121	68.8	78.9	77.5	77.2
Kansas	25,140	22,230	18,985	18,877	83.8	82.1	74.2	73.5
Kentucky	20,696	22,730	23,252	23,242	89.1	89.7	89.2	89.6
Louisiana	32,493	30,735	25,198	25,586	86.0	77.9	69.8	71.1
Maine	8,587	7,298	6,417	6,391	92.9	88.5	90.0	89.7
Maryland	24,716	25,629	24,816	24,683	87.0	81.4	85.6	85.8
Massachusetts	49,765	49,805	42,880	42,801	91.3	88.9	87.2	87.2
Michigan	43,271	42,615	39,894	39,545	87.5	84.1	84.8	84.3
Minnesota	41,163	38,813	29,434	28,529	93.8	92.1	91.0	90.2
Mississippi	15,247	15,815	16,489	16,447	94.9	92.7	88.7	88.3
Missouri	39,891	38,586	37,839	37,519	75.7	70.4	68.3	68.1
Montana	6,415	5,973	4,943	4,799	89.0	77.9	70.7	69.3
Nebraska	16,166	14,989	12,630	12,522	89.0	83.8	78.6	77.6
Nevada	3,645	3,657	4,735	4,717	91.2	65.9	80.9	78.8
New Hampshire	6,877	7,158	6,932	6,906	92.8	91.3	90.1	89.6
New Jersey	40,397	45,837	45,917	45,486	91.9	87.8	89.9	88.0
New Mexico	6,051	6,503	5,555	5,645	86.8	89.2	82.1	83.1
New York	103,409	112,957	109,044	108,077	96.0	93.7	92.4	91.6
North Carolina	35,511	36,658	37,199	37,486	92.7	88.6	83.8	84.4
North Dakota	6,868	6,343	5,629	5,733	96.4	91.2	87.4	90.0
Ohio	79,026	81,946	79,234	78,673	73.9	78.0	85.2	85.0
Oklahoma	26,377	23,833	19,227	19,491	77.8	70.3	66.5	67.0
Oregon	11,673	9,990	7,549	7,498	84.1	74.0	61.8	61.3
Pennsylvania	84,843	83,880	81,014	80,253	91.6	88.2	91.2	90.2
Rhode Island	8,823	9,041	8,043	8,053	91.8	88.0	91.4	91.6
South Carolina	14,568	15,739	17,133	17,240	87.3	86.9	88.0	87.9
South Dakota	7,926	7,059	6,497	6,471	95.5	90.0	81.9	93.9
Tennessee	33,929	34,714	31,927	31,437	91.5	89.9	85.6	84.4
Texas	89,354	85,275	91,099	92,133	72.6	68.2	69.7	69.1
Utah	5,832	5,703	5,361	5,448	82.1	74.5	64.9	65.0
Vermont	1,792	3,349	2,931	2,833	96.2	89.5	89.5	87.2
Virginia	28,119	27,091	28,314	28,308	93.5	88.5	88.1	87.5
Washington	24,954	21,158	18,065	17,578	87.7	81.7	82.7	80.8
West Virginia	10,216	10,334	9,557	9,448	93.7	90.5	88.2	87.6
Wisconsin	43,998	38,911	30,618	29,801	90.2	83.9	84.8	83.1
Wyoming	2,661	2,605	2,427	2,401	87.7	83.5	81.9	80.9

*Percentage of beds occupied (number of nursing home residents per 100 nursing home beds).
Notes: Annual numbers of nursing homes, beds, and residents are based on the Online Survey Certification and Reporting Database reporting cycle.

SOURCE: Adapted from "Table 109. Nursing Homes, Beds, Residents, and Occupancy Rates, by State: United States, Selected Years 1995–2011," in *Health, United States, 2012: With Special Feature on Emergency Care,* National Center for Health Statistics, 2013, http://www.cdc.gov/nchs/data/hus/hus12.pdf#109 (accessed June 1, 2013). Non-government data from Cowles Research Group.

indicates that about 3.3 million Americans spent at least part of 2012 in a nursing home in the United States.

DIVERSIFICATION OF NURSING HOMES. To remain competitive with home health care and the increasing array of alternative living arrangements for older adults, many nursing homes have begun offering specialized services. The National Nursing Home Survey (http://www.cdc.gov/nchs/nnhs.htm), a continuing series of national sample surveys of nursing homes, their residents, and their staff, finds that in 2004 (the most recent survey for which data were available as of July 2013) more than

TABLE 3.7

Medicare-certified providers, selected years 1975–2010

[Data are compiled from various Centers for Medicare & Medicaid Services data systems]

Providers or suppliers	1975	1980	1985	1990	1996	2000	2004	2006	2008	2010
					Number of providers or suppliers					
Skilled nursing facilities	—	5,052	6,451	8,937	—	14,841	14,968	15,028	15,032	15,084
Home health agencies	2,242	2,924	5,679	5,730	8,437	7,857	7,519	8,618	9,407	10,914
Clinical laboratory improvement amendments facilities	—	—	—	—	159,907	171,018	189,340	199,817	210,872	224,679
End-stage renal disease facilities	—	999	1,393	1,937	2,876	3,787	4,618	4,892	5,317	5,631
Outpatient physical therapy	117	419	854	1,195	2,302	2,867	2,971	3,009	2,781	2,536
Portable X-ray	132	216	308	443	555	666	608	549	547	561
Rural health clinics	—	391	428	551	2,775	3,453	3,536	3,723	3,757	3,845
Comprehensive outpatient rehabilitation facilities	—	—	72	186	307	522	635	589	476	354
Ambulatory surgical centers	—	—	336	1,197	2,112	2,894	4,136	4,707	5,174	5,316
Hospices	—	—	164	825	1,927	2,326	2,645	3,071	3,346	3,509
Critical access hospitals	—	—	—	—	—	—	—	—	1,302	1,325

—Data not available.
Notes: Data for 1975–1990 are as of July 1. Data for 1996–2010 are as of December 31.

SOURCE: "Table 110. Medicare-Certified Providers and Suppliers: United States, Selected Years 1975–2010," in *Health, United States 2012: With Special Feature on Emergency Care*, National Center for Health Statistics, 2013, http://www.cdc.gov/nchs/data/hus/hus12.pdf#109 (accessed June 1, 2013)

half of all nursing homes offered programs such as hospice (end-of-life) care, pain management, and wound treatment programs. According to the Alzheimer's Association, in *2013 Alzheimer's Disease Facts and Figures* (March 2013, http://www.alz.org/downloads/facts _figures_2013.pdf), in 2012 about 5% of nursing home beds, or 79,937 beds in Alzheimer's special care units, were reserved for people suffering from Alzheimer's disease or another dementia (loss of intellectual functioning accompanied by memory loss and personality changes). (Alzheimer's disease is a progressive form of dementia that is characterized by impairment of memory and intellectual functions.)

Matt Sedensky observes in "For Nursing Homes, 'It's Diversify or Die'" (Associated Press, September 7, 2010) that many nursing homes are expanding their service offerings to include home-based services such as delivered meals, transportation, and assisted living to increase revenue. Elinor Ginzler, an expert in long-term care with the advocacy group AARP, asserts that "nursing homes are waking up more and more to the reality that their old model of doing business is not going to hold up in the 21st century."

Collaborating with other providers of health care services or on their own, many nursing homes also offer services such as adult day care and visiting nurse services for people who still live at home. Other programs include respite plans that allow caregivers who need to travel for business or vacation to leave an older relative in the nursing home temporarily.

THE PIONEER NETWORK. In response to concerns about quality of life and quality of care issues in nursing homes, leaders in nursing home reform efforts from around the United States established in 2000 the Pioneer Network as a forum for the culture change movement. The culture change in this instance was a focus on person-directed values that affirm and support each person's individuality and abilities and that apply to elders and to those who work with them. The Pioneer Network explains in "Mission, Vision and Values" (2013, http://www.pioneernetwork.net/AboutUs/Values/) that it commits to the following values:

- Know each person

- Each person can and does make a difference

- Relationship is the fundamental building block of a transformed culture

- Respond to spirit, as well as mind and body

- Risk taking is a normal part of life

- Put person before task

- All elders are entitled to self-determination wherever they live

- Community is the antidote to institutionalization

- Do unto others as you would have them do unto you

- Promote the growth and development of all

- Shape and use the potential of the environment in all its aspects: physical, organizational, psycho/social/ spiritual

- Practice self-examination, searching for new creativity and opportunities for doing better

- Recognize that culture change and transformation are not destinations but a journey, always a work in progress

INNOVATION AND CULTURE CHANGE IMPROVE THE QUALITY OF LIFE FOR RESIDENTS. Industry observers frequently decry the care that is provided in nursing homes. The media publicizes instances of elder abuse (neglect, exploitation, or mistreatment of older adults) and other quality of care issues. However, several organizations have actively sought to develop models of health service delivery that improve the clinical care and quality of life for nursing home residents.

The Innovations Exchange program (http://www.innovations.ahrq.gov/) by the Agency for Healthcare Research and Quality (AHRQ) offers profiles of nursing home innovations and assessments of the effectiveness of these innovations in terms of improving residents' quality of life and satisfaction. The program also examines nursing homes' ability to attract and retain staff and their financial performance. By sharing and publicizing these innovations, the AHRQ aims to improve the quality of nursing home care.

For example, in "Creation of Households Program in Nursing Home Improves Residents' Health Status, Reduces Staff Turnover, and Boosts Demand for Services" (April 3, 2013, http://www.innovations.ahrq.gov/content.aspx?id=2051), the AHRQ describes the renovation of a 126-bed nursing home in Kansas to create living areas that enable residents to feel as if they live in their own home. Residents have privacy, can decorate their "household," and can have pets. They are able to control their own schedules and activities. These changes not only improved residents' quality of life and engagement but also increased staff job satisfaction and reduced staff turnover. The AHRQ reports that nursing home administrators from 42 states and 14 countries have visited the facility to experience firsthand how they might apply some of these innovations.

Besides physical modifications of the nursing homes to create more homelike dining rooms and bathrooms, the AHRQ reports in "Nursing Homes Create Home-Like, Resident-Focused Environment and Culture, Leading to Better Quality and Financial Performance, Higher Resident Satisfaction, and Lower Staff Turnover" (February 6, 2013, http://www.innovations.ahrq.gov/content.aspx?id=2621) on innovations that encourage communal "neighborhood" activities in nursing homes, such as decorating common areas or holding neighborhood celebrations of residents' birthdays. Instead of having the nursing home staff rotate through the facility, they are permanently assigned to a specific neighborhood so they can get to know the residents and develop ongoing relationships. Staff members are given more scheduling flexibility, to better accommodate individual residents' preferences. At each nursing home a "quality of life specialist" visits with residents daily to assess and improve their comfort and quality of life.

The AHRQ reports that this initiative has resulted in improved quality of care as measured by key quality measures such as fewer reports of pain and fewer pressure ulcers (injuries to the skin and underlying tissue usually over a bony prominence that result from continuous pressure or friction in the area) as well as fewer formal complaints. Resident and family member satisfaction ratings rose from 59.5% in 2006 to 65% in 2007. Likewise, staff satisfaction increased between 2006 and 2007, from 58% to 75%. Staff retention also improved: the annual turnover rate of nursing assistants declined from 143% in 2005 to 96% in 2008.

The initiative has also improved the nursing homes' financial performance. Between 2005 and 2007 the nursing homes' average census grew from 825 to 859, and this 10% increase meant the facilities were operating very close to their capacity. Higher census counts and reduced staff turnover also significantly improved the nursing homes' net revenues, which tripled during this period.

THE EDEN ALTERNATIVE. Developed in 1991 by William Thomas, the Eden Alternative is a movement that, like the Pioneer Network, seeks to transform nursing homes. The Eden Alternative strives to create nursing homes that are rich and vibrant human habitats where plants, children, and animals bring life-enriching energy to residents. The philosophy of the Eden Alternative is that providing a stimulant-rich environment will help minimize the hopelessness that is often felt by nursing home residents. Nursing homes based on this model are being opened across the country.

By providing gardenlike settings filled with plants and encouraging relationships with children and pets, the Eden Alternative hopes to improve the human spirit and dispel loneliness. The 10 principles (2013, http://www.edenalt.org/about/our-10-principles.html) of an Eden Alternative nursing home are:

1. The three plagues of loneliness, helplessness, and boredom account for the bulk of suffering among our Elders.

2. An Elder-centered community commits to creating a human habitat where life revolves around close and continuing contact with plants, animals, and children. It is these relationships that provide the young and old alike with a pathway to a life worth living.

3. Loving companionship is the antidote to loneliness. Elders deserve easy access to human and animal companionship.

4. An Elder-centered community creates opportunity to give as well as receive care. This is the antidote to helplessness.

5. An Elder-centered community imbues daily life with variety and spontaneity by creating an environment

in which unexpected and unpredictable interactions and happenings can take place. This is the antidote to boredom.

6. Meaningless activity corrodes the human spirit. The opportunity to do things that we find meaningful is essential to human health.

7. Medical treatment should be the servant of genuine human caring, never its master.

8. An Elder-centered community honors its Elders by de-emphasizing top-down bureaucratic authority, seeking instead to place the maximum possible decision-making authority into the hands of the Elders or into the hands of those closest to them.

9. Creating an Elder-centered community is a never-ending process. Human growth must never be separated from human life.

10. Wise leadership is the lifeblood of any struggle against the three plagues. For it, there can be no substitute.

Thomas's initiatives also include the Green House Project—the construction of small group homes for older adults, built to a residential scale that situates necessary clinical care within a social model in which primacy is given to the older adults' quality of life. The goal of this social model is to provide frail older adults with an environment that promotes autonomy, dignity, privacy, and choice.

Green Houses are designed to feel more like homes than typical long-term care institutions and to blend easily into their community or surroundings. The first Green House in the nation opened in May 2003 in Tupelo, Mississippi, developed by United Methodist Senior Services of Mississippi. The Robert Wood Johnson Foundation (http://www.rwjf.org/en/grants/grantees/the-green-house-project.html) reports that in 2013 more than 260 Green Houses were operating or under way in 32 states.

Characteristics of People in Residential Care

In "Residents Living in Residential Care Facilities: United States, 2010" (*NCHS Data Brief*, no. 91, April 2012), Christine Caffrey et al. present the key findings from the NCHS 2010 National Survey of Residential Care Facilities. In 2010 the overwhelming majority (91%) of residents were non-Hispanic white and nearly three-quarters (70%) were women. (See Figure 3.4.) More than half (54%) were aged 85 years and older and over one-quarter (27%) were aged 75 to 84 years.

Caffrey et al. report that the mean (average) monthly charge per person for residential care was $3,165 and that Medicaid (a federal and state health care program for people below the poverty level) helped pay some of the

FIGURE 3.4

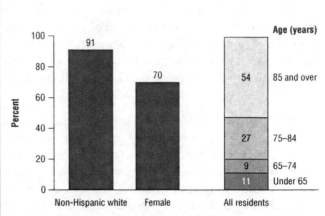

Selected characteristics of people in residential care, 2010

Note: Estimates may not add to 100% due to rounding.

SOURCE: Christine Caffrey et al., "Figure 1. Selected Characteristics of Residential Care Residents: United States, 2010," in "Residents Living in Residential Care Facilities: United States, 2010," *NCHS Data Brief*, no. 91, April 2012, http://www.cdc.gov/nchs/data/databriefs/db91.htm (accessed June 1, 2013)

FIGURE 3.5

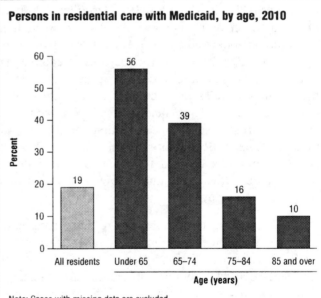

Persons in residential care with Medicaid, by age, 2010

Note: Cases with missing data are excluded.

SOURCE: Christine Caffrey et al., "Figure 2. Residential Care Residents with Medicaid, by Age: United States, 2010," in "Residents Living in Residential Care Facilities: United States, 2010," *NCHS Data Brief*, no. 91, April 2012, http://www.cdc.gov/nchs/data/databriefs/db91.htm (accessed June 1, 2013)

cost of residential care for about one-fifth (19%) of residents. (See Figure 3.5.) Younger residents were more likely to have Medicaid coverage than were older residents. More than half (56%) of residents under the age of 65 years had Medicaid, compared with 39% of residents aged 65 to 74 years, 16% of residents aged 75 to 84 years, and 10% of residents aged 85 years and older.

FIGURE 3.6

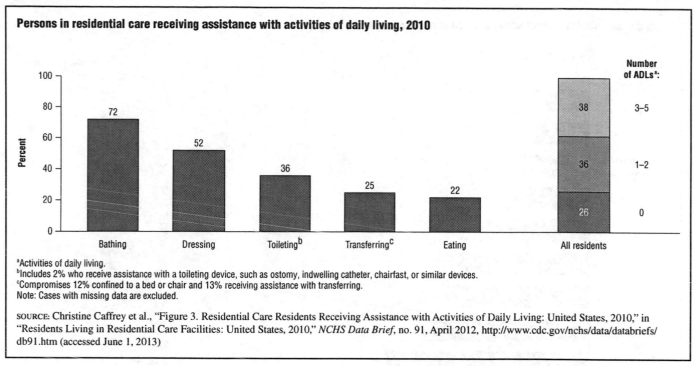

Persons in residential care receiving assistance with activities of daily living, 2010

[a]Activities of daily living.
[b]Includes 2% who receive assistance with a toileting device, such as ostomy, indwelling catheter, chairfast, or similar devices.
[c]Compromises 12% confined to a bed or chair and 13% receiving assistance with transferring.
Note: Cases with missing data are excluded.

SOURCE: Christine Caffrey et al., "Figure 3. Residential Care Residents Receiving Assistance with Activities of Daily Living: United States, 2010," in "Residents Living in Residential Care Facilities: United States, 2010," *NCHS Data Brief*, no. 91, April 2012, http://www.cdc.gov/nchs/data/databriefs/db91.htm (accessed June 1, 2013)

Most residents received help with the activities of daily living such as bathing (72%) and dressing (52%). (See Figure 3.6.) Nearly four out of 10 (38%) required help with three or more activities of daily living. Sixty-eight percent of residents had been diagnosed with at least two to three of the 10 most chronic conditions. (See Figure 3.7.)

Assisted Living

Assisted living arose to bridge a gap in long-term care. It is a type of residential care intended to meet the needs of older adults who wish to live independently in the community but require some of the services (e.g., housekeeping, meals, transportation, and assistance with other activities of daily living) provided by a nursing home. Assisted living offers a flexible array of services that enable older adults to maintain as much independence as they can, for as long as possible.

Because assisted living refers to a concept and philosophy as opposed to a regulated provider of health services such as a hospital or SNF, there is no uniform description of the services an assisted living residence must offer, and as a result there is considerable variation among assisted living facilities. These residences are regulated on a state level, and each state has its own definition of what constitutes an assisted living facility and its own set of rules that govern them. The AHRQ defines in "Assisted Living Defined" (2013, http://www.ahrq.gov/professionals/systems/long-term-care/resources/facilities/ltcscan/ltc3.html) the term *assisted living* as "a type of residential long-term care setting known by nearly 30 different names" that includes "24-hour service and oversight, services that meet scheduled and unscheduled needs, and care/services that promote independence, with an emphasis on dignity, autonomy, choice, privacy, and home-like environment."

In "Assisted Living" (2013, http://www.alfa.org/alfa/Assisted_Living_Information.asp), the Assisted Living Federation of America describes the goal of assisted living: "To provide personalized, resident centered care in order to meet individual preferences and needs. Assisted living treats all residents with dignity, provides privacy and encourages independence and freedom of choice. Residents' family members and friends are encouraged to get involved in the assisted living community."

Assisted living residences may be located on the grounds of retirement communities or in nursing homes, or they may be freestanding residential facilities. They vary in size, location, and services. Some are high-rise apartment complexes, whereas others are converted private homes. Most contain between 25 and 120 units, which vary in size from one room to a full apartment.

Assisted living licensing regulations vary from state to state. Most states require staff certification and training and all assisted living facilities must comply with local building codes and fire safety regulations.

BOARD-AND-CARE FACILITIES. Board-and-care facilities were the earliest form of assisted living. In *Licensed Board and Care Homes: Preliminary Findings from the 1991 National Health Provider Inventory* (April 11, 1994,

FIGURE 3.7

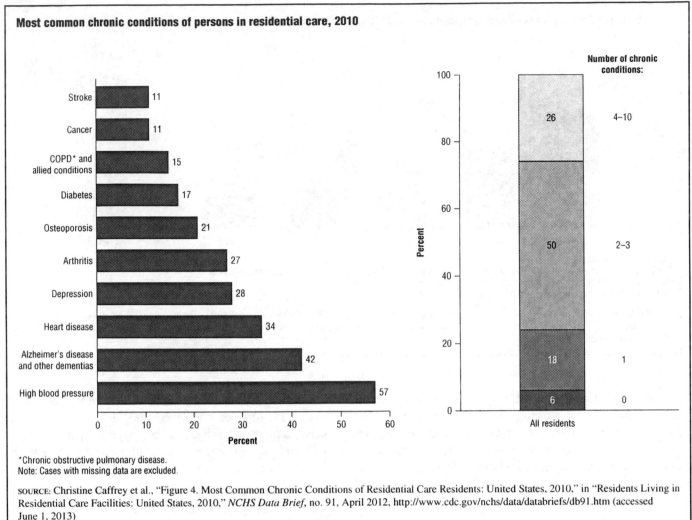

Most common chronic conditions of persons in residential care, 2010

*Chronic obstructive pulmonary disease.
Note: Cases with missing data are excluded.

SOURCE: Christine Caffrey et al., "Figure 4. Most Common Chronic Conditions of Residential Care Residents: United States, 2010," in "Residents Living in Residential Care Facilities: United States, 2010," *NCHS Data Brief*, no. 91, April 2012, http://www.cdc.gov/nchs/data/databriefs/db91.htm (accessed June 1, 2013)

http://aspe.hhs.gov/daltcp/reports/licbchom.htm), Robert F. Clark et al. define the term *board-and-care homes* as "non-medical community-based facilities that provide protective oversight and/or personal care in addition to meals and lodging to one or more residents with functional or cognitive limitations." Typically, board-and-care residents have their own bedrooms and bathrooms or share them with one other person, whereas other living areas are shared.

Although many board-and-care facilities offer residents safe, homelike environments and attentive caregivers, there have been many well-publicized instances of fraud and abuse. Observers attribute the variability in quality of these facilities to the fact that they are unregulated in many states and as a result receive little oversight.

In an attempt to stem abuses, the federal government passed the Keys Amendment in 1978. Under the terms of this legislation, residents living in board-and-care facilities that fail to provide adequate care are subject to reduced SSI payments. This move was intended to penalize substandard board-and-care operators, but advocates for older adults contend that it actually penalizes the SSI recipients and that it has not reduced reports of abuse. With the 1992 reauthorization of the Older Americans Act of 1965, Congress provided for long-term care ombudsman programs that are designed to help prevent the abuse, exploitation, and neglect of residents in long-term care facilities such as board-and-care residences and nursing homes. Paid and volunteer ombudsmen monitor facilities and act as advocates for residents.

COSTS OF ASSISTED LIVING. The cost of assisted living varies based on geography, unit size, and the services needed. The MetLife Mature Market Institute explains in *Market Survey of Long-Term Care Costs: The 2012 MetLife Market Survey of Nursing Home, Assisted Living, Adult Day Services, and Home Care Costs* (November 2012, https://www.metlife.com/assets/cao/mmi/publications/studies/2012/studies/mmi-2012-market-survey-long-term-care-costs.pdf) that the "national average assisted living base rates increased by 2.1%, from $3,477 monthly or $41,724 annually in 2011, to $3,550 monthly or $42,600 annually in 2012." Most assisted living facilities charge monthly rates and some require long-term leases.

The MetLife Mature Market Institute report considers the cost for assisted living communities based on the number of services included in their base rates. Communities that included five or fewer services were "basic" and had an average monthly cost of $2,751, those providing six to nine services were "standard" and had an average monthly cost of $3,486, and those providing 10 or more services in their base rates were "inclusive" and had an average monthly cost of $3,789.

Residents or their families generally pay for assisted living using their own financial resources. Some health insurance programs or long-term care insurance policies reimburse for specific health-related care that is provided, and some state and local governments offer subsidies for rent or services for low-income older adults. Others may provide subsidies in the form of an additional payment for those who receive SSI or Medicaid.

Continuing Care Retirement Communities

Continuing care retirement communities (CCRCs), also known as life care communities, offer a continuum of care (independent living, assisted living, and nursing home care) in a single facility or on common grounds. The goal of CCRCs is to enable residents to age in place (remaining in their own home rather than relocating to assisted living facilities or other supportive housing). When residents become ill or disabled, for example, they do not have to relocate to a nursing home, because medical care is available on the CCRC campus.

Like assisted living facilities, CCRCs vary in location, design, and amenities. They range from urban high rises to semirural campuses and from 100 to over 1,000 residents. Most include common dining rooms, activity and exercise areas, indoor and outdoor recreation areas, and swimming pools.

Typically, residents are required to pay an entrance fee and a fixed monthly fee in return for housing, meals, personal care, recreation, and nursing services. Many CCRCs offer other payment options, including both entrance fee and fee-for-service (paid for each visit, procedure, or treatment delivered) arrangements. In the past entrance fees were nonrefundable; by 2011, however, many newer CCRCs offered refundable or partially refundable entrance fees.

CCRCs may be operated by private, nonprofit, and/or religious organizations. According to Ashlea Ebeling, in "Continuing Care Communities: A Big Investment with Catches" (Forbes.com, September 26, 2011), there are nearly 2,000 CCRCs in the United States and the average vacancy rate is 11%. With few exceptions, none of the costs of CCRCs are covered by government or private insurance. The AARP reports in "About Continuing Care Communities" (September 2010, http://www.aarp.org/relationships/caregiving-resource-center/info-09-2010/ho_continuing_care_retirement_communities.html) that entrance fees range from $100,000 to $1 million and monthly fees range from $3,000 to $5,000.

Shared Housing and Cohousing

Older adults may share living quarters to reduce expenses, share household and home maintenance responsibilities, and gain companionship. Many choose to share the same homes in which they raised their families because these houses are often large enough to accommodate more than one or two people. Shared housing is often called cohousing, but the terms are not exactly the same.

Most shared housing consists of a single homeowner taking a roommate to share living space and expenses. Shared housing can also include households with three or more roommates and family-like cooperatives in which large groups of people live together. In contrast, cohousing usually refers to planned or intentional communities of private dwellings with shared common areas that include dining rooms, meeting rooms, and recreation facilities. Shared housing and cohousing are cost-effective alternatives for those who wish to remain in their own home and for older adults who cannot afford assisted living or CCRCs.

The cohousing concept originated in Denmark during the 1960s and spread to the United States during the 1980s. According to the Cohousing Association of the United States (http://www.cohousing.org/directory), in 2013 there were more than 200 cohousing communities in various stages of development in 38 states. Cohousing participants are involved in planning the community and maintaining it, and most cohousing groups make their decisions by consensus.

Shared housing or intergenerational cohousing may also meet the needs of younger as well as older people. Along with the benefits of cost-sharing and companionship, home sharers and cohousing residents may exchange services—for example, help with household maintenance in exchange for babysitting.

Elder Cottage Housing Opportunity Units

Elder cottage housing opportunity (ECHO) units, or "granny flats," are small, freestanding, removable housing units that are located on the same lot as a single-family house. Another name used by local zoning authorities is accessory apartments or units. Accessory apartments are self-contained second living units built into or attached to an existing single-family dwelling. They are generally smaller than the primary unit, and usually contain one or two bedrooms, a bathroom, a sitting room, and a kitchen.

Generally, families construct ECHO units and accessory apartments for parents or grandparents so that the older adults can be nearby while maintaining their independence. Existing zoning laws and concerns about property values are obstacles to the construction of ECHO units, but as this alternative becomes more popular, local jurisdictions may be pressured to allow multifamily housing in neighborhoods that traditionally have had only single-family homes.

According to Tim Newcomb, in "Need Extra Income? Put a Cottage in Your Backyard" (Time.com, May 28, 2011), accessory dwelling units are appearing in communities across the country, most notably in Seattle, Washington; Portland, Oregon; Berkeley, California; Denver, Colorado; and Burlington, Vermont. Newcomb indicates that the units cost about $100 per square foot to construct and that they are generally between 400 and 800 square feet (37 and 74 square m) in size.

Retirement Communities

Developers such as the industry leader Del Webb (a division of Pulte Homes) have constructed communities and even entire small "cities" exclusively for older adults. Examples include the Sun City communities in Arizona, Florida, and Texas. The Arizona and Florida communities opened during the 1960s and the Texas community in 1996.

In 2013 Del Webb (http://www.delwebb.com/index .aspx) boasted over 50 communities in 22 states. Homes in most of these properties were available only to those families in which at least one member was 55 years or older, and no one under the age of 19 years was allowed to reside permanently. Sun City communities offer clubs, golf courses, social organizations, fitness clubs, organized travel, and recreational complexes. Medical facilities are located nearby.

Housing Slump Imperils Older Adults and Limits Their Mobility

Many older adults and baby boomers aspire to relocate to CCRCs or purchase new homes in active retirement communities, but it is likely that only those with considerable financial resources will be able to do so. The decline in residential real estate prices, which began in 2006 and persisted in many parts of the country throughout 2013, made it difficult for older adults to sell their homes. Besides losing equity in their homes as prices declined, many older adults also saw their retirement assets erode. Although retirement accounts had generally rebounded by 2013, the aftereffects of the Great Recession worried older adults, prompting many to forgo or postpone plans to relocate.

Mark Miller observes in "Time not on the Side of Older Americans in Housing Slump" (Reuters.com, July 26, 2012) that "even if a housing recovery does get underway, older homeowners who are underwater aren't likely to have sufficient time to wait out a full recovery, which likely will take years, if not decades."

OWNING AND RENTING A HOME

In the press release "Residential Vacancies and Homeownership in the First Quarter 2013" (April 30, 2013, http://www.census.gov/housing/hvs/files/qtr113/ q113press.pdf), the Census Bureau notes that the overall homeownership rate during the first quarter of 2013 was 65%, down slightly from the highest rate of 69.2% during the fourth quarter of 2004. (See Table 3.8.) During the first quarter of 2013, 80.2% of adults aged 65 to 69 years, 82.8% of adults aged 70 to 74 years, and 79.2% of adults aged 75 years and older owned their own home. (See Table 3.9.)

The AoA reports in *Profile of Older Americans* that in 2011 nearly half of older adults devoted more than a quarter of their income to housing costs—43% of homeowners and 71% of renters. In 2011 the median value (the middle value; half of all homes are lower and half are

TABLE 3.8

Homeownership rates, 1995–2013

[In percent]

| Year | Homeownership rates | | | |
	First quarter	Second quarter	Third quarter	Fourth quarter
2013	65.0			
2012	65.4	65.5	65.5	65.4
2011	66.4	65.9	66.3	66.0
2010	67.1	66.9	66.9	66.5
2009	67.3	67.4	67.6	67.2
2008	67.8	68.1	67.9	67.5
2007	68.4	68.2	68.2	67.8
2006	68.5	68.7	69.0	68.9
2005	69.1	68.6	68.8	69.0
2004	68.6	69.2	69.0	69.2
2003	68.0	68.0	68.4	68.6
2002*	67.8	67.6	68.0	68.3
2002	67.8	67.6	68.0	68.3
2001	67.5	67.7	68.1	68.0
2000	67.1	67.2	67.7	67.5
1999	66.7	66.6	67.0	66.9
1998	65.9	66.0	66.8	66.4
1997	65.4	65.7	66.0	65.7
1996	65.1	65.4	65.6	65.4
1995	64.2	64.7	65.0	65.1

*Revised in 2002 to incorporate information collected in Census 2000.

SOURCE: Robert R. Callis and Melissa Kresin, "Table 4. Homeownership Rates for the United States: 1995 to 2013," in *Residential Vacancies and Homeownership in the First Quarter 2013*, U.S. Census Bureau, April 30, 2013, http://www.census.gov/housing/hvs/files/qtr113/q113press.pdf (accessed June 3, 2013)

Bravve, Bolton, and Crowley indicate that in 2011, 35% of all households were renters and that same year the number of renter households increased by 1 million—the single largest annual increase since the early 1980s. In 2012 rents rose 3.8% from 2011. The rental vacancy rate fell from 8% in 2009 to 4.5% in 2012. In 2013 the average hourly wage was $14.32; the researchers observe, however, that renters must earn $18.79 per hour to afford an apartment while spending no more than 30% of their income on housing. In all but one state the wages needed to rent a two-bedroom apartment exceeded the average renter's wages. Older adults relying solely on SSI payments (an estimated 57% of the 8 million SSI recipients depended on SSI alone in 2013) could not afford rental housing. Bravve, Bolton, and Crowley state, "Among those reliant on SSI, there is not a single county in the U.S. where even a modest efficiency apartment, priced according to the FMR, is affordable."

HOUSING CHALLENGES FOR OLDER ADULTS
Physical Hazards and Accommodations

Home characteristics that are considered desirable by younger householders may present challenges to older adults. For example, the staircase in a two-story house may become a formidable obstacle to an older adult suffering from arthritis, heart disease, or other disabling conditions. Narrow halls and doorways cannot accommodate walkers and wheelchairs. High cabinets and shelves may be beyond the reach of an arthritis sufferer. Although houses can be modified to meet the physical needs of older or disabled people, some older houses cannot be remodeled as easily, and retrofitting them may be quite costly. Owners of condominiums in Florida, whose young-old (aged 65 to 74 years) residents once prized second- and third-floor units for their breezes and golf course views, are now considering installing elevators for residents in their 80s and 90s who find climbing stairs more difficult.

Older adults, as well as advocates on their behalf, express a strong preference for aging in place. Much research confirms that most people over the age of 55 years want to remain in familiar surroundings rather than move to alternative housing. To live more comfortably, those older adults who have the means can redesign and reequip their home to accommodate the physical changes that are associated with aging.

Simple adaptations include replacing doorknobs with levers that can be pushed downward with a fist or elbow, requiring no gripping or twisting; replacing light switches with flat "touch" switches; placing closet rods at adjustable heights; installing stoves with front- or side-mounted controls; and marking steps with bright colors. More complex renovations include replacing a bathroom with a wet room (a tiled space that is large enough to accommodate a wheelchair and equipped with a showerhead, waterproof chair, and sloping floor for a drain), placing electrical outlets higher than usual, and widening passageways and doorways for walkers, wheelchairs, or scooters.

Anticipating the increase in the older population, some real estate developers are manufacturing houses that are designed to meet the needs of older adults and prolong their ability to live independently. These houses feature accommodations such as nonskid flooring, walls strong enough to support grab bars, outlets at convenient heights, levers instead of knobs on doors and plumbing fixtures, and doorways and hallways wide enough for wheelchair access.

More technologically advanced homes, called smart homes, feature an array of adaptive technologies, such as embedded computers, sensors that detect motion and falls, and automated blood pressure monitoring, that aim to help older adults remain in their homes and age in place. For example, the article "'Magic Carpet' Could Help Prevent Falls" (September 4, 2012, http://www.manchester.ac.uk/aboutus/news/display/?id=8648) notes that researchers at the University of Manchester developed a carpet with optical fibers that sense and map walking patterns. By analyzing the movements of a person walking on it, the carpet can identify if the person's gait is unsteady or if the person has tripped or fallen. According to the article "12 Unusual Housing Trends to Track in 2013" (Forbes.com, 2013), the smart home market will grow from $16.9 million in 2011 to $35.6 million by 2016.

PUBLIC HOUSING

Congress passed the U.S. Housing Act of 1937 to create low-income public housing, but according to the Milbank Memorial Fund and the Council of Large Public Housing Authorities, in *Public Housing and Supportive Services for the Frail Elderly: A Guide for Housing Authorities and Their Collaborators* (September 2006, http://www.milbank.org/reports/0609publichousing/0609publichousing.pdf), by 1952 only a small percentage of available housing was occupied by older adults. After 1956, when Congress authorized the development of dedicated public housing for the elderly and specifically made low-income older adults eligible for such housing, the situation improved. During the 1960s and 1970s many developments for low-income older adults were constructed. These apartments were sufficient for most residents, but they were not designed to enable residents to age in place. They lacked the flexibility and the range of housing options necessary to meet the needs of frail older adults. Residents who entered public housing as young-old aged in place and are now the older-old (aged 75 years and older) and are in need of more supportive and health services than they were two decades ago.

TABLE 3.9

Homeownership rates, by age of householder, first quarter 2012 and 2013

[In percent]

Age of householder	First quarter 2012	First quarter 2013
United States	65.4	65.0
Under 25 years	21.3	20.8
25 to 29 years	34.2	34.4
30 to 34 years	48.3	48.9
35 to 39 years	56.4	55.3
40 to 44 years	65.9	64.4
45 to 49 years	69.5	69.4
50 to 54 years	73.0	73.1
55 to 59 years	76.7	75.7
60 to 64 years	79.0	78.5
65 to 69 years	81.6	80.2
70 to 74 years	83.9	82.8
75 years and over	79.0	79.2
Under 35 years	36.8	36.8
35 to 44 years	61.4	60.1
45 to 54 years	71.3	71.3
55 to 64 years	77.8	77.0
65 years and over	80.9	80.4

SOURCE: Adapted from "Table 7. Homeownership Rates by Age of Householder," in *Housing Vacancies and Homeownership (CPS/HVS): 2013*, U.S. Census Bureau, April 30, 2013, http://www.census.gov/housing/hvs/data/q113ind.html (accessed June 3, 2013)

higher) of homes owned by older adults was $150,000, but because the median purchase price of these homes was just $55,000, 65% of older homeowners had no mortgage debt—they owned their homes free and clear.

Renters generally pay a higher percentage of their income for housing than do homeowners. Unlike most homeowners, who pay fixed monthly mortgage payments, renters often face annual rent increases. Many older adult renters living on fixed incomes are unprepared to pay these increases. Homeowners also benefit from their home equity and can borrow against it in times of financial need. In contrast, renters do not build equity and do not get a return on their investment. Also, mortgage payments are tax deductible, whereas rent payments are not.

Strategic Defaults

Faced with job losses, declining home values, or mounting medical bills, some older homeowners choose to walk away from their mortgages. Called strategic default, this practice, which was once considered as shameful as filing for bankruptcy, is no longer as stigmatized and occurs more frequently among older adults. In "What Happens When You Walk Away from Your Home?" (Reuters.com, January 27, 2012), Chris Taylor explains that although homeowners should consider strategic default a last resort, it may be the right solution for those who have exhausted efforts to refinance or participate in government programs designed to keep people in their homes.

Reverse Mortgages

To supplement their retirement income or to pay for health care, many older Americans turn to reverse mortgages. Reverse mortgages allow homeowners to convert some of their home equity into cash, making it possible for them to avoid selling their home.

With a traditional mortgage homeowners make monthly payments to the lender. In a reverse mortgage the lender pays the homeowner in monthly installments and in most cases no repayment is due until the homeowner dies, sells the house, or moves. Reverse mortgages help homeowners who have considerable equity in their home to stay in their home and still meet their financial obligations.

A key disadvantage of a reverse mortgage is that when the home is no longer used as the primary residence of the borrower, the cash, interest, and finance charges must be repaid. This is generally accomplished by selling the home, and the spouse or heirs only receive any funds in excess of this obligation.

In *Changing Attitudes, Changing Motives: The MetLife Study of How Aging Homeowners Use Reverse Mortgages* (March 2012, https://www.metlife.com/assets/cao/mmi/publications/studies/2012/studies/mmi-changing-attitudes-changing-motives.pdf), a market research study that examines the attitudes of older homeowners toward reverse mortgages, the National Council on Aging and the MetLife Mature Market Institute find that the average age of borrowers is 73. However, almost half (46%) of borrowers considering a reverse mortgage are under the age of 70 years.

Sale/Leaseback with Life Tenancy

Another option for older homeowners is a sale/leaseback in which the homeowner gives up ownership of the home and becomes a renter. The former homeowner frequently requests life tenancy—retaining the right to live in the house as a renter for the rest of his or her life. The buyer pays the former homeowner in monthly installments and is responsible for property taxes, insurance, maintenance, and repairs.

Renting Is Often Unaffordable

Elina Bravve, Megan Bolton, and Sheila Crowley of the National Low Income Housing Coalition document in *Out of Reach 2013* (March 2013, http://nlihc.org/sites/default/files/oor/2013_OOR.pdf) income and rental housing cost data for the 50 states, the District of Columbia, and Puerto Rico. For each area, the researchers calculate the income that is needed to be able to afford the fair market rent (FMR) of the housing. They also calculate the number of full-time minimum-wage jobs that are necessary to afford the FMR, which highlights the hardships that are faced by many families with varying numbers of wage earners.

Public housing itself has also aged—most of it is more than 40 years old. Many developments are badly rundown and in need of renovation. Most are unequipped to offer the range of supportive services that are required by increasingly frail and dependent residents. Absent supportive services, the bleak alternative may be moving older people into costly, isolated institutions. Older adults may suffer unnecessary institutionalization, and nursing home care is far more costly than community-based services.

Section 202 Supportive Housing for the Elderly Act was passed in 2010. The act supports the development and maintenance of housing options for older adults with very low incomes. It encourages the enhancement of existing units and expanding access to assisted living facilities and programs that enable older adults to remain in the community. It also supports the Department of Housing and Urban Development's creation of an information clearing house of affordable housing projects for older adults.

In "HUD's Public Housing Program" (2013, http://portal.hud.gov/hudportal/HUD?src=/topics/rental_assistance/phprog), the Department of Housing and Urban Development reports that in 2013 there were approximately 1.2 million households living in public housing units and 3,300 housing authorities that managed the housing for low-income residents. Eligibility for public housing is based on income (income limits vary by location), age, disability, family status, and U.S citizenship or eligible immigration status.

Alisha Sanders describes in "Every Cloud Has a Silver Lining: Could It Be Affordable Senior Housing?" (February 26, 2013, http://www.leadingage.org/Every_Cloud_Has_a_Silver_Lining_Could_it_be_Affordable_Senior_Housing.aspx) the policy challenges of meeting the needs of an aging population with sharply limited budgets, specifically:

- Many older adults struggle financially while experiencing multiple chronic conditions and functional limitations. Affordable housing can help improve the health and well-being of this vulnerable population.

- State and federal policy makers are seeking ways to expand and enhance community-based living options that will improve older adults' health and well-being and conserve public expenditures.

- Policy makers depend on affordable housing communities to help them achieve the objective of providing low-income residents with the services and supports they need to remain healthy and independent.

Sanders acknowledges that regulations, reimbursement levels, and individual needs can undermine housing communities' ability to assist low-income older adults to live independently. She observes, however, that communities such as Park Danforth in Portland, Maine, have developed creative ways to contain costs and continue to offer residents needed services.

CHAPTER 4
WORKING AND RETIREMENT: NEW OPTIONS FOR OLDER ADULTS

Americans head off to their jobs each day as much for daily meaning as for daily bread.

—Studs Terkel, *Working: People Talk about What They Do All Day and How They Feel about What They Do* (1974)

Historically, Americans aged 65 years and older have made substantial contributions to society. Examples of accomplished older adults include:

- Benjamin Franklin (1706–1790)—writer, scientist, inventor, and statesman—helped draft the Declaration of Independence at age 70.

- Thomas Alva Edison (1847–1931) worked on inventions, including the lightbulb, the microphone, and the phonograph, until his death at the age of 84.

- Rear Admiral Grace Murray Hopper (1906–1992), one of the early computer scientists and a coauthor of the computer language COBOL, maintained an active speaking and consulting schedule until her death at age 85.

- Margaret Mead (1901–1978), the noted anthropologist, returned to New Guinea when she was 72 and exhausted a much younger television film crew as they tried to keep up with her.

- Albert Einstein (1879–1955), who formulated the theory of relativity, was working on a unifying theory of the universe when he died at age 76.

- Georgia O'Keeffe (1887–1986) created masterful paintings when she was more than 80 years of age.

Older adults continue to play vital roles in industry, government, and the arts. Notable examples include:

- Former senator John Glenn (1921–), who piloted the first manned U.S. spacecraft to orbit the earth, returned to space at age 77 as a payload specialist.

- T. Boone Pickens (1928–) is a financier and chairman of BP Capital Management; in 2012 *Forbes* ranked him as the 360th-richest person in the United States.

- U.S. Senator John McCain (1936–; R-AZ) was 76 years old when he was elected in 2012 to a 14th term as senator. He was the Republican presidential candidate in the 2008 election.

- Madeleine Albright (1937–), the U.S. secretary of state from 1997 to 2001, is the president of the Harry S. Truman Scholarship Foundation and chair of the National Democratic Institute for International Affairs. She also serves as cochair of the Commission on Legal Empowerment of the Poor and of the Pew Global Attitudes Project.

- James E. Hansen (1941–), the former head of the National Aeronautics and Space Administration's Goddard Institute for Space Studies and adjunct professor in the Department of Earth and Environmental Sciences at Columbia University, is known for increasing public awareness of global warming and its effects on climate change.

- Robert Redford (1937–) is an Academy Award–winning actor, director, producer, businessman, environmentalist, philanthropist, and founder of the Sundance Film Festival.

- Hillary Rodham Clinton (1947–) was the 67th U.S. secretary of state from 2009 to 2013. She was also the First Lady of the United States from 1993 to 2001 and a U.S. senator for New York from 2001 to 2009.

- Nancy Pelosi (1940–; D-CA) served as the Speaker of the U.S. House of Representatives from January 2007 to January 2011. She was the first woman to hold that position.

DEFINING AND REDEFINING RETIREMENT

Retirement in the United States is usually defined by withdrawal from the paid labor force and receipt of income from pension plans, Social Security, or other retirement plans. There are, however, many people who may be viewed as being retired, although they do not fulfill the criteria of the generally accepted definition of retirement. For example, workers who retire from the military or other federal employment, which provide pension benefits after 20 years of service, may choose to continue to work and remain in the labor force for years, collecting both a salary and a pension. Other workers retire from full-time employment but continue to work part time to supplement their pension, Social Security, or retirement benefits. As a result, not all workers collecting pensions are retired, and some workers collecting salaries are retired.

Besides expanding the definition of the term *retirement*, an increasing number of older Americans are not subscribing to the traditional timing and lifestyle of retirement. Retirement is no longer an event, it is a process, and work and retirement are no longer mutually exclusive. Although many older adults still choose to retire from full-time employment at age 65, they remain active by exploring new careers, working part time, volunteering, and engaging in a variety of leisure activities. An increasing proportion of older adults work well beyond age 65, and some choose not to retire at all.

In 2013 prospective retirees included the baby boom generation (people born between 1946 and 1964). This generation faces unique difficulties when contemplating retirement—declining home values, high unemployment, low interest rates, and a depressed economy. In "Boomers Aren't Working Forever, after All" (Reuters.com, May 30, 2013), Mark Miller reports that although some boomers say they plan to postpone retirement and reinvent the last third of their lives, the oldest boomers, those born in 1946, appear to be following conventional retirement schedules. According to Miller, "more than half the oldest boomers . . . had fully retired by the end of the year in which they turned 66."

The MetLife Mature Market Institute confirms in *The Oldest Boomers: Healthy, Retiring Rapidly and Collecting Social Security* (May 2013, https://www.metlife.com/assets/cao/mmi/publications/studies/2013/mmi-oldest-boomers.pdf) that more than half (52%) of the oldest boomers (people born in 1946) had retired by 2012, up from 45% in 2011. Many of those who retired said they did so in response to job loss or health challenges. The majority (86%) were collecting Social Security benefits and 43% began collecting benefits earlier than they had originally planned. Two-thirds (20% very confident and 46% somewhat confident) said they are confident "in Social Security's ability to provide them with adequate lifetime benefits."

Of those who were still working in 2012, about 7% were planning to postpone retirement and 13% anticipated being able to retire early. One-third of these working oldest boomers anticipated a lower standard of living in retirement, but among those who were retired, just one out of five said their standard of living declined in retirement.

RECASTING WORK AND RETIREMENT

Throughout much of human history the average length of life was relatively short. According to Laura B. Shrestha of the Congressional Research Service, in *Life Expectancy in the United States* (August 16, 2006, http://aging.senate.gov/crs/aging1.pdf), in 1900 life expectancy was just 49.2 years. In a world where most people did not expect to live beyond age 50, it was essential that personal, educational, and professional milestones be attained by certain ages. Obtaining an education, job training, marriage, parenthood, and retirement not only were designated to particular periods of life but also were expected generally to occur only once in a lifetime.

This regimented pattern of life was maintained by tradition and reinforced by laws and regulations. In the United States government regulations and institutional rules prescribed the ages at which education began, work-life ended, and pension and Social Security benefits commenced. This timetable was based on the assumptions that these activities were to be performed "on time" and in sequence and that most growth and development occurred during the first half of life, whereas the second half was, in general, characterized by decline and disinvestment.

Social and demographic trends (including increased longevity and improved health), technological advances, and economic realities have transformed the size and composition of the labor force as well as the nature of family and work. Examples of these changes include:

- Marriage and childbearing are often postponed in favor of pursuing education and careers. Advances in reproductive technology have enabled women to delay having children by 20 years. Table 4.1 shows that the rate of women aged 40 to 44 years giving birth rose from 10.2 births per 1,000 women in 2010 to 10.3 births per 1,000 women in 2011.

- Formal learning was once the exclusive province of the young; however, middle-aged and older adults are increasingly returning to school. According to the U.S. Census Bureau, in the press release "Back to School: 2012–2013" (July 24, 2012, http://www.census.gov/newsroom/releases/archives/facts_for_features_special_editions/cb11-_ff15.html), 16% of all college students were aged 35 years and older in 2010, and 34% of these students attended school part time. Distance learning programs and classes offered online have created opportunities for older adults who wish to continue their education.

- Career changes and retraining have become the norm rather than the exception. Americans once pursued a

TABLE 4.1

Birth rates, by age of mother, 2010 and 2011

[Data for 2011 are based on a continuous file of records received from the states. Figures for 2011 are based on weighted data rounded to the nearest individual, so categories may not add to totals. Rates are per 1,000 women. Population estimates as of July 1 for 2011 and based on counts enumerated as of April 1 for 2010.]

Age and race	2011		2010	
	Number	Rate	Number	Rate
All races and origins[a]				
Total[b]	3,953,593	63.2	3,999,386	64.1
10–14 years	3,974	0.4	4,497	0.4
15–19 years	329,797	31.3	367,678	34.2
15–17 years	95,554	15.4	109,173	17.3
18–19 years	234,242	54.1	258,505	58.2
20–24 years	925,213	85.3	951,688	90.0
25–29 years	1,127,592	107.2	1,133,713	108.3
30–34 years	986,661	96.5	962,170	96.5
35–39 years	463,815	47.2	464,870	45.9
40–44 years	108,891	10.3	107,045	10.2
45–54 years[c]	7,651	0.7	7,725	0.7

[a]Includes births to race and origin groups not shown separately, such as white Hispanic and black Hispanic women, and births with origin not stated.
[b]The total number includes births to women of all ages. The rate shown for all ages is the fertility rate, which is defined as the total number of births (regardless of the age of the mother) per 1,000 women aged 15–44.
[c]The birth rate for women aged 45–49 is computed by relating the number of births to women aged 45 and over to women aged 45–49 because most of the births in this group are to women aged 45–49.

SOURCE: Adapted from Brady E. Hamilton, Joyce A. Martin, and Stephanie J. Ventura, "Table 2. Births by Age, Race, and Hispanic Origin of Mother: United States, Final 2010 and Preliminary 2011," in "Births: Preliminary Data for 2011," *National Vital Statistics Reports*, vol. 61, no. 5, October 3, 2012, http://www.cdc.gov/nchs/data/nvsr/nvsr61/nvsr61_05.pdf (accessed June 4, 2013)

single career during their lifetime; many workers now change jobs and even careers several times. According to the American Council on Education (2013, http://www.acenet.edu), an increasing number of adults, from military veterans to people aged 50 years and older, are returning to work in second, third, or even fifth careers.

- Age-based mandatory retirement no longer exists in most private-sector industries. Historically, mandatory retirement ages were justified by the argument that some occupations were either too dangerous for older workers or required high levels of physical and mental acuity. Mandatory retirement is still compulsory for federal law officers, correctional officers, firefighters, air traffic controllers, and commercial airline pilots. However, mandatory retirement ages have been faulted because they are arbitrary and are not based on actual physical evaluations of individual workers. As a result, some detractors view the practice of age-based mandatory retirement as a form of age discrimination.

Although a conventional American life generally included education, work, and recreation/retirement, in this order, the current cohort (a group of individuals that shares a common characteristic such as birth years and is studied over time) of workers and retirees has the opportunity to blend, reorder, and repeat these activities as desired. Many gerontologists (professionals who study the social, psychological, and biological aspects of aging)

and other aging researchers posit that there is a "third age"—a stage of working life when older workers can actively renegotiate their relationship with the labor force. Their choices, depending on life circumstances, may include remaining in the workforce, retiring, or returning to work for periods of part-time, full-time, or part-season employment. Not all workers and retirees will choose to stray from the conventional course, but increasingly they have the option to do so.

A CHANGING ECONOMY AND CHANGING ROLES

From Agricultural ...

When the U.S. economy was predominantly agricultural, children were put to work as soon as they were able to contribute to the family upkeep. Similarly, workers who lived beyond age 65 did not retire; they worked as long as they were physically able. When older adults were no longer able to work, younger family members cared for them. Older people were valued and respected for their accumulated knowledge and experience and were integral members of the interconnected family and labor systems.

... to Industrial ...

The Industrial Revolution shifted workers from the farm to manufacturing jobs. The work was physically demanding, the hours long, and the tasks rigidly structured.

Women labored in factories and at home caring for the family. Older people found themselves displaced—their skills and experience were not relevant to new technologies and they could not physically compete with the large number of young workers eager to exploit new economic opportunities.

As industrial workers matured, some were promoted to positions as supervisors and managers. For older workers who had been with the same company for many years, labor unions provided a measure of job security through the seniority system ("first hired, last fired"). However, in an increasingly youth-oriented society older workers were often rejected in favor of younger laborers. Frequent reports of age discrimination prompted Congress to pass the Age Discrimination in Employment Act (ADEA). Enacted in 1967 to protect workers aged 40 to 65 years, ADEA made it illegal for employers or unions to discharge, refuse to hire, or otherwise discriminate on the basis of age. Victims are eligible for lost wages—the amount is doubled in the most blatant cases—and workers wrongfully terminated may also seek reinstatement. The ADEA Amendments of 1978 made 70 the upper age limit and prohibited mandatory retirement for most workers in the private sector and in the federal government. In 1986 Congress again amended the act to eliminate the upper age limit.

... to Service and Information

The U.S. economy continued its dramatic shift away from smokestack industries such as mining and manufacturing to an economy in which service occupations and the production and dissemination of information predominate. As a result, the demand for highly educated workers has grown, and the demand for workers who perform physical labor has slackened. Many information-age careers such as those in the fields of health, law, information technology, and communications, are ideally suited for older workers because they do not require physical labor, and employers benefit from the cumulative experience of older workers.

THE AGING LABOR FORCE

As the baby boom generation approaches retirement age, the proportion of the U.S. population aged 65 years and older will increase significantly. However, the U.S. labor force is already undergoing a shift toward a greater number of older workers and a relative scarcity of new entrants.

According to the U.S. Bureau of Labor Statistics (BLS), the median age (the middle value; half are younger and half are older) of the U.S. labor force is increasing, from 34.6 years in 1980, to 41.7 years in 2010, to a projected 42.8 years in 2020. (See Table 4.2.)

TABLE 4.2

Median age of the labor force, 1980, 1990, 2000, 2010 and projected 2020

Group	1980	1990	2000	2010	2020
Total	**34.6**	**36.4**	**39.3**	**41.7**	**42.8**
Sex					
Men	35.1	36.5	39.2	41.5	42.4
Women	33.9	36.2	39.3	42.0	43.3
Race					
White	34.8	36.6	39.6	42.3	43.3
Black	33.3	34.8	37.4	39.3	40.4
Asian	34.1	35.8	37.9	41.2	44.0
Ethnicity					
Hispanic origin	32.0	31.2	33.7	36.9	38.7
White non-Hispanic	35.2	37.1	40.5	43.6	44.8

SOURCE: "Table 6. Median Age of the Labor Force, by Sex, Race and Ethnicity, 1980, 1990, 2000, 2010 and Projected 2020," in *Employment Projections*, U.S. Bureau of Labor Statistics, Office of Occupational Statistics and Employment Projections, February 1, 2012, http://www.bls.gov/emp/ep_table_306.htm (accessed June 4, 2013)

Older Adults in the Labor Force

The BLS (February 2013, http://www.bls.gov/cps/cpsaat03.pdf) reports that in 2012 older workers accounted for 17.3% of the entire U.S. labor force. In *Older Workers* (July 2008, http://www.bls.gov/spotlight/2008/older_workers/pdf/older_workers_bls_spotlight.pdf), the BLS notes that between 1948 and 2007 the labor force participation of men aged 65 years and older generally declined until the late 1990s, when rates leveled off or even rose slightly. The observed decline in older adults' participation in the labor force during the 1970s and into the 1980s has been attributed to widespread mandatory retirement practices in many industries that forced workers to retire at age 65. In addition, the eligibility age for Social Security benefits was reduced from 65 to 62 years of age during the 1960s, enabling workers to retire earlier. The relatively stable proportion of older workers in the labor force since that time is in part because of the elimination of mandatory retirement and the liberalization of the Social Security earnings test—the earnings limits that prompt a reduction of Social Security benefits. The labor force participation rate for older workers was at record lows during the 1980s and early 1990s but has been increasing since the late 1990s—a larger share of older workers are remaining in or returning to the labor force.

The BLS indicates that between 1977 and 2007 the employment of workers aged 65 years and older increased by 101%. The number of employed men over the age of 65 years increased by 75% and the number of employed women rose by 147%. Although the overall percentage of workers aged 75 years and older was small, 0.8% in 2007, it increased a staggering 172% between 1977 and 2007. This increase in older workers may reflect several factors, including economic necessity, the fact that older adults are seeking to remain vital and active into their 70s, a desire for the challenge and social interactions that work offers, or some combination of these.

Unemployment Is High among Older Adults

The BLS reports in "Record Unemployment among Older Workers Does Not Keep Them out of the Job Market" (March 2010, http://www.bls.gov/opub/ils/pdf/opbils81.pdf) that the unemployment rate for workers aged 55 years and older has significantly increased since December 2007. In February 2010, 7.1% of older adults were unemployed. Although there are fewer unemployed older adults than younger adults, older unemployed people are jobless longer than younger people—an average of 35.5 weeks, compared with 23.3 weeks for people aged 16 to 24 years and 30.3 weeks for those aged 25 to 54 years.

Despite persisting high unemployment rates, older adults continue to participate in the labor force. Table 4.3 shows that the unemployment rate for older adults decreased in 2012, and except for a slight increase in January 2013, continued to decline in 2013.

Older Women Opt to Work Rather Than Retire

Between 1990 and 2010 labor force participation rates generally rose among women aged 55 years and older, from 22.9% in 1990 to 26.1% in 2000 to 35.1% in 2010. (See Table 4.4.) The BLS projects that the participation rate of women aged 55 years and older will increase to 39.3% by 2020. Between 1990 and 2010 the participation rate for women aged 62 to 64 years rose from 30.7% to 45.3%, and among women aged 65 to 69 years the rate increased from 17% to 27%. Likewise, the labor force participation of women aged 70 to 74 years grew from 8.2% in 1990 to 14.7% in 2010, and among women aged 75 to 79 years from 3.9% to 8.2%. These increases have narrowed the gap in labor force participation rates between men and women.

Most older women in the 21st century spent some time in the labor force when they were younger. However, the older the woman the less likely she is to have ever worked outside the home. In the United States the group of women in their late 50s and early 60s that was the first to work outside the home in large numbers is approaching retirement. Women in this cohort who are single, widowed, or divorced often continue to work to support themselves because they do not have sufficient Social Security credits to retire.

Married older women are increasingly choosing to keep working after their husband retires, breaking with the practice of joining their husband in retirement. In 1977 about one-third of employed women aged 65 years and older were married, but the BLS reports in *Women in the Labor Force: A Databook* (February 2013, http://www.bls.gov/cps/wlf-databook-2012.pdf) that in 2011 more than half (56.8%) of married women were employed. Historically, some of the reasons cited for the growing proportion of older married women in the workforce are:

- Older women have careers they find personally satisfying as well as financially rewarding.

- They need to secure their retirement to prevent the poverty that has historically afflicted widows.

- Their income helps maintain the family standard of living and may be vital when their husband has been pressured to retire by his employer or suffers failing health.

TABLE 4.3

Unemployment rates by age, 2012 and January–April 2013

[Seasonally adjusted. Percent.]

Age	2012									2013			
	Apr.	May	June	July	Aug.	Sept.	Oct.	Nov.	Dec.	Jan.	Feb.	Mar.	Apr.
Total, 16 years and over	8.1	8.2	8.2	8.2	8.1	7.8	7.9	7.8	7.8	7.9	7.7	7.6	7.5
16 to 19 years	24.9	24.4	23.7	23.9	24.5	23.7	23.7	23.6	23.5	23.4	25.1	24.2	24.1
16 to 17 years	26.0	26.3	26.7	26.8	29.3	25.5	25.3	28.4	25.8	28.4	27.6	27.1	27.3
18 to 19 years	24.8	23.3	21.9	22.2	22.7	22.7	22.7	20.4	22.6	20.8	23.0	22.1	22.6
20 years and over	7.5	7.6	7.6	7.6	7.4	7.2	7.3	7.1	7.2	7.3	7.1	6.9	6.9
20 to 24 years	13.2	13.0	13.7	13.5	13.8	12.4	13.2	12.6	13.7	14.2	13.1	13.3	13.1
25 years and over	6.8	6.9	6.9	6.9	6.7	6.6	6.6	6.5	6.5	6.5	6.3	6.2	6.1
25 to 54 years	6.9	7.1	7.2	7.2	7.0	6.8	6.8	6.7	6.7	6.7	6.5	6.4	6.4
25 to 34 years	8.1	8.2	8.2	8.2	8.3	8.1	8.2	7.9	7.7	7.7	7.8	7.4	7.4
35 to 44 years	6.5	6.8	7.0	6.8	6.6	6.3	6.3	6.2	6.6	6.5	6.2	6.0	5.8
45 to 54 years	6.2	6.3	6.3	6.5	6.3	6.0	6.1	6.0	5.8	6.0	5.5	5.7	5.9
55 years and over	6.3	6.5	6.1	6.1	5.9	5.9	5.8	5.8	5.9	6.0	5.8	5.5	5.5

SOURCE: Adapted from "A-10. Unemployment Rates by Age, Sex, and Marital Status, Seasonally Adjusted," in *Labor Force Statistics from the Current Population Survey*, U.S. Bureau of Labor Statistics, Division of Labor Force Statistics, May 3, 2013, http://www.bls.gov/web/empsit/cpseea10.htm (accessed June 4, 2013)

TABLE 4.4

Labor force participation rates, by age and gender, 1990, 2000, 2010, and projected 2020

[In percent]

Group	Participation rate				Percentage-point change			Annual growth rate		
	1990	2000	2010	2020	1990–2000	2000–2010	2010–2020	1990–2000	2000–2010	2010–2020
Total, 16 years and older	**66.5**	**67.1**	**64.7**	**62.5**	**0.6**	**−2.4**	**−2.2**	**0.1**	**−0.4**	**−0.3**
16 to 24	67.3	65.4	55.2	48.2	−1.9	−10.2	−7.0	−0.3	−1.7	−1.3
16 to 19	53.7	52.0	34.9	26.5	−1.7	−17.1	−8.4	−0.3	−3.9	−2.7
20 to 24	77.8	77.8	71.4	65.9	0.0	−6.4	−5.5	0.0	−0.9	−0.8
25 to 54	83.5	84.0	82.2	81.3	0.5	−1.8	−0.9	0.1	−0.2	−0.1
25 to 34	83.6	84.6	82.2	80.6	1.0	−2.4	−1.6	0.1	−0.3	−0.2
35 to 44	85.2	84.8	83.2	82.6	−0.4	−1.6	−0.6	0.0	−0.2	−0.1
45 to 54	80.7	82.5	81.2	80.8	1.8	−1.3	−0.4	0.2	−0.2	0.0
55 and older	30.1	32.4	40.2	43.0	2.3	7.8	2.8	0.7	2.2	0.7
55 to 64	55.9	59.3	64.9	68.8	3.4	5.6	3.9	0.6	0.9	0.6
55 to 59	67.0	68.9	73.3	76.3	1.9	4.4	3.0	0.3	0.6	0.4
60 to 64	44.8	47.2	55.2	60.9	2.4	8.0	5.7	0.5	1.6	1.0
60 to 61	55.1	57.1	62.5	64.2	2.0	5.4	1.7	0.4	0.9	0.3
62 to 64	38.0	40.2	49.8	58.5	2.2	9.6	8.7	0.6	2.2	1.6
65 and older	11.8	12.9	17.4	22.6	1.1	4.5	5.2	0.9	3.0	2.6
65 to 74	16.7	19.2	25.7	31.0	2.5	6.5	5.3	1.4	3.0	1.9
65 to 69	21.0	24.5	31.5	37.8	3.5	7.0	6.3	1.6	2.5	1.8
70 to 74	11.3	13.5	18.0	22.8	2.2	4.5	4.8	1.8	2.9	2.4
75 and older	4.3	5.3	7.4	10.0	1.0	2.1	2.6	2.1	3.4	3.1
75 to 79	6.1	7.5	10.9	15.2	1.4	3.4	4.3	2.1	3.8	3.4
Men, 16 years and older	**76.4**	**74.8**	**71.2**	**68.2**	**−1.6**	**−3.6**	**−3.0**	**−0.2**	**−0.5**	**−0.4**
16 to 24	71.8	68.6	56.8	50.6	−3.2	−11.8	−6.2	−0.5	−1.9	−1.1
16 to 19	55.7	52.8	34.9	27.9	−2.9	−17.9	−7.0	−0.5	−4.1	−2.2
20 to 24	84.4	82.6	74.5	69.4	−1.8	−8.1	−5.1	−0.2	−1.0	−0.7
25 to 54	93.4	91.6	89.3	88.1	−1.8	−1.9	−1.6	−0.2	−0.2	−0.2
25 to 34	94.1	93.4	90.3	86.9	−0.7	−3.1	−3.4	−0.1	−0.3	−0.4
35 to 44	94.3	92.7	91.5	91.3	−1.6	−1.2	−0.2	−0.2	−0.1	0.0
45 to 54	90.7	88.6	86.8	86.0	−2.1	−1.8	−0.8	−0.2	−0.2	−0.1
55 and older	39.4	40.1	46.4	47.3	0.7	6.3	0.9	0.2	1.5	0.2
55 to 64	67.8	67.3	70.0	71.1	−0.5	2.7	1.1	−0.1	0.4	0.2
55 to 59	79.9	77.1	78.5	78.6	−2.8	1.4	0.1	−0.4	0.2	0.0
60 to 64	55.5	55.0	60.0	63.2	−0.5	5.0	3.2	−0.1	0.9	0.5
60 to 61	68.8	66.0	67.4	62.9	−2.8	1.4	−4.5	−0.4	0.2	−0.7
62 to 64	46.5	47.0	54.6	63.4	0.5	7.6	8.8	0.1	1.5	1.5
65 and older	16.3	17.7	22.1	26.7	1.4	4.4	4.6	0.8	2.2	1.9
65 to 74	21.4	24.6	30.4	35.1	3.2	5.8	4.7	1.4	2.1	1.4
65 to 69	26.0	30.3	36.5	41.4	4.3	6.2	4.9	1.5	1.9	1.3
70 to 74	15.4	18.0	22.0	27.0	2.6	4.0	5.0	1.6	2.0	2.1
75 and older	7.1	8.1	10.4	12.8	1.0	2.3	2.4	1.3	2.5	2.1
75 to 79	9.5	10.7	14.5	18.2	1.2	3.8	3.7	1.2	3.1	2.3
Women, 16 years and older	**57.5**	**59.9**	**58.6**	**57.1**	**2.4**	**−1.3**	**−1.5**	**0.4**	**−0.2**	**−0.3**
16 to 24	62.9	63.0	53.6	45.7	0.1	−9.4	−7.9	0.0	−1.6	−1.6
16 to 19	51.6	51.2	35.0	25.2	−0.4	−16.2	−9.8	−0.1	−3.7	−3.2
20 to 24	71.3	73.1	68.3	62.3	1.8	−4.8	−6.0	0.2	−0.7	−0.9
25 to 54	74.0	76.7	75.2	74.6	2.7	−1.5	−0.6	0.4	−0.2	−0.1
25 to 34	73.5	76.1	74.7	74.2	2.6	−1.4	−0.5	0.3	−0.2	−0.1
35 to 44	76.4	77.2	75.2	74.0	0.8	−2.0	−1.2	0.1	−0.3	−0.2
45 to 54	71.2	76.8	75.7	75.7	5.6	−1.1	0.0	0.8	−0.1	0.0
55 and older	22.9	26.1	35.1	39.3	3.2	9.0	4.2	1.3	3.0	1.1
55 to 64	45.2	51.9	60.2	66.6	6.7	8.3	6.4	1.4	1.5	1.0
55 to 59	55.3	61.4	68.4	74.1	6.1	7.0	5.7	1.1	1.1	0.8
60 to 64	35.5	40.2	50.7	58.8	4.7	10.5	8.1	1.3	2.3	1.5
60 to 61	42.9	49.0	58.0	65.4	6.1	9.0	7.4	1.3	1.7	1.2
62 to 64	30.7	34.1	45.3	54.1	3.4	11.2	8.8	1.1	2.9	1.8
65 and older	8.6	9.4	13.8	19.2	0.8	4.4	5.4	0.9	3.9	3.4
65 to 74	13.0	14.9	21.6	27.5	1.9	6.7	5.9	1.4	3.8	2.4
65 to 69	17.0	19.5	27.0	34.5	2.5	7.5	7.5	1.4	3.3	2.5
70 to 74	8.2	10.0	14.7	19.2	1.8	4.7	4.5	2.0	3.9	2.7
75 and older	2.7	3.6	5.3	8.0	0.9	1.7	2.7	2.9	3.9	4.2
75 to 79	3.9	5.3	8.2	13.0	1.4	2.9	4.8	3.1	4.5	4.7

Note: Details may not sum to totals because of rounding.

SOURCE: Adapted from Mitra Toossi, "Table 3. Civilian Labor Force Participation Rates, by Age, Gender, Race and Ethnicity, 1990, 2000, 2010, and Projected 2020," in "Employment Outlook: 2010–2020—Labor Force Projections to 2020: A More Slowly Growing Workforce," *Monthly Labor Review*, January 2012, http://www.bls.gov/opub/mlr/2012/01/art3full.pdf (accessed June 4, 2013)

- They enjoy social interactions at the workplace—women value relationships with coworkers more than men, and as a result women often find retirement more isolating.

The Aging Labor Force

In "Employment Outlook: 2010–2020 Labor Force Projections to 2020: A More Slowly Growing Workforce" (*Monthly Labor Review*, January 2012), Mitra Toossi of the BLS observes that older workers are the only group in which the labor participation rate has been rising substantially. The 55 and older age group accounted for 11.9% of the labor force in 1990 and 19.5% in 2010, and is projected to reach 25.2% in 2020. (See Table 4.5.)

Part-Time versus Full-Time Work

Kevin E. Cahill, Michael D. Giandrea, and Joseph F. Quinn observe in "Older Workers and Short-Term Jobs: Patterns and Determinants" (*Monthly Labor Review*, May 2012) that adults who had never held a full-time career job were more likely to work part time after age 50. Interestingly, between 1992 and 2008 the percentage of older adults with a history of full-time career work that were working part time increased. Among people aged 51 to 61 years, 10% of men and 15% of women who had held a full-time career job were working part time in 1992. (See Figure 4.1.) By 2008 this percentage had increase to 55% of men and 49% of women.

Older workers may find increasing opportunities for flexible employment and alternative work arrangements, such as working as independent contractors or on-call workers rather than as employees or daily workers. For employers, hiring older part-time workers is often an attractive alternative to hiring younger full-time workers. Some employers value older workers' maturity, dependability, and experience. Others hire older workers to reduce payroll expenses. This reduction is achieved when part-time workers are hired as independent contractors and do not receive benefits.

According to the AARP, in "2013 Best Employers for Workers over 50 Announced" (2013, http://www.aarp.org/work/employee-benefits/best_employers/), employers from a variety of industries value older workers and actively seek to recruit and retain them. In 2013 the AARP and the Society for Human Resource Management recognized the top-50 employers for workers aged 50 years and older. Six of the top 10 employers—the National Institutes of Health, Scripps Health, the Atlantic Health System, the University of Texas MD Anderson Cancer Center, the Mercy Health System, the YMCA of Greater Rochester, West Virginia University, Bon Secours Virginia, the National Rural Electric Cooperative Association, and the WellStar Health System—were in the health care industry.

Employers Favor Older Workers

In "Adecco Staffing Mature Worker Survey" (2013, http://www.adeccousa.com/), a survey of 501 hiring managers, Adecco Staffing finds that hiring managers view older workers favorably. The managers indicated that they are three times more likely to hire a worker aged 50 years or older (60%) than they are to hire a Millennial (people born between 1981 and 2000; 20%). Hiring managers characterized older workers as reliable (91%), professional (88%), and good listeners (77%), and 39% said there are no challenges inherent in hiring older workers.

DISPELLING MYTHS AND STEREOTYPES ABOUT OLDER WORKERS

Older workers are often stereotyped by the mistaken belief that performance declines with age. Performance studies, however, reveal that older workers perform intellectually as well as or better than workers 30 years younger by maintaining their problem-solving, communication, and creative skills. The Adecco Staffing survey confirms that managers feel older adults have better time-management skills than Millennials. Nearly half (46%) of managers said Millennials need to improve their time-management skills, compared with just 10% of older workers.

Myth: Older Workers Have Overly Increased Absenteeism

Because aging is associated with declining health, older workers are often assumed to have markedly higher rates of illnesses and absences from work. Somewhat surprisingly, the chronic (long-term) health conditions that older adults may suffer tend to be manageable and do not affect attendance records. In fact, absence rates for older full-time wage and salary workers are comparable to those of younger workers. According to the BLS, in 2012 the absence rate for workers aged 55 years and older was 3.4%, compared with 3% for those aged 25 to 54 years. (See Table 4.6.)

Myth: It Costs More to Hire Older Workers

One widely accepted myth is that hiring and training older workers is not a sound investment because they will not remain on the job long. The BLS, however, indicates that in January 2012 workers aged 55 to 64 years had a median job tenure of 10.3 years, which was more than three times longer than the 3.2 years for workers aged 25 to 34 years. (See Table 4.7.) Research conducted by the AARP repeatedly demonstrates that workers between the ages of 50 and 60 work for an average of 15 years. Furthermore, the Mature Workers Employment Alliance, an organization that assists older workers to transition to new positions, asserts that the future work life of employees over the age of 50 generally exceeds the life of the technology for which they are trained.

In "Myths about Older Workers" (March 2009, http://www.aging.unc.edu/programs/nccolle/files/MythsAboutOlderWorkers.pdf), the North Carolina Collaboration on

TABLE 4.5

Labor force participation rates, by age and gender, race and ethnicity, 1990, 2000, 2010, and projected 2020

[Numbers in thousands]

Group	Level 1990	Level 2000	Level 2010	Level 2020	Change 1990–2000	Change 2000–2010	Change 2010–2020	Percent change 1990–2000	Percent change 2000–2010	Percent change 2010–2020	Percent distribution 1990	Percent distribution 2000	Percent distribution 2010	Percent distribution 2020	Annual growth rate 1990–2000	Annual growth rate 2000–2010	Annual growth rate 2010–2020
Total, 16 years and older	125,840	142,583	153,889	164,360	16,743	11,306	10,471	13.3	7.9	6.8	100.0	100.0	100.0	100.0	1.3	0.8	0.7
Age, years																	
16 to 24	22,492	22,520	20,934	18,330	28	−1,586	−2,604	0.1	−7.0	−12.4	17.9	15.8	13.6	11.2	0.0	−0.7	−1.3
25 to 54	88,322	101,394	102,940	104,619	13,072	1,546	1,679	14.8	1.5	1.6	70.2	71.1	66.9	63.7	1.4	0.2	0.2
55 and older	15,026	18,669	30,014	41,411	3,643	11,345	11,397	24.2	60.8	38.0	11.9	13.1	19.5	25.2	2.2	4.9	3.3
Gender																	
Men	69,011	76,280	81,985	87,128	7,269	5,705	5,143	10.5	7.5	6.3	54.8	53.5	53.3	53.0	1.0	0.7	0.6
Women	56,829	66,303	71,904	77,232	9,474	5,601	5,328	16.7	8.4	7.4	45.2	46.5	46.7	47.0	1.6	0.8	0.7
Race																	
White	107,447	118,545	125,084	130,516	11,098	6,539	5,432	10.3	5.5	4.3	85.4	83.1	81.3	79.4	1.0	0.5	0.4
Black	13,740	16,397	17,862	19,676	2,657	1,465	1,814	19.3	8.9	10.2	10.9	11.5	11.6	12.0	1.8	0.9	1.0
Asian	4,653	6,270	7,248	9,430	1,617	978	2,182	34.8	15.6	30.1	3.7	4.4	4.7	5.7	3.0	1.5	2.7
All other groups*	—	1,371	3,694	4,738	—	2,323	1,044	—	169.4	28.3	—	1.0	2.4	2.9	—	10.4	2.5
Ethnicity																	
Hispanic origin	10,720	16,689	22,748	30,493	5,969	6,059	7,745	55.7	36.3	34.0	8.5	11.7	14.8	18.6	4.5	3.1	3.0
Other than Hispanic origin	115,120	125,894	131,141	133,867	10,774	5,247	2,726	9.4	4.2	2.1	91.5	88.3	85.2	81.4	0.9	0.4	0.2
White non-Hispanic	97,818	102,729	103,947	102,371	4,911	1,218	−1,576	5.0	1.2	−1.5	77.7	72.0	67.5	62.3	0.5	0.1	−0.2
Age of baby boomers	26 to 44	36 to 54	46 to 64	56 to 74													

*The "all other groups" category includes (1) those classified as being of multiple racial origin and (2) the racial categories of (2a) American Indian and Alaska Native and (2b) Native Hawaiian and other Pacific Islanders.

Note : Dash indicates no data collected for category. Details may not sum to totals because of rounding.

SOURCE: Mitra Toossi, "Table 1. Civilian Labor Force, by Age, Gender, Race and Ethnicity, 1990, 2000, 2010, and Projected 2020," in "Employment Outlook: 2010–2020—Labor Force Projections to 2020: A More Slowly Growing Workforce," Monthly Labor Review, January 2012. http://www.bls.gov/opub/mlr/2012/01/art3full.pdf (accessed June 4, 2013)

FIGURE 4.1

Percentage of older adults working part time by full-time career job status, 1992–2008

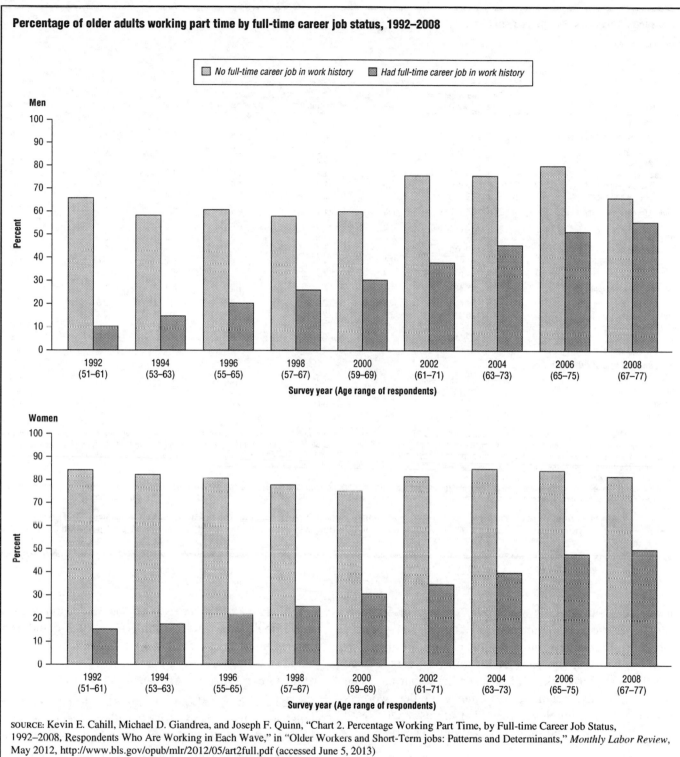

SOURCE: Kevin E. Cahill, Michael D. Giandrea, and Joseph F. Quinn, "Chart 2. Percentage Working Part Time, by Full-time Career Job Status, 1992–2008, Respondents Who Are Working in Each Wave," in "Older Workers and Short-Term jobs: Patterns and Determinants," *Monthly Labor Review*, May 2012, http://www.bls.gov/opub/mlr/2012/05/art2full.pdf (accessed June 5, 2013)

Lifelong Learning and Engagement observes that older workers are less likely to change jobs frequently, which reduces the expenses that are associated with employee turnover. It also notes that some older workers willingly forgo benefits because they have insurance from previous employers or through Medicare.

The AARP indicates that although older workers' health, disability, and life insurance costs are higher than those of younger workers, they are offset by lower costs because of fewer dependents. Older workers have generally earned more vacation time and have higher pension costs, and they take fewer risks, which means they have

TABLE 4.6

Absences from work, by age and sex, 2012

[Numbers in thousands]

	Full-time wage and salary workers[a]	2012 Absence rate[a]			Lost worktime rate[b]		
Characteristic		Total	Illness or injury	Other reasons	Total	Illness or injury	Other reasons
Age and sex							
Total, 16 years and over	102,590	3.1	2.1	1.0	1.5	1.0	0.5
16 to 19 years	1,060	3.8	2.6	1.2	1.3	0.8	0.5
20 to 24 years	7,932	3.0	2.0	1.0	1.2	0.7	0.5
25 years and over	93,598	3.1	2.1	1.0	1.6	1.1	0.5
25 to 54 years	73,940	3.0	2.0	1.0	1.5	1.0	0.6
55 years and over	19,658	3.4	2.7	0.7	1.8	1.5	0.3
Men, 16 years and over	57,159	2.3	1.7	0.6	1.1	0.9	0.2
16 to 19 years	627	3.2	2.4	0.8	1.0	0.8	0.2
20 to 24 years	4,512	2.4	1.8	0.6	0.9	0.6	0.3
25 years and over	52,019	2.3	1.7	0.6	1.1	0.9	0.2
25 to 54 years	41,424	2.1	1.5	0.6	1.0	0.8	0.3
55 years and over	10,595	2.9	2.4	0.5	1.6	1.4	0.2
Women, 16 years and over	45,431	4.1	2.6	1.5	2.1	1.3	0.8
16 to 19 years	433	4.8	2.9	1.9	1.7	0.8	0.9
20 to 24 years	3,419	3.8	2.3	1.6	1.5	0.7	0.8
25 years and over	41,579	4.1	2.7	1.4	2.1	1.3	0.8
25 to 54 years	32,516	4.2	2.6	1.6	2.2	1.2	0.9
55 years and over	9,062	4.0	3.1	0.9	2.1	1.6	0.4
Race and Hispanic or Latino ethnicity							
White	81,756	3.1	2.1	0.9	1.5	1.0	0.5
Black or African American	12,156	3.6	2.4	1.2	1.9	1.3	0.6
Asian	5,772	2.3	1.5	0.8	1.2	0.7	0.5
Hispanic or Latino	16,249	3.0	2.0	1.0	1.4	0.9	0.5

[a]Absences are defined as instances when persons who usually work 35 or more hours per week (full time) worked less than 35 hours during the reference week for one of the following reasons: own illness, injury, or medical problems; child care problems; other family or personal obligations; civic or military duty; and maternity or paternity leave. Excluded are situations in which work was missed due to vacation or personal days, holiday, labor dispute, and other reasons. For multiple jobholders, absence data refer only to work missed at their main jobs. The absence rate is the ratio of workers with absences to total full-time wage and salary employment.
[b]Hours absent as a percent of hours usually worked.
Note: Estimates for the above race groups (white, black or African American, and Asian) do not sum to totals because data are not presented for all races. Persons whose ethnicity is identified as Hispanic or Latino may be of any race. All self-employed workers are excluded, both those with incorporated businesses and those with unincorporated businesses.

SOURCE: "46. Absences from Work of Employed Full-time Wage and Salary Workers by Age, Sex, Race, and Hispanic or Latino Ethnicity," in *Labor Force Statistics from the Current Population Survey*, U.S. Department of Labor, U.S. Bureau of Labor Statistics, 2013, http://www.bls.gov/cps/cpsaat46.pdf (accessed June 5, 2013)

---

lower accident rates. Workers over the age of 50 years file fewer workers' compensation claims than younger workers—the largest numbers of claims are filed by workers between the ages of 30 and 34 years. Fringe benefit costs for workers of all ages are about the same overall. Finally, retaining experienced older workers actually reduces employer costs that are associated with recruiting, hiring, and training new, younger workers.

Myth: Older Workers Are Technophobes

There is a pervasive myth that older adults are unable to learn or use new information technology. In "Don't Be the Office Tech Dinosaur" (WSJ.com, April 16, 2013), Sue Shellenbarger observes that although older workers' lagging technology skills may contribute to higher rates of job loss, many have taken steps to become and stay up to date with social media, mobile apps, and blogs. Shellenbarger explains that even Doug Gould, an award-winning advertising executive, has to continue to learn and adopt new technology. Gould asserts, "There is new technology out there I don't know the first thing about, that could easily turn me into a dinosaur if I don't continue to adapt."

Myth: Older Workers Are Not Innovators

The stereotype of older workers as slow to learn new skills, unwilling to take risks, and unable to adapt to change is fading as older entrepreneurs and innovators gain recognition. Tom Agan, the cofounder and managing partner of Rivia, an innovation and brand consulting firm, asserts in "Why Innovators Get Better with Age" (NYTimes.com, March 30, 2013) that "less gray hair sharply reduces an organization's innovation potential, which over the long term can greatly outweigh short-term gains." He observes that the directors of the top-five films in 2012 and the best-selling fiction writers are in their 40s and 50s. Agan notes that the age when Nobel Prize winners make their discoveries has risen from 32 in 1900 to 38 in 2000. He also cites research revealing that

TABLE 4.7

Median years of tenure with current employer for employed workers, by age and sex, selected years 2002–12

Age and sex	January 2002	January 2004	January 2006	January 2008	January 2010	January 2012
Total						
16 years and over	3.7	4.0	4.0	4.1	4.4	4.6
16 to 17 years	0.7	0.7	0.6	0.7	0.7	0.7
18 to 19 years	0.8	0.8	0.7	0.8	1.0	0.8
20 to 24 years	1.2	1.3	1.3	1.3	1.5	1.3
25 years and over	4.7	4.9	4.9	5.1	5.2	5.4
25 to 34 years	2.7	2.9	2.9	2.7	3.1	3.2
35 to 44 years	4.6	4.9	4.9	4.9	5.1	5.3
45 to 54 years	7.6	7.7	7.3	7.6	7.8	7.8
55 to 64 years	9.9	9.6	9.3	9.9	10.0	10.3
65 years and over	8.6	9.0	8.8	10.2	9.9	10.3
Men						
16 years and over	3.9	4.1	4.1	4.2	4.6	4.7
16 to 17 years	0.8	0.7	0.7	0.7	0.7	0.6
18 to 19 years	0.8	0.8	0.7	0.8	1.0	0.8
20 to 24 years	1.4	1.3	1.4	1.4	1.6	1.4
25 years and over	4.9	5.1	5.0	5.2	5.3	5.5
25 to 34 years	2.8	3.0	2.9	2.8	3.2	3.2
35 to 44 years	5.0	5.2	5.1	5.2	5.3	5.4
45 to 54 years	9.1	9.6	8.1	8.2	8.5	8.5
55 to 64 years	10.2	9.8	9.5	10.1	10.4	10.7
65 years and over	8.1	8.2	8.3	10.4	9.7	10.2
Women						
16 years and over	3.4	3.8	3.9	3.9	4.2	4.6
16 to 17 years	0.7	0.6	0.6	0.6	0.7	0.7
18 to 19 years	0.8	0.8	0.7	0.8	1.0	0.8
20 to 24 years	1.1	1.3	1.2	1.3	1.5	1.3
25 years and over	4.4	4.7	4.8	4.9	5.1	5.4
25 to 34 years	2.5	2.8	2.8	2.6	3.0	3.1
35 to 44 years	4.2	4.5	4.6	4.7	4.9	5.2
45 to 54 years	6.5	6.4	6.7	7.0	7.1	7.3
55 to 64 years	9.6	9.2	9.2	9.8	9.7	10.0
65 years and over	9.4	9.6	9.5	9.9	10.1	10.5

Note: Updated population controls are introduced annually with the release of January data.

SOURCE: "Table 1. Median Years of Tenure with Current Employer for Employed Wage and Salary Workers by Age and Sex, Selected Years, 2002–2012," in *Employee Tenure in 2012*, U.S. Department of Labor, U.S. Bureau of Labor Statistics, September 18, 2012, http://www.bls.gov/news.release/pdf/tenure.pdf (accessed June 6, 2013)

people aged 55 to 65 years have more potential to innovate than do people aged 25 years.

AGE DISCRIMINATION

Although the 1967 ADEA and its amendments were enacted to ban discrimination against workers based on their age, the act was also intended to promote the employment of older workers based on their abilities. Besides making it illegal for employers to discriminate based on age in hiring, discharging, and compensating employees, the act also prohibited companies from coercing older workers into accepting incentives to early retirement. In 1990 ADEA was strengthened with the passing of the Older Workers Benefit Protection Act. Besides prohibiting discrimination in employee benefits based on age, it provides that an employee's waiver of the right to sue for age discrimination, a clause sometimes included in severance packages, is invalid unless it is "voluntary and knowing."

However, age bias and discrimination persist, even though age discrimination in the workplace is against the law. More than 15,000 claims of age discrimination are filed with the Equal Employment Opportunity Commission (EEOC) every year. Most cases involve older workers who believe they were terminated unfairly, but a number of the cases involve workers who feel they have met age discrimination in hiring practices.

The number of claims received by the EEOC rose from 19,921 in fiscal year (FY) 2002 to 22,857 in FY 2012. (See Table 4.8.) Agency data reveal that most claimants do not win. Of the claims that were resolved in FY 2012, the EEOC found "reasonable cause" that age discrimination may have occurred in just 770 cases and found "no reasonable cause" in 19,239 cases.

Pressure to Retire

There are many forms of subtle discrimination against older workers as well as ways that employers

TABLE 4.8

Age Discrimination in Employment Act (ADEA) charges, fiscal years 1997–2012

	Fiscal year 1997	Fiscal year 1998	Fiscal year 1999	Fiscal year 2000	Fiscal year 2001	Fiscal year 2002	Fiscal year 2003	Fiscal year 2004	Fiscal year 2005	Fiscal year 2006	Fiscal year 2007	Fiscal year 2008	Fiscal year 2009	Fiscal year 2010	Fiscal year 2011	Fiscal year 2012
Receipts	15,785	15,191	14,141	16,008	17,405	19,921	19,124	17,837	16,585	16,548	19,103	24,582	22,778	23,264	23,465	22,857
Resolutions	18,279	15,995	15,448	14,672	15,155	18,673	17,352	15,792	14,076	14,146	16,134	21,415	20,529	24,800	26,080	27,335
Resolutions by type																
Settlements	642	755	816	1,156	1,006	1,222	1,285	1,377	1,326	1,417	1,795	1,974	1,935	2,250	2,231	2,001
	3.5%	4.7%	5.3%	7.9%	6.6%	6.5%	7.4%	8.7%	9.4%	10.0%	11.1%	9.2%	9.4%	9.1%	8.6%	7.3%
Withdrawals with benefits	762	580	578	560	551	671	710	787	764	767	958	1,252	1,161	1,322	1,369	1,280
	4.2%	3.6%	3.7%	3.8%	3.6%	3.6%	4.1%	5.0%	5.4%	5.4%	5.9%	5.8%	5.7%	5.3%	5.2%	4.7%
Administrative closures	4,986	4,175	3,601	3,232	3,963	6,254	2,824	3,550	2,537	2,639	2,754	6,387	4,031	4,167	4,230	4,045
	27.3%	26.1%	23.3%	22.0%	26.1%	33.5%	16.3%	22.5%	18.0%	18.7%	17.1%	29.8%	19.6%	16.8%	16.2%	14.8%
No reasonable cause	11,163	9,863	9,172	8,517	8,388	9,725	11,976	9,563	8,866	8,746	10,002	11,124	12,788	16,308	17,454	19,239
	61.1%	61.7%	59.4%	58.0%	55.3%	52.1%	69.0%	60.6%	63.0%	61.8%	62.0%	51.9%	62.3%	65.8%	66.9%	70.4%
Reasonable cause	726	622	1,281	1,207	1,247	801	557	515	583	612	625	678	614	753	796	770
	4.0%	3.9%	8.3%	8.2%	8.2%	4.3%	3.2%	3.3%	4.1%	4.3%	3.9%	3.2%	3.0%	3.0%	3.1%	2.8%
Successful conciliations	74	119	184	241	409	208	166	139	169	177	186	220	202	252	273	343
	0.4%	0.7%	1.2%	1.6%	2.7%	1.1%	1.0%	0.9%	1.2%	1.3%	1.2%	1.0%	1.0%	1.0%	1.0%	1.3%
Unsuccessful conciliations	652	503	1,097	966	838	593	391	376	414	435	439	458	412	501	523	427
	3.6%	3.1%	7.1%	6.6%	5.5%	3.2%	2.3%	2.4%	2.9%	3.1%	2.7%	2.1%	2.0%	2.0%	2.0%	1.6%
Merit resolutions	2,130	1,957	2,675	2,923	2,804	2,694	2,552	2,679	2,673	2,796	3,378	3,904	3,710	4,325	4,396	4,051
	11.7%	12.2%	17.3%	19.9%	18.5%	14.4%	14.7%	17.0%	19.0%	19.8%	20.9%	18.2%	18.1%	17.4%	16.9%	14.8%
Monetary benefits (millions)*	$44.3	$34.7	$38.6	$45.2	$53.7	$55.7	$48.9	$69.0	$77.7	$51.5	$66.8	$82.8	$72.1	$93.6	$95.2	$91.6

*Does not include monetary benefits obtained through litigation.
Notes: The total of individual percentages may not always sum to 100% due to rounding.

SOURCE: "Age Discrimination in Employment Act FY 1997–FY 2012," U.S. Equal Opportunity Commission, 2013. http://www.eeoc.gov/eeoc/statistics/enforcement/adea.cfm (accessed June 7, 2013)

can directly or indirectly exert pressure on older employees to resign or retire. This form of discrimination is "under the radar" and in many instances violates the spirit, if not the letter, of ADEA.

From an employer's standpoint, age discrimination is simply the consequence of efforts to reduce payroll expenses. Employment decisions are not only based on how much an employee contributes to the company but also on the salary and benefits the company must provide the employee, relative to the cost of other employees. Because salary tends to increase with longevity on the job, older workers usually receive higher wages than younger workers. Thus, if two employees are equally productive and the older one has a higher salary, a company has an economic incentive to lay off the older worker or strongly encourage early retirement.

For many workers, early retirement is untenable. Early retirement benefits are usually less than regular retirement benefits and may be insufficient to allow a retiree to live comfortably without working. Finding a new job is more challenging for older workers, particularly during periods of high unemployment, and they are frequently unemployed for longer periods than are younger job seekers. Furthermore, workers who refuse to accept early retirement may find themselves without jobs at all, perhaps with no pension and no severance pay.

Some labor economists contend that early retirements, whether voluntary or coerced, deprive the nation of skilled workers needed for robust growth and divest the government of the revenue that these workers would have contributed in payroll taxes.

Filing ADEA Claims: Suing the Company

The costs involved in filing an age discrimination suit are high. Besides the financial outlay for legal representation, workers who sue their employers may be stigmatized and face further discrimination—future employers' reluctance to hire a worker who has filed a discrimination suit against a former employer. Workers caught in this scenario can suffer emotional and financial damage that may adversely affect them for the rest of their life. Nonetheless, many workers do choose to sue their employers.

U.S. Supreme Court Decisions Augment ADEA

In response to the so-called Great Recession (which lasted from late 2007 to mid-2009) and the continuing economic uncertainty in 2013, many companies instituted layoffs and reductions in force in an effort to reduce costs and remain viable. Because reductions in force aim to reduce payroll, some target higher-paid workers, who are often older adults with longer tenures. ADEA is violated if an employment policy that seems neutral, such as the criteria for workers to be laid off, actually exerts a statistically significant adverse or "disparate impact" when applied to workers aged 40 years and older versus younger workers.

The 2005 U.S. Supreme Court decision in *Smith v. City of Jackson* (544 U.S. 228), that workers aged 40 years and older may prove discrimination under ADEA using a disparate impact theory, strengthened protections for older workers. The court stated that plaintiffs in age discrimination lawsuits do not have to prove that employers intended to discriminate, only that layoffs had a "disparate impact" on older workers. This ruling is significant because claimants are not required to show that an employer deliberately targeted a single employee or group of employees. Instead, claimants can prevail if they are able to demonstrate that an employer used a neutral business practice—with no intent to discriminate—that had an adverse impact on people aged 40 years and older.

In 2008 the Supreme Court ruled in *Meacham et al. v. Knolls Atomic Power Laboratory* (No. 06-1505) that an employer defending against a disparate impact age bias claim, and not the employee making the charge, bears the burden of proving that the adverse action—in this case a reduction in workforce plan—was based on a reasonable factor other than age. The disparate impact theory is based on the principle that a policy that appears neutral may still have an adverse impact on a protected class, in this case, older workers.

The Supreme Court ruling in *Gross v. FBL Financial Services, Inc.* (No. 08-441 [2009]) essentially reversed its earlier position, making it more difficult for older workers to prevail in age discrimination suits. The ruling eliminated the requirement that employers prove they had a legitimate reason other than age for laying off older workers. Instead, the burden of proof now falls to older workers, who must prove that age was the key factor. The ruling reversed a jury verdict in favor of an insurance adjuster in Iowa who filed a claim because his company demoted him and gave his job to a younger worker. According to David G. Savage, in "Supreme Court Makes Age Bias Suits Harder to Win" (LATimes.com, June 19, 2009), the high court opined that "the judge had erred by allowing the plaintiff to win without proving he had been demoted because of his age." In "Reductions in Force: The Supreme Court Escalates the Legal Risks" (July 2008, http://www.lorman.com/news letters/article.php?article_id=1028&newsletter_id=223 &category_id=8&topic=LIT), Frank C. Morris Jr. of Epstein Becker & Green P.C. states that "precisely at a time when the economy may force employers to make more [reductions in force] decisions, the Supreme Court has made defending such decisions decidedly harder for employers."

RECENT AGE DISCRIMINATION CASES AND COURT DECISIONS. Dan Fastenberg reports in "Worker Debra Moreno Wins $193,000 in Age Discrimination Lawsuit" (HuffingtonPost.com, July 25, 2012) that Debra Moreno, a 54-year-old office worker in Maui, Hawaii, won $193,236 in a lawsuit that accused her employer of "outlandish discrimination." Moreno explained that although her supervisor described her as an efficient worker, the owner of the company said she looked and sounded old. The EEOC filed the suit on Moreno's behalf, averring, "What makes this case especially appalling is the flagrant disregard for a worker's abilities, coupled with disparaging ageist remarks and thinking."

The article "3M Settles Age-Discrimination Suit for up to $12M" (Associated Press, March 19, 2011) reports that in March 2011 3M Co. settled an age discrimination suit filed in 2004 that charged the company with downgrading older workers' performance reviews and favoring younger workers for training and advancement. Although a company spokesperson said the proposed settlement, which applied to about 7,000 current and former employees, was not "an admission of liability," 3M agreed in August 2011 to pay $3 million to the plaintiffs in this case.

BABY BOOMERS AND RETIREES WANT TO DO GOOD WORK

Baby Boomers Will Transform Retirement

Large numbers of boomers are crafting their encores and helping to create a movement for personal renewal and social good.

—Marci Alboher, in *The Encore Career Handbook: How to Make a Living and a Difference in the Second Half of Life* (2013)

In *Encore Career Choices: Purpose, Passion and a Paycheck in a Tough Economy* (November 2011, http://www.encore.org/files/EncoreCareerChoices.pdf), the MetLife Foundation and Civic Ventures indicate that about 31 million Americans aged 44 to 70 years are interested in launching so-called encore careers. The following are the key findings of the survey:

- Nearly two-thirds (64%) of people plan to keep working—because they want to use their skills in paid or volunteer positions (31%) or because they need the income and employer-sponsored health insurance coverage (33%).

- Although more than a quarter (27%) of survey respondents are likely to try an encore career "in the next five years," about half (51%) view the economy as a potential obstacle to changing jobs or entering an encore career.

- Survey respondents already in encore careers anticipate working to age 69.1, and those interested in encore careers say they will work until age 68.6. Both groups are planning to work more than three years longer than they thought they would three years ago.

- Among those in encore careers, one out of five cited the desire to make a difference as a primary motivation for continuing to work.

- Workers in encore careers work an estimated 16.7 billion hours in education, health care, government, and nonprofit organizations. This estimate represents more than twice the 8.1 billion hours contributed annually by volunteers of all ages.

- Nearly three-quarters (70%) say it is very important to them to leave the world a better place as a result of their work. About the same proportion (73%) anticipate that today's children will be worse off as adults than most people are now.

- One-quarter of survey respondents are very interested in encore careers, down from 34% in 2008.

- The economic circumstances of those who want encore careers and those who do not are comparable. Both groups have median incomes of $45,000 to $59,999 per year. About half of both groups report household assets of less than $150,000, and roughly one-third of both groups say their assets do not exceed $50,000.

- The commitment to service of the current group of older adults is attributable not only to their idealism but also to their historic effort to find meaning and identity in work and the desire to work with others who share common goals.

The survey concludes that the option of pursuing an encore career is considered desirable by a large number of older adults. The MetLife Foundation and Civic Ventures researchers assert, "The ability to combine income and altruism should be accessible to those who want it— both because it will increase individual satisfaction and economic security and because it will help the nation meet growing fiscal and social needs. It creates a virtue out of necessity and represents a win-win of monumental proportions."

Volunteerism in Retirement

Volunteerism among older adults is a relatively new phenomenon. Historically, older adults were seen as the segment of society most in need of care and support. As medical technology enables people to live longer, healthier lives, and as stereotypes about aging shatter, the older population is being recognized as a valuable resource for volunteer organizations.

Every day millions of older Americans perform volunteer work in their communities. With free time as well as the wisdom and experience derived from years of living, they make ideal volunteers. Older adult volunteers are educated and skilled and can offer volunteer organizations many of the professional services they would otherwise have to purchase, such as legal, accounting, public relations, information systems support, and human resource management. Perhaps more important, they have empathy and compassion because they have encountered many of the same problems that are faced by those they seek to help.

According to the BLS, in *Volunteering in the United States—2012* (February 22, 2013, http://www.bls.gov/news.release/pdf/volun.pdf), volunteer rates in September 2012 were the lowest for young adults aged 16 to 24 years (22.6% of the population) and those aged 25 to 34 years (23.2%), followed by adults aged 65 years and older (24.4%). (See Table 4.9.) Volunteers aged 65 years and older did, however, devote the most time—a median of 90 hours during the year—to volunteer activities. (See Table 4.10.) Older volunteers were more likely to work for religious organizations than younger volunteers. The BLS notes that 46.5% of volunteers aged 65 years and older volunteered primarily for religious organizations, compared with 25.1% of volunteers aged 20 to 24 years. (See Table 4.11.)

NATIONAL SERVICE ORGANIZATIONS. Efforts to establish a national senior service during the administration of President John F. Kennedy (1917–1963) are described by Peter Shapiro in *A History of National Service in America* (1994). In 1963 Kennedy proposed the National Service Corps (NSC) "to provide opportunities for service for those aged persons who can assume active roles in community volunteer efforts." When the NSC was proposed, a scant 11% of the older population was involved in any kind of volunteerism. The plan to engage older adults in full-time, intensive service, with a minimum one-year commitment, to combat urban and rural poverty was viewed as revolutionary. Although the NSC proposal was championed by the Kennedy administration and widely supported in the public and private sectors, it was defeated in Congress, where reactionary lawmakers linked it to efforts aimed at promoting racial integration in the South.

Despite the defeat of the NSC, the idea of harnessing the volunteer power of older adults caught on. The Economic Opportunity Act of 1964 gave rise to the Volunteers in Service to America (VISTA) and eventually led to the launch of service programs involving low-income older adults, such as the Foster Grandparent, Senior Companion, and Senior Community Service Employment Programs. The Foster Grandparent Program matched 1,000 older adults aged 60 years and older with 2,500 children living in orphanages and other institutions. The older adults would spend four hours a day, five days a week, feeding, cuddling, rocking, and exercising disabled children.

The success of the Foster Grandparent Program exceeded all expectations. In 1971 the program was incorporated into the newly created ACTION agency, along with the Peace Corps, VISTA, the Service Corps of Retired Executives (SCORE), and the Active Corps of Executives. The Foster Grandparent Program has since become part of the Senior Corps, a network of programs that tap the experience, skills, and talents of older adults to meet community challenges. Through its three programs—Foster Grandparent, Senior Companion, and Retired and Senior Volunteer Programs—over 300,000 Americans aged 55 years and older assisted local nonprofits, public agencies, and faith-based organizations in 2012. The Corporation for National and Community Service notes in "Senior Corps Fact Sheet" (February 2012, http://www.nationalservice.gov/newsroom/marketing/fact-sheets/senior-corps) that Senior Corps volunteers spent 96.2 million hours working with 312,000 children and 737,000 elderly in 2012.

Another successful national volunteer program involving older adults is SCORE, which uses retired business executives as counselors and consultants to small businesses. Established by the Small Business Administration (SBA) in 1964, the program works with recipients of SBA loans and others, assisting them to draft business plans, evaluate profitability, and develop marketing strategies. One objective of the program is to reduce default rates on these loans. SCORE mentors business owners and provides one-on-one counseling, consultation via e-mail, and training sessions.

Other volunteer service organizations that offer opportunities for older adults to contribute their time, energy, and talents include the AARP-sponsored Create the Good (http://createthegood.org/), which connects people to volunteer programs and projects, and the Experience Corps (http://www.aarp.org/experience-corps/), in which volunteers tutor and mentor students, providing literacy coaching and homework help, while serving as consistent role models.

TABLE 4.9

Volunteers by age groups and other selected characteristics, September 2012

[Numbers in thousands]

Characteristics in September 2012	Total, both sexes			Men			Women		
	Civilian noninstitutional population	Volunteers		Civilian noninstitutional population	Volunteers		Civilian noninstitutional population	Volunteers	
		Number	Percent of population		Number	Percent of population		Number	Percent of population
Age									
Total, 16 years and over	**243,772**	**64,513**	**26.5**	**117,600**	**27,238**	**23.2**	**126,172**	**37,274**	**29.5**
16 to 24 years	38,800	8,776	22.6	19,556	3,914	20.0	19,244	4,862	25.3
16 to 19 years	16,931	4,644	27.4	8,628	2,166	25.1	8,303	2,478	29.8
20 to 24 years	21,869	4,132	18.9	10,928	1,748	16.0	10,941	2,384	21.8
25 years and over	204,973	55,737	27.2	98,045	23,324	23.8	106,928	32,413	30.3
25 to 34 years	41,072	9,513	23.2	20,263	3,813	18.8	20,810	5,700	27.4
35 to 44 years	39,632	12,527	31.6	19,412	5,130	26.4	20,221	7,397	36.6
45 to 54 years	43,608	12,777	29.3	21,294	5,569	26.2	22,314	7,208	32.3
55 to 64 years	38,442	10,619	27.6	18,475	4,547	24.6	19,966	6,072	30.4
65 years and over	42,219	10,301	24.4	18,601	4,265	22.9	23,618	6,036	25.6
Race and Hispanic or Latino ethnicity									
White	193,503	53,778	27.8	94,429	22,961	24.3	99,074	30,817	31.1
Black or African American	29,991	6,316	21.1	13,550	2,429	17.9	16,441	3,886	23.6
Asian	12,875	2,524	19.6	6,040	1,057	17.5	6,835	1,467	21.5
Hispanic or Latino ethnicity	36,969	5,635	15.2	18,546	2,422	13.1	18,424	3,213	17.4
Educational attainment[a]									
Less than a high school diploma	24,697	2,177	8.8	12,293	956	7.8	12,404	1,221	9.8
High school graduates, no college[b]	60,767	10,527	17.3	29,747	4,391	14.8	31,020	6,136	19.8
Some college or associate degree	55,081	15,832	28.7	25,004	6,123	24.5	30,077	9,709	32.3
Bachelor's degree and higher[c]	64,428	27,202	42.2	31,000	11,855	38.2	33,427	15,346	45.9
Marital status									
Single, never married	72,102	14,920	20.7	38,024	6,501	17.1	34,078	8,419	24.7
Married, spouse present	123,194	39,290	31.9	61,981	17,711	28.6	61,213	21,579	35.3
Other marital status[d]	48,476	10,302	21.3	17,595	3,027	17.2	30,881	7,276	23.6
Presence of own children under 18 years[e]									
Without own children under 18	176,911	42,105	23.8	88,080	18,248	20.7	88,831	23,857	26.9
With own children under 18	66,861	22,408	33.5	29,521	8,991	30.5	37,340	13,417	35.9
Employment status									
Civilian labor force	156,594	44,974	28.7	83,124	20,882	25.1	73,469	24,092	32.8
Employed	144,450	42,083	29.1	76,695	19,681	25.7	67,755	22,402	33.1
Full time[f]	115,983	32,568	28.1	66,207	16,873	25.5	49,775	15,695	31.5
Part time[g]	28,468	9,515	33.4	10,488	2,807	26.8	17,980	6,707	37.3
Unemployed	12,144	2,891	23.8	6,430	1,202	18.7	5,714	1,689	29.6
Not in the labor force	87,179	19,539	22.4	34,476	6,356	18.4	52,703	13,183	25.0

[a]Data refer to persons 25 years and over.
[b]Includes persons with a high school diploma or equivalent.
[c]Includes persons with bachelor's, professional, and doctoral degrees.
[d]Includes divorced, separated, and widowed persons.
[e]Own children include sons, daughters, stepchildren, and adopted children. Not included are nieces, nephews, grandchildren, and other related and unrelated children.
[f]Usually work 35 hours or more a week at all jobs.
[g]Usually work less than 35 hours a week at all jobs.
Note: Data on volunteers relate to persons who performed unpaid volunteer activities for an organization at any point from September 1, 2011, through the survey period in September 2012. Estimates for the above race groups (white, black or African American, and Asian) do not sum to totals because data are not presented for all races. Persons whose ethnicity is identified as Hispanic or Latino may be of any race.

SOURCE: "Table 1. Volunteers by Selected Characteristics, September 2012," in *Volunteering in the United States, 2012*, U.S. Department of Labor, U.S. Bureau of Labor Statistics, February 22, 2013, http://www.bls.gov/news.release/pdf/volun.pdf (accessed June 7, 2013)

TABLE 4.10

Volunteers by annual hours volunteered and other selected characteristics, September 2012

Characteristics in September 2012	Total volunteers (thousands)	Total	Percent distribution of total annual hours spent volunteering at all organizations						Median annual hours[a]
			1 to 14 hour(s)	15 to 49 hours	50 to 99 hours	100 to 499 hours	500 hours and over	Not reporting annual hours	
Sex									
Total, both sexes	64,513	100.0	21.7	24.5	15.3	27.4	5.8	5.3	50
Men	27,238	100.0	21.4	24.8	15.3	27.3	6.0	5.2	50
Women	37,274	100.0	21.9	24.3	15.4	27.5	5.6	5.3	51
Age									
Total, 16 years and over	64,513	100.0	21.7	24.5	15.3	27.4	5.8	5.3	50
16 to 24 years	8,776	100.0	25.1	25.4	14.8	22.9	4.6	7.2	40
16 to 19 years	4,644	100.0	24.6	27.4	16.5	21.7	3.3	6.5	40
20 to 24 years	4,132	100.0	25.6	23.1	12.9	24.3	6.0	8.0	40
25 years and over	55,737	100.0	21.2	24.4	15.4	28.1	6.0	4.9	52
25 to 34 years	9,513	100.0	29.0	26.1	15.8	20.9	3.5	4.8	32
35 to 44 years	12,527	100.0	23.6	26.1	15.8	25.6	4.5	4.5	46
45 to 54 years	12,777	100.0	20.9	25.3	15.2	28.5	5.5	4.6	52
55 to 64 years	10,619	100.0	18.4	24.0	15.9	30.2	6.4	5.1	56
65 years and over	10,301	100.0	14.3	20.1	14.4	35.1	10.2	5.9	90
Race and Hispanic or Latino ethnicity									
White	53,778	100.0	21.3	25.0	15.5	27.6	5.6	5.0	50
Black or African American	6,316	100.0	21.7	22.2	13.5	27.9	7.6	7.2	52
Asian	2,524	100.0	28.5	22.4	16.7	22.7	3.6	6.1	40
Hispanic or Latino ethnicity	5,635	100.0	22.8	26.0	15.6	24.1	5.8	5.7	48
Educational attainment[b]									
Less than a high school diploma	2,177	100.0	25.5	18.7	16.1	27.5	6.1	6.0	52
High school graduates, no college[c]	10,527	100.0	22.4	24.0	14.6	27.2	6.3	5.4	50
Some college or associate degree	15,832	100.0	22.0	24.7	14.9	27.0	6.3	5.1	50
Bachelor's degree and higher[d]	27,202	100.0	19.9	24.8	15.9	29.1	5.6	4.6	52
Marital status									
Single, never married	14,920	100.0	26.4	24.9	14.9	22.7	4.5	6.7	40
Married, spouse present	39,290	100.0	20.3	24.6	15.8	29.1	5.8	4.5	52
Other marital status[e]	10,302	100.0	20.3	23.9	14.4	27.7	7.7	6.0	52
Presence of own children under 18 years[f]									
Men									
No own children under 18 years old	18,248	100.0	20.5	25.0	14.6	27.1	6.9	5.9	52
With own children under 18 years old	8,991	100.0	23.3	24.3	16.5	27.7	4.3	3.9	50
Women									
No own children under 18 years old	23,857	100.0	20.5	23.4	15.0	29.0	6.2	5.8	52
With own children under 18 years old	13,417	100.0	24.5	26.0	16.1	24.7	4.4	4.3	44
Employment status									
Civilian labor force	44,974	100.0	23.0	25.8	15.7	25.8	4.7	5.0	48
Employed	42,083	100.0	23.0	25.9	15.8	25.7	4.5	5.0	48
Full time[g]	32,568	100.0	23.5	26.2	15.8	25.2	4.2	5.0	45
Part time[h]	9,515	100.0	21.3	24.9	16.0	27.5	5.4	4.9	52
Unemployed	2,891	100.0	23.3	23.8	13.6	27.6	7.6	4.1	52
Not in the labor force	19,539	100.0	18.7	21.7	14.5	31.0	8.2	5.9	61

[a]For those reporting annual hours.
[b]Data refer to persons 25 years and over.
[c]Includes persons with a high school diploma or equivalent.
[d]Includes persons with bachelor's, professional, and doctoral degrees.
[e]Includes divorced, separated, and widowed persons.
[f]Own children include sons, daughters, stepchildren, and adopted children. Not included are nieces, nephews, grandchildren, and other related and unrelated children.
[g]Usually work 35 hours or more a week at all jobs.
[h]Usually work less than 35 hours a week at all jobs.
Note: Data on volunteers relate to persons who performed unpaid volunteer activities for an organization at any point from September 1, 2011, through the survey period in September 2012. Estimates for the above race groups (white, black or African American, and Asian) do not sum to totals because data are not presented for all races. Persons whose ethnicity is identified as Hispanic or Latino may be of any race.

SOURCE: "Table 2. Volunteers by Annual Hours of Volunteer Activities and Selected Characteristics, September 2012," in *Volunteering in the United States, 2012*, U.S. Department of Labor, U.S. Bureau of Labor Statistics, February 22, 2013, http://www.bls.gov/news.release/pdf/volun.pdf (accessed June 7, 2013)

TABLE 4.11

Volunteers by type of organization and other selected characteristics, September 2012

Characteristics in September 2012	Total volunteers (thousands)	Percent distribution of volunteers by type of main organization[a]										
		Total	Civic, political, professional, or international	Educational or youth service	Environmental or animal care	Hospital or other health	Public safety	Religious	Social or community service	Sport, hobby, cultural, or arts	Other	Not determined
Sex												
Total, both sexes	**64,513**	**100.0**	**5.5**	**25.5**	**2.6**	**7.8**	**1.2**	**33.1**	**14.2**	**3.8**	**4.0**	**2.3**
Men	27,238	100.0	6.8	23.8	2.5	6.2	1.9	32.9	14.8	4.5	4.4	2.2
Women	37,274	100.0	4.6	26.7	2.7	9.0	0.6	33.2	13.8	3.3	3.7	2.3
Age												
Total, 16 years and over	**64,513**	**100.0**	**5.5**	**25.5**	**2.6**	**7.8**	**1.2**	**33.1**	**14.2**	**3.8**	**4.0**	**2.3**
16 to 24 years	8,776	100.0	4.7	27.4	3.1	9.9	1.4	26.5	16.1	3.1	4.5	3.3
16 to 19 years	4,644	100.0	4.2	30.9	2.4	8.0	0.9	27.7	15.8	2.8	4.1	3.2
20 to 24 years	4,132	100.0	5.2	23.4	3.8	12.0	2.0	25.1	16.5	3.4	5.0	3.5
25 years and over	55,737	100.0	5.6	25.2	2.6	7.5	1.1	34.1	13.9	3.9	3.9	2.1
25 to 34 years	9,513	100.0	4.2	31.7	3.2	8.3	1.6	27.9	14.3	3.2	3.5	2.0
35 to 44 years	12,527	100.0	4.0	40.2	2.4	5.5	1.1	26.5	11.6	3.8	3.4	1.5
45 to 54 years	12,777	100.0	4.9	28.6	2.5	7.5	1.0	33.0	12.8	3.7	3.8	2.2
55 to 64 years	10,619	100.0	7.6	14.5	3.1	8.8	1.1	38.2	14.5	4.9	4.6	2.8
65 years and over	10,301	100.0	7.8	7.5	1.8	7.9	0.9	46.5	17.1	4.2	4.2	2.2
Race and Hispanic or Latino ethnicity												
White	53,778	100.0	5.7	25.1	2.8	8.2	1.3	32.3	14.3	4.0	4.0	2.2
Black or African American	6,316	100.0	4.5	24.6	1.2	5.3	0.4	40.7	13.4	2.9	3.9	3.1
Asian	2,524	100.0	4.1	31.4	1.7	7.8	—	34.0	12.2	2.7	3.3	2.8
Hispanic or Latino ethnicity	5,635	100.0	3.7	31.2	1.9	6.5	0.8	35.0	12.3	2.8	3.0	2.8
Educational attainment[b]												
Less than a high school diploma	2,177	100.0	3.6	23.2	0.6	3.5	1.4	48.6	12.0	2.8	2.6	1.8
High school graduates, no college[c]	10,527	100.0	5.1	21.4	2.9	7.0	1.7	40.0	13.5	3.3	3.3	1.8
Some college or associate degree	15,832	100.0	5.5	25.2	2.3	7.8	1.4	34.5	13.9	3.3	4.2	2.0
Bachelor's degree and higher[d]	27,202	100.0	6.0	26.8	2.8	7.9	0.7	30.5	14.3	4.7	4.1	2.3
Marital status												
Single, never married	14,920	100.0	5.6	25.8	3.7	10.1	1.4	24.0	17.3	3.7	5.1	3.3
Married, spouse present	39,290	100.0	5.1	26.9	2.1	6.7	1.1	36.5	12.3	4.0	3.4	1.8
Other marital status[e]	10,302	100.0	6.7	19.6	3.0	8.7	1.2	33.3	16.9	3.5	4.4	2.5
Presence of own children under 18 years[f]												
Men												
No own children under 18 years old	18,248	100.0	7.9	16.4	3.1	7.1	2.1	34.3	17.2	4.3	5.1	2.6
With own children under 18 years old	8,991	100.0	4.6	38.8	1.2	4.4	1.5	30.3	10.0	4.8	3.0	1.4
Women												
No own children under 18 years old	23,857	100.0	5.7	15.8	3.4	11.1	0.7	36.4	16.0	3.9	4.4	2.7
With own children under 18 years old	13,417	100.0	2.5	46.2	1.5	5.3	0.5	27.6	10.0	2.3	2.5	1.6
Employment status												
Civilian labor force	44,974	100.0	5.5	27.4	2.9	7.8	1.4	30.9	14.0	4.0	3.9	2.3
Employed	42,083	100.0	5.4	27.6	2.9	7.9	1.4	30.9	13.8	4.1	3.8	2.3
Full time[g]	32,568	100.0	5.6	27.7	2.8	8.2	1.4	30.0	14.1	4.2	3.8	2.3
Part time[h]	9,515	100.0	5.0	27.2	3.2	6.8	1.1	33.8	12.8	4.1	3.8	2.2
Unemployed	2,891	100.0	5.8	24.6	2.3	6.5	1.9	31.7	16.8	2.7	5.5	2.3
Not in the labor force	19,539	100.0	5.6	21.1	2.1	8.0	0.6	38.1	14.8	3.4	4.1	2.3

[a]Main organization is defined as the organization for which the volunteer worked the most hours during the year.
[b]Data refer to persons 25 years and over.
[c]Includes persons with a high school diploma or equivalent.
[d]Includes persons with bachelor's, professional, and doctoral degrees.
[e]Includes divorced, separated, and widowed persons.
[f]Own children include sons, daughters, stepchildren, and adopted children. Not included are nieces, nephews, grandchildren, and other related and unrelated children.
[g]Usually work 35 hours or more a week at all jobs.
[h]Usually work less than 35 hours a week at all jobs.
Note: Data on volunteers relate to persons who performed unpaid volunteer activities for an organization at any point from September 1, 2011, through the survey period in September 2012. Estimates for the above race groups (white, black or African American, and Asian) do not sum to totals because data are not presented for all races. Persons whose ethnicity is identified as Hispanic or Latino may be of any race.

SOURCE: "Table 4. Volunteers by Type of Main Organization for Which Volunteer Activities Were Performed and Selected Characteristics, September 2012," in *Volunteering in the United States, 2012*, U.S. Department of Labor, U.S. Bureau of Labor Statistics, February 22, 2013, http://www.bls.gov/news.release/pdf/volun.pdf (accessed June 7, 2013)

CHAPTER 5
EDUCATION, VOTING, AND POLITICAL BEHAVIOR

EDUCATIONAL ATTAINMENT OF OLDER AMERICANS

Educational attainment influences employment and socioeconomic status, which in turn affect the quality of life of older adults. Higher levels of education are often associated with greater earning capacity, higher standards of living, and better overall health status.

As of 2010, 80% of the older population had earned a high school diploma and 23% had obtained an undergraduate college degree. (See Figure 5.1.) These figures are in contrast to those from 1965, when just 24% of older adults had earned a high school diploma and only 5% had graduated from college.

Although educational attainment has increased among older adults, significant differences remain between racial and ethnic groups. Among adults aged 65 years and older in 2010, 84% of non-Hispanic whites and 74% of Asian Americans had graduated from high school, compared with 65% of African Americans and 47% of Hispanics. (See Figure 5.2.) Older Asian Americans were the most likely to have graduated from college (35%), followed by older non-Hispanic whites (24%); just 15% of African Americans and 10% of Hispanics aged 65 years and older had earned a bachelor's degree.

Lifelong Learning

Live as if you were to die tomorrow. Learn as if you were to live forever.

—Mohandas Gandhi

Campuses are graying as a growing number of older people head back to school. Older adults are major participants in programs once called adult education (college courses that do not lead to a formal degree). They are also attending two- and four-year colleges to pursue undergraduate and graduate degrees, as well as taking personal enrichment classes and courses that are sponsored by community senior centers and parks and recreation facilities.

For example, in "2013 Community College Fast Facts" (2013, http://www.aacc.nche.edu/AboutCC/Pages/fastfacts factsheet.aspx), the American Association of Community Colleges indicates that as of 2011, 15% of community college students were aged 40 years and older. In 2011 an estimated 3.8 million (17.9%) students in degree-granting programs were aged 35 years and older. (See Table 5.1.) By 2021 this number is anticipated to increase to 4.5 million (19%).

The American Association of Community Colleges notes in *The Plus 50 Initiative Evaluation: Initiative Impact* (January 2012, http://plus50.aacc.nche.edu/Documents/ThePlus50InitiativeEvaluation_InitiativeImpact.pdf) that the Plus 50 Initiative was established in 2008 to help a pilot group of 13 community colleges expand their offerings for students aged 50 years and older. By 2010 the number of students had increased by 15,000, doubling in size in just two years. Another ambitious initiative, the Plus 50 Encore Completion Program (2013, http://plus50.aacc.nche.edu/aboutplus50/pages/default.aspx), will "help 10,000 baby boomers earn high-value degrees or certificates in fields that give back (education, health care, social services) and are hiring."

Older adults' motivations for returning to school have changed over time. Although they once may have taken courses primarily for pleasure, older students in the 21st century are as likely to return to school for work-related education. They are learning new skills, retraining for new careers, or enhancing their existing skills to remain competitive. Homemakers displaced by divorce or widowhood are often seeking training to enable them to reenter the workforce.

In "Back on Campus to Experience Road Not Taken" (NYTimes.com, March 18, 2013), Robert Strauss looks at older adults who have returned to school. He observes that, traditionally, older students returned to school because they were seeking intellectual stimulation or career enhancement.

FIGURE 5.1

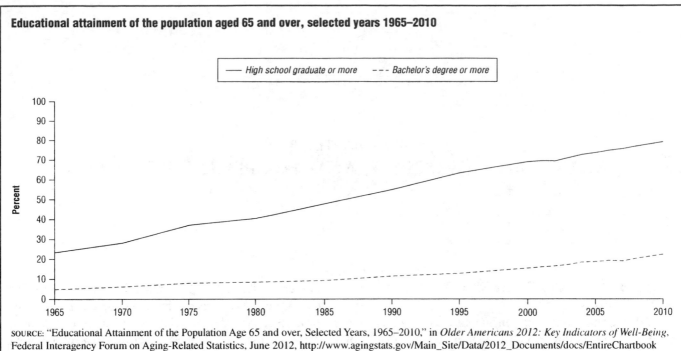

Educational attainment of the population aged 65 and over, selected years 1965–2010

— High school graduate or more   - - - Bachelor's degree or more

SOURCE: "Educational Attainment of the Population Age 65 and over, Selected Years, 1965–2010," in *Older Americans 2012: Key Indicators of Well-Being*, Federal Interagency Forum on Aging-Related Statistics, June 2012, http://www.agingstats.gov/Main_Site/Data/2012_Documents/docs/EntireChartbook .pdf (accessed May 28, 2013)

FIGURE 5.2

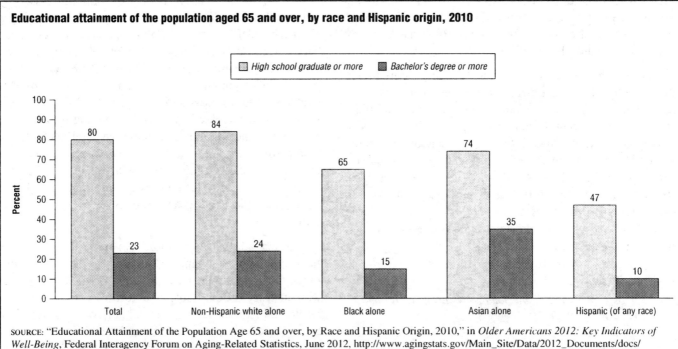

Educational attainment of the population aged 65 and over, by race and Hispanic origin, 2010

☐ High school graduate or more   ■ Bachelor's degree or more

SOURCE: "Educational Attainment of the Population Age 65 and over, by Race and Hispanic Origin, 2010," in *Older Americans 2012: Key Indicators of Well-Being*, Federal Interagency Forum on Aging-Related Statistics, June 2012, http://www.agingstats.gov/Main_Site/Data/2012_Documents/docs/ EntireChartbook.pdf (accessed May 28, 2013)

However, Strauss profiles older adults with another motivation: the desire to pursue a course of education they had passed up when they were younger. For example, Richard Hendrix wanted to study law but instead became an English professor and university administrator. At 68, he decided to revisit his long-standing desire and entered law school.

TABLE 5.1

Enrollment in degree-granting institutions, by sex, and age, selected years 1970–2021

[In thousands]

Attendance status, sex, and age	1970	1980	1990	2000	2003	2004	2005	2006	2007	2008	2009	2010	Projected 2011	2012	2013	2016	2021
1	2	3	4	5	6	7	8	9	10	11	12	13	14	15	16	17	18
All students	8,581	12,097	13,819	15,312	16,911	17,272	17,487	17,759	18,248	19,103	20,428	21,016	20,994	21,253	21,485	22,194	23,755
14 to 17 years old	263	257	153	13	169	166	187	184	200	195	217	202	202	207	208	219	244
18 and 19 years old	2,579	2,852	2,777	3,258	3,355	3,367	3,444	3,561	3,690	3,813	4,041	4,056	4,025	4,343	4,331	4,358	4,765
20 and 21 years old	1,885	2,395	2,593	3,005	3,391	3,516	3,563	3,573	3,570	3,649	3,945	4,101	4,174	4,386	4,368	4,361	4,603
22 to 24 years old	1,469	1,947	2,202	2,600	3,086	3,166	3,114	3,185	3,280	3,443	3,594	3,758	3,708	3,823	3,922	3,996	4,037
25 to 29 years old	1,091	1,843	2,083	2,044	2,311	2,418	2,469	2,506	2,651	2,840	3,096	3,253	3,319	3,057	3,116	3,389	3,545
30 to 34 years old	527	1,227	1,384	1,333	1,418	1,440	1,438	1,472	1,519	1,609	1,741	1,805	1,807	1,678	1,726	1,833	2,037
35 years old and over	767	1,577	2,627	2,942	3,181	3,199	3,272	3,277	3,339	3,554	3,794	3,840	3,758	3,759	3,812	4,038	4,524
Males	5,044	5,874	6,284	6,722	7,260	7,387	7,456	7,575	7,816	8,189	8,770	9,045	9,026	9,107	9,160	9,261	9,741
14 to 17 years old	125	106	66	53	67	62	68	69	88	93	103	94	95	90	90	92	101
18 and 19 years old	1,355	1,368	1,298	1,464	1,474	1,475	1,523	1,604	1,669	1,704	1,806	1,820	1,819	1,896	1,886	1,876	2,040
20 and 21 years old	1,064	1,219	1,259	1,411	1,541	1,608	1,658	1,628	1,634	1,695	1,876	1,948	1,973	2,102	2,088	2,060	2,154
22 to 24 years old	1,004	1,075	1,129	1,222	1,411	1,437	1,410	1,445	1,480	1,555	1,606	1,723	1,682	1,760	1,798	1,799	1,792
25 to 29 years old	796	983	1,024	903	1,007	1,039	1,057	1,040	1,148	1,222	1,382	1,410	1,442	1,354	1,370	1,452	1,491
30 to 34 years old	333	564	605	581	602	619	591	628	638	691	709	731	715	691	707	729	792
35 years old and over	366	559	902	1,077	1,158	1,147	1,149	1,160	1,159	1,228	1,287	1,320	1,300	1,215	1,223	1,252	1,372
Females	3,537	6,223	7,535	8,591	9,651	9,885	10,032	10,184	10,432	10,914	11,658	11,971	11,968	12,146	12,325	12,933	14,014
14 to 17 years old	137	151	87	73	102	104	119	115	112	102	114	108	108	118	119	127	143
18 and 19 years old	1,224	1,484	1,479	1,794	1,880	1,892	1,920	1,956	2,021	2,109	2,236	2,236	2,206	2,447	2,446	2,482	2,725
20 and 21 years old	821	1,177	1,334	1,593	1,851	1,908	1,905	1,945	1,936	1,954	2,069	2,154	2,201	2,284	2,280	2,301	2,449
22 to 24 years old	464	871	1,073	1,373	1,675	1,729	1,704	1,740	1,800	1,888	1,987	2,036	2,027	2,063	2,125	2,197	2,245
25 to 29 years old	296	859	1,059	1,135	1,304	1,379	1,413	1,466	1,502	1,618	1,713	1,844	1,877	1,703	1,746	1,937	2,055
30 to 34 years old	194	663	779	752	816	821	847	844	881	918	1,032	1,074	1,092	987	1,020	1,103	1,246
35 years old and over	401	1,018	1,725	1,865	2,023	2,052	2,123	2,117	2,180	2,326	2,507	2,520	2,458	2,544	2,590	2,786	3,152
Full-time	5,816	7,098	7,821	9,010	10,326	10,610	10,797	10,957	11,270	11,748	12,723	13,082	13,001	13,146	13,262	13,586	14,497
14 to 17 years old	246	231	134	121	146	138	152	148	169	168	181	170	171	163	164	174	194
18 and 19 years old	2,374	2,544	2,471	2,823	2,934	2,960	3,026	3,120	3,244	3,359	3,513	3,495	3,413	3,644	3,637	3,665	4,014
20 and 21 years old	1,649	2,007	2,137	2,452	2,841	2,926	2,976	2,972	2,985	3,043	3,271	3,363	3,392	3,438	3,427	3,426	3,623
22 to 24 years old	904	1,181	1,405	1,714	2,083	2,143	2,122	2,127	2,205	2,347	2,535	2,584	2,504	2,689	2,758	2,808	2,846
25 to 29 years old	426	641	791	886	1,086	1,132	1,174	1,225	1,299	1,369	1,520	1,605	1,628	1,477	1,507	1,641	1,723
30 to 34 years old	113	272	383	418	489	517	547	571	556	571	663	744	759	646	665	705	785
35 years old and over	104	221	500	596	747	795	800	794	812	890	1,041	1,121	1,135	1,088	1,104	1,168	1,312
Males	3,504	3,689	3,808	4,111	4,638	4,739	4,803	4,879	5,029	5,234	5,671	5,837	5,793	5,843	5,873	5,931	6,263
14 to 17 years old	121	95	55	51	58	49	53	52	74	73	78	71	75	58	58	60	67
18 and 19 years old	1,261	1,219	1,171	1,252	1,291	1,297	1,339	1,404	1,465	1,516	1,580	1,574	1,532	1,588	1,581	1,578	1,722
20 and 21 years old	955	1,046	1,035	1,156	1,305	1,360	1,398	1,372	1,366	1,407	1,547	1,586	1,591	1,642	1,632	1,617	1,698
22 to 24 years old	686	717	768	834	995	1,001	982	992	1,043	1,105	1,177	1,214	1,171	1,269	1,296	1,301	1,305
25 to 29 years old	346	391	433	410	503	498	506	533	578	597	665	714	736	640	649	693	719
30 to 34 years old	77	142	171	186	209	231	225	235	231	249	281	301	296	291	298	310	341
35 years old and over	58	80	174	222	277	302	300	291	273	287	343	376	392	355	359	371	412

TABLE 5.1

Enrollment in degree-granting institutions, by sex, and age, selected years 1970–2021 [CONTINUED]

[In thousands]

| Attendance status, sex, and age | 1970 | 1980 | 1990 | 2000 | 2003 | 2004 | 2005 | 2006 | 2007 | 2008 | 2009 | 2010 | 2011 | 2012 | Projected | | |
| | | | | | | | | | | | | | | | 2013 | 2016 | 2021 |
1	2	3	4	5	6	7	8	9	10	11	12	13	14	15	16	17	18
Females	**2,312**	**3,409**	**4,013**	**4,899**	**5,688**	**5,871**	**5,994**	**6,078**	**6,240**	**6,513**	**7,052**	**7,245**	**7,208**	**7,303**	**7,388**	**7,655**	**8,234**
14 to 17 years old	125	136	78	70	88	89	98	95	95	95	103	99	96	104	105	113	127
18 and 19 years old	1,113	1,325	1,300	1,571	1,643	1,662	1,687	1,716	1,779	1,843	1,933	1,921	1,880	2,057	2,056	2,087	2,292
20 and 21 years old	693	961	1,101	1,296	1,536	1,566	1,578	1,601	1,619	1,636	1,724	1,777	1,801	1,797	1,794	1,808	1,925
22 to 24 years old	218	464	638	880	1,088	1,142	1,140	1,135	1,163	1,242	1,358	1,370	1,333	1,421	1,462	1,507	1,540
25 to 29 years old	80	250	358	476	583	634	668	692	721	772	855	890	892	837	858	948	1,004
30 to 34 years old	37	130	212	232	280	286	322	336	324	322	382	444	463	355	367	395	445
35 years old and over	46	141	326	374	471	493	500	503	539	603	697	745	743	733	745	797	900
Part-time	**2,765**	**4,999**	**5,998**	**6,303**	**6,585**	**6,662**	**6,690**	**6,802**	**6,978**	**7,355**	**7,705**	**7,934**	**7,993**	**8,107**	**8,224**	**8,608**	**9,258**
14 to 17 years old	16	26	19	10	23	28	36	36	31	27	36	32	31	45	44	46	50
18 and 19 years old	205	308	306	435	421	407	417	440	446	453	528	561	612	699	694	693	751
20 and 21 years old	236	388	456	553	551	590	586	601	585	606	674	739	782	947	942	936	980
22 to 24 years old	564	765	796	886	1,003	1,023	992	1,058	1,074	1,096	1,059	1,174	1,204	1,134	1,164	1,188	1,192
25 to 29 years old	665	1,202	1,291	1,158	1,224	1,286	1,296	1,282	1,352	1,471	1,576	1,649	1,692	1,580	1,609	1,748	1,823
30 to 34 years old	414	954	1,001	915	929	923	891	901	963	1,037	1,078	1,060	1,047	1,032	1,061	1,128	1,252
35 years old and over	663	1,356	2,127	2,345	2,434	2,404	2,472	2,483	2,527	2,664	2,753	2,719	2,624	2,671	2,708	2,870	3,212
Males	**1,540**	**2,185**	**2,476**	**2,611**	**2,622**	**2,648**	**2,653**	**2,696**	**2,786**	**2,955**	**3,099**	**3,208**	**3,233**	**3,264**	**3,287**	**3,329**	**3,478**
14 to 17 years old	4	12	11	7	9	13	15	17	14	20	25	23	20	31	31	32	34
18 and 19 years old	94	149	127	212	183	178	184	200	204	188	226	245	287	308	305	298	318
20 and 21 years old	108	172	224	255	236	248	260	257	269	289	329	362	382	460	456	443	456
22 to 24 years old	318	359	361	388	416	436	428	452	438	450	430	508	510	491	502	498	487
25 to 29 years old	450	592	591	498	504	540	551	507	570	625	717	695	706	714	721	759	772
30 to 34 years old	257	422	435	395	392	388	365	393	406	442	428	430	419	400	408	419	451
35 years old and over	309	479	728	855	882	845	850	869	886	941	944	944	908	859	864	881	960
Females	**1,225**	**2,814**	**3,521**	**3,692**	**3,963**	**4,014**	**4,038**	**4,106**	**4,192**	**4,401**	**4,606**	**4,726**	**4,760**	**4,843**	**4,936**	**5,279**	**5,780**
14 to 17 years old	12	14	9	3	14	15	21	20	17	7	11	9	12	13	13	14	15
18 and 19 years old	112	159	179	223	238	230	233	240	242	265	303	316	325	390	389	395	433
20 and 21 years old	128	216	233	298	315	342	327	344	317	318	345	377	400	487	486	492	524
22 to 24 years old	246	407	435	497	587	588	564	605	637	646	629	666	694	643	663	690	705
25 to 29 years old	216	609	700	660	721	746	745	774	781	846	858	953	985	866	888	989	1,050
30 to 34 years old	158	532	567	520	537	535	526	508	557	595	651	630	629	632	653	709	801
35 years old and over	354	876	1,399	1,491	1,552	1,560	1,623	1,614	1,640	1,723	1,810	1,775	1,716	1,812	1,844	1,989	2,252

Note: Distributions by age are estimates based on samples of the civilian noninstitutional population from the U.S. Census Bureau's Current Population Survey. Data through 1995 are for institutions of higher education, while later data are for degree-granting institutions. Degree-granting institutions grant associate's or higher degrees and participate in Title IV federal financial aid programs. The degree-granting classification is very similar to the earlier higher education classification, but it includes more 2-year colleges and excludes a few higher education institutions that did not grant degrees. Detail may not sum to totals because of rounding.

SOURCE: "Table 224. Total Fall Enrollment in Degree-Granting Institutions, by Attendance Status, Sex, and Age: Selected Years, 1970 through 2021," in *Advance Release of Selected 2012 Digest Tables*, National Center for Education Statistics, 2012. http://nces.ed.gov/programs/digest/d12/tables/dt12_224.asp (accessed June 7, 2013)

ROAD SCHOLAR MEETS OLDER ADULTS' NEEDS FOR EDUCATION AND ADVENTURE. Founded in 1975, Road Scholar (formerly known as Elderhostel) is a nonprofit organization that offers learning adventures for people aged 55 years and older. In *2012 Annual Report* (2013, http://www.roadscholar.org/ebook/2013/RSAnnualReport 2012/RoadScholar_AnnualReport2012.html), Road Scholar states that it provided educational opportunities to nearly 100,000 older adults in 2012. Approximately 6,500 Road Scholar programs per year are conducted around the world. Programs include three- to five-day classes, field trips, and cultural excursions. They provide older adults with opportunities to study diverse cultures, explore ancient histories, study literature and art, and learn about modern peoples and issues. Some participants attend programs that are held on local college and university campuses, whereas others embark on programs that involve transcontinental travel.

Adventure programs combine learning with outdoor sports such as walking, hiking, camping, kayaking, and biking. For example, a bicycle tour of the Netherlands also includes instruction about the country's history, art, and people. Shipboard programs explore history, art, ecology, and culture aboard a floating classroom.

Service-learning programs involve both education and hands-on work to serve the needs of a community. Older adults conduct wildlife or marine research, tutor children, or build affordable housing. The organization also offers a series of intergenerational programs in which older adults and their grandchildren explore subjects that appeal to both young and old, including dinosaurs, hot-air ballooning, and space travel.

Participants in Road Scholar programs in 2012 reported the following benefits:

- 92% of participants learned something new
- 43% were revitalized by their program experience
- 27% had their perspective on the world changed
- 25% stepped outside their comfort zone
- 17% fulfilled a lifelong dream

OLDER ADULTS ARE ONLINE. Rapid technological change has intensified the need for information management skills and ongoing technology training. The growing importance of knowledge- and information-based jobs has created a workforce that is rapidly becoming accustomed to continuous education, training, and retraining throughout one's work life.

Computer technology, especially use of the Internet, has also gained importance in Americans' lives outside of work, facilitating communication via e-mail and enabling interactions and transactions that once required travel to now occur in their home. Examples include online banking and shopping, e-mail communication with physicians and other health care providers, and participation in online support groups.

In *Older Adults and Internet Use* (June 6, 2012, http://www.pewinternet.org/~/media//Files/Reports/2012/PIP_Older_adults_and_internet_use.pdf), Kathryn Zickuhr and Mary Madden of the Pew Research Center's Internet and American Life Project report high Internet use by older adults—in 2012 more than half (53%) of adults aged 65 years and older were using the Internet or e-mail.

Zickuhr and Madden note that 39% of adults aged 65 years and older had a broadband Internet connection at home in 2012, up from 8% in 2005. The percentage of adults with broadband service decreased with advancing age: 77% of adults aged 30 to 49 years, 62% of adults aged 50 to 64 years, and 39% of adults aged 65 years and older. Older adults who are online have made Internet use a regular part of their lives—70% use the Internet daily.

Older adults use the Internet to conduct research, exchange e-mail, and purchase products, whereas younger adults use it for socializing and entertainment. According to Zickuhr and Madden, of older adults who went online in 2012, the vast majority sent and received e-mail—86% of adults aged 65 years and older used e-mail, and 59% used e-mail on a typical day.

In 2012, 48% of adults aged 65 years and older owned a desktop computer, 32% owned a laptop, and 69% owned a cell phone. Just 10% of adults aged 65 years and older owned a smartphone (a mobile phone with advanced capabilities including Internet access).

OLDER ADULTS JOIN SOCIAL NETWORKS. Zickuhr and Madden find that although young people are still much more likely than older Internet users to participate in social networking sites, in February 2012 one-third (34%) of adults aged 65 years and older used social networking sites such as Facebook and 18% accessed social networking sites on a typical day. There was less use of social networking sites by adults aged 76 years and older. Just 20% of these older adults used social networking sites and only 8% accessed the sites on a typical day in 2012.

According to Maeve Duggan and Joanna Brenner of the Pew Research Center's Internet and American Life Project, in *The Demographics of Social Media Users— 2012* (February 14, 2013, http://www.pewinternet.org/~/media//Files/Reports/2013/PIP_SocialMediaUsers.pdf), by December 2012 more than half (52%) of adults aged 50 to 64 years said they use social networking sites. In "Old School, Meet New School: Seniors Tackle Social Networks" (CNBC.com, March 10, 2013), Cadie Thompson explains that AARP offered its first "Facebook 101 class" in 2010 and the class was filled to capacity with standing room only. Other organizations are teaching older adults how to navigate social networking sites. Thompson quotes

Tom Kamber of Older Adults Technology Services in New York City, who asserted, "Social media is the fastest growing area of new applications for older adults using technology. For us, it's the number one thing people are asking us for. It's the most requested class that we offer."

Online communities and social networks can help older adults stay in touch with family and friends, preventing social isolation. There is also evidence that using social media can help support the health of older adults. Anja K. Leist of the University of Luxembourg explains in "Social Media Use of Older Adults: A Mini-Review" (*Gerontology*, vol. 59, no. 4, 2013) that social media provides the opportunity for older adults to engage in meaningful social contact, exchange health information, share experiences managing illnesses, and provide and receive social support.

THEY ALSO TEXT, BLOG, AND TWEET. There are few reliable statistics about the numbers of older adults who use smartphones and who create and maintain blogs, send text messages, or "tweet" (post or enter a status update on Twitter, a blogging service that limits entries to 140 characters), but the ranks of older bloggers and Twitterers are growing.

Duggan and Brenner report that between November 2010 and December 2012 the percentage of all Internet users on Twitter rose to 16%. Among those aged 50 to 64 years, just 10% said they use Twitter, and a scant 2% of those over the age of 65 years said they tweet.

OLDER ADULTS PLAY VIDEO GAMES. Video games are popular among older adults. For some, console game versions of their once-favorite sports help them to stay "in the game," even when an injury, disability, or illness prevents them from actually participating in tennis, bowling, or golf. Others feel that playing video games helps them to exercise their brains, eye-hand coordination, and reflexes. Still others simply find video games as diverting and entertaining as do younger players.

According to Ian Sherr, in "Study Points to Video-game Popularity among Boomer Women" (WSJ.com, December 6, 2012), gamers aged 50 years and older spent an average of 24.7 hours per week playing video games in 2012, compared with 15.6 hours spent by gamers under the age of 50 years. Sherr cites a study conducted by Trinity University that found that nearly two-thirds (62%) of baby boom gamers were female, compared with 39% of gamers under the age of 50 years. Multiplayer games, long believed to be played largely by teenaged boys, also attract older adults—11% of gamers over the age of 50 years said they play these games online.

Jason C. Allaire et al. find in "Successful Aging through Digital Games: Socioemotional Differences between Older Adult Gamers and Non-gamers" (*Computers in Human Behavior*, vol. 29, no. 4, July 2013) that

adults aged 63 years and older who played video games, even those who played only occasionally, reported higher levels of emotional and social well-being and less depression than did nongamers.

Playing video games may also improve a number of cognitive functions. In "A Randomized Controlled Trial of Cognitive Training Using a Visual Speed of Processing Intervention in Middle Aged and Older Adults" (*PLOS One*, vol. 8, no. 5, May 2013), Fredric D. Wolinsky et al. looked at whether playing the video game *Road Tour* for a total of 10 hours would prevent age-related declines and potentially improve cognitive function in older adults. Approximately 700 older adults were assigned to either complete crossword puzzles or play the video game, which involves matching fleeting images of car types and road signs. The older adults who played the video game showed greater improvements in memory, attention, problem-solving skills, and perception one year after the study was completed than did those who had completed crossword puzzles.

THE POLITICS OF OLDER ADULTS

Older adults are vitally interested in politics and government, and they are especially interested in the issues that directly influence their lives, including eligibility for and reform to Social Security as well as benefits and coverage by Medicare (a medical insurance program for older adults and people with disabilities). Historically, they are more likely to vote than adults in other age groups, and because many have retired from the workforce they have time to advocate for the policies and candidates they favor.

David Leonhardt explains in "Old vs. Young" (NYTimes.com, June 22, 2012) that during the 1980s and 1990s older and younger Americans voted similarly, but beginning around 2004 older voters shifted to the right whereas younger voters moved to the left. Although not all young people are liberal or Democrats, on the whole they are more positive about immigrants, same-sex marriage, military cuts, and the future of the United States. In contrast, many older adults feel they are alienated from the Democratic Party, which they believe is too socially liberal.

Financial Outlook Divides Older and Younger Americans

In *Young Americans Most Positive about Direction of Finances* (April 29, 2013, http://www.gallup.com/poll/162095/young-americans-positive-direction-finances.aspx), Frank Newport and Igor Himelfarb of the Gallup Organization explain that "age is one of the most powerful correlates of Americans' outlook for their personal financial situations," and Gallup poll data support this claim. An April 2013 Gallup poll found that although slightly less than half of Americans of all ages described their current financial situation as "excellent/good," young adults aged 18 to 29 years were the most likely to report that their circumstances were "getting better." Nearly three-quarters (73%) said their financial situation was improving, compared with 37% of adults aged 50 to 64 years and 23% of adults aged 65 years and older. (See Table 5.2.)

TABLE 5.2

Ratings of personal financial situation as "good" or "excellent" and "getting better," by age group, 2013

HOW WOULD YOU RATE YOUR FINANCIAL SITUATION TODAY—AS EXCELLENT, GOOD, ONLY FAIR, OR POOR? RIGHT NOW, DO YOU THINK THAT YOUR FINANCIAL SITUATION AS A WHOLE IS GETTING BETTER OR GETTING WORSE?

	% excellent/good	% getting better
18 to 29	48	73
30 to 49	43	53
50 to 64	44	37
65+	48	23

SOURCE: Frank Newport and Igor Himelfarb, "How Would You Rate Your Financial Situation Today—As Excellent, Good, Only Fair, or Poor? Right Now, Do You Think That Your Financial Situation As A Whole Is Getting Better or Getting Worse? By Age," in *Young Americans Most Positive about Direction of Finances*, The Gallup Organization, April 29, 2013, http://www.gallup.com/poll/162095/young-americans-positive-direction-finances.aspx (accessed June 11, 2013). Copyright © 2013 Gallup, Inc. All rights reserved. The content is used with permission; however, Gallup retains all rights of republication.

Older Adults' Views on Major Social Issues

Joy Wilke and Lydia Saad of the Gallup Organization observe in *Older Americans' Moral Attitudes Changing* (June 3, 2013, http://www.gallup.com/poll/162881/older-americans-moral-attitudes-changing.aspx) that younger and older Americans differ in terms of their views about the moral acceptability of a wide range of social and political issues. For example, more than twice as many adults aged 18 to 34 years than adults aged 55 years and older consider pornography, sex between teenagers, polygamy (having more than one spouse at the same time), and cloning humans to be morally acceptable. (See Table 5.3.)

Between 2001 and 2013 older Americans' acceptance of same-sex relationships increased 27 percentage points, from 27% to 51%. (See Figure 5.3.) Similarly, their acceptance of premarital sex increased from 34% to 56% during this same period. Older Americans are also more tolerant of divorce—the perceived moral acceptability of divorce increased 21 percentage points between 2001 and 2013 among adults aged 55 years and older.

Another shift among older adults concerns their view about stem cell research. Between 2001 and 2013 the moral acceptability of stem cell research involving stem cells from human embryos increased 21 percentage points among adults aged 55 years and older, from 48% to 69%. (See Figure 5.4.)

TABLE 5.3

Percentage of Americans considering social issues morally acceptable, by age group, 2013

Next, I'm going to read you a list of issues. Regardless of whether or not you think it should be legal, for each one, please tell me whether you personally believe that in general it is morally acceptable or morally wrong.

	18 to 34 years	35 to 54 years	55 and older	Net support among 18–34 vs. 55+
	%	%	%	%
Pornography	49	28	19	+30
Sex between teenagers	48	30	22	+26
Gay or lesbian relations	74	54	51	+23
Sex between an unmarried man and woman	72	63	56	+16
Having a baby outside of marriage	71	67	57	+14
Polygamy	19	15	8	+11
Abortion	48	40	38	+10
Cloning humans	19	11	9	+10
Cloning animals	37	35	32	+5
Gambling	66	65	62	+4
Doctor-assisted suicide	46	47	43	+3
Suicide	17	15	16	+1
Married men and women having an affair	7	6	6	+1
Divorce	68	66	69	−1
Buying and wearing clothes made of animal fur	58	61	59	−1
Medical research using stem cells from human embryos	58	59	63	−5
The death penalty	57	66	63	−6
Medical testing on animals	47	60	61	−14

SOURCE: Joy Wilke and Lydia Saad, "Americans' Views on the Morality of Major Societal Issues," in *Older Americans' Moral Attitudes Changing*, The Gallup Organization, June 3, 2013, http://www.gallup.com/poll/162881/older-americans-moral-attitudes-changing.aspx (accessed June 11, 2013). Copyright © 2013 Gallup, Inc. All rights reserved. The content is used with permission; however, Gallup retains all rights of republication.

FIGURE 5.3

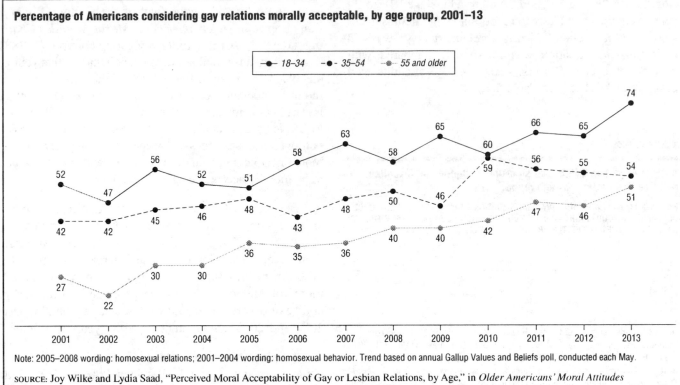

Percentage of Americans considering gay relations morally acceptable, by age group, 2001–13

FIGURE 5.4

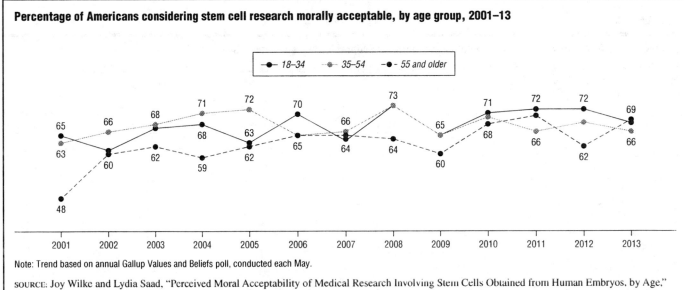

Percentage of Americans considering stem cell research morally acceptable, by age group, 2001–13

However, Paul Steinhauser reports in "Polls Suggest Congress Might Have Waited Too Long on Gun Control" (CNN.com, March 27, 2013) that although support for gun control was high in the immediate aftermath of the shootings in Newtown, Connecticut, in December 2012, by March 2013 support for stricter gun laws declined among adults aged 50 years and older. He indicates that support for gun control among older adults fell 16 percentage points by the end of the first quarter of 2013.

U.S. Politicians Are Growing Older

In "The Grayest Congress" (NBCNews.com, 2013), Jennifer Colby reports that in 2013 Congress was the oldest it has ever been. The average age of a U.S. senator was 60, and the average age of a member of the U.S. House of Representatives was 55. During the 113th Congress (2013–2014) Senators Dianne Feinstein (1933–; D-CA) and Chuck Grassley (1933–; R-IA) were 80, and Orrin G. Hatch (1934–; R-UT) and Richard Shelby (1934–; R-AL) were 79. In the House Ralph Hall (1923–; D-TX) was 90; John D. Dingell (1926–; D-MI) was 87; John Conyers Jr. (1929–; D-MI) and Louise M. Slaughter (1929–; D-NY) were 84; Charles B. Rangel (1930–; D-NY) and Sam Johnson (1930–; R-TX) were 83; and Howard Coble (1931–; R-NC) was 82.

"GRAY POWER": A POLITICAL BLOC

AARP believes strongly in the principles of collective purpose, collective voice and the collective power of the 50 and over population to change the market based on their needs. These principles guide our efforts.

—AARP, "What We Do" (2013)

Adults aged 55 to 74 years vote more than any other age group, and it is inevitable that the increasing number of Americans in this cohort (a group of individuals that shares a common characteristic such as birth years and is studied over time) will wield an enormous political impact. With 37 million members, the AARP (2013, http://www.aarp.org/about-aarp/?intcmp=FTR-LINKS) exercises considerable influence when lobbying political leaders about the issues that concern older Americans.

As part of its mission, the AARP advocates on behalf of older adults. It is known as a powerful advocate on a range of legislative, consumer, and legal issues. To this end, the organization monitors issues that are pertinent to the lives of older Americans, assesses public opinion on such issues, and keeps policy makers apprised of these opinions. Advocacy efforts include becoming involved in litigation when the decision could have a significant effect on the lives of older Americans. In cases regarding age discrimination, pensions, health care, economic security, and consumer issues, AARP lawyers file amicus briefs (legal documents filed by individuals or groups that are not actual parties to a lawsuit but that are interested in influencing the outcome of the lawsuit) and support third-party lawsuits to promote the interests of older people.

The AARP responds to political and policy issues of concern to its constituency. For example, it asserts in the press release "AARP Statement on 2013 Social Security Trustees Report" (May 31, 2013, http://www.aarp.org/about-aarp/press-center/info-06-2013/AARP-Statement-on-2013-Social-Security-Trustees-Report.html) that it is "is fighting to stop short-sighted changes that will cut Social Security to reduce the deficit, and instead calling for a separate debate about responsible solutions that will secure and strengthen Social Security for today's seniors and their kids and grandkids."

CHAPTER 6
ON THE ROAD: OLDER ADULT DRIVERS

Readily available transportation is a vital factor in the quality of life of older adults. Transportation is essential for accessing health care, establishing and maintaining social and family relationships, obtaining food and other necessities, and preserving independence and self-esteem.

The ability to drive often determines whether an older adult is able to live independently. Driving is the primary mode of transportation in the United States, and personal vehicles remain the transportation mode of choice for almost all Americans, including older people. Surveys conducted by the AARP repeatedly confirm that people over the age of 65 years make nearly all their trips in private vehicles, either as drivers or passengers. Even in urban areas where public transit is readily available, private vehicles are still used by most older people, and nondrivers rely on family members or friends for transport. The National Highway Traffic Safety Administration (NHTSA) confirms in "Alternative Transportation—It Could Work for You" (2013, http://www.nhtsa.gov/people/injury/olddrive/Driving%20Safely%20Aging%20Web/page6.html) that older adult nondrivers rely on alternative forms of transportation, such as rides from family or friends, public transportation, walking, or senior vans or taxicabs.

The NHTSA states in *Older Driver Program: Five-Year Strategic Plan 2012–2017* (December 2010, http://www.nhtsa.gov/staticfiles/nti/pdf/811432.pdf) that people aged 65 years and older are a significant and growing segment of the driving population. In "Older Adult Drivers: Get the Facts" (January 31, 2013, http://www.cdc.gov/Motorvehiclesafety/Older_Adult_Drivers/adult-drivers_fact sheet.html), the Centers for Disease Control and Prevention (CDC) reports that the number of older drivers increased 23% between 1999 and 2009, when 33 million adults aged 65 years and older were licensed drivers.

Federal Highway Administration data reveal that in 2011 the percentage of older drivers was comparable for men and women aged 65 to 74 years, but for people aged 75 years and older slightly more women than men were licensed drivers. (See Table 6.1.) Donald H. Camph notes in *A New Vision of America's Highways: Long-Distance Travel, Recreation, Tourism, and Rural Travel* (March 2007, http://www.pdfio.com/k-2010906.html) that as the baby boomers (people born between 1946 and 1964) join the ranks of older adults, the number of drivers aged 65 years and older will continue to grow, exceeding 40 million by 2020.

Camph observes, however, that although many older adults drive and many more are expected to in the future, driving is not a viable alternative for a significant number of older people. Many older adults choose to stop or limit their driving for health or safety reasons. Others do not have access to a vehicle. Camph also asserts that "more than 50 percent of non-drivers age 65 and older—or 3.6 million Americans—stay home on any given day at least partially because they lack transportation options."

Limited income also restricts many older adults' use of automobiles. According to the U.S. Bureau of Labor Statistics, car ownership costs are the second-largest household expense in the United States, and the average household spends nearly as much to own and operate a car as it does on food and health care combined. Table 6.2 shows that the average costs associated with car ownership rose from $7,417 in 2000 to $7,658 in 2009, largely due to increased spending on gas and motor oil. The cost of owning and operating an automobile, especially during periods of rising fuel prices, may be prohibitive for older adults living on fixed incomes. As a result, an ever-increasing proportion of the older population depends on alternative forms of transport in those areas where such transport is available; however,

TABLE 6.1

Licensed drivers, by sex and percentage in each age group and relation to population, 2011

[March 2013]

	Male drivers			Female drivers			Total drivers		
Age	Number	Percent of total drivers	Drivers as percent of age group*	Number	Percent of total drivers	Drivers as percent of age group*	Number	Percent of total drivers	Drivers as percent of age group*
Under 16	180,236	0.2	8.5	180,810	0.2	8.9	361,046	0.2	8.7
16	585,450	0.6	26.9	582,091	0.5	28.2	1,167,541	0.6	27.5
17	986,128	0.9	44.3	963,922	0.9	45.8	1,950,050	0.9	45.0
18	1,363,555	1.3	60.2	1,286,280	1.2	60.3	2,649,835	1.3	60.3
19	1,605,232	1.5	69.2	1,524,549	1.4	69.5	3,129,781	1.5	69.3
(19 and under)	4,720,601	4.5	42.5	4,537,652	4.2	43.1	9,258,253	4.4	42.8
20	1,724,122	1.6	73.4	1,659,530	1.6	73.9	3,383,652	1.6	73.6
21	1,786,515	1.7	76.2	1,744,844	1.6	77.6	3,531,359	1.7	76.9
22	1,790,106	1.7	79.5	1,760,400	1.6	81.6	3,550,506	1.7	80.5
23	1,792,594	1.7	81.4	1,779,147	1.7	84.3	3,571,741	1.7	82.8
24	1,806,120	1.7	83.4	1,805,910	1.7	86.9	3,612,030	1.7	85.1
(20–24)	8,899,457	8.5	78.7	8,749,831	8.2	80.7	17,649,288	8.3	79.7
25–29	9,251,814	8.8	86.0	9,363,999	8.8	89.0	18,615,814	8.8	87.5
30–34	9,051,625	8.6	88.0	9,224,935	8.6	90.2	18,276,560	8.6	89.1
35–39	8,786,828	8.4	90.0	8,891,794	8.3	90.4	17,678,623	8.3	90.2
40–44	9,599,452	9.2	91.8	9,660,828	9.0	91.4	19,260,281	9.1	91.6
45–49	10,130,142	9.7	92.5	10,241,364	9.6	91.4	20,371,506	9.6	91.9
50–54	10,292,465	9.8	93.0	10,508,380	9.8	91.4	20,800,845	9.8	92.2
55–59	9,313,456	8.9	94.9	9,574,420	9.0	91.7	18,887,876	8.9	93.2
60–64	8,131,920	7.8	95.2	8,377,738	7.8	90.4	16,509,658	7.8	92.7
65–69	5,894,680	5.6	97.1	6,079,104	5.7	89.4	11,973,784	5.7	93.0
70–74	4,176,442	4.0	94.8	4,361,670	4.1	83.8	8,538,112	4.0	88.9
75–79	3,004,712	2.9	92.9	3,220,510	3.0	77.5	6,225,222	2.9	84.3
80–84	2,092,065	2.0	89.4	2,341,405	2.2	67.9	4,433,470	2.1	76.6
85 and over	1,554,233	1.5	82.1	1,841,125	1.7	47.9	3,395,359	1.6	59.2
Total	**104,899,893**	**100.0**	**86.0**	**106,974,756**	**100.0**	**83.3**	**211,874,649**	**100.0**	**84.6**

*These percentages are computed using population estimates of the Bureau of the Census. Under-16 age group is compared to 14 and 15-year-old population estimates; the other age brackets coincide with those from the Bureau of the Census.

SOURCE: "Distribution of Licensed Drivers—2011 by Sex and Percentage in Each Age Group and Relation to Population," in *Highway Statistics 2011*, U.S. Department of Transportation, Federal Highway Administration, March 2013, http://www.fhwa.dot.gov/policyinformation/statistics/2011/pdf/dl20.pdf (accessed June 12, 2013)

some older adults remain isolated and immobilized by the absence of accessible, affordable transportation in their communities.

According to the U.S. Government Accountability Office (GAO), in *Transportation-Disadvantaged Populations: Federal Coordination Efforts Could Be Further Strengthened* (June 2012, http://www.gao.gov/assets/600/591707.pdf), of the 80 federal programs that fund services for transportation-disadvantaged populations, one program—the U.S. Department of Transportation (DOT) Capital Assistance Program for Elderly Persons and Persons with Disabilities—focuses specifically on supporting transportation services for transportation-disadvantaged older adults.

TRANSPORTATION INITIATIVES ADDRESS NEEDS OF OLDER ADULTS

Because ensuring access to transportation is key to older adults' independence and quality of life, several federal agencies and initiatives aim to address this need. The Federal Interagency Coordinating Council on Access and Mobility sponsors United We Ride, a national interagency initiative that supports states and their localities to develop coordinated human service delivery systems. The National Center on Senior Transportation (NCST) aims to assist older adults to remain active vital members of their communities by offering a range of transportation options and alternatives. The NCST-sponsored Senior Transportation program is a collaborative effort that coordinates research and services intended to develop new transportation solutions, especially for rural areas. The program also champions the creative use of technology to connect volunteers, older drivers, and older adults in need of transportation services. The NCST is overseen by the Easter Seals Inc. and receives funding via the DOT's Federal Transit Administration.

In "Enhancing Older Adult Mobility through Person-Centered Mobility Management" (April 2012, http://www.n4a.org/pdf/NCST_Announces_Mobility_Management_Grantees.pdf), the NCST describes the eight grants it funded in 2012. The grants range from $34,889 to $50,000 and the grantees will develop solutions to mobility problems using strategies that include:

TABLE 6.2

Average annual expenditures of all consumer units, by selected types of expenditures, selected years 1990–2009

[In dollars, except as indicated (96,968 represents $96,968,000). Based on Consumer Expenditure Survey. Data are averages for the noninstitutional population. Expenditures reported here are out-of-pocket. Consumer units include families, single persons living alone or sharing a household with others but who are financially independent, or two or more persons living together who share expenses.]

Type of expenditure	1990	1995	2000	2005	2006	2007	2008	2009
Number of consumer units (1,000)	96,968	103,123	109,367	117,356	118,843	120,171	120,770	120,847
Expenditures, Total* (dol.)	28,381	32,264	38,045	46,409	48,398	49,638	50,486	49,067
Food	4,296	4,505	5,158	5,931	6,111	6,133	6,443	6,372
Food at home*	2,485	2,803	3,021	3,297	3,417	3,465	3,744	3,753
Meats, poultry, fish, and eggs	668	752	795	764	797	777	846	841
Dairy products	295	297	325	378	368	387	430	406
Fruits and vegetables	408	457	521	552	592	600	657	656
Other food at home	746	856	927	1,158	1,212	1,241	1,305	1,343
Food away from home	1,811	1,702	2,137	2,634	2,694	2,668	2,698	2,619
Alcoholic beverages	293	277	372	426	497	457	444	435
Housing*	8,703	10,458	12,319	15,167	16,366	16,920	17,109	16,895
Shelter	4,836	5,928	7,114	8,805	9,673	10,023	10,183	10,075
Utilities, fuels, and public services	1,890	2,191	2,489	3,183	3,397	3,477	3,649	3,645
Apparel and services	1,618	1,704	1,856	1,886	1,874	1,881	1,801	1,725
Transportation*	5,120	6,014	7,417	8,344	8,508	8,758	8,604	7,658
Vehicle purchases	2,129	2,638	3,418	3,544	3,421	3,244	2,755	2,657
Gasoline and motor oil	1,047	1,006	1,291	2,013	2,227	2,384	2,715	1,986
Other vehicle expenses	1,642	2,015	2,281	2,339	2,355	2,592	2,621	2,536
Health care	1,480	1,732	2,066	2,664	2,766	2,853	2,976	3,126
Entertainment	1,422	1,612	1,863	2,388	2,376	2,698	2,835	2,693
Reading	153	162	146	126	117	118	116	110
Tobacco products, smoking supplies	274	269	319	319	327	323	317	380
Personal insurance and pensions	2,592	2,964	3,365	5,204	5,270	5,336	5,605	5,471
Life and other personal insurance	345	373	399	381	322	309	317	309
Pensions and Social Security	2,248	2,591	2,966	4,823	4,948	5,027	5,288	5,162

*Includes expenditures not shown separately.

SOURCE: "Table 684. Average Annual Expenditures of All Consumer Units by Selected Major Types of Expenditure: 1990–2009," in *Statistical Abstract of the United States: 2012*, 131st ed., U.S. Census Bureau, 2012, http://www.census.gov/prod/2011pubs/12statab/income.pdf (accessed June 12, 2013)

- Encouraging collaboration between various networks and creating community coalitions and stakeholder groups to better address the mobility needs of older adults

- Organizing and conducting consumer market research to better understand the ideas and opinions of older adults who receive mobility counseling

- Developing approaches to meet the unique needs of particular population groups and addressing special circumstances such as the transportation needs in rural areas

- Designing tool kits, training curricula, and marketing materials

Department of Transportation's Initiatives

In his speech to the Atlantic Generations Forum in Washington, D.C., on May 22, 2013, Ray H. LaHood (1945–; http://www.dot.gov/briefing-room/atlantic-genera tions-forum), the former U.S. secretary of transportation, addressed the DOT's efforts to repair and rebuild the U.S. transportation system. He described grant programs in excess of $3 billion that support 200 local community transportation initiatives in 50 states and asserted that "by updating our transportation network, we make getting around safer for all Americans at any age—children, young professionals, and seniors."

Hood explained that the DOT aims to provide safe, reliable, and convenient transportation options for older adults and cited examples of accommodations for older adults, such as communities replacing "worn out signs and traffic signals, you'll see larger signs with taller letters, signs placed in a way to give motorists more time to react, and even bigger lenses on traffic signals." He also noted that the timing of pedestrian signals is being adjusted to give pedestrians enough time to safely cross streets.

MOTOR VEHICLE ACCIDENTS

The Insurance Institute for Highway Safety (IIHS), a nonprofit organization dedicated to reducing the losses from motor vehicle accidents, reports that apart from the youngest drivers, older drivers have the highest rates of fatal crashes per mile driven. Although older drivers tend to limit their number of miles driven as they age and they drive at the safest times (in daylight and avoiding rush-hour traffic), their rate of accidents per mile is extremely high. In "Fatality Facts 2011: Older People" (2013, http://www .iihs.org/research/fatality.aspx?topicName=Older-people),

FIGURE 6.1

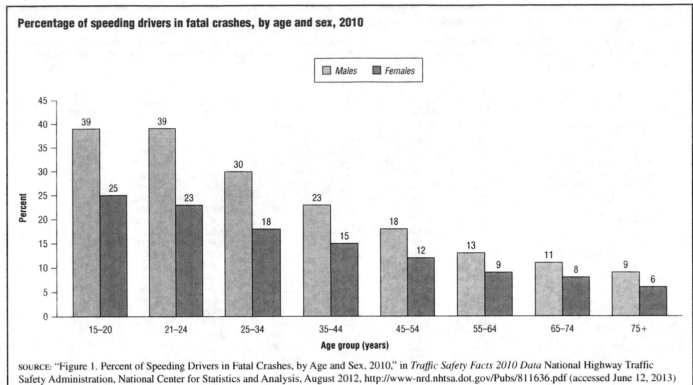

Percentage of speeding drivers in fatal crashes, by age and sex, 2010

SOURCE: "Figure 1. Percent of Speeding Drivers in Fatal Crashes, by Age and Sex, 2010," in *Traffic Safety Facts 2010 Data* National Highway Traffic Safety Administration, National Center for Statistics and Analysis, August 2012, http://www-nrd.nhtsa.dot.gov/Pubs/811636.pdf (accessed June 12, 2013)

the IIHS observes that among drivers involved in fatal crashes in 2011, the proportion in multiple-vehicle crashes at intersections increased with driver age, starting at ages 70 to 74. Nearly four out of 10 (39%) fatal motor vehicle accidents among drivers aged 80 years and older were multiple-vehicle crashes, compared with about 18% for drivers aged 20 to 49 years.

The oldest and youngest drivers have the highest fatality rates on a per-mile-driven basis, but a key difference between the two age groups is that older drivers involved in crashes are less likely than younger drivers to hurt others—older drivers pose more of a danger to themselves. Drivers under the age of 35 years are also more likely to be speeding and are responsible for far more of the speeding-related fatal crashes than are older adult drivers. (See Figure 6.1.).

Table 6.3 shows that in 2010 the death rate (the number of deaths per 100,000 people) for motor vehicle–related injuries for adults aged 65 years and older was 16%, compared with 11.9% for adults aged 45 to 64 years. The higher fatality rates of adults aged 75 to 84 years and 85 years and older who were involved in crashes—18.8% and 23.8%, respectively—are attributable to older adults' fragility as opposed to the likelihood of being involved in an accident. Older people are more susceptible to injury, especially chest injuries, and are more likely to die as a result of those injuries. However, the IIHS indicates that relatively few deaths (less than

1%) of adults aged 70 years and older are attributable to motor vehicle accidents.

The IIHS reports that in 2011, 76% of motor vehicle crash fatalities among people aged 70 years and older involved occupants in passenger vehicles and 16% were pedestrians. The death rate per 100,000 people for pedestrians aged 70 years and older in 2011 was higher than for pedestrians in all younger age groups.

In 2011, 75% of fatal crashes involving drivers aged 85 years and older were multiple-vehicle accidents. Of those, over four out of 10 (44%) occurred at intersections. The IIHS observes that older drivers are more likely than younger drivers to have accidents when making left turns and attributes this to the fact that older drivers take longer to make turns, increasing the risk of a crash.

Older adults also suffer nonfatal injuries as drivers or passengers in motor vehicle crashes. In 2011 the National Center for Injury Prevention and Control recorded 261,123 nonfatal motor vehicle injuries in adults aged 65 to 85 years. (See Table 6.4; this figure shows the 194,678 injuries to occupants of vehicles and the 66,445 injuries attributable to other transport.) Motor vehicle accidents (called unintentional MV-occupant) were the fourth-leading cause of nonfatal injuries among adults aged 65 to 85 years in the United States in 2011.

The data about older drivers are not all bad. According to the CDC, in "New Data on Older Adult Drivers" (April 19, 2011, http://www.cdc.gov/features/dsolder

TABLE 6.3

Death rates for motor vehicle-related injuries, by selected characteristics, selected years 1950–2010

[Data are based on death certificates]

Sex, race, Hispanic origin, and age	1950[a]	1960[a]	1970	1980	1990	2000	2009	2010
All persons				Deaths per 100,000 resident population				
All ages, age-adjusted[b]	24.6	23.1	27.6	22.3	18.5	15.4	11.6	11.3
All ages, crude	23.1	21.3	26.9	23.5	18.8	15.4	11.8	11.4
Under 1 year	8.4	8.1	9.8	7.0	4.9	4.4	2.4	2.0
1–14 years	9.8	8.6	10.5	8.2	6.0	4.3	2.5	2.3
1–4 years	11.5	10.0	11.5	9.2	6.3	4.2	2.9	2.8
5–14 years	8.8	7.9	10.2	7.9	5.9	4.3	2.4	2.2
15–24 years	34.4	38.0	47.2	44.8	34.1	26.9	17.6	16.6
15–19 years	29.6	33.9	43.6	43.0	33.1	26.0	15.2	13.6
20–24 years	38.8	42.9	51.3	46.6	35.0	28.0	20.2	19.7
25–34 years	24.6	24.3	30.9	29.1	23.6	17.3	14.5	14.0
35–44 years	20.3	19.3	24.9	20.9	16.9	15.3	12.2	11.6
45–64 years	25.2	23.0	26.5	18.0	15.7	14.3	12.2	11.9
45–54 years	22.2	21.4	25.5	18.6	15.6	14.2	12.7	12.0
55–64 years	29.0	25.1	27.9	17.4	15.9	14.4	11.5	11.9
65 years and over	43.1	34.7	36.2	22.5	23.1	21.4	15.8	16.0
65–74 years	39.1	31.4	32.8	19.2	18.6	16.5	12.7	12.3
75–84 years	52.7	41.8	43.5	28.1	29.1	25.7	18.6	18.8
85 years and over	45.1	37.9	34.2	27.6	31.2	30.4	20.9	23.8
Male								
All ages, age-adjusted[b]	38.5	35.4	41.5	33.6	26.5	21.7	16.8	16.2
All ages, crude	35.4	31.8	39.7	35.3	26.7	21.3	16.9	16.3
Under 1 year	9.1	8.6	9.3	7.3	5.0	4.6	2.6	2.2
1–14 years	12.3	10.7	13.0	10.0	7.0	4.9	2.9	2.7
1–4 years	13.0	11.5	12.9	10.2	6.9	4.7	3.4	3.0
5–14 years	11.9	10.4	13.1	9.9	7.0	5.0	2.7	2.5
15–24 years	56.7	61.2	73.2	68.4	49.5	37.4	24.5	23.1
15–19 years	46.3	51.7	64.1	62.6	45.5	33.9	19.2	17.8
20–24 years	66.7	73.2	84.4	74.3	53.3	41.2	30.0	28.5
25–34 years	40.8	40.1	49.4	46.3	35.7	25.5	21.7	21.0
35–44 years	32.5	29.9	37.7	31.7	24.7	22.0	18.2	16.9
45–64 years	37.7	33.3	38.9	26.5	21.9	20.2	18.2	17.9
45–54 years	33.6	31.6	37.2	27.6	22.0	20.4	19.0	17.9
55–64 years	43.1	35.6	40.9	25.4	21.7	19.8	17.2	17.8
65 years and over	66.6	52.1	54.4	33.9	32.1	29.5	22.0	22.2
65–74 years	59.1	45.8	47.3	27.3	24.2	21.7	17.5	17.1
75–84 years	85.0	66.0	68.2	44.3	41.2	35.6	25.8	25.9
85 years and over	78.1	62.7	63.1	56.1	64.5	57.5	35.3	40.2
Female								
All ages, age-adjusted[b]	11.5	11.7	14.9	11.8	11.0	9.5	6.7	6.5
All ages, crude	10.9	11.0	14.7	12.3	11.3	9.7	6.9	6.8
Under 1 year	7.6	7.5	10.4	6.7	4.9	4.2	2.1	1.8
1–14 years	7.2	6.3	7.9	6.3	4.9	3.7	2.2	2.0
1–4 years	10.0	8.4	10.0	8.1	5.6	3.8	2.5	2.5
5–14 years	5.7	5.4	7.2	5.7	4.7	3.6	2.0	1.8
15–24 years	12.6	15.1	21.6	20.8	17.9	15.9	10.5	9.9
15–19 years	12.9	16.0	22.7	22.8	20.0	17.5	10.9	9.2
20–24 years	12.2	14.0	20.4	18.9	16.0	14.2	10.0	10.5
25–34 years	9.3	9.2	13.0	12.2	11.5	8.8	7.2	6.9
35–44 years	8.5	9.1	12.9	10.4	9.2	8.8	6.2	6.2
45–64 years	12.6	13.1	15.3	10.3	10.1	8.7	6.5	6.3
45–54 years	10.9	11.6	14.5	10.2	9.6	8.2	6.6	6.3
55–64 years	14.9	15.2	16.2	10.5	10.8	9.5	6.3	6.3
65 years and over	21.9	20.3	23.1	15.0	17.2	15.8	11.1	11.3
65–74 years	20.6	19.0	21.6	13.0	14.1	12.3	8.5	8.2
75–84 years	25.2	23.0	27.2	18.5	21.9	19.2	13.5	13.7
85 years and over	22.1	22.0	18.0	15.2	18.3	19.3	14.0	15.9
White male[c]								
All ages, age-adjusted[b]	37.9	34.8	40.4	33.8	26.3	21.8	17.3	16.7
All ages, crude	35.1	31.5	39.1	35.9	26.7	21.6	17.5	17.0
Under 1 year	9.1	8.8	9.1	7.0	4.8	4.2	2.5	2.0
1–14 years	12.4	10.6	12.5	9.8	6.6	4.8	2.8	2.7
15–24 years	58.3	62.7	75.2	73.8	52.5	39.6	26.6	24.6
25–34 years	39.1	38.6	47.0	46.6	35.4	25.1	21.8	21.4
35–44 years	30.9	28.4	35.2	30.7	23.7	21.8	18.5	17.4
45–64 years	36.2	31.7	36.5	25.2	20.6	19.7	18.7	18.3
65 years and over	67.1	52.1	54.2	32.7	31.4	29.4	22.3	22.7

TABLE 6.3

Death rates for motor vehicle-related injuries, by selected characteristics, selected years 1950–2010 [CONTINUED]

[Data are based on death certificates]

[a]Includes deaths of persons who were not residents of the 50 states and the District of Columbia (D.C.).
[b]Age-adjusted rates are calculated using the year 2000 standard population. Prior to 2001, age-adjusted rates were calculated using standard million proportions based on rounded population numbers. Starting with 2001 data, unrounded population numbers are used to calculate age-adjusted rates.
[c]The race groups, white, black, Asian or Pacific Islander, and American Indian or Alaska Native, include persons of Hispanic and non-Hispanic origin. Persons of Hispanic origin may be of any race. Death rates for the American Indian or Alaska Native, Asian or Pacific Islander, and Hispanic populations are known to be underestimated.
Notes: Starting with *Health, United States, 2003*, rates for 1991–1999 were revised using intercensal population estimates based on the 1990 and 2000 censuses. For 2000, population estimates are bridged-race April 1 census counts. Starting with *Health, United States, 2012*, rates for 2001–2009 were revised using intercensal population estimates based on the 2000 and 2010 censuses. For 2010, population estimates are bridged-race April 1 census counts. Age groups were selected to minimize the presentation of unstable age-specific death rates based on small numbers of deaths and for consistency among comparison groups. Starting with 2003 data, some states allowed the reporting of more than one race on the death certificate. The multiple-race data for these states were bridged to the single-race categories of the 1977 Office of Management and Budget standards, for comparability with other states.

SOURCE: Adapted from "Table 33. Death Rates for Motor Vehicle-Related Injuries, by Sex, Race, Hispanic Origin, and Age: United States, Selected Years 1950–2010," in *Health, United States, 2012: With Special Feature on Emergency Care*, National Center for Health Statistics, 2013, http://www.cdc.gov/nchs/data/hus/2012/033.pdf (accessed June 12, 2013)

TABLE 6.4

Ten leading causes of nonfatal injuries, ages 65–85, 2011

[2011, all races, both sexes, disposition: all cases]

Rank	Age groups 65–85	
1	Unintentional fall	2,403,146
2	Unintentional struck by/against	269,421
3	Unintentional overexertion	203,047
4	Unintentional motor vehicle-occupant	194,678
5	Unintentional cut/pierce	148,065
6	Unintentional poisoning	95,841
7	Unintentional other bite/sting	93,856
8	Unintentional other specified	74,873
9	Unintentional other transport	66,445
10	Unintentional unknown/unspecified	56,754

SOURCE: "10 Leading Causes of Nonfatal Injury, United States 2011, All Races, Both Sexes, Disposition: All Cases," National Center for Injury Prevention and Control, 2013, http://webapp.cdc.gov/cgi-bin/broker.exe?_PROGRAM=wisqnf.nfilead.sas&_SERVICE=v8prod&log=0&rept=nfil&year1=2011&year2=2011&Racethn=0&Sex=0&disp=0&ranking=10&PRTFMT=FRIENDLY&lcnifmt=custom&intent=0&c_age1=65&c_age2=85&_debug=0 (accessed June 12, 2013)

FIGURE 6.2

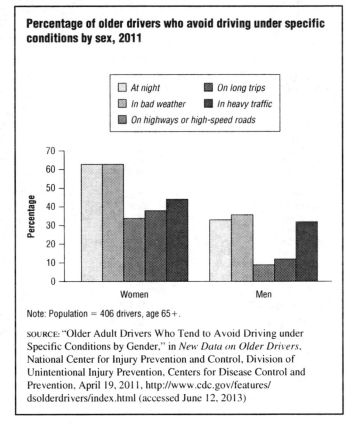

Percentage of older drivers who avoid driving under specific conditions by sex, 2011

Legend: At night; In bad weather; On highways or high-speed roads; On long trips; In heavy traffic

Note: Population = 406 drivers, age 65+.

SOURCE: "Older Adult Drivers Who Tend to Avoid Driving under Specific Conditions by Gender," in *New Data on Older Drivers*, National Center for Injury Prevention and Control, Division of Unintentional Injury Prevention, Centers for Disease Control and Prevention, April 19, 2011, http://www.cdc.gov/features/dsolderdrivers/index.html (accessed June 12, 2013)

drivers/index.html), older drivers take fewer risks than younger drivers by limiting their driving on high-speed roads, during bad weather and at night, and in heavy traffic. Figure 6.2 shows the percentages of older adult drivers who tend to avoid driving under certain conditions.

AGE-RELATED CHANGES MAY IMPAIR OLDER DRIVERS' SKILLS

Most older adults retain their driving skills, but some age-related changes in vision, hearing, cognitive functions (attention, memory, and reaction times), reflexes, and flexibility of the head and neck may impair the skills that are critical for safe driving. For example, reaction time becomes slower and more variable with advancing age, and arthritis (inflammation that causes pain and loss of movement of the joints) in the neck or shoulder may limit sufferers' ability to turn their neck well enough to merge into traffic, see when backing up, and navigate

intersections where the angle of intersecting roads is less than perpendicular.

Changes such as reduced muscle mass and the resultant reduction in strength, as well as decreases in the efficiency of the circulatory, cardiac, and respiratory systems are strictly related to aging. Others are attributable to the fact that certain diseases, such as arthritis and glaucoma (a disease in which fluid pressure inside the eyes slowly rises, leading to vision loss or blindness), tend to strike at later ages. The functional losses that are associated with these conditions are usually gradual, and many afflicted older drivers are able to adapt to them. Most older adults do not experience declines until very old age, and most learn to adjust to the limitations imposed by age-related changes. Still, a substantial proportion of older adults do stop driving in response to age-related changes. In "New Data on Older Drivers," the CDC reports that of older adults who reduced their driving, 40% said they did so because of vision problems. The IIHS adds in "Q&A: Older Drivers" (March 2013, http://www.iihs.org/research/qanda/older_people.aspx) that lifestyle changes such as becoming widowed or divorced influence older adults' driving patterns as do problems with mobility or memory.

The *Physician's Guide to Assessing and Counseling Older Drivers* (February 2010, http://www.ama-assn.org/resources/doc/public-health/older-drivers-guide.pdf), published by the American Medical Association (AMA) and the NHTSA, details medical conditions and their potential effect on driving and highlights treatment methods and counseling measures that can minimize these effects. The AMA and the NHTSA identify motor vehicle injuries as the leading cause of injury-related deaths among 65- to 75-year-olds and the second-leading cause of deaths among 75- to 84-year-olds. They posit that significant growth in the older population and an increase in miles driven by older adults could act to triple the number of traffic fatalities in the coming years. Believing that the medical community can help stem this increase, the AMA and the NHTSA call on physicians to help their patients maintain or even improve their driving skills by periodically assessing them for disease- and medication-related conditions that might impair their capacity to function as safe drivers.

Acute and Chronic Medical Problems

According to the AMA and the NHTSA, in *Physician's Guide to Assessing and Counseling Older Drivers*, patients discharged from the hospital following treatment for serious illnesses may be temporarily, or even permanently, unable to drive safely. Examples of acute (short-term) medical problems that can impair driving performance include:

- Acute myocardial infarction (heart attack)
- Stroke (sudden death of a portion of the brain cells due to a lack of blood flow and oxygen) and other traumatic brain injury
- Syncope (fainting) and vertigo (dizziness)
- Seizures (sudden attacks or convulsions characterized by generalized muscle spasms and loss of consciousness)
- Surgery
- Delirium (altered mental state characterized by wild, irregular, and incoherent thoughts and actions) from any cause

The AMA and the NHTSA note that a variety of chronic (long-term) medical conditions can also compromise driving function, including:

- Visual disorders such as cataracts, diabetic retinopathy (damage to the blood vessels that supply the retina that can result in blindness), macular degeneration (a degenerative condition that can cause blurred vision), glaucoma, retinitis pigmentosa (an inherited condition that causes night blindness and tunnel vision), and low visual acuity (the inability to distinguish fine details) even after correction with lenses. Along with visual acuity, other visual functions decline with advancing age. For example, sensitivity to glare increases and may be exacerbated by cataracts. Because driving is largely a visual task, impaired vision can significantly compromise the ability to read signs, see lane lines, and identify pedestrians in the dark or during inclement weather.

- Cardiovascular disorders such as angina (chest pain from a blockage in a coronary artery that prevents oxygen-rich blood from reaching part of the heart) or syncope pose dangers to drivers because acute pain or even transient loss of consciousness increases the risk of accidents.

- Neurologic diseases such as seizures, dementia (loss of intellectual functioning accompanied by memory loss and personality changes), multiple sclerosis (a progressive nerve disease that can result in the loss of the ability to walk or speak), Parkinson's disease (a degenerative disease that causes tremors and slowed movement and speech), peripheral neuropathy (numbness or tingling in the hands and/or feet), and residual deficits (losses or disability) resulting from stroke all may impair the driver's ability to operate a vehicle and/or exercise sufficient caution when driving.

- Psychiatric diseases, especially those mental disorders in which patients suffer hallucinations, severe anxiety, and irrational thoughts and are unable to distinguish between reality and imagination, can affect judgment and impair the driver's ability to operate a vehicle.

- Metabolic diseases, such as diabetes mellitus (a condition in which there is increased sugar in the blood and urine because the body is unable to use sugar to produce energy) and hypothyroidism (decreased production of the thyroid hormone by the thyroid gland), can act to impair judgment and response time.

- Musculoskeletal disabilities, such as arthritis and injuries, can impair response time.

The AMA and the NHTSA observe that driving requires a range of sophisticated cognitive skills, which is why some cognitive changes can compromise driving ability. It is not unusual for memory, attention, processing speed, and executive skills (the capacity for logical analysis) to decline with advancing age. Weakening memory may make it difficult for some older drivers to process information from traffic signs and to navigate correctly. As multiple demands are made on older drivers' attention, the AMA and the NHTSA state that "drivers must possess selective attention—the ability to prioritize stimuli and focus on only the most important—in order to attend to urgent stimuli (such as traffic signs) while not being distracted by irrelevant ones (such as roadside ads)." Selective attention problems challenge older drivers to distinguish the most critical information when they are faced with many signs and signals. Drivers have to divide their attention to concentrate "on the multiple stimuli required by most driving tasks." Processing speed affects perception-reaction time and is critical in situations where drivers must immediately choose between actions such as accelerating, braking, or steering. Executive skills enable drivers to make correct decisions after evaluating the stimuli that are related to driving, such as to stop at a red light or stop at a crosswalk when a pedestrian is crossing the street.

Medications

The AMA and the NHTSA indicate in *Physician's Guide to Assessing and Counseling Older Drivers* that many commonly used prescription and over-the-counter (nonprescription) medications can impair driving performance. In general, drugs with strong central nervous system effects, such as antidepressants, antihistamines, muscle relaxants, narcotic analgesics (painkillers), anticonvulsants (used to prevent seizures), and stimulants, have the potential to adversely affect the ability to operate a motor vehicle. The extent to which driving skills are compromised varies from person to person and between different medications that are used for the same purpose. The effects of prescription and over-the-counter medications may be intensified in combination with other drugs or alcohol.

Driving performance may also be affected by medication side effects, such as "drowsiness, dizziness, blurred vision, unsteadiness, fainting, [and] slowed reaction time." Generally, these side effects are dose-dependent and lessen over time, but older adults are often more sensitive to the effects of medications and may take longer to metabolize them, prolonging their effects. Medications such as prescription sleep aids "that cause drowsiness, euphoria, and/or anterograde amnesia may also diminish insight, and the patient may experience impairment without being aware of it."

Some Fears about Older Drivers Are Unwarranted

As the ranks of older adults swell, many states and organizations—the AMA and the NHTSA are chief among these groups—are taking action to ensure driver safety. Concern about older driver safety has intensified in recent years in response to a spate of media reports describing serious crashes involving older drivers. However, some of this concern may be unwarranted. In "Fatality Facts 2011," the IIHS observes that between 1995 and 2011 fatal crash involvement rates for drivers aged 70 years and older declined 45%—from 25.9 to 14.2 deaths per 100,000 in the United States.

These findings contradict earlier research, which predicted that older drivers would make up a substantially larger proportion of drivers in fatal crashes. According to Tara Parker-Pope, in "Declining Car Risk for Older Drivers" (NYTimes.com, January 12, 2009), research suggests that older drivers are in better overall health than their counterparts were during the late 1990s, so they are less likely to make a driving mistake that can lead to an accident. The IIHS explains in "Q&A: Older Drivers" that older drivers largely threaten their own safety and their passengers' safety. In 2011 drivers aged 70 years and older accounted for 77% of fatal crashes—62% involved the drivers themselves and 15% involved older passengers. Although drivers aged 75 years and older kill fewer pedestrians, bicyclists, motorcyclists, and occupants of other vehicles than do drivers aged 30 to 59 years, drivers aged 75 to 79 years file more insurance claims for damage to other vehicles than do drivers aged 35 to 69 years.

Ensuring the Safety of Older Drivers

In *Physician's Guide to Assessing and Counseling Older Drivers*, the AMA and the NHTSA advocate coordinated efforts among the medical and research communities, policy makers, community planners, the automobile industry, and government agencies to achieve the common goal of safe transportation for the older population. The AMA and the NHTSA call for refined diagnostic tools to assist physicians in assessing patients' crash risk, improved access to driver assessment and rehabilitation, safer roads and vehicles, and better alternatives to driving for older adults.

Some auto insurance companies reduce payments for older adults who successfully complete driving classes such as the AARP Driver Safety Program. The AARP notes in "AARP Driver Safety: History and Facts" (January 1, 2010, http://www.aarp.org/home-garden/transportation/info-05-2010/dsp_article_program_history_and_facts.html) that since 2006 it has offered an online classroom refresher course that provides guidance in assessing physical abilities and making adjustments accordingly. By 2010, 36 states and the District of Columbia granted insurance discounts to drivers who have taken the course. The American Automobile Association offers a similar program called Safe Driving for Mature Operators that aims to improve the skills of older drivers. These courses address the aging process and help drivers adjust to age-related changes that can affect driving. Both organizations provide resources that help older drivers and their families determine whether they can safely continue driving.

As of July 2013, there were no upper age limits for driving. The National Institute on Aging observes that because people age at different rates, it is not possible to choose a specific age at which to suspend driving. Setting an age limit would leave some drivers on the road too long, whereas others would be forced to stop driving prematurely. Heredity, general health, lifestyle, and surroundings all influence how people age.

Many states are acting to reduce risks for older drivers by improving roadways to make driving less hazardous. According to the GAO, in *Older Driver Safety: Knowledge Sharing Should Help States Prepare for Increase in Older Driver Population* (April 2007, http://www.gao.gov/new.items/d07413.pdf), several states have adopted Federal Highway Administration practices to help older drivers, including:

- Wider highway lanes
- Intersections that give drivers a longer view of oncoming traffic and allow more time for left turns
- Road signs with larger, more visible letters and numbers
- Advance street name signs before intersections

In 2010 the NHTSA released *Older Driver Program: Five-Year Strategic Plan 2012–2017* to assist the states to prepare for the more than 40 million drivers aged 65 years and older who will take to the roads in the coming decade. The plan calls for enhanced communication and education about older drivers and the development of older driver licensing policies, such as policies that restrict, rather than rescind, older drivers' licenses. It suggests the development of screening programs for Departments of Motor Vehicles to use in the license renewal process and enhanced training of law enforcement personnel on how to interact with older drivers.

Technology Aids Older Drivers

Advances in automotive technology such as global positioning system navigation devices that provide turn-by-turn directions can help older adults drive more safely and comfortably. In "Best New-Cars (and Features) for Senior Drivers" (Forbes.com, January 10, 2013), Jim Gorzelany reports that adjustable and heated seats can make older drivers more comfortable, and thicker steering wheels and larger knobs can make handling easier for older adults with arthritis. Large, more legible gauges, high-intensity high beams, and auto-dimming rear- and side-view mirrors help minimize glare, enabling older adults with vision problems to see the road. Parking aids can help people with limited mobility, and some collision warning and prevention systems not only alert drivers to dangers but also automatically apply the brakes if sensors detect a person or object in the vehicle's pathway.

PROVIDING ALTERNATIVE MEANS OF TRANSPORTATION

In *Transportation-Disadvantaged Populations*, the GAO considers issues and services for "transportation-disadvantaged" older adults—those who cannot drive or have limited their driving, or those who have an income restraint, disability, or medical condition that limits their ability to travel. The GAO identifies the federal programs that address this population's mobility issues, the extent to which these programs meet their mobility needs, the cost-effectiveness of service delivery, obstacles to addressing mobility needs, and strategies for overcoming these obstacles. According to the GAO, there are 80 federal programs designed to meet the transportation needs of older adults. For example, the U.S. Department of Health and Human Services funds Community Services Block Grant Programs, which provide taxicab vouchers and bus tokens that enable low-income older adults to take general trips, and Social Services Block Grants, which provide assistance for transport to and from medical or social service appointments.

The GAO points out that besides the programs that are intended to provide assistance specifically to older people, there are other programs that are designed to aid transportation-disadvantaged segments of the population, including older adults. For example, the Americans with Disabilities Act (ADA) of 1990 required that changes to public transportation be made to provide better accessibility for people with disabilities; about half of ADA-eligible riders are aged 65 years and older. Also, the Transportation Equity Act for the 21st Century, enacted in 1998, authorized funds for several programs, including a formula grant that supported states' efforts to meet the special transportation needs of older adults and people with disabilities.

The IIHS observes in "Q&A: Older Drivers" that public transportation is not available in many parts of the country and that although volunteer drivers and van programs meet some older adults' needs, rural communities often lack viable alternatives to driving for older adults.

Types of Transportation for Nondrivers

Transportation for older adults can include door-to-door services such as taxis or van services, public buses that travel along fixed routes, or ride sharing in carpools. According to the Administration on Aging (AoA), in *Because We Care: A Guide for People Who Care* (2009, http://www.uwex.edu/CES/flp/families/documents/Because

WeCare.pdf), there are three general classes of alternative transportation for older adults:

- Demand response generally requires advance reservations and provides door-to-door service from one specific location to another. Such systems offer older adults comfortable and relatively flexible transport, with the potential for adapting to the needs of individual riders. Payment of fares for demand-response transport is usually required on a per-ride basis.

- Fixed route and scheduled services follow a predetermined route, stopping at established locations at specific times to allow passengers to board and disembark. This type of service typically requires payment of fares on a per-ride basis. Older adults are often eligible for discounted rates.

- Ride sharing programs connect people who need rides with drivers who have room in their cars and are willing to take passengers. This system generally offers scheduled transportation to a particular destination, such as a place of employment, a senior center, or a medical center.

Meeting the Transportation Needs of Older Adults

In *Transportation-Disadvantaged Seniors: Efforts to Enhance Senior Mobility Could Benefit from Additional Guidance and Information* (August 2004, http://www .gao.gov/new.items/d04971.pdf), the GAO cites research by the Beverly Foundation that identifies five attributes that are necessary for alternative transportation services for older adults:

- Availability—older adults can travel to desired locations at the times they want to go.

- Accessibility—vehicles can be accessed by those with disabilities, services can be door-to-door or door-through-door as necessary, and stops are pedestrian-friendly. Door-through-door transport offers personal, hands-on assistance for older adults who may have difficulties exiting their homes, disembarking from vehicles, and/or opening doors. It is also called assisted transportation, supported (or supportive) transportation, and escorted transportation.

- Acceptability—transport is safe, clean, and easy to use.

- Affordability—financial assistance is available if necessary.

- Adaptability—multiple trips and special equipment can be accommodated.

The GAO highlights specific unmet needs: "Seniors who rely on alternative transportation have difficulty making trips for which the automobile is better suited, such as trips that involve carrying packages;... life-enhancing needs are less likely to be met than life-sustaining needs; and... mobility needs are less likely to be met in nonurban communities (especially rural communities) than in urban communities." It also identifies obstacles to addressing transportation-disadvantaged older adults' mobility needs, potential strategies that federal and other government entities might take to better meet these needs, and trade-offs that are associated with implementing each strategy. For example, the GAO finds that older drivers are not encouraged to investigate or plan for a time when they will be unable to drive. One way to address this obstacle might be to institute educational programs that would ease older adults' transition from driver to nondriver. This strategy does, however, have the potential to increase demand for alternative transportation services and the costs that are associated with their provision.

To increase and improve alternative transportation services, the GAO suggests enlisting the aid of volunteer drivers, sponsoring demonstration programs, identifying best practices, increasing cooperation among federal programs, and establishing a central clearinghouse of information that could be accessed by stakeholders in the various programs. It recommends that the AoA improve the value and consistency of information pertaining to older adults' transportation needs that is received from area agencies on aging, including providing guidance for those agencies on assessing mobility needs. The AoA is also called on to keep older adults and their caregivers better informed of alternative transportation programs and to ensure that the best methods and practices are shared among transportation and social service providers to enhance the older population's mobility.

CHAPTER 7
THE HEALTH AND MEDICAL PROBLEMS OF OLDER ADULTS

Among the fears many people have about aging is coping with losses—not only declining mental and physical abilities but also the prospect of failing health, chronic (long-term) illness, and disability. Although aging is associated with physiological changes, the rate and extent of these changes varies widely. One person may be limited by arthritis at age 65, whereas another is vigorous and active at age 90.

Despite the increasing proportion of active healthy older adults, it is true that the incidence (the rate of new cases of a disorder over a specified period) and prevalence (the total number of cases of a disorder in a given population at a specific time) of selected diseases as well as the utilization of health care services increase with advancing age. For example, the incidence of some diseases, such as diabetes, heart disease, breast cancer, Parkinson's disease, and Alzheimer's disease (a progressive disease that is characterized by memory loss, impaired thinking, and declining ability to function), increases with age. In contrast, the incidence of other diseases, such as human immunodeficiency virus (HIV) infection, multiple sclerosis, and schizophrenia, decreases with age.

This chapter considers the epidemiology of aging (the distribution and determinants of health and illness in the population of older adults). It describes trends in aging and the health of aging Americans; distinctions among healthy aging, disease, and disability; health promotion and prevention as applied to older people; and selected diseases and conditions that are common in old age.

GENERAL HEALTH OF OLDER AMERICANS

The proportion of adults rating their health as fair or poor increases with advancing age. In 2011, 19.1% of adults aged 55 to 64 years, 21.5% of adults aged 65 to 74 years, and 28.6% of adults aged 75 years and older considered themselves to be in fair or poor health, compared with just 6.5% of adults aged 18 to 44 years. (See Table 7.1.)

The Federal Interagency Forum on Aging-Related Statistics indicates in *Older Americans 2012: Key Indicators of Well-Being* (June 2012, http://www.aging stats.gov/Main_Site/Data/2012_Documents/docs/Entire Chartbook.pdf) that in 2008–10, 82% of non-Hispanic whites aged 65 to 74 years said their health was good or better than good, compared with just 69% of non-Hispanic whites aged 85 years and older. (See Figure 7.1.) Older people of other races and ethnic categories followed this same pattern. Across all older age groups, non-Hispanic white respondents were more likely to report good health than non-Hispanic African American and Hispanic respondents.

The Federal Interagency Forum on Aging-Related Statistics notes that most older people have at least one chronic condition and many have several. Among the most frequently occurring conditions of older adults in 2009–10 were hypertension (54% of men and 57% of women), arthritic symptoms (45% of men and 56% of women), all types of heart disease (37% of men and 26% of women), and cancer (28% of men and 21% of women). (See Figure 7.2.)

Figure 7.3 shows that rates of chronic conditions that limited one to two activities of daily living (ADLs) among Americans aged 65 years and older decreased from 20% in 1992 to 18% in 2009 and that the percentage reporting difficulty with five to six activities decreased from 4% to 3% during the same period. (ADLs are generally considered to include eating, bathing, dressing, getting to and using the bathroom, getting in or out of bed or a chair, and mobility.) The National Center for Health Statistics (NCHS) reports in *Health, United States, 2012* (May 2013, http://www.cdc.gov/nchs/data/hus/hus12.pdf) that between 2001 and 2011 the percentage of people who were limited in their ability to perform complex functions such as working, maintaining a household, living independently, or participating in community

TABLE 7.1

Percentage of adults who reported their health as fair or poor, by selected characteristics, selected years 1991–2011

[Data are based on household interviews of a sample of the civilian noninstitutionalized population]

Characteristic	1991[a]	1995[a]	1997	2000	2005	2009	2010	2011
	\multicolumn{8} Percent of persons with fair or poor health							
All ages, age-adjusted[b, c]	10.4	10.6	9.2	9.0	9.2	9.4	9.6	9.8
All ages, crude[c]	10.0	10.1	8.9	8.9	9.3	9.9	10.1	10.4
Age								
Under 18 years	2.6	2.6	2.1	1.7	1.8	1.8	2.0	2.0
Under 6 years	2.7	2.7	1.9	1.5	1.6	1.3	1.8	1.5
6–17 years	2.6	2.5	2.1	1.8	1.9	2.0	2.2	2.2
18–44 years	6.1	6.6	5.3	5.1	5.5	6.3	6.3	6.5
18–24 years	4.8	4.5	3.4	3.3	3.3	3.6	3.9	4.2
25–44 years	6.4	7.2	5.9	5.7	6.3	7.2	7.2	7.3
45–54 years	13.4	13.4	11.7	11.9	11.6	13.1	13.3	14.1
55–64 years	20.7	21.4	18.2	17.9	18.3	19.1	19.4	19.1
65 years and over	29.0	28.3	26.7	26.9	26.6	24.0	24.4	24.7
65–74 years	26.0	25.6	23.1	22.5	23.4	19.9	21.2	21.5
75 years and over	33.6	32.2	31.5	32.1	30.2	28.9	28.3	28.6
Sex[b]								
Male	10.0	10.1	8.8	8.8	8.8	9.1	9.2	9.4
Female	10.8	11.1	9.7	9.3	9.5	9.7	10.0	10.1
Race[b, d]								
White only	9.6	9.7	8.3	8.2	8.6	8.7	8.8	9.0
Black or African American only	16.8	17.2	15.8	14.6	14.3	14.2	14.9	15.0
American Indian or Alaska Native only	18.3	18.7	17.3	17.2	13.2	16.3	17.8	14.4
Asian only	7.8	9.3	7.8	7.4	6.8	8.4	8.1	8.7
Native Hawaiian or other Pacific Islander only	—	—	—	*	*	*	*	*
2 or more races	—	—	—	16.2	14.5	15.3	15.6	14.2
Black or African American; white	—	—	—	*14.5	8.3	18.0	*16.7	16.7
American Indian or Alaska Native; white	—	—	—	18.7	17.2	15.2	19.0	16.5
Hispanic origin and race[b, d]								
Hispanic or Latino	15.6	15.1	13.0	12.8	13.3	13.3	13.1	13.2
Mexican	17.0	16.7	13.1	12.8	14.3	13.7	13.7	14.0
Not Hispanic or Latino	10.0	10.1	8.9	8.7	8.7	8.9	9.2	9.4
White only	9.1	9.1	8.0	7.9	8.0	8.0	8.2	8.4
Black or African American only	16.8	17.3	15.8	14.6	14.4	14.2	14.9	15.0
Percent of poverty level[b, e]								
Below 100%	22.8	23.7	20.8	19.6	20.4	21.8	20.9	21.5
100%–199%	14.7	15.5	13.9	14.1	14.4	14.9	15.2	15.0
200%–399%	7.9	7.9	8.2	8.4	8.3	8.6	8.3	8.7
400% or more	4.9	4.7	4.1	4.5	4.7	4.3	4.3	4.3
Hispanic origin and race and percent of poverty level[b, d, e]								
Hispanic or Latino:								
Below 100%	23.6	22.7	19.9	18.7	20.2	22.1	19.2	21.0
100%–199%	18.0	16.9	13.5	15.3	15.3	16.2	15.6	14.4
200%–399%	10.3	10.1	10.0	10.3	10.3	9.7	10.3	10.8
400% or more	6.6	4.0	5.7	5.5	7.6	5.6	6.4	5.0
Not Hispanic or Latino:								
White only:								
Below 100%	21.9	22.8	19.7	18.8	20.1	20.5	20.9	21.2
100%–199%	14.0	14.8	13.3	13.4	13.8	14.6	14.8	15.0
200%–399%	7.5	7.3	7.7	7.9	7.9	8.1	7.7	8.1
400% or more	4.7	4.6	3.9	4.2	4.3	4.0	4.0	4.1
Black or African American only:								
Below 100%	25.8	27.7	25.3	23.8	23.3	25.2	23.9	24.7
100%–199%	17.0	19.3	19.2	18.2	17.6	16.6	18.3	18.5
200%–399%	12.0	11.4	12.2	11.7	11.2	11.0	11.2	10.7
400% or more	5.9	6.5	6.1	7.3	7.1	5.9	6.8	6.9

activities increased with advancing age. The Federal Interagency Forum on Aging-Related Statistics indicates that measures of disability—in terms of difficulty with basic actions such as limitations in movement or in emotional, sensory, or cognitive functioning (thinking and reasoning) associated with a health problem—were higher for women than men in the same age group.

Instrumental activities of daily living (IADLs) and measures of physical, cognitive, and social functioning are ways to assess disability and often determine whether older adults can live independently in the community. IADLs include activities such as light housework, meal preparation, doing the laundry, grocery shopping, getting around outside the home, managing money, taking

TABLE 7.1

Percentage of adults who reported their health as fair or poor, by selected characteristics, selected years 1991–2011 [CONTINUED]

[Data are based on household interviews of a sample of the civilian noninstitutionalized population]

Characteristic	1991[a]	1995[a]	1997	2000	2005	2009	2010	2011
Disability measure among adults 18 years and over[b, f]	Percent of persons with fair or poor health							
Any basic actions difficulty or complex activity limitation	—	—	27.0	27.6	28.5	30.3	28.7	30.1
Any basic actions difficulty	—	—	27.3	27.7	29.1	30.9	28.9	30.6
Any complex activity limitation	—	—	42.9	45.6	46.3	48.8	46.0	48.3
No disability	—	—	3.4	3.8	3.6	3.6	3.5	3.6
Geographic region[b]								
Northeast	8.3	9.1	8.0	7.6	7.5	8.4	7.9	8.4
Midwest	9.1	9.7	8.1	8.0	8.3	8.6	9.0	8.8
South	13.1	12.3	10.8	10.7	11.0	10.9	11.1	11.2
West	9.7	10.1	8.8	8.8	8.6	8.8	9.2	9.5
Location of residence[b]								
Within MSA[g]	9.9	10.1	8.7	8.5	8.7	9.1	9.2	9.4
Outside MSA[g]	11.9	12.6	11.1	11.1	11.2	11.2	11.9	11.7

—Data not available.

*Estimates are considered unreliable.

[a]Data prior to 1997 are not strictly comparable with data for later years due to the 1997 questionnaire redesign.

[b]Estimates are age-adjusted to the year 2000 standard population using six age groups: under 18 years, 18–44 years, 45–54 years, 55–64 years, 65–74 years, and 75 years and over. The disability measure is age-adjusted using the five adult age groups.

[c]Includes all other races not shown separately and unknown disability status.

[d]The race groups, white, black, American Indian or Alaska Native, Asian, Native Hawaiian or other Pacific Islander, and 2 or more races, include persons of Hispanic and non-Hispanic origin. Persons of Hispanic origin may be of any race. Starting with 1999 data, race-specific estimates are tabulated according to the 1997 Revisions to the Standards for the Classification of Federal Data on Race and Ethnicity and are not strictly comparable with estimates for earlier years. The five single-race categories plus multiple-race categories shown in the table conform to the 1997 Standards. Starting with 1999 data, race-specific estimates are for persons who reported only one racial group; the category 2 or more races includes persons who reported more than one racial group. Prior to 1999, data were tabulated according to the 1977 Standards with four racial groups, and the Asian only category included Native Hawaiian or Other Pacific Islander. Estimates for single-race categories prior to 1999 included persons who reported one race or, if they reported more than one race, identified one race as best representing their race. Starting with 2003 data, race responses of other race and unspecified multiple race were treated as missing, and then race was imputed if these were the only race responses. Almost all persons with a race response of other race were of Hispanic origin.

[e]Percent of poverty level is based on family income and family size and composition using U.S. Census Bureau poverty thresholds. Missing family income data were imputed for 1991 and beyond.

[f]Any basic actions difficulty or complex activity limitation is defined as having one or more of the following limitations or difficulties: movement difficulty, emotional difficulty, sensory (seeing or hearing) difficulty, cognitive difficulty, self-care (activities of daily living or instrumental activities of daily living) limitation, social limitation, or work limitation. Starting with 2007 data, the hearing question, a component of the basic actions difficulty measure, was revised. Consequently, data prior to 2007 are not comparable with data for 2007 and beyond.

[g]MSA is metropolitan statistical area. Starting with 2006 data, MSA status is determined using 2000 census data and the 2000 standards for defining MSAs.

SOURCE: "Table 50. Respondent-Assessed Health Status, by Selected Characteristics: United States, Selected Years 1991–2011," in *Health, United States, 2012: With Special Feature on Emergency Care*, National Center for Health Statistics, 2013, http://www.cdc.gov/nchs/data/hus/2012/050.pdf (accessed June 12, 2013)

medications as prescribed, and using the telephone. Non-institutionalized individuals (people who are not in the U.S. military, school, jail, or mental health facilities) are considered chronically disabled if they cannot perform one or more IADL for 90 days or longer. Measures of physical functioning, such as the ability to stoop or kneel, lift heavy objects, walk a few blocks, or reach above the head, are also used to monitor progressive disability. In 2009, 19% of men aged 65 years and older and 30% of women said they had trouble with at least one ADL. (See Figure 7.4.) Along with IADLs (which are also called basic actions), limitations or difficulties with complex activities such as working, maintaining a household, living independently, or participating in community activities increase with advancing age. Figure 7.5 shows that, overall, the prevalence of such limitations is higher for women than men.

Hospital Utilization and Physician Visits

Adults aged 65 years and older have the highest rates of inpatient hospitalization and the longest average lengths of stay (ALOS). In 2009–10 people aged 65 years and older had 3,436.1 hospital discharges per 10,000 population—nearly three times the number of discharges of adults aged 45 to 64 years. (See Table 7.2.) The highest number of discharges and the longest ALOS were among adults aged 75 to 84 years (3,982.8 and 5.7 days, respectively) and 85 years and older (5,667.7 and 5.6 days, respectively).

The ALOS for adults aged 65 years and older was 5.6 days in 2009–10, compared with 5 days for people aged 45 to 64 years. (See Table 7.2.) The ALOS among all age groups had declined since 1980, from a high of 7.5 days to 4.8 days in 2009–10. Among patients aged 75 years and older, the ALOS decreased by half, from 11.4 days in 1980 to 5.7 days in 2009–10.

Shorter stays are in part because of the federal government's introduction of diagnosis-related groups (DRG) during the mid-1980s. (DRGs are categories of illnesses that prescribe, and allow for, a set duration of treatment.) DRG-based reimbursement encourages hospitals to discharge patients as quickly as possible by

FIGURE 7.1

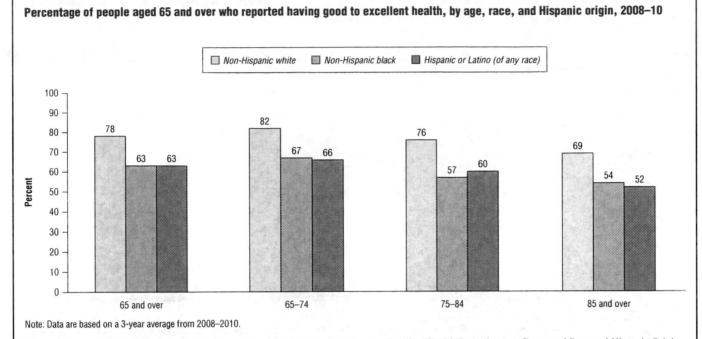

Percentage of people aged 65 and over who reported having good to excellent health, by age, race, and Hispanic origin, 2008–10

Note: Data are based on a 3-year average from 2008–2010.

SOURCE: "Percentage of People Age 65 and over with Respondent-Reported Good to Excellent Health Status by Age Group and Race and Hispanic Origin, 2008–2010," in *Older Americans 2012: Key Indicators of Well-Being*, Federal Interagency Forum on Aging-Related Statistics, June 2012,http://www .agingstats.gov/Main_Site/Data/2012_Documents/docs/EntireChartbook.pdf (accessed May 28, 2013)

FIGURE 7.2

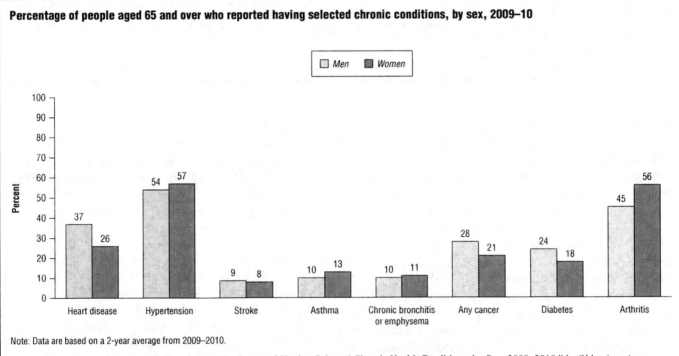

Percentage of people aged 65 and over who reported having selected chronic conditions, by sex, 2009–10

Note: Data are based on a 2-year average from 2009–2010.

SOURCE: "Percentage of People Age 65 and over Who Reported Having Selected Chronic Health Conditions, by Sex, 2009–2010," in *Older Americans 2012: Key Indicators of Well-Being*, Federal Interagency Forum on Aging-Related Statistics, June 2012, http://www.agingstats.gov/Main_Site/Data/2012_ Documents/docs/EntireChartbook.pdf (accessed May 28, 2013)

compensating hospitals for a predetermined number of days per diagnosis, regardless of the actual length of stay. Shorter lengths of stay are also attributable to the increas-ing use of outpatient settings as opposed to hospital admission for an expanding range of procedures such as hernia repairs, gallbladder removal, and cataract surgery.

FIGURE 7.3

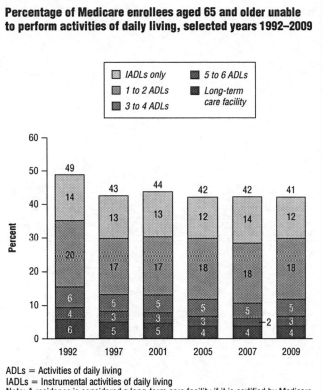

Percentage of Medicare enrollees aged 65 and older unable to perform activities of daily living, selected years 1992–2009

ADLs = Activities of daily living
IADLs = Instrumental activities of daily living
Note: A residence is considered a long-term care facility if it is certified by Medicare or Medicaid; has three or more beds, is licensed as a nursing home or other long-term care facility, and provides at least one personal care service; or provides 24-hour, 7-day-a-week supervision by a caregiver. ADL limitations refer to difficulty performing (or inability to perform for a health reason) one or more of the following tasks: bathing, dressing, eating, getting in/out of chairs, walking, or using the toilet. IADL limitations refer to difficulty performing (or inability to perform for a health reason) one or more of the following tasks: using the telephone, light housework, heavy housework, meal preparation, shopping, or managing money.

SOURCE: "Percentage of Medicare Enrollees Age 65 and over Who Have Limitations in Activities of Daily Living (ADLs) or Instrumental Activities of Daily Living (IADLs), or Who Are in a Long-Term Care Facility, Selected Years 1992–2009," in *Older Americans 2012: Key Indicators of Well-Being,* Federal Interagency Forum on Aging-Related Statistics, June 2012, http://www.agingstats.gov/Main_Site/Data/2012_Documents/docs/EntireChartbook.pdf (accessed May 28, 2013)

The growing older population also uses more physician services. Visit rates increase with age among adults aged 65 years and older and were two and a half times as high as visit rates for children under the age of 18 years in 2010. (See Table 7.3.) Although women generally make more visits than men, the gender gap practically disappears among older adults. Older adults also make more visits to primary care physicians (general and family practitioners and specialists in internal medicine) and to physician specialists. (See Table 7.4.)

CHRONIC DISEASES AND CONDITIONS

Chronic diseases are prolonged illnesses such as arthritis, asthma, heart disease, diabetes, and cancer that do not resolve spontaneously and are rarely cured. According to the Centers for Disease Control and Prevention (CDC), in "Chronic Diseases and Health Promotion" (August 13, 2012, http://www.cdc.gov/chronicdisease/overview/index.htm), chronic illnesses account for 70% of all deaths in the United States annually. In 2010 five of the seven leading causes of death among adults aged 65 years and older were chronic diseases: heart disease, malignant neoplasms (cancer), chronic lower respiratory diseases, cerebrovascular diseases (stroke), and diabetes mellitus (a condition in which there is increased sugar in the blood and urine because the body is unable to use sugar to produce energy). (See Table 7.5.) Although other chronic conditions such as arthritis, asthma, and chronic bronchitis are not immediately life threatening, they compromise the quality of life of affected individuals and place an enormous financial burden on individuals, families, and the U.S. health care system.

The prevalence of some chronic conditions such as hypertension (high blood pressure) and diabetes is increasing in the general population and among older adults. In 2009–10 more than half (55.9%) of people aged 65 years and older had hypertension and 20.5% suffered from diabetes. (See Table 7.6.) Between 1997–98 and 2009–10 the rate of diabetes increased dramatically, from 13% to 20.5%. (See Table 7.7.) The rate of hypertension also witnessed an increase during this same period, from 46.5% to 55.9%. The increase in these conditions is largely attributable to increasing rates of obesity, which is implicated in the development of these and many other chronic conditions.

Arthritis

The word *arthritis* literally means "joint inflammation," and it is applied to dozens of related diseases known as rheumatic diseases. When a joint (the point where two bones meet) becomes inflamed, swelling, redness, pain, and loss of motion occur. In the most serious forms of the disease, the loss of motion can be physically disabling.

More than 100 types of arthritis have been identified, but four major types affect large numbers of older Americans:

- Osteoarthritis—the most common type, generally affects people as they grow older. Sometimes called degenerative arthritis, it causes the breakdown of bones and cartilage (connective tissue that attaches to bones) and pain and stiffness in the fingers, knees, feet, hips, and back. In *A National Public Health Agenda for Osteoarthritis 2010* (February 2010, http://www.arthritis.org/files/images/Ad%20Council%20101/OA_Agenda_2010.pdf), the Arthritis Foundation and the CDC report that approximately 27 million Americans are affected by osteoarthritis. About half of all adults will develop symptomatic osteoarthritis

FIGURE 7.4

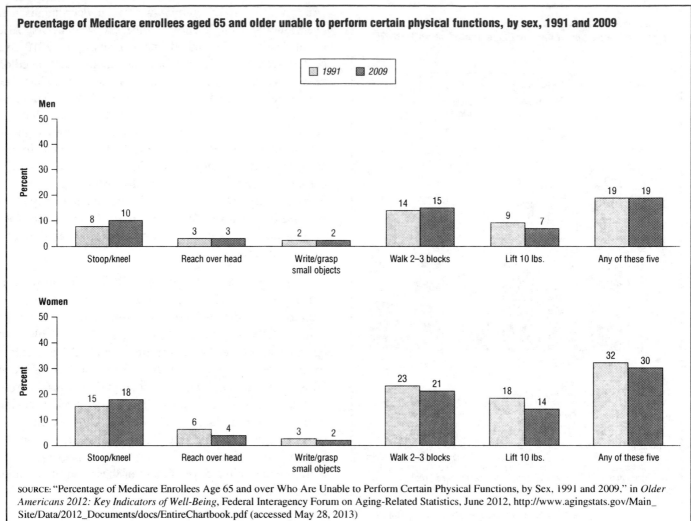

Percentage of Medicare enrollees aged 65 and older unable to perform certain physical functions, by sex, 1991 and 2009

☐ 1991   ■ 2009

Men

SOURCE: "Percentage of Medicare Enrollees Age 65 and over Who Are Unable to Perform Certain Physical Functions, by Sex, 1991 and 2009," in *Older Americans 2012: Key Indicators of Well-Being*, Federal Interagency Forum on Aging-Related Statistics, June 2012, http://www.agingstats.gov/Main_Site/Data/2012_Documents/docs/EntireChartbook.pdf (accessed May 28, 2013)

of the knee at some point during their life, and this risk increases with obesity to two of every three obese adults.

- Fibromyalgia—affects the muscles and connective tissues and causes widespread pain, as well as fatigue, sleep problems, and stiffness. Fibromyalgia also causes "tender points" that are more sensitive to pain than other areas of the body. The National Fibromyalgia Association estimates in "Fibromyalgia Fact Sheet" (2013, http://www.fmaware.org/PageServerc 145.html?pagename=fibromyalgia_fmFactSheet) that 10 million Americans suffer from this condition.

- Rheumatoid arthritis—an inflammatory form of arthritis caused by a flaw in the body's immune system. The result is inflammation and swelling in the joint lining, followed by damage to bone and cartilage in the hands, wrists, feet, knees, ankles, shoulders, or elbows. The Arthritis Foundation indicates in "What Is Rheumatoid Arthritis?" (2013, http://www.arthritis today.org/conditions/rheumatoid-arthritis/all-about-ra/

what-is-ra.php) that rheumatoid arthritis affects approximately 1.5 million Americans.

- Gout—inflammation of a joint caused by an accumulation of a natural substance, uric acid, in the joint, usually the big toe, knee, or wrist. The uric acid forms crystals in the affected joint, causing severe pain and swelling. This form affects more men than women, claiming about a million sufferers.

PREVALENCE. Arthritis is a common problem and is the leading cause of disability in the United States. In "Quick Stats on Arthritis" (August 1, 2011, http://www .cdc.gov/arthritis/resources/quickstats.htm), the CDC reports that 50 million Americans—one out of five adults—have been diagnosed with arthritis and 21 million adults have activity limitations that are attributable to the disease. The CDC predicts in "NHIS Arthritis Surveillance" (October 20, 2010, http://www.cdc.gov/arthritis/data _statistics/national_nhis.htm) that the total number of people suffering from arthritis will increase to 67 million by 2030. (See Figure 7.6.)

FIGURE 7.5

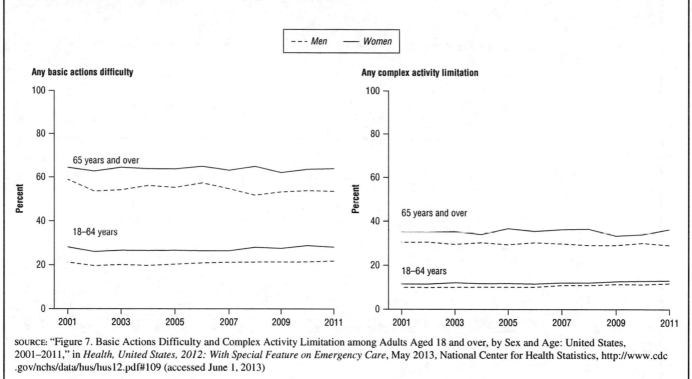

Difficulties with basic and complex actions, by age and sex, 2001–11

--- Men — Women

Any basic actions difficulty

Any complex activity limitation

SOURCE: "Figure 7. Basic Actions Difficulty and Complex Activity Limitation among Adults Aged 18 and over, by Sex and Age: United States, 2001–2011," in *Health, United States, 2012: With Special Feature on Emergency Care*, May 2013, National Center for Health Statistics, http://www.cdc.gov/nchs/data/hus/hus12.pdf#109 (accessed June 1, 2013)

Osteoporosis

Osteoporosis is a skeletal disorder characterized by compromised bone strength, which predisposes affected individuals to increased risk of fracture, especially of the hip, spine, and wrist, although any bone can be affected. The National Osteoporosis Foundation (NOF) observes in "Learn about Osteoporosis" (2013, http://www.nof.org/node/40) that although some bone loss occurs naturally with advancing age, the stooped posture (kyphosis) and loss of height (greater than 1 to 2 inches [2.5 to 5.1 cm]) that are experienced by many older adults result from vertebral fractures caused by osteoporosis.

According to the NOF, in "What Is Osteoporosis?" (2013, http://www.nof.org/articles/7), 9 million Americans have osteoporosis and another 48 million have low bone density, which means they are considered to be at risk of developing the condition. The NOF states, "Nearly 60% of adults age 50 and older are at risk of breaking a bone and should be concerned about bone health." Like other chronic conditions that disproportionately affect older adults, the prevalence of bone disease and fractures is projected to increase markedly as the population ages.

The NOF reports that one out of two women and one out of four men over the age of 50 will have an osteoporosis-related fracture in their remaining lifetime. The aging of the population and the historic lack of focus on bone health may together cause the number of fractures due to osteoporosis in the United States to exceed 3 million by 2025.

One of the goals of the treatment of osteoporosis is to maintain bone health by preventing bone loss and by building new bone. Another goal is to minimize the risk and impact of falls, because they can cause fractures. Figure 7.7 shows the pyramid of prevention and treatment of osteoporosis. At its base is nutrition (with adequate intake of calcium, vitamin D, and other minerals), physical exercise, and preventive measures to reduce the risk of falls. The second layer of the pyramid involves identifying and treating diseases that can cause osteoporosis, such as thyroid disease. The peak of the pyramid involves drug therapy for osteoporosis. There are two primary types of drugs used to treat osteoporosis. Antiresorptive agents act to reduce bone loss, and anabolic agents are drugs that build bone. Antiresorptive therapies include use of bisphosphonates, estrogen, selective estrogen receptor modulators, and calcitonin. They reduce bone loss, stabilize the architecture of the bone, and decrease bone turnover (the continuous process of remodeling in which bone is lost through resorption and new bone is formed).

Diabetes

Diabetes is a disease that affects the body's use of food, causing blood glucose (sugar levels in the blood) to

TABLE 7.2

Hospital discharges, days of care, and average length of stay, by selected characteristics, selected years 1980–2010

[Data are based on a sample of the civilian noninstitutionalized population]

Sex and age	All persons[a]			Not Hispanic or Latino						Mexican[b, c]		
				White only[b]			Black or African American only[b]					
	1988–1994	1999–2002	2007–2010	1988–1994	1999–2002	2007–2010	1988–1994	1999–2002	2007–2010	1988–1994	1999–2002	2007–2010
	Percent of population with at least one prescription drug in past 30 days											
Both sexes, age-adjusted[d]	39.1	45.2	47.5	41.1	48.7	52.8	36.9	40.1	42.3	31.7	31.7	33.9
Male	32.7	39.8	42.8	34.2	43.0	47.5	31.1	35.4	36.7	27.5	25.8	31.0
Female	45.0	50.3	52.0	47.6	54.3	57.9	41.4	43.8	46.8	36.0	37.8	37.0
Both sexes, crude	37.8	45.0	48.5	41.4	50.7	56.2	31.2	36.0	40.2	24.0	23.6	26.4
Male	30.6	38.6	43.0	33.5	43.8	50.3	25.5	30.7	33.9	20.1	18.8	23.7
Female	44.6	51.1	53.8	48.9	57.5	61.8	36.2	40.6	45.7	28.1	28.9	29.4
Under 18 years	20.5	23.8	24.0	22.9	27.0	28.1	14.8	18.5	21.7	16.1	15.8	16.8
18–44 years	31.3	35.9	38.7	34.3	41.3	47.5	27.8	28.5	28.5	21.1	19.1	19.4
45–64 years	54.8	64.1	66.2	55.5	66.1	69.7	57.5	62.3	64.2	48.1	49.3	49.7
65 years and over	73.6	84.7	89.7	74.0	85.4	90.2	74.5	81.1	89.1	67.7	72.0	86.2
Male												
Under 18 years	20.4	25.7	24.5	22.3	29.9	27.4	15.5	19.6	24.8	16.3	16.2	17.6
18–44 years	21.5	27.1	29.5	23.5	31.2	37.1	21.1	21.5	18.8	14.9	13.0	16.7
45–64 years	47.2	55.6	61.3	48.1	57.4	65.2	48.2	54.0	54.6	43.8	36.4	43.9
65 years and over	67.2	80.1	88.8	67.4	81.0	90.1	64.4	78.1	85.3	61.3	66.8	80.2
Female												
Under 18 years	20.6	21.7	23.5	23.6	24.0	28.8	14.2	17.3	18.6	16.0	15.4	16.0
18–44 years	40.7	44.6	47.6	44.7	51.7	57.6	33.4	34.2	36.7	28.1	26.2	22.8
45–64 years	62.0	72.0	70.8	62.6	74.7	74.1	64.4	69.0	72.1	52.2	62.4	55.7
65 years and over	78.3	88.1	90.4	78.8	88.8	90.2	81.3	83.1	91.5	73.0	76.3	91.1
	Percent of population with three or more prescription drugs in past 30 days											
Both sexes, age-adjusted[d]	11.8	17.8	20.8	12.4	18.9	22.4	12.6	16.5	20.7	9.0	11.2	15.0
Male	9.4	14.8	19.1	9.9	15.9	20.6	10.2	14.5	17.7	7.0	9.5	13.4
Female	13.9	20.4	22.5	14.6	21.8	24.3	14.3	18.1	22.9	11.0	12.8	16.6
Both sexes, crude	11.0	17.6	21.7	12.5	20.6	25.8	9.2	13.5	18.6	4.8	6.1	9.0
Male	8.3	13.9	19.0	9.5	16.5	22.9	7.0	10.9	15.0	3.4	4.8	7.6
Female	13.6	21.1	24.2	15.4	24.5	28.6	11.1	15.7	21.7	6.4	7.5	10.6
Under 18 years	2.4	4.1	3.8	3.2	4.9	4.0	1.5	2.5	3.9	1.2*	2.0	2.6
18–44 years	5.7	8.4	9.7	6.3	10.1	12.3	5.4	6.6	7.7	3.0	2.7	3.0*
45–64 years	20.0	30.8	34.4	20.9	31.6	36.6	21.9	31.1	36.9	16.0	20.7	24.1
65 years and over	35.3	51.8	66.6	35.0	52.6	66.8	41.2	50.3	66.7	31.3	39.5	61.6
Male												
Under 18 years	2.6	4.3	4.4	3.3	5.2	4.5	1.7	3.0	5.6	0.9*	1.9	3.1
18–44 years	3.6	6.7	7.1	4.1	8.4	9.1	4.2	4.4	5.3*	1.8*	1.7*	2.6
45–64 years	15.1	23.6	30.4	15.8	24.0	32.7	18.7	26.3	29.5	11.6	18.2	19.7
65 years and over	31.3	46.3	66.8	30.9	47.2	67.8	31.7	48.7	60.6	27.6	34.2	56.6
Female												
Under 18 years	2.3	3.9	3.1	3.0	4.7	3.6	1.2*	2.0*	2.3*	1.5*	2.2	2.1
18–44 years	7.6	10.2	12.2	8.5	11.9	15.3	6.4	8.5	9.7	4.3	4.0	3.5*
45–64 years	24.7	37.5	38.1	25.8	39.1	40.4	24.3	35.0	43.1	20.3	23.3	28.5
65 years and over	38.2	55.9	66.4	38.0	56.7	66.1	47.7	51.3	70.6	34.5	44.0	65.7

TABLE 7.2

Hospital discharges, days of care, and average length of stay, by selected characteristics, selected years 1980–2010 [CONTINUED]

[Data are based on a sample of the civilian noninstitutionalized population]

Sex and age	All persons[a]			Not Hispanic or Latino						Mexican[b,c]		
				White only[a]			Black or African American only[b]					
	1988–1994	1999–2002	2007–2010	1988–1994	1999–2002	2007–2010	1988–1994	1999–2002	2007–2010	1988–1994	1999–2002	2007–2010
	Percent of population with five or more prescription drugs in past 30 days											
Both sexes, age-adjusted[d]	4.0	7.5	10.1	4.2	7.8	10.7	3.8	7.7	10.8	2.9	4.4	7.9
Male	2.9	6.1	9.2	3.1	6.3	9.8	2.9	6.4	9.1	2.0	3.5	7.2
Female	4.9	8.7	11.0	5.1	9.2	11.6	4.5	8.7	12.0	3.7	5.2	8.7
Both sexes, crude	3.6	7.4	10.6	4.2	8.7	12.6	2.6	6.2	9.4	1.4	2.1	4.1
Male	2.5	5.6	9.1	2.9	6.6	11.0	1.8	4.8	7.5	0.9	1.6	3.4
Female	4.7	9.1	12.1	5.4	10.8	14.2	3.3	7.4	11.1	1.9	2.7	4.9
Under 18 years	*	0.8*	0.8	*	0.9*	0.9	*	*	1.0*	*	0.3*	*
18–44 years	1.2	2.3	3.1	1.4	2.5	3.9	1.0	3.2	2.2*	*	*	*
45–64 years	7.4	13.3	16.8	7.8	13.6	17.7	7.1	14.3	19.9	5.4	8.3	12.1
65 years and over	13.8	27.1	39.7	13.9	28.6	39.4	14.3	24.6	41.4	11.6	17.4	39.4
Male												
Under 18 years	*	*	0.8	*	*	*	*	*	1.6*	*	*	*
18–44 years	0.8*	1.7	2.1	0.8*	1.9	2.8*	*	1.9*	*	*	*	*
45–64 years	4.8	9.5	14.4	5.0	9.4	15.2	5.9	13.0	17.4	3.5*	5.9*	10.4
65 years and over	11.3	24.7	39.5	11.6	25.9	39.9	9.9	21.0	34.1	8.7*	15.3	36.3
Female												
Under 18 years	*	0.8*	0.7*	*	*	*	*	*	*	*	*	*
18–44 years	1.7	2.8	4.0	1.8	3.0*	4.9	1.2	4.3*	3.1*	0.6*	*	*
45–64 years	9.7	16.8	19.1	10.3	17.6	20.2	8.0	15.3	22.0	7.2*	10.8	13.9
65 years and over	15.6	28.9	39.8	15.7	30.6	39.0	17.4	27.1	46.0	14.0	19.2	41.9

*Estimates are considered unreliable.

[a]Includes persons of all races and Hispanic origins, not just those shown separately.

[b]Starting with 1999 data, race-specific estimates are tabulated according to the 1997 Revisions to the Standards for the Classification of Federal Data on Race and Ethnicity and are not strictly comparable with estimates for earlier years. The two non-Hispanic race categories shown in the table conform to the 1997 Standards. Starting with 1999 data, race-specific estimates are for persons who reported only one racial group. Prior to data year 1999, estimates were tabulated according to the 1977 Standards. Estimates for single-race categories prior to 1999 included persons who reported more than one race or, if they reported more than one race, identified one race as best representing their race.

[c]Persons of Mexican origin may be of any race.

[d]Age-adjusted to the 2000 standard population using four age groups: Under 18 years, 18–44 years, 45–64 years, and 65 years and over. Age-adjusted estimates in this table may differ from other age-adjusted estimates based on the same data and presented elsewhere if different age groups are used in the adjustment procedure.

SOURCE: "Table 94. Discharges, Days of Care, and Average Length of Stay in Nonfederal Short-Stay Hospitals, by Selected Characteristics: United States, Selected Years 1980 through 2009–2010," in Older Americans 2012: Key Indicators of Well-Being, Federal Interagency Forum on Aging-Related Statistics, June 2012, http://www.agingstats.gov/Main_Site/Data/2012_Documents/docs/EntireChartbook.pdf (accessed May 28, 2013)

TABLE 7.3

Visits to physician offices, hospital outpatient departments, and emergency departments, by age, sex and race, 1995–2010

[Data are based on reporting by a sample of office-based physicians, hospital outpatient departments, and hospital emergency departments]

Age, sex, and race	All places[a]				Physician offices			
	1995	2000	2009	2010	1995	2000	2009	2010
Age	Number of visits, in thousands							
Total	860,859	1,014,848	1,270,001	1,239,387	697,082	823,542	1,037,796	1,008,802
Under 18 years	194,644	212,165	239,590	246,228	150,351	163,459	183,999	191,500
18–44 years	285,184	315,774	341,209	342,797	219,065	243,011	257,890	261,941
45–64 years	188,320	255,894	374,775	352,001	159,531	216,783	316,395	296,385
45–54 years	104,891	142,233	190,701	171,039	88,266	119,474	158,120	140,819
55–64 years	83,429	113,661	184,074	180,962	71,264	97,309	158,275	155,566
65 years and over	192,712	231,014	314,428	298,362	168,135	200,289	279,514	258,976
65–74 years	102,605	116,505	153,884	151,075	90,544	102,447	137,452	132,201
75 years and over	90,106	114,510	160,544	147,287	77,591	97,842	142,062	126,775
	Number of visits per 100 persons							
Total, age-adjusted[b]	334	374	414	401	271	304	337	325
Total, crude	329	370	421	408	266	300	344	332
Under 18 years	275	293	322	331	213	226	247	257
18–44 years	264	291	309	310	203	224	234	237
45–64 years	364	422	475	441	309	358	401	371
45–54 years	339	385	431	388	286	323	358	320
55–64 years	401	481	532	505	343	412	457	434
65 years and over	612	706	829	767	534	612	737	666
65–74 years	560	656	749	713	494	577	669	624
75 years and over	683	766	923	831	588	654	817	715
Sex and age								
Male, age-adjusted[b]	290	325	358	350	232	261	290	283
Male, crude	277	314	356	350	220	251	289	283
Under 18 years	273	302	334	340	209	231	257	262
18–44 years	190	203	201	205	139	148	145	151
45–54 years	275	316	361	324	229	260	296	265
55–64 years	351	428	473	460	300	367	403	396
65–74 years	508	614	731	680	445	539	654	597
75 years and over	711	771	907	871	616	670	807	760
Female, age-adjusted[b]	377	420	469	452	309	345	383	367
Female, crude	378	424	483	464	310	348	397	379
Under 18 years	277	285	310	322	217	221	237	252
18–44 years	336	377	416	415	265	298	322	323
45–54 years	400	451	499	450	339	384	417	372
55–64 years	446	529	586	546	382	453	507	469
65–74 years	603	692	764	741	534	609	681	647
75 years and over	666	763	934	804	571	645	823	685
Race and age[c]								
White, age-adjusted[b]	339	380	421	408	282	315	351	336
White, crude	338	381	434	421	281	316	365	349
Under 18 years	295	306	339	341	237	243	269	270
18–44 years	267	301	312	319	211	239	244	249
45–54 years	334	386	432	389	286	330	369	326
55–64 years	397	480	531	505	345	416	466	440
65–74 years	557	641	752	727	496	568	678	642
75 years and over	689	764	936	838	598	658	835	723
Black or African American, age-adjusted[b]	309	353	459	439	204	239	314	316
Black or African American, crude	281	324	438	425	178	214	296	303
Under 18 years	193	264	315	351	100	167	198	241
18–44 years	260	257	373	339	158	149	228	222
45–54 years	387	383	486	466	281	269	329	339
55–64 years	414	495	645	617	294	373	478	481
65–74 years	553	656	821	715	429	512	667	565
75 years and over	534	745	908	845	395	568	718	682

become too high. People with diabetes can convert food to glucose, but there is a problem with insulin. In one type of diabetes (insulin-dependent diabetes, or type 1), the pancreas does not manufacture enough insulin, and in another type (noninsulin-dependent, or type 2), the body has insulin but cannot use the insulin effectively (this latter condition is called insulin resistance). When insulin is either absent or ineffective, glucose cannot get into the cells to be used for energy. Instead, the unused glucose builds up in the bloodstream and circulates through the kidneys. If the blood-glucose level rises high enough, the excess glucose "spills" over into the urine, causing

TABLE 7.3

Visits to physician offices, hospital outpatient departments, and emergency departments, by age, sex and race, 1995–2010 [CONTINUED]

[Data are based on reporting by a sample of office-based physicians, hospital outpatient departments, and hospital emergency departments]

[a]All places includes visits to physician offices and hospital outpatient and emergency departments.
[b]Estimates are age-adjusted to the year 2000 standard population using six age groups: under 18 years, 18–44 years, 45–54 years, 55–64 years, 65–74 years, and 75 years and over.
[c]Estimates by racial group should be used with caution because information on race was collected from medical records. In 2010, race data were missing and imputed for 23% of visits to physician offices, 14% of visits to hospital outpatient departments, and 11% of visits to hospital emergency departments. Starting with 1999 data, the instruction for the race item on the patient record form was changed so that more than one race could be recorded. In previous years only one race could be checked. Estimates for race in this table are for visits where only one race was recorded. Because of the small number of responses with more than one racial group checked, estimates for visits with multiple races checked are unreliable and are not presented.
Notes: Rates for 1995–2000 were computed using 1990-based postcensal estimates of the civilian noninstitutionalized population as of July 1, adjusted for net underenumeration using the 1990 National Population Adjustment Matrix from the U.S. Census Bureau. Starting with 2001 data, rates were computed using 2000-based postcensal estimates of the civilian noninstitutionalized population as of July 1. The difference between rates for 2000 computed using 1990-based on postcensal estimates and rates computed using estimates based on 2000 census counts is minimal. Rates will be overestimated to the extent that visits by institutionalized persons are counted in the numerator (for example, hospital emergency department visits by nursing home residents) and institutionalized persons are omitted from the denominator (the civilian noninstitutionalized population). Starting with *Health, United States, 2005*, data for physician offices for 2001 and beyond use a revised weighting scheme.

SOURCE: Adapted from "Table 88. Visits to Physician Offices, Hospital Outpatient Departments, and Hospital Emergency Departments, by Age, Sex, and Race: United States, Selected Years 1995–2010," in *Health, United States, 2012: With Special Feature on Emergency Care*, May 2013, National Center for Health Statistics, http://www.cdc.gov/nchs/data/hus/hus12.pdf#109 (accessed June 1, 2013)

frequent urination. This leads to an increased feeling of thirst as the body tries to compensate for the fluid that is lost through urination.

Type 2 diabetes is most often seen in adults and is the most common type of diabetes in the United States. In type 2 diabetes the pancreas produces insulin, but it is not used effectively and the body resists responding to it. Heredity is a predisposing factor in the genesis of diabetes, but because the pancreas continues to produce insulin in people suffering from type 2 diabetes, the disease is considered to be more of a problem of insulin resistance, in which the body is not using the hormone efficiently.

Complications can threaten the lives of diabetics. The healing process of the body is slowed and there is an increased risk of infection. Diabetics are at greater risk of heart disease; circulatory problems, especially in the legs, which are sometimes severe enough to require surgery or even amputation; diabetic retinopathy, a condition that can cause blindness; kidney disease that may require dialysis; and dental problems. Close attention to preventive health care, such as regular eye, dental, and foot examinations and control of blood sugar levels, can prevent or delay some of the consequences of diabetes.

The relatively recent rise in type 2 diabetes is in part attributed to rising obesity among adults. Between 1997 and 2012 the percentage of adults aged 18 years and older diagnosed with diabetes increased from 5.1% to 9.2%. (See Figure 7.8.) The NCHS indicates in *Early Release of Selected Estimates Based on Data from the January–March 2012 National Health Interview Survey* (September 2012, http://www.cdc.gov/nchs/data/nhis/earlyrelease/earlyrelease201209.pdf) that of all the adult age groups in 2012, the highest rate of diagnosed diabetes was among adults aged 65 years and older, at 20.8%. However, these rates may significantly underestimate the true prevalence of diabetes in the United States in view of National Health and Nutrition Survey findings, which show that sizable numbers of adults have undiagnosed diabetes.

Prostate Problems

Prostate problems typically occur after age 50. There are three common prostate disorders: prostatitis (inflammation of the prostate gland), benign prostatic hyperplasia (BPH; noncancerous enlargement of the prostate), and prostate cancer. Prostatitis causes painful or difficult urination and frequently occurs in younger men. According to the National Kidney and Urologic Diseases Information Clearinghouse, in "Prostate Enlargement: Benign Prostatic Hyperplasia" (March 23, 2012, http://kidney.niddk.nih.gov/kudiseases/pubs/prostateenlargement/), up to 90% of men in their 70s and 80s are believed to have some symptoms of BPH.

Prostate cancer is the second-most common cause of cancer death after lung cancer in American men and the sixth-leading cause of death of men overall. The American Cancer Society reports in *Cancer Facts and Figures, 2013* (2013, http://www.cancer.org/acs/groups/content/@epidemiologysurveilance/documents/document/acspc-036845.pdf) that an estimated 238,590 men were diagnosed with prostate cancer in 2013 and 29,720 died from it. When diagnosed and treated early, prostate cancer is generally not life threatening, because it progresses slowly and remains localized for a long time. As a result, many men who are diagnosed late in life do not die from this disease.

Urinary Incontinence

Urinary incontinence is the uncontrollable loss of urine that is so severe that it has social or hygienic consequences. In *Urological Diseases in America 2012* (April 2012, http://udaonline.net/pdf-compendium/Sections/Urologic_Diseases_in_America.4.13.12.pdf), the National Institutes of Health reports that about 50% of women aged 65 to 74 years suffer from incontinence.

TABLE 7.4

Visits to primary care physicians, by age, sex, and race, selected years 1980–2010

[Data are based on reporting by a sample of office-based physicians]

| | Type of primary care generalist physician[a] | | | | | | | | | | | |
| | All primary care generalists | | | | General and family practice | | | | Internal medicine | | | |
Age, sex, and race	1980	1990	2000	2010	1980	1990	2000	2010	1980	1990	2000	2010
Age						Percent distribution						
Total	66.2	63.6	58.9	55.2	33.5	29.9	24.1	21.1	12.1	13.8	15.3	13.9
Under 18 years	77.8	79.5	79.7	80.9	26.1	26.5	19.9	15.3	2.0	2.9	*	*
18–44 years	65.3	65.2	62.1	62.7	34.3	31.9	28.2	27.8	8.6	11.8	12.7	11.6
45–64 years	60.2	55.5	51.2	46.7	36.3	32.1	26.4	23.1	19.5	18.6	20.1	18.5
45–54 years	60.2	55.6	52.3	48.7	37.4	32.0	27.8	26.2	17.1	17.1	18.7	15.7
55–64 years	60.2	55.5	49.9	44.8	35.4	32.1	24.7	20.4	21.8	20.0	21.7	21.0
65 years and over	61.6	52.6	46.5	38.3	37.5	28.1	20.2	16.4	22.7	23.3	24.5	20.5
65–74 years	61.2	52.7	46.6	37.3	37.4	28.1	19.7	17.5	22.1	23.0	24.5	18.2
75 years and over	62.3	52.4	46.4	39.2	37.6	28.0	20.8	15.4	23.5	23.7	24.5	22.8
Sex and age												
Male:												
Under 18 years	77.3	78.1	77.7	80.1	25.6	24.1	18.3	15.7	2.0	3.0	*	*
18–44 years	50.8	51.8	51.5	51.7	38.0	35.9	34.2	33.7	11.5	15.0	14.4	16.4
45–64 years	55.6	50.6	49.4	43.7	34.4	31.0	28.7	24.4	20.5	19.2	19.8	19.1
65 years and over	58.2	51.2	43.1	36.6	35.6	27.7	19.3	16.2	22.3	23.3	23.8	20.3
Female:												
Under 18 years	78.5	81.1	82.0	81.7	26.6	29.1	21.7	14.9	2.0	2.8	*	*
18–44 years	72.1	71.3	67.2	67.9	32.5	30.0	25.3	25.0	7.3	10.3	11.9	9.4
45–64 years	63.4	58.8	52.5	48.9	37.7	32.8	24.9	22.2	18.9	18.2	20.2	18.1
65 years and over	63.9	53.5	48.9	39.6	38.7	28.3	20.9	16.7	22.9	23.3	25.0	20.5
Race and age[b]												
White:												
Under 18 years	77.6	79.2	78.5	79.6	26.4	27.1	21.2	15.6	2.0	2.3	*	*
18–44 years	64.8	64.4	61.4	61.2	34.5	31.9	29.2	27.9	8.6	10.6	11.0	11.1
45–64 years	59.6	54.2	49.3	45.2	36.0	31.5	27.3	22.8	19.2	17.6	17.1	17.5
65 years and over	61.4	51.9	45.1	37.6	36.6	27.5	20.3	16.6	23.3	23.1	23.0	19.7
Black or African American:												
Under 18 years	79.9	85.5	87.3	88.0	23.7	20.2	*	*16.5	*2.2	9.8	*	*
18–44 years	68.5	68.3	65.0	72.6	31.7	31.9	22.0	29.4	9.0	18.1	20.9	*14.0
45–64 years	66.1	61.6	61.7	57.0	38.6	31.2	23.3	26.7	22.6	26.9	35.9	24.5
65 years and over	64.6	58.6	52.8	45.2	49.0	28.9	*18.5	*18.6	14.2	28.7	33.4	*25.4

*Estimates are considered unreliable. Data preceded by an asterisk have a relative standard error (RSE) of 20%–30%. Data not shown have a RSE greater than 30%.
[a]Type of physician is based on physician's self-designated primary area of practice. Primary care generalist physicians are defined as practitioners in the fields of general and family practice, general internal medicine, general obstetrics and gynecology, and general pediatrics and exclude primary care specialists. Primary care generalists in general and family practice exclude primary care specialties, such as sports medicine and geriatrics. Primary care internal medicine physicians exclude internal medicine specialists, such as allergists, cardiologists, and endocrinologists. Primary care obstetrics and gynecology physicians exclude obstetrics and gynecology specialties, such as gynecological oncology, maternal and fetal medicine, obstetrics and gynecology critical care medicine, and reproductive endocrinology. Primary care pediatricians exclude pediatric specialists, such as adolescent medicine specialists, neonatologists, pediatric allergists, and pediatric cardiologists.
[b]Estimates by racial group should be used with caution because information on race was collected from medical records. In 2010, race data were missing and imputed for 23% of visits. Information on the race imputation process used in each data year is available in the public-use file documentation. Starting with 1999 data, the instruction for the race item on the patient record form was changed so that more than one race could be recorded. In previous years only one racial category could be checked. Estimates for racial groups presented in this table are for visits where only one race was recorded. Because of the small number of responses with more than one racial group checked, estimates for visits with multiple races checked are unreliable and are not presented.
Notes: This table presents data on visits to physician offices and excludes visits to other sites, such as hospital outpatient and emergency departments. In 1980, the survey excluded Alaska and Hawaii. Data for all other years include all 50 states and the District of Columbia. Visits with specialty of physician unknown are excluded. Starting with *Health, United States, 2005*, data for 2001 and later years for physician offices use a revised weighting scheme.
SOURCE: Adapted from "Table 89. Visits to Primary Care Generalist and Specialty Care Physicians, by Selected Characteristics and Type of Physician: United States, Selected Years 1980–2010," in *Health, United States, 2012: With Special Feature on Emergency Care*, 2013, National Center for Health Statistics, http://www.cdc.gov/nchs/data/hus/hus12.pdf#109 (accessed June 1, 2013)

The problem is more common in women than in men, although it affects men of all ages. Urinary incontinence can lead to many complications. For example, if untreated it increases the risk of developing serious bladder and kidney infections, skin rashes, and pressure sores.

Age-related changes affect the ability to control urination. The maximum capacity of urine that the bladder can hold diminishes, as does the ability to postpone urination when a person feels the urge to urinate. As a person ages, the rate of urine flow out of the bladder and through the urethra slows, and the volume of urine remaining in the bladder after urination is finished increases. In women the urethra shortens and its lining becomes thinner as the level of estrogen declines during menopause, decreasing the ability of the urinary sphincter to close tightly. Among older men, the prostate gland enlarges, sometimes blocking the flow of urine through the urethra.

TABLE 7.5

Leading causes of death and numbers of deaths, by age, 1980 and 2010

[Data are based on death certificates]

Age and rank order	1980 Cause of death	Deaths	2010 Cause of death	Deaths
25–44 years				
Rank	All causes	108,658	All causes	112,292
1	Unintentional injuries	26,722	Unintentional injuries	29,365
2	Malignant neoplasms	17,551	Malignant neoplasms	15,428
3	Diseases of heart	14,513	Diseases of heart	13,816
4	Homicide	10,983	Suicide	12,306
5	Suicide	9,855	Homicide	6,731
6	Chronic liver disease and cirrhosis	4,782	Chronic liver disease and cirrhosis	2,910
7	Cerebrovascular diseases	3,154	Human immunodeficiency virus (HIV) disease	2,639
8	Diabetes mellitus	1,472	Cerebrovascular diseases	2,421
9	Pneumonia and influenza	1,467	Diabetes mellitus	2,395
10	Congenital anomalies	817	Influenza and pneumonia	1,158
45–64 years				
Rank	All causes	425,338	All causes	494,009
1	Diseases of heart	148,322	Malignant neoplasms	159,712
2	Malignant neoplasms	135,675	Diseases of heart	104,806
3	Cerebrovascular diseases	19,909	Unintentional injuries	33,690
4	Unintentional injuries	18,140	Chronic lower respiratory diseases	18,694
5	Chronic liver disease and cirrhosis	16,089	Chronic liver disease and cirrhosis	18,415
6	Chronic obstructive pulmonary diseases	11,514	Diabetes mellitus	17,287
7	Diabetes mellitus	7,977	Cerebrovascular diseases	16,603
8	Suicide	7,079	Suicide	15,183
9	Pneumonia and influenza	5,804	Nephritis, nephrotic syndrome and nephrosis	7,304
10	Homicide	4,019	Septicemia	6,937
65 years and over				
Rank	All causes	1,341,848	All causes	1,798,276
1	Diseases of heart	595,406	Diseases of heart	477,338
2	Malignant neoplasms	258,389	Malignant neoplasms	396,670
3	Cerebrovascular diseases	146,417	Chronic lower respiratory diseases	118,031
4	Pneumonia and influenza	45,512	Cerebrovascular diseases	109,990
5	Chronic obstructive pulmonary diseases	43,587	Alzheimer's disease	82,616
6	Atherosclerosis	28,081	Diabetes mellitus	49,191
7	Diabetes mellitus	25,216	Influenza and pneumonia	42,846
8	Unintentional injuries	24,844	Nephritis, nephrotic syndrome and nephrosis	41,994
9	Nephritis, nephrotic syndrome, and nephrosis	12,968	Unintentional injuries	41,300
10	Chronic liver disease and cirrhosis	9,519	Septicemia	26,310

SOURCE: Adapted from "Table 23. Leading Causes of Death and Numbers of Deaths, by Age: United States, 1980 and 2010," in *Health, United States, 2012: With Special Feature on Emergency Care*, 2013, National Center for Health Statistics, http://www.cdc.gov/nchs/data/hus/hus12.pdf#109 (accessed June 1, 2013)

Although urinary incontinence is common, highly treatable, and frequently curable, it is underdiagnosed and often untreated because sufferers do not seek treatment. Many older adults are fearful, embarrassed, or incorrectly assume that incontinence is a normal consequence of growing old. The disorder exacts a serious emotional toll—sufferers are often homebound, isolated, or depressed and are more likely to report their health as fair to poor than their peers. Urinary incontinence may lead to institutionalization, because many of those afflicted have some activity limitations and because incontinence is difficult for caregivers to manage.

Malnutrition

The older population is vulnerable to nutrition-related health problems. As people age, their energy needs decline, and it is vital for them to consume nutrient-dense foods in a lower calorie diet. According to the National Resource Center on Nutrition, Physical Activity, and Aging, in "Malnutrition and Older Americans" (2013, http://nutritionandaging.fiu.edu/aging_network/malfact2.asp), 35% to 50% of older adults in long-term care facilities and up to 65% of older adults in hospitals are at risk for malnutrition. Concerning homebound older adults, an estimated 1 million are also at risk for malnutrition.

Older adults' nutrition may be affected by many factors, including loneliness, depression, a cognitive disorder, poor appetite, or a lack of transportation. An older adult may forgo meal preparation when there is no longer someone else to cook for or eat with; and a bereaved or frail older adult may not have the stamina or motivation to shop or cook. Malnutrition may also be the result of poverty. When faced with fixed incomes and competing needs, older adults may be forced to choose between buying food or the prescription medications they need.

TABLE 7.6

Percentage of people aged 65 and over who reported having selected chronic conditions, by sex, race, and Hispanic origin, 2009–10

	Heart disease	Hypertension	Stroke	Asthma	Chronic bronchitis or emphysema	Any cancer	Diabetes	Arthritis
Total	**30.4**	**55.9**	**8.6**	**11.3**	**10.3**	**24.0**	**20.5**	**51.2**
Men	36.9	54.1	9.1	9.7	9.6	27.6	23.5	44.8
Women	25.5	57.2	8.2	12.5	10.8	21.2	18.2	56.1
Non-Hispanic white	32.1	54.2	8.5	11.3	10.9	26.9	18.0	52.6
Non-Hispanic black	25.1	69.2	11.7	11.5	8.4	13.9	31.6	51.0
Hispanic	22.2	57.2	7.2	11.1	7.1	10.4	32.5	43.8

Note: Data are based on a two-year average from 2009–10.

SOURCE: "Table 16a. Percentage of People Age 65 and over Who Reported Having Selected Chronic Health Conditions, by Sex and Race and Hispanic Origin, 2009–2010," in *Older Americans 2012: Key Indicators of Well-Being*, Federal Interagency Forum on Aging-Related Statistics, June 2012, http://www .agingstats.gov/Main_Site/Data/2012_Documents/docs/EntireChartbook.pdf (accessed May 28, 2013)

TABLE 7.7

Percentage of people aged 65 and over who reported having selected chronic conditions, selected years 1997–2010

Year	Heart disease	Hypertension	Stroke	Emphysema	Asthma	Chronic bronchitis	Any cancer	Diabetes	Arthritis
1997–1998	32.3	46.5	8.2	5.2	7.7	6.4	18.7	13.0	—
1999–2000	29.8	47.4	8.2	5.2	7.4	6.2	19.9	13.7	—
2001–2002	31.5	50.2	8.9	5.0	8.3	6.1	20.8	15.4	—
2003–2004	31.8	51.9	9.3	5.2	8.9	6.0	20.7	16.9	50.0
2005–2006	30.9	53.3	9.3	5.7	10.6	6.1	21.1	18.0	49.5
2007–2008	31.9	55.7	8.8	5.1	10.4	5.4	22.5	18.6	49.5
2009–2010	30.4	55.9	8.6	6.2	11.3	6.2	24.0	20.5	51.2

— Not available.
Note: Data are based on two-year averages.

SOURCE: "Table 16b. Percentage of People Age 65 and over Who Reported Having Selected Chronic Health Conditions, 1997–1998 through 2009–2010," in *Older Americans 2012: Key Indicators of Well-Being*, Federal Interagency Forum on Aging-Related Statistics, June 2012, http://www.agingstats.gov/Main_Site/ Data/2012_Documents/docs/EntireChartbook.pdf (accessed May 28, 2013)

FIGURE 7.6

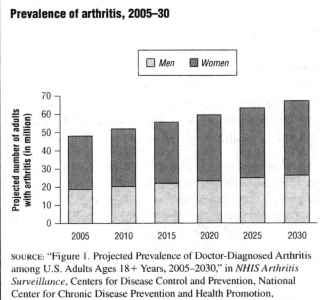

Prevalence of arthritis, 2005–30

☐ Men ☑ Women

Projected number of adults with arthritis (in million)

SOURCE: "Figure 1. Projected Prevalence of Doctor-Diagnosed Arthritis among U.S. Adults Ages 18+ Years, 2005–2030," in *NHIS Arthritis Surveillance*, Centers for Disease Control and Prevention, National Center for Chronic Disease Prevention and Health Promotion, October 20, 2010, http://www.cdc.gov/arthritis/data_statistics/national_ nhis.htm#disability (accessed June 14, 2013)

Hearing Loss

There are many causes of hearing loss, the most common being age-related changes in the ear's mechanism. Hearing loss is a common problem among older adults and can seriously compromise quality of life. People suffering from hearing loss may withdraw from social contact and are sometimes misdiagnosed as cognitively impaired or mentally ill. In 2010, 46% of older men and 31% of older women reported having trouble hearing. (See Figure 7.9.)

In "Hearing Loss Prevalence and Risk Factors among Older Adults in the United States" (*Journals of Gerontology, Series A: Biological Sciences and Medical Sciences*, vol. 66, no. 5, May 2011), Frank R. Lin et al. analyze the relationship between hearing loss and cognitive and functional decline (diminished abilities to think, reason, and perform the ADLs). The researchers find that hearing loss is associated with an increased risk of cognitive decline in older adults. Lin et al. report in "Hearing Loss and Incident Dementia" (*Archives of Neurology*, vol. 68, no. 2, February 2011) a relationship between

FIGURE 7.7

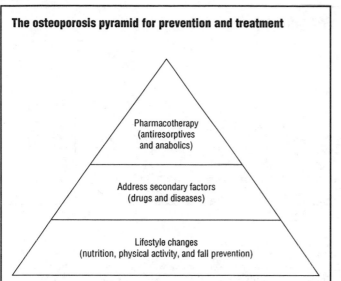

The osteoporosis pyramid for prevention and treatment

Pharmacotherapy
(antiresorptives
and anabolics)

Address secondary factors
(drugs and diseases)

Lifestyle changes
(nutrition, physical activity, and fall prevention)

Note:

The base of the pyramid: The first step in the prevention and treatment of osteoporosis and the prevention of fractures is to build a foundation of nutrition and lifestyle measures that maximize bone health. The diet should not only be adequate in calcium and vitamin D, but should have a healthy balance of other nutrients. A weight-bearing exercise program should be developed. Cigarette smoking and excessive alcohol use must be avoided. In the older individual, at high risk for fractures, the changes in lifestyle would include a plan not only to maximize physical activity, but also to minimize the risk of falls. The use of hip protectors can be considered in some high-risk patients. Diseases that increase the risk of falls by causing visual impairment, postural hypotension (a drop in blood pressure on standing, which leads to dizziness), or poor balance should be treated. Drugs that cause bone loss or increase the risk of falls should be avoided or given at the lowest effective dose.

The second level of the pyramid: The next step is to identify and treat diseases that produce secondary osteoporosis or aggravate primary osteoporosis. These measures are the foundation upon which specific pharmacotherapy is built and should never be forgotten.

The third level of the pyramid: If there is sufficiently high risk of fracture to warrant pharmacotherapy, the patient is usually started on antiresorptives. Anabolic agents are used in individuals in whom antiresorptive therapy is not adequate to prevent bone loss or fractures.

SOURCE: "Figure 9-1. The Osteoporosis Pyramid for Prevention and Treatment," in *Bone Health and Osteoporosis: A Report of the Surgeon General*, U.S. Department of Health and Human Services, Public Health Service, Office of the Surgeon General, October 14, 2004, http://www.surgeongeneral.gov/library/reports/bonehealth/chapter_9 .html (accessed June 14, 2013)

hearing loss and Alzheimer's disease. The researchers find that mild hearing loss is associated with a slight increase in the risk of Alzheimer's and that the worse the hearing loss, the greater the risk for Alzheimer's. It is not yet known whether hearing loss is a marker or an early indicator of Alzheimer's disease, or whether correcting hearing loss might serve to prevent the onset of Alzheimer's.

Dane J. Genther et al. note in "Association of Hearing Loss with Hospitalization and Burden of Disease in Older Adults" (*Journal of the American Medical Association*, vol. 309, no. 22, June 12, 2013) that nearly two out of every three adults aged 70 years and older suffer from hearing loss and that the incidence markedly increases with advancing age. Because hearing loss is associated with poorer cognitive and physical functioning, the researchers wanted to determine if hearing loss can also be associated with other health and economic outcomes such as hospitalization. Genther et al. find that compared with older adults with normal hearing, those with hearing loss were more likely to have risk factors for heart disease and stroke and were more likely to have been hospitalized during the prior year—18.7% and 23.8%, respectively. Those with hearing loss also had more hospitalizations.

There is an expanding array of devices and services to mitigate the effects of hearing loss. Hearing-impaired people may benefit from high-tech hearing aids, amplifiers for doorbells and telephones, infrared amplifiers, and even companion dogs that are trained to respond to sounds for their owner.

Vision Changes

Almost no one escapes age-related changes in vision. Over time it becomes increasingly difficult to read small print or thread a needle at the usual distance. For many older adults, night vision declines. This is often caused by a condition called presbyopia (tired eyes) and is a common occurrence. People who were previously nearsighted may actually realize some improvement in eyesight as they become slightly farsighted. In 2010, 13% of men and 15% of women aged 65 years and older reported vision problems. (See Figure 7.9.)

Major Eye Diseases

Cataracts, glaucoma, age-related macular degeneration, and diabetic retinopathy are the leading causes of vision impairment and blindness in older adults. Cataracts are the leading cause of blindness in the world. Glaucoma is a chronic disease that often requires lifelong treatment to control. Age-related macular degeneration is the most common cause of blindness and vision impairment in Americans aged 60 years and older. Diabetic retinopathy is a common complication of diabetes and is considered to be a leading cause of blindness in the industrialized world.

CATARACTS. A cataract is an opacity, or clouding, of the naturally clear lens of the eye. The prevalence of cataracts increases dramatically with age and most develop slowly over time as they progressively compromise vision. Once a clouded lens develops, surgery to remove the affected lens and replace it with an artificial lens is the recommended treatment. The AARP reports in "Eye Diseases of the Aging—Symptoms, Causes and Treatments" (2013, http://www.aarp.org/health/conditions-treatments/info-05-2013/eye-diseases-of-aging.html) that cataracts affect nearly 25 million Americans over the

FIGURE 7.8

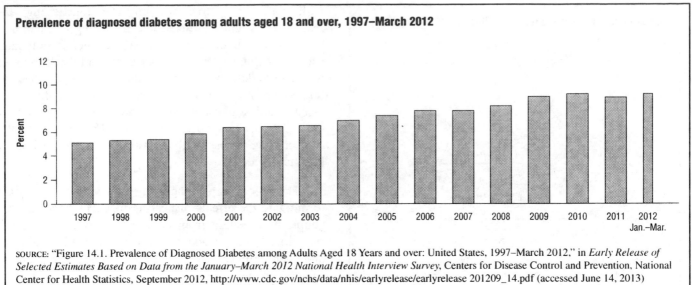

Prevalence of diagnosed diabetes among adults aged 18 and over, 1997–March 2012

SOURCE: "Figure 14.1. Prevalence of Diagnosed Diabetes among Adults Aged 18 Years and over: United States, 1997–March 2012," in *Early Release of Selected Estimates Based on Data from the January–March 2012 National Health Interview Survey*, Centers for Disease Control and Prevention, National Center for Health Statistics, September 2012, http://www.cdc.gov/nchs/data/nhis/earlyrelease/earlyrelease 201209_14.pdf (accessed June 14, 2013)

FIGURE 7.9

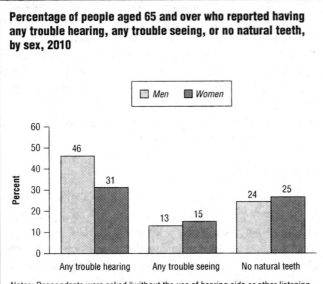

Percentage of people aged 65 and over who reported having any trouble hearing, any trouble seeing, or no natural teeth, by sex, 2010

Notes: Respondents were asked "without the use of hearing aids or other listening devices, is your hearing excellent, good, a little trouble hearing, moderate trouble, a lot of trouble, or are you deaf?" For the purposes of this indicator, the category "Any trouble hearing" includes: "a little trouble hearing, moderate trouble, a lot of trouble, and deaf." Regarding their vision, respondents were asked "Do you have any trouble seeing, even when wearing glasses or contact lenses?" The category "Any trouble seeing" includes those who responded yes or in a subsequent question report themselves as blind. Lastly, respondents were asked in one question, "Have you lost all of your upper and lower natural (permanent) teeth?"

SOURCE: "Percentage of People Age 65 and over Who Reported Having Any Trouble Hearing, Trouble Seeing, or No Natural Teeth, by Sex, 2010," in *Older Americans 2012: Key Indicators of Well-Being*, Federal Interagency Forum on Aging-Related Statistics, June 2012, http://www.agingstats.gov/Main_Site/Data/2012_Documents/Docs/EntireChartbook.pdf (accessed May 28, 2013)

information from the eye to the brain. The loss of vision is not experienced until a significant amount of nerve damage has occurred. Because the onset is gradual, as many as half of all people with glaucoma are unaware that they have the disease. In "Vision Problems in the U.S." (2012, http://www.visionproblemsus.org), Prevent Blindness America indicates that in 2010 glaucoma affected approximately 2.7 million Americans over the age of 40 years.

Routine glaucoma testing is especially important for older people. There is no cure for glaucoma and no way to restore lost vision; however, medication can generally manage the condition. At later stages, laser therapy and surgery are effective in preventing further damage.

AGE-RELATED MACULAR DEGENERATION. Age-related macular degeneration (AMD) is a condition in which the macula, a specialized part of the retina that is responsible for sharp central and reading vision, is damaged. Symptoms include blurred vision, a dark spot in the center of the vision field, and vertical line distortion. Prevent Blindness America notes in "Vision Problems in the U.S." that in 2010 nearly 2.1 million adults aged 50 years and older had the advanced form of the condition.

In "Forecasting Age-Related Macular Degeneration through the Year 2050: The Potential Impact of New Treatments" (*Archives of Ophthalmology*, vol. 127, no. 4, April 2009), David B. Rein et al. predict that the prevalence of early AMD will increase substantially, from 9.1 million in 2010 to 17.8 million in 2050.

DIABETIC RETINOPATHY. Diabetic retinopathy occurs when the small blood vessels in the retina become blocked, break down, leak fluid that distorts vision, and

age of 40 years and more than half of Americans aged 65 years and older.

GLAUCOMA. Glaucoma is a disease that causes gradual damage to the optic nerve, which carries visual

sometimes release blood into the center of the eye, causing blindness. Photocoagulation (laser treatment) can help reduce the risk of loss of vision in advanced cases. The disorder is a leading cause of blindness, but is less common among older adults than other types of visual impairment. According to Prevent Blindness America, in "Vision Problems in the U.S.," in 2010 diabetic retinopathy affected 7.7 million Americans aged 40 years and older. The prevalence of diabetic retinopathy increases with age, reflecting the higher rates of diabetes in older people.

Oral Health Problems

According to the CDC, in "Oral Health—Preventing Cavities, Gum Disease, Tooth Loss, and Oral Cancers: At a Glance 2011" (July 29, 2011, http://www.cdc.gov/chronicdisease/resources/publications/AAG/doh.htm), one-fourth of adults aged 65 years and older have lost all their teeth. Figure 7.9 shows that in 2010, 24% of men and 25% of women aged 65 years and older had no natural teeth. For people aged 85 years and older, 32.5% had none of their teeth in 2010. (See Table 7.8.) Older adults living in poverty (42.3%) were nearly twice as likely to have lost their teeth than those living above poverty (21.6%).

Parkinson's Disease

According to the Parkinson's Disease Foundation, in "Statistics on Parkinson's" (2013, www.pdf.org/en/parkinson_statistics), Parkinson's disease (PD) affects about 1 million people in the United States. An estimated 60,000 people in the United States are diagnosed with PD each year and thousands of others have the disease but are not diagnosed. The incidence of PD increases with advancing age—just 4% of cases are diagnosed in people under the age of 50 years. In "Movement Disorders" (*Medical Clinics of North America*, vol. 93, no. 2, March 2009), Meghan K. Harris et al. observe that the prevalence of PD is 1% to 2% in the population aged 65 years and older and up to 4% in individuals older than 85. PD usually begins during the 70s, but up to 10% of those affected are aged 50 years and younger.

PD is caused by the death of about half a million brain cells in the basal ganglia. These cells secrete dopamine, a neurotransmitter (chemical messenger), whose function is to allow nerve impulses to move smoothly from one nerve cell to another. These nerve cells, in turn, transmit messages to the muscles of the body to begin movement. When the normal supply of dopamine is reduced, the messages are not sent correctly, and the symptoms—mild tremor (shaking), change in walking, or a decreased arm swing—of PD begin to appear.

The four early warning signs of PD are tremors, muscle stiffness, unusual slowness (bradykinesia), and a stooped posture. Medications can control initial symptoms, but over time they become less effective. As the disease worsens, patients develop more severe tremors, causing them to fall or jerk uncontrollably. (The jerky body movements PD patients experience are called dyskinesias.) At other times, rigidity sets in, rendering them unable to move. About one-third of patients also develop dementia (loss of intellectual functioning accompanied by memory loss and personality changes).

TREATMENT OF PARKINSON'S DISEASE. Management of PD is individualized and includes drug therapy and daily exercise. Exercise can often lessen the rigidity of muscles, prevent weakness, and improve the ability to walk.

The main goal of drug treatment is to restore the chemical balance between dopamine and another neurotransmitter, acetylcholine. Most patients are given levodopa (L-dopa), a compound that the body converts into dopamine. Treatment with L-dopa does not, however, slow the progressive course of the disease or even delay the changes in the brain PD produces, and it may produce some unpleasant side effects such as dyskinesias.

TABLE 7.8

Percentage of people aged 65 and over who reported having any trouble hearing, any trouble seeing, or no natural teeth, by selected characteristics, 2010

Sex, age, and poverty status	Any trouble hearing	Any trouble seeing	No natural teeth
Both sexes			
65 and over	37.5	14.0	24.3
65–74	31.2	12.2	19.3
75–84	40.3	13.8	29.8
85 and over	58.6	22.5	32.5
Below poverty	31.4	24.0	42.3
Above poverty	37.5	13.1	21.6
Men			
65 and over	46.1	12.7	23.5
65–74	41.0	10.5	18.4
75–84	50.8	14.6	30.0
85 and over	61.7	19.5	33.4
Women			
65 and over	30.9	14.9	24.9
65–74	22.8	13.6	20.0
75–84	32.4	13.2	29.6
85 and over	57.1	23.9	32.1

Note: Respondents were asked "without the use of hearing aids or other listening devices, is your hearing excellent, good, a little trouble hearing, moderate trouble, a lot of trouble, or are you deaf?" For the purposes of this indicator, the category "Any trouble hearing" includes: "a little trouble hearing, moderate trouble, a lot of trouble, and deaf."
Regarding their vision, respondents were asked "Do you have any trouble seeing, even when wearing glasses or contact lenses?" The category "Any trouble seeing" includes those who responded yes or in a subsequent question report themselves as blind. Lastly, respondents were asked in one question, "Have you lost all of your upper and lower natural (permanent) teeth?"

SOURCE: "Table 17a. Percentage of People Age 65 and over Who Reported Having Any Trouble Hearing, Trouble Seeing, or No Natural Teeth, by Selected Characteristics, 2010," in *Older Americans 2012: Key Indicators of Well-Being*, Federal Interagency Forum on Aging-Related Statistics, June 2012, http://www.agingstats.gov/Main_Site/Data/2012_Documents/docs/EntireChartbook.pdf (accessed May 28, 2013)

INFECTIOUS DISEASES

Infectious (contagious) diseases are caused by microorganisms (viruses, bacteria, parasites, or fungi) that are transmitted from one person to another through casual contact, such as with the transmittal of influenza; through bodily fluids, such as with the transmittal of HIV; or from contaminated food, air, or water supplies. The CDC reports that in 2010 influenza and pneumonia remained among the top-10 causes of death for older adults, responsible for 42,846 deaths of people aged 65 years and older. (See Table 7.5.) Influenza-related deaths can result from pneumonia as well as from exacerbation of chronic diseases.

Influenza

Influenza (flu) is a contagious respiratory disease caused by a virus. The virus is expelled by an infected individual in droplets into the air and may be inhaled by anyone nearby. It can also be transmitted by direct hand contact. The flu primarily affects the lungs, but the whole body experiences symptoms. Influenza is an acute (short-term) illness characterized by fever, chills, weakness, loss of appetite, and aching muscles in the head, back, arms, and legs. The accompanying fever rises quickly—sometimes reaching 104 degrees Fahrenheit (40 degrees Celsius)—but usually subsides after two or three days. Influenza leaves the patient exhausted.

For healthy individuals, the flu is typically a moderately severe illness, but for older people who are not in good general health, the flu can be severe and even fatal. Complications such as secondary bacterial infections may develop, taking advantage of the body's weakened condition and lowered resistance. The most common bacterial complication is pneumonia, affecting the lungs, but sinuses, bronchi (larger air passages of the lungs), and inner ears can also become secondarily infected. Less common but serious complications include viral pneumonia, encephalitis (inflammation of the brain), acute renal (kidney) failure, and nervous system disorders. These complications can be fatal.

Influenza can be prevented by inoculation with a current influenza vaccine, which is formulated annually to contain the influenza viruses expected to cause the flu the upcoming year. Immunization produces antibodies to the influenza viruses, which become most effective after one or two months. The CDC advises that older adults get flu shots early in the fall, because peak flu activity usually occurs around the beginning of the new calendar year. In 2010, 66% of non-Hispanic white, 54% of Hispanic, and 52% of non-Hispanic African American older adults reported receiving influenza shots within the past 12 months. (See Figure 7.10.) In "Seasonal Flu Shot: Questions & Answers" (July 16, 2012, http://www.cdc.gov/flu/about/

FIGURE 7.10

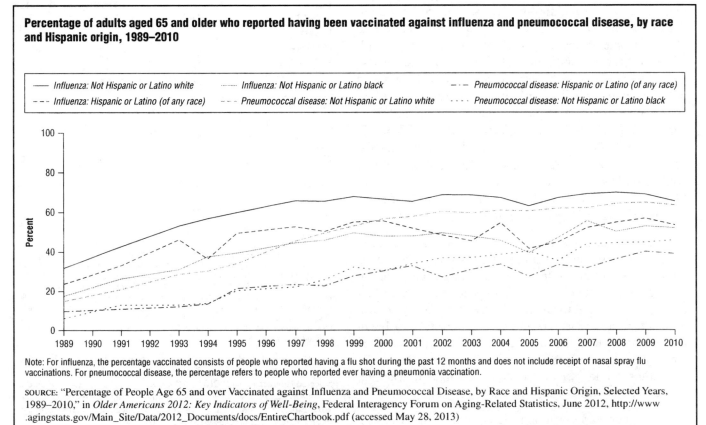

Percentage of adults aged 65 and older who reported having been vaccinated against influenza and pneumococcal disease, by race and Hispanic origin, 1989–2010

Note: For influenza, the percentage vaccinated consists of people who reported having a flu shot during the past 12 months and does not include receipt of nasal spray flu vaccinations. For pneumococcal disease, the percentage refers to people who reported ever having a pneumonia vaccination.

SOURCE: "Percentage of People Age 65 and over Vaccinated against Influenza and Pneumococcal Disease, by Race and Hispanic Origin, Selected Years, 1989–2010," in *Older Americans 2012: Key Indicators of Well-Being*, Federal Interagency Forum on Aging-Related Statistics, June 2012, http://www .agingstats.gov/Main_Site/Data/2012_Documents/docs/EntireChartbook.pdf (accessed May 28, 2013)

qa/flushot.htm), the CDC asserts that adults aged 65 years and older are at high risk of developing serious complications such as pneumonia should they contract the flu.

Pneumonia

Pneumonia is a serious lung infection. Symptoms of pneumonia are fever, chills, cough, shortness of breath, chest pain, and increased sputum production. Pneumonia may be caused by viruses, bacteria, or fungi; the pneumococcus bacterium, however, is the most important cause of serious pneumonia.

Older adults are two to three times more likely than other adults to develop pneumococcal infections. A single vaccination can prevent most cases of pneumococcal pneumonia. The CDC recommends that all people aged 65 years and older receive the pneumonia vaccine, and since 1998 an increasing proportion of the older population reports having been vaccinated. (See Figure 7.10.) In 2010, 64% of non-Hispanic white, 46% of non-Hispanic African American, and 39% of Hispanic older adults had received a pneumococcal vaccination.

MANDATORY IMMUNIZATION FOR NURSING HOME RESIDENTS. Nursing home residents are required to be immunized against influenza and pneumonia; nursing homes that fail to enforce this requirement risk losing reimbursement from the Medicare (a medical insurance program for older adults and people with disabilities) and Medicaid (a federal and state health care program for people below the poverty level) programs. The regulation, which was issued by the Centers for Medicare and Medicaid Services in August 2005, intends to ensure that the most vulnerable older adults receive their flu and pneumococcal vaccinations. People aged 65 years and older are among the most vulnerable, especially those in the close quarters of nursing homes, where infection can spread more easily.

DISABILITY IN THE OLDER POPULATION

Americans are not only living longer but also are developing fewer chronic diseases and disabilities. The current cohort (a group of individuals that shares a common characteristic such as birth years and is studied over time) of older Americans are defying the stereotype that aging is synonymous with increasing disability and dependence.

In "Recent Declines in Chronic Disability in the Elderly U.S. Population: Risk Factors and Future Dynamics" (*Annual Review of Public Health*, vol. 29, April 2008), Kenneth G. Manton of Duke University reports on data from the 1982 and 2004–05 National Long-Term Care Surveys, which surveyed approximately 20,000 Medicare enrollees. Manton notes that the proportion of Americans aged 65 years and older with a chronic disability significantly declined about 2.2% per year during this period due to improved nutrition, sanitation, and education. However, he cautions that obesity may threaten the downward trend in disability because it increases the risk of developing potentially disabling chronic diseases such as heart disease, type 2 diabetes, high blood pressure, stroke, and osteoarthritis. Among adults aged 65 to 74 years, the percentage of obese men increased from 24% in 1988–94 to 43% in 2009–10. (See Figure 7.11.) Likewise, the

FIGURE 7.11

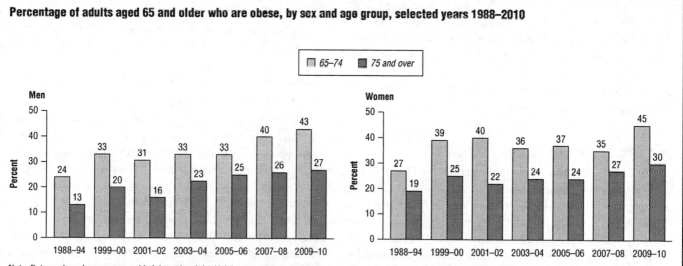

Percentage of adults aged 65 and older who are obese, by sex and age group, selected years 1988–2010

Note: Data are based on a measured height and weight. Height was measured without shoes. Obese is defined by a body mass index (BMI) of 30 kilograms/meter² or greater. The percentage of people who are obese is a subset of the percentage of those who are overweight.

SOURCE: "Percentage of Population Age 65 and over Who Are Obese, by Sex and Age Group, Selected Years, 1988–2010," in *Older Americans 2012: Key Indicators of Well-Being*, Federal Interagency Forum on Aging-Related Statistics, June 2012, http://www.agingstats.gov/Main_Site/Data/2012_Documents/docs/EntireChartbook.pdf (accessed May 28, 2013)

FIGURE 7.12

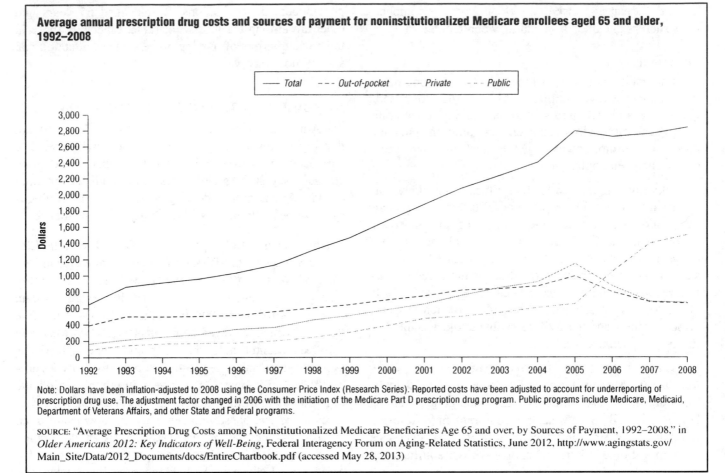

Average annual prescription drug costs and sources of payment for noninstitutionalized Medicare enrollees aged 65 and older, 1992–2008

Note: Dollars have been inflation-adjusted to 2008 using the Consumer Price Index (Research Series). Reported costs have been adjusted to account for underreporting of prescription drug use. The adjustment factor changed in 2006 with the initiation of the Medicare Part D prescription drug program. Public programs include Medicare, Medicaid, Department of Veterans Affairs, and other State and Federal programs.

SOURCE: "Average Prescription Drug Costs among Noninstitutionalized Medicare Beneficiaries Age 65 and over, by Sources of Payment, 1992–2008," in *Older Americans 2012: Key Indicators of Well-Being*, Federal Interagency Forum on Aging-Related Statistics, June 2012, http://www.agingstats.gov/Main_Site/Data/2012_Documents/docs/EntireChartbook.pdf (accessed May 28, 2013)

percentage of obese women rose from 27% to 45% during the same period.

Manton's concern that obesity would reverse the downward trend in disability has become reality. Toby A. White and Elena A. Erosheva find in "Using Group-Based Latent Class Transition Models to Analyze Chronic Disability Data from the National Long-Term Care Survey 1984–2004" (*Statistics in Medicine*, April 1, 2013) that the declines in chronic disability observed at the end of the 20th century have not continued in the 21st century.

DRUG USE AMONG OLDER ADULTS

According to the National Institute on Drug Abuse, in *Prescription Drugs: Abuse and Addiction* (October 2011, http://www.drugabuse.gov/sites/default/files/rrprescription.pdf), although adults aged 65 years and older make up 13% of the population, they account for approximately one-third of all medications that are prescribed in the United States.

Prescription drug costs have skyrocketed since the early 1990s. In 2008 the average cost per person was $2,834. (See Figure 7.12.) Out-of-pocket costs for prescription drugs have increased, creating serious financial hard-

ships for many older adults. The American Federation of State, County, and Municipal Employees indicates in "Affordable Prescription Drugs" (June 2012, http://www.afscme.org/members/conventions/resolutions-and-amendments/2012/resolutions/affordable-prescription-drugs) that the prices of the most commonly used drugs rose 25% between 2005 and 2009—almost twice the rate of inflation.

Older Adults Respond Differently to Drugs

Many factors influence the efficacy (the ability of an intervention to produce the intended diagnostic or therapeutic effect in optimal circumstances), safety, and success of drug therapy with older patients. These factors include the effects of aging on pharmacokinetics—the absorption, distribution, metabolism, and excretion of drugs. Of the four, absorption is the least affected by aging. In older people, absorption is generally complete, just slower. The distribution of most medications is related to body weight and composition changes that occur with aging, such as decreased lean muscle mass, increased fat mass, and decreased total body water.

Health professionals who care for older adults know that drug dosages must often be modified based on changing organ function and estimates of lean body mass. They coined the adage "start low and go slow" to guide prescribing drugs for older adults. For example, some initial doses of drugs should be lower because older adults have decreased total body water, which might increase the concentration of the drug. Fat-soluble drugs may also have to be administered in lower doses because they may accumulate in fatty tissues, resulting in longer durations of action. The mechanism used to clear a drug via metabolism in the liver or clearance (excretion) through the kidneys changes with aging and is affected by interactions with other medications. Pharmacodynamics (tissue sensitivity to drugs) also changes with advancing age. Among older adults, the complete elimination of a drug from body tissues, including the brain, can take weeks longer than it might in younger people.

Adherence, Drug-Drug Interactions, and Polypharmacy

Adherence (taking prescription medications regularly and correctly) is a challenge for older people who may suffer from memory loss, impaired vision, or arthritis. Abigail Flinders et al. note in "Prescribing for Older People" (*Nursing Older People*, vol. 21, no. 2, March 2009) that about half of older adults fail to take their medications at the right times and in the right amounts. Strategies to improve adherence include weekly pill boxes, calendars, and easy-to-open bottles with large-print labels.

Drug-drug interactions are more frequent among older adults because they are more likely than people of other ages to be taking multiple medications. Dangerous drug-drug interactions may occur when two or more drugs act together to either intensify or diminish one another's potency and effectiveness or when in combination they produce adverse side effects. For example, a person who takes heparin, a blood-thinning medication, should not take aspirin, which also acts to thin the blood. Similarly, antacids can interfere with the absorption of certain drugs that are used to treat Parkinson's disease, hypertension, and heart disease.

Polypharmacy is the use of many medications at the same time. It also refers to prescribing more medication than is needed or a medication regimen that includes at least one unnecessary medication. The major risk associated with polypharmacy is the potential for adverse drug reactions and interactions. Drug-induced adverse events may masquerade as other illnesses or precipitate confusion, falls, and incontinence, potentially prompting the physician to prescribe yet another drug. This "prescribing cascade" is easily prevented. It requires that physicians ensure that all medications prescribed are appropriate, safe, effective, and taken correctly.

In "Polypharmacy in Older Adults at Home: What It Is and What to Do about It—Implications for Home Healthcare and Hospice" (*Home Healthcare Nurse*, vol. 30, no. 8, September 2012), Gretchen I. Riker and Stephen M. Setter find that increasing prescription drug use increases the likelihood of polypharmacy. Because polypharmacy is potentially dangerous, Riker and Setter suggest that "periodic medication reviews and effective and constant communication between healthcare providers and patients can help to identify potentially inappropriate medications."

LEADING CAUSES OF DEATH

The two leading causes of death among adults aged 65 years and older—heart disease and malignant neoplasms—were unchanged between 1980 and 2010. (See Table 7.5.) In 2010 chronic lower respiratory diseases rose to the third-leading cause of death, while cerebrovascular diseases dropped to fourth place. Alzheimer's disease held fifth place on the list and was responsible for 82,616 deaths.

Heart Disease

Although deaths from heart disease have declined, it still kills more Americans than any other single disease. According to the American Heart Association, in "Older Americans and Cardiovascular Diseases" (March 2013, http://www.heart.org/idc/groups/heart-public/@wcm/@sop/@smd/documents/downloadable/ucm_319574.pdf), 80% of people who die of heart disease are aged 65 years and older. Among adults aged 60 to 79 years, 21.1% of men and 10.6% of women have heart disease. Among those aged 80 years and older the percentages increase to 34.6% of men and 18.6% of women. The average age of a first heart attack is 64.7 for men and 72.2 for women. Because women are generally older when they suffer heart attacks, they are more likely to die within weeks of the attack.

Table 7.5 shows the decrease in the numbers of deaths from cerebrovascular diseases between 1980 and 2010. Several factors account for the decreasing numbers of deaths from heart disease, including better control of hypertension and cholesterol levels and changes in exercise and diet. The increasing ranks of trained paramedics and the widespread use of cardiopulmonary resuscitation and immediate treatment have also increased the likelihood of surviving an initial heart attack.

The growing use of statin drugs (drugs that reduce blood cholesterol levels) to reduce the risk of heart disease as well as procedures such as cardiac catheterization, coronary bypass surgery, pacemakers, angioplasty (a procedure to open narrowed or blocked blood vessels of the heart), and stenting (using wire scaffolds that hold arteries open) have improved the quality, and in some instances extended the lives, of people with heart disease.

However, the Mayo Clinic explains in "Statins: Are These Cholesterol-Lowering Drugs Right for You?" (March 13, 2012, http://www.mayoclinic.com/health/statins/CL00010) that statin use may produce side effects such as joint and muscle pain, nausea, diarrhea, and constipation. Although these common side effects often subside with continued use of the drugs, less frequent but serious side effects such as liver and kidney damage, severe muscle pain, and elevated blood sugar may occur with statin treatment.

Cancer

Cancer is the second-leading cause of death among older adults. (See Table 7.5.) The American Cancer Society indicates in *Cancer Facts and Figures, 2013* that about 77% of all cancers are diagnosed after age 55. The likelihood of dying of cancer increases every decade after the age of 30. In 2010 among adults aged 65 to 74 years, there were 666.1 deaths per 100,000 people; for adults aged 75 to 84 years, this rate was 1,202.2 deaths per 100,000 people; and for adults aged 85 years and older, it was 1,729.5 deaths per 100,000 people. (See Table 7.9.)

The National Comprehensive Cancer Network explains in "Cancer and the Elderly" (2013, http://www.nccn.com/component/content/article/54-cancer-basics/1728-cancer-and-the-elderly.html) that cancer risk increases with advancing age because some age-related changes such as diminished immunity, decreased ability of the hormone insulin to regulate blood sugar, and chronic inflammation may spur the growth of cancer. Older adults may also be more susceptible to cancer-causing agents in the environment such as secondhand smoke and chemical pollutants (e.g., asbestos and radiation).

Success in treating certain cancers, such as Hodgkin's disease and some forms of leukemia, has been offset by the rise in rates of other cancers, such as breast and lung cancers. Table 7.5 shows that the number of cancer deaths among adults aged 65 years and older rose sharply from 258,389 in 1980 to 396,670 in 2010. Progress in treating cancer has largely been related to screenings, early diagnoses, and new drug therapies.

Stroke

Stroke (cerebrovascular disease or "brain attack") is the fourth-leading cause of death and is the principal cause of disability among older adults. (See Table 7.5.) In "Older Americans and Cardiovascular Diseases," the American Heart Association reports that among adults aged 60 to 79 years the risk of stroke is 6.2% for men and 6.9% for women. Among those aged 80 years and older the risk rises to 13.9% for men and 13.8% for women.

According to the NCHS, in *Health, United States, 2012*, in 1980 strokes killed 146,417 people aged 65 years and older. In 2010, among people aged 65 years and older, 109,990 deaths were attributable to stroke. (See Table 7.5.) The death rate for people aged 65 to 74 years declined as well, from 219 per 100,000 population in 1980 to 81.7 per 100,000 population in 2010. (See Table 7.10.) There was a comparable decline for people aged 75 to 84 years. There were 288.3 deaths per 100,000 population for this age group in 2010, down from 786.9 deaths per 100,000 population in 1980. The improvement was even greater for people aged 85 years and older. There were 993.8 deaths per 100,000 population for this age group in 2010, less than half the rate of 2,283.7 per 100,000 population in 1980. The Mayo Clinic explains in "Stroke: Definition" (July 3, 2012, http://www.mayoclinic.com/health/stroke/DS00150) that "better control of major stroke risk factors—high blood pressure, smoking and high cholesterol—may be responsible for the decline."

In "Stroke Recovery: Regaining Arm Use" (May 10, 2012, http://www.webmd.com/stroke/regaining-arm-use-after-stroke-10/slideshow-stroke), WebMD observes that about 80% of stroke victims suffer some weakness or paralysis on the opposite side of the body from where the stroke occurred in the brain. Although stroke rehabilitation improves the chances of recovery, some stroke survivors must learn to live with disability.

HEALTHY AGING

According to the CDC, ample research demonstrates that healthy lifestyles have a greater effect than genetic factors in helping to prevent the deterioration that is traditionally associated with aging. People who are physically active, eat a healthy diet, and do not smoke reduce their risk for chronic diseases, have half the rate of disability of those who do not, and can delay disability by as many as 10 years.

Among the recommended health practices for older adults is participating in early detection practices such as screenings for hypertension, cancer, diabetes, and depression. Screening detects diseases early in their course, when they are most treatable; however, many older adults do not obtain the recommended screenings. For example, although immunizations reduce the risk for hospitalization and death from influenza and pneumonia, the Federal Interagency Forum on Aging-Related Statistics notes in *Older Americans 2012* that in 2010, 36.7% of older adults had not received flu shots and 40.3% of older adults had not been vaccinated against pneumonia.

Because falls are the most common cause of injuries in older adults, injury prevention is a vitally important way to prevent disability. The CDC reports in "Falls among Older Adults: An Overview" (September 20,

TABLE 7.9

Death rates for malignant neoplasms, selected characteristics, selected years 1950–2010

[Data are based on death certificates]

Race, Hispanic origin, and age	1950[a]	1960[a]	1970	1980	1990	2000	2009	2010
All females				Deaths per 100,000 resident population				
All ages, age-adjusted[b]	31.9	31.7	32.1	31.9	33.3	26.8	22.3	22.1
All ages, crude	24.7	26.1	28.4	30.6	34.0	29.2	26.1	26.1
Under 25 years	*	*	*	*	*	*	*	*
25–34 years	3.8	3.8	3.9	3.3	2.9	2.3	1.7	1.6
35–44 years	20.8	20.2	20.4	17.9	17.8	12.4	10.5	9.8
45–54 years	46.9	51.4	52.6	48.1	45.4	33.0	26.2	25.7
55–64 years	69.9	70.8	77.6	80.5	78.6	59.3	47.9	47.7
65–74 years	95.0	90.0	93.8	101.1	111.7	88.3	73.4	73.9
75–84 years	139.8	129.9	127.4	126.4	146.3	128.9	112.6	109.1
85 years and over	195.5	191.9	157.1	169.3	196.8	205.7	178.0	185.8
White[c]								
All ages, age-adjusted[b]	32.4	32.0	32.5	32.1	33.2	26.3	21.9	21.5
All ages, crude	25.7	27.2	29.9	32.3	35.9	30.7	27.4	27.3
35–44 years	20.8	19.7	20.2	17.3	17.1	11.3	9.0	8.8
45–54 years	47.1	51.2	53.0	48.1	44.3	31.2	24.8	23.9
55–64 years	70.9	71.8	79.3	81.3	78.5	57.9	46.4	45.9
65–74 years	96.3	91.6	95.9	103.7	113.3	89.3	73.2	73.3
75–84 years	143.6	132.8	129.6	128.4	148.2	130.2	113.1	110.2
85 years and over	204.2	199.7	161.9	171.7	198.0	205.5	179.2	186.8
Black or African American[c]								
All ages, age-adjusted[b]	25.3	27.9	28.9	31.7	38.1	34.5	30.2	30.3
All ages, crude	16.4	18.7	19.7	22.9	29.0	27.9	26.9	27.5
35–44 years	21.0	24.8	24.4	24.1	25.8	20.9	17.6	18.3
45–54 years	46.5	54.4	52.0	52.7	60.5	51.5	40.6	40.9
55–64 years	64.3	63.2	64.7	79.9	93.1	80.9	68.5	70.5
65–74 years	67.0	72.3	77.3	84.3	112.2	98.6	92.4	97.4
75–84 years[d]	81.0	87.5	101.8	114.1	140.5	139.8	136.4	123.2
85 years and over	—	92.1	112.1	149.9	201.5	238.7	201.9	214.6
American Indian or Alaska Native[c]								
All ages, age-adjusted[b]	—	—	—	10.8	13.7	13.6	12.2	11.5
All ages, crude	—	—	—	6.1	8.6	8.7	8.4	8.0
35–44 years	—	—	—	*	*	*	*	*
45–54 years	—	—	—	*	23.9	14.4	12.0	13.2
55–64 years	—	—	—	*	*	40.0	29.9	25.2
65–74 years	—	—	—	*	*	42.5	51.3	34.3
75–84 years	—	—	—	*	*	71.8	53.2	61.1
85 years and over	—	—	—	*	*	*	*	*
Asian or Pacific Islander[c]								
All ages, age-adjusted[b]	—	—	—	11.9	13.7	12.3	11.1	11.9
All ages, crude	—	—	—	8.2	9.3	10.2	10.1	10.8
35–44 years	—	—	—	10.4	8.4	8.1	5.4	5.4
45–54 years	—	—	—	23.4	26.4	22.3	15.5	17.0
55–64 years	—	—	—	35.7	33.8	31.3	28.8	28.4
65–74 years	—	—	—	*	38.5	34.7	34.6	37.9
75–84 years	—	—	—	*	48.0	37.5	46.4	53.2
85 years and over	—	—	—	*	*	68.2	72.9	77.5
Hispanic or Latina[c, e]								
All ages, age-adjusted[b]	—	—	—	—	19.5	16.9	14.8	14.4
All ages, crude	—	—	—	—	11.5	9.7	9.4	9.2
35–44 years	—	—	—	—	11.7	8.7	7.0	6.2
45–54 years	—	—	—	—	32.8	23.9	19.0	18.6
55–64 years	—	—	—	—	45.8	39.1	32.6	32.7
65–74 years	—	—	—	—	64.8	54.9	46.3	49.0
75–84 years	—	—	—	—	67.2	74.9	72.4	61.8
85 years and over	—	—	—	—	102.8	105.8	111.4	117.8

2012, http://www.cdc.gov/HomeandRecreationalSafety/Falls/adultfalls.html) that over one-third of adults aged 65 years and older fall each year, and of those who fall, 20% to 30% suffer injuries that impair mobility and independence. Removing tripping hazards in the home, such as rugs, and installing grab bars in bathrooms are simple measures that can greatly reduce older Americans' risk for falls and fractures.

The current cohort of older adults is better equipped to prevent the illness, disability, and death associated with many chronic diseases than any previous generation.

[Data are based on death certificates]

They are less likely to smoke, drink, or experience detrimental stress than younger people, and older adults have better eating habits than their younger counterparts. For example, the percentage of men aged 65 years and older who smoke cigarettes declined from 29% in 1965 to 10% in 2010. (See Figure 7.13.) In contrast, the percentage of women the same age who smoke remained relatively constant during this period, decreasing slightly from 10% to 9%.

Older adults are, however, less likely to exercise than younger adults. In 2010 only 11% of adults aged 65 years and older said they regularly engaged in leisure-time physical activity, and the percentage participating declined with advancing age—just 4% of adults aged 85 years and older engaged in regular physical activity. (See Figure 7.14.) Increasing evidence suggests that behavior change, even late in life, is beneficial and can improve disease control and enhance quality of life.

Maintaining a Healthy Weight

The United States is in the throes of an obesity epidemic. Obesity is defined as a body mass index (a number that shows body weight adjusted for height) greater than or equal to 30 kilograms per meters squared. In 2012, 27.9% of adults aged 60 years and older were obese, and the group of adults aged 40 to 59 years that will soon join the ranks of older Americans reported the highest rate of obesity, at 33.1%. (See Figure 7.15.) Furthermore, the percentages of older adults who are obese have increased from 1988–94, when just 24% of men and 27% of women aged 65 to 74 years and 13% of men and 19% of women aged 75 years and older were obese. (See Figure 7.11.) By 2009–10, 43% of men and 45% of women aged 65 to 74 years and 27% of men and 30% of women aged 75 years and older were obese.

Obesity increases the risk for multiple health problems, including hypertension, high cholesterol, type 2 diabetes, coronary heart disease, congestive heart failure, stroke, arthritis, obstructive sleep apnea, and other serious conditions.

Smoking

According to the Federal Interagency Forum on Aging-Related Statistics, in *Older Americans 2012*, the per capita tobacco consumption declined in the United States during the last decades of the 20th century. By 2010 fewer people over the age of 65 (9.7% of men and 9.3% of women) smoked than all other age groups. Data from the 2012 National Health Interview Survey reveal that adults aged 65 years and older were the least likely to be current smokers—just 8.9%, compared with 20.4% of adults aged 18 to 44 years and 19.4% of those aged 45 to 64 years. (See Figure 7.16.)

The U.S. surgeon general explains that even older adult smokers realize health benefits from quitting. For example, a smoker's risk of heart disease begins to decline almost immediately after quitting, regardless of how long the person smoked.

Physical Activity

Regular physical activity comes closer to being a fountain of youth than any prescription medicine. Along with helping older adults to remain mobile and independent, exercise can lower the risk of obesity, heart disease, stroke, diabetes, and some cancers. It can also delay osteoporosis and arthritis, reduce symptoms of depression, and improve sleep quality and memory. Despite these benefits, in 2012 less than half (44.9%) of adults aged 65 to 74 years and 28.9% of adults aged 75 years and older met the 2008 federal physical activity guidelines for aerobic activity through leisure-time physical

TABLE 7.10

Death rates for cerebrovascular disease, selected characteristics, selected years 1950–2010

[Data are based on death certificates]

Sex, race, Hispanic origin, and age	1950[a]	1960[a]	1970	1980	1990	2000	2009	2010
All persons				Deaths per 100,000 resident population				
All ages, age-adjusted[b]	180.7	177.9	147.7	96.2	65.3	60.9	39.6	39.1
All ages, crude	104.0	108.0	101.9	75.0	57.8	59.6	42.0	41.9
Under 1 year	5.1	4.1	5.0	4.4	3.8	3.3	3.7	3.3
1–4 years	0.9	0.8	1.0	0.5	0.3	0.3	0.3	0.3
5–14 years	0.5	0.7	0.7	0.3	0.2	0.2	0.2	0.2
15–24 years	1.6	1.8	1.6	1.0	0.6	0.5	0.4	0.4
25–34 years	4.2	4.7	4.5	2.6	2.2	1.5	1.3	1.3
35–44 years	18.7	14.7	15.6	8.5	6.4	5.8	4.6	4.6
45–54 years	70.4	49.2	41.6	25.2	18.7	16.0	13.7	13.1
55–64 years	194.2	147.3	115.8	65.1	47.9	41.0	29.7	29.3
65–74 years	554.7	469.2	384.1	219.0	144.2	128.6	82.8	81.7
75–84 years	1,499.6	1,491.3	1,254.2	786.9	498.0	461.3	294.9	288.3
85 years and over	2,990.1	3,680.5	3,014.3	2,283.7	1,628.9	1,589.2	992.2	993.8
Male								
All ages, age-adjusted[b]	186.4	186.1	157.4	102.2	68.5	62.4	39.9	39.3
All ages, crude	102.5	104.5	94.5	63.4	46.7	46.9	34.5	34.5
Under 1 year	6.4	5.0	5.8	5.0	4.4	3.8	4.4	3.2
1–4 years	1.1	0.9	1.2	0.4	0.3	*	0.3	0.3
5–14 years	0.5	0.7	0.8	0.3	0.2	0.2	0.2	0.3
15–24 years	1.8	1.9	1.8	1.1	0.7	0.5	0.5	0.5
25–34 years	4.2	4.5	4.4	2.6	2.1	1.5	1.5	1.3
35–44 years	17.5	14.6	15.7	8.7	6.8	5.8	5.1	5.0
45–54 years	67.9	52.2	44.4	27.2	20.5	17.5	15.3	14.9
55–64 years	205.2	163.8	138.7	74.6	54.3	47.2	35.0	34.7
65–74 years	589.6	530.7	449.5	258.6	166.6	145.0	94.2	92.0
75–84 years	1,543.6	1,555.9	1,361.6	866.3	551.1	490.8	300.9	295.2
85 years and over	3,048.6	3,643.1	2,895.2	2,193.6	1,528.5	1,484.3	891.6	892.0
Female								
All ages, age-adjusted[b]	175.8	170.7	140.0	91.7	62.6	59.1	38.8	38.3
All ages, crude	105.6	111.4	109.0	85.9	68.4	71.8	49.2	49.1
Under 1 year	3.7	3.2	4.0	3.8	3.1	2.7	3.0	3.4
1–4 years	0.7	0.7	0.7	0.5	0.3	0.4	0.3	0.3
5–14 years	0.4	0.6	0.6	0.3	0.2	0.2	0.1	0.2
15–24 years	1.5	1.6	1.4	0.8	0.6	0.5	0.4	0.4
25–34 years	4.3	4.9	4.7	2.6	2.2	1.5	1.2	1.2
35–44 years	19.9	14.8	15.6	8.4	6.1	5.7	4.2	4.2
45–54 years	72.9	46.3	39.0	23.3	17.0	14.5	12.2	11.4
55–64 years	183.1	131.8	95.3	56.8	42.2	35.3	24.8	24.3
65–74 years	522.1	415.7	333.3	188.7	126.7	115.1	72.9	72.8
75–84 years	1,462.2	1,441.1	1,183.1	740.1	466.2	442.1	290.6	283.4
85 years and over	2,949.4	3,704.4	3,081.0	2,323.1	1,667.6	1,632.0	1,040.2	1,043.0
White male[c]								
All ages, age-adjusted[b]	182.1	181.6	153.7	98.7	65.5	59.8	38.0	37.6
All ages, crude	100.5	102.7	93.5	63.1	46.9	48.4	35.7	35.8
45–54 years	53.7	40.9	35.6	21.7	15.4	13.6	12.7	12.2
55–64 years	182.2	139.0	119.9	64.0	45.7	39.7	29.3	29.0
65–74 years	569.7	501.0	420.0	239.8	152.9	133.8	86.2	83.3
75–84 years	1,556.3	1,564.8	1,361.6	852.7	539.2	480.0	292.9	288.3
85 years and over	3,127.1	3,734.8	3,018.1	2,230.8	1,545.4	1,490.7	896.0	903.2
Black or African American male[c]								
All ages, age-adjusted[b]	228.8	238.5	206.4	142.0	102.2	89.6	58.8	56.6
All ages, crude	122.0	122.9	108.8	73.0	53.0	46.1	35.0	34.5
45–54 years	211.9	166.1	136.1	82.1	68.4	49.5	34.5	33.6
55–64 years	522.8	439.9	343.4	189.7	141.7	115.4	84.5	83.2
65–74 years	783.6	899.2	780.1	472.3	326.9	268.5	182.8	182.6
75–84 years[d]	1,504.9	1,475.2	1,445.7	1,066.3	721.5	659.2	412.7	398.0
85 years and over	—	2,700.0	1,963.1	1,873.2	1,421.5	1,458.8	887.4	804.5

activity. (See Figure 7.17.) The 2008 guidelines recommend that adults perform at least 150 minutes per week of moderate-intensity aerobic physical activity, or 75 minutes per week of vigorous-intensity aerobic physical activity, or an equivalent combination of moderate- and vigorous-intensity activity.

Use of Preventive Health Services

More widespread use of preventive services is a key to preserving and extending the health and quality of life of older Americans. Screening for early detection of selected cancers—such as breast, cervical, and colorectal—as well as diabetes, cardiovascular disease, and glaucoma can save

TABLE 7.10

Death rates for cerebrovascular disease, selected characteristics, selected years 1950–10 [CONTINUED]

[Data are based on death certificates]

*Rates based on fewer than 20 deaths are considered unreliable and are not shown.
—Data not available.
aIncludes deaths of persons who were not residents of the 50 states and the District of Columbia (D.C.).
bAge-adjusted rates are calculated using the year 2000 standard population. Prior to 2001, age-adjusted rates were calculated using standard million proportions based on rounded population numbers. Starting with 2001 data, unrounded population numbers are used to calculate age-adjusted rates.
cThe race groups, white, black, Asian or Pacific Islander, and American Indian or Alaska Native, include persons of Hispanic and non-Hispanic origin. Persons of Hispanic origin may be of any race. Death rates for the American Indian or Alaska Native, Asian or Pacific Islander, and Hispanic populations are known to be underestimated.
dIn 1950, rate is for the age group 75 years and over.
Notes: Starting with *Health, United States, 2003*, rates for 1991–1999 were revised using intercensal population estimates based on the 1990 and 2000 censuses. For 2000, population estimates are bridged-race April 1 census counts. Starting with *Health, United States, 2012*, rates for 2001–2009 were revised using intercensal population estimates based on the 2000 and 2010 censuses. For 2010, population estimates are bridged-race April 1 census counts. Age groups were selected to minimize the presentation of unstable age-specific death rates based on small numbers of deaths and for consistency among comparison groups. Starting with 2003 data, some states allowed the reporting of more than one race on the death certificate. The multiple-race data for these states were bridged to the single-race categories of the 1977 Office of Management and Budget standards, for comparability with other states.

SOURCE: Adapted from "Table 27. Death Rates for Cerebrovascular Diseases, by Sex, Race, Hispanic Origin, and Age: United States, Selected Years 1950–2010," in *Health, United States, 2012: With Special Feature on Emergency Care*, 2013, National Center for Health Statistics, http://www.cdc.gov/nchs/data/hus/hus12.pdf#109 (accessed June 1, 2013)

FIGURE 7.13

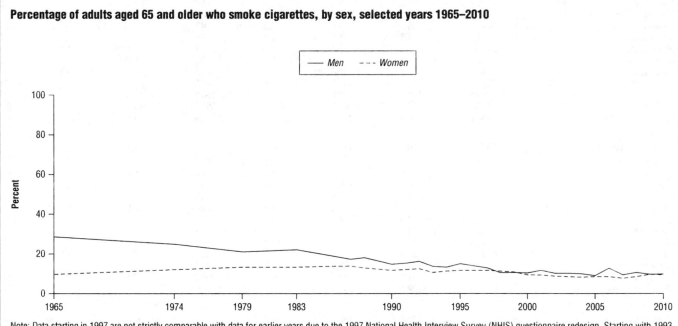

Percentage of adults aged 65 and older who smoke cigarettes, by sex, selected years 1965–2010

Note: Data starting in 1997 are not strictly comparable with data for earlier years due to the 1997 National Health Interview Survey (NHIS) questionnaire redesign. Starting with 1993 data, current cigarette smokers were defined as ever smoking 100 cigarettes in their lifetime and smoking now on every day or some days.

SOURCE: "Percentage of People Age 65 and over Who Are Current Cigarette Smokers, by Sex, Selected Years, 1965–2010," in *Older Americans 2012: Key Indicators of Well-Being*, Federal Interagency Forum on Aging-Related Statistics, June 2012, http://www.agingstats.gov/Main_Site/Data/2012_Documents/docs/EntireChartbook.pdf (accessed May 28, 2013)

lives and slow the progress of chronic disease. People with a regular source of medical care are more likely to receive basic medical services, such as routine checkups, which present the opportunity to receive preventive services, and in 2012, 96.1% of adults aged 65 years and older reported having a regular source of medical care. (See Figure 7.18.) Given that Medicare covers a comprehensive range of preventive services and screenings, such as screening for heart disease, cancer, diabetes, glaucoma, and depression, it seems unlikely that cost prevents older adults from obtaining these services. Data from the 2012 National Health Interview Survey reveal that just 2.3% of respondents aged 65 years and older reported that they failed to obtain needed medical care because of cost during the 12 months preceding the interview. (See Figure 7.19.)

SEXUALITY IN AGING

Despite the popular belief that sexuality is exclusively for the young, sexual interest, activity, and capabilities are often lifelong. Although the growing population of older adults will likely spur additional research,

FIGURE 7.14

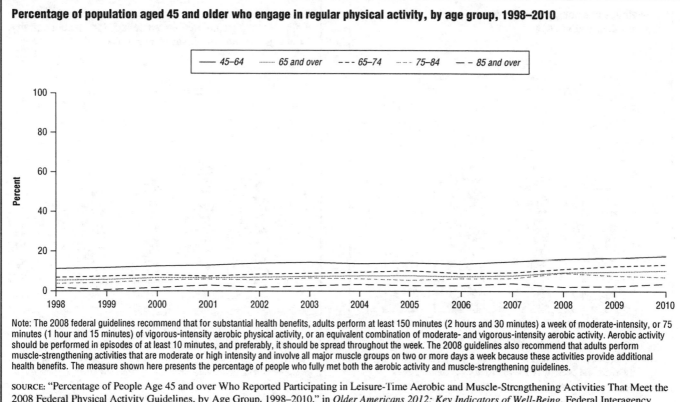

Percentage of population aged 45 and older who engage in regular physical activity, by age group, 1998–2010

— 45–64   ⋯⋯ 65 and over   - - - 65–74   ⋯ - 75–84   — - 85 and over

Note: The 2008 federal guidelines recommend that for substantial health benefits, adults perform at least 150 minutes (2 hours and 30 minutes) a week of moderate-intensity, or 75 minutes (1 hour and 15 minutes) of vigorous-intensity aerobic physical activity, or an equivalent combination of moderate- and vigorous-intensity aerobic activity. Aerobic activity should be performed in episodes of at least 10 minutes, and preferably, it should be spread throughout the week. The 2008 guidelines also recommend that adults perform muscle-strengthening activities that are moderate or high intensity and involve all major muscle groups on two or more days a week because these activities provide additional health benefits. The measure shown here presents the percentage of people who fully met both the aerobic activity and muscle-strengthening guidelines.

SOURCE: "Percentage of People Age 45 and over Who Reported Participating in Leisure-Time Aerobic and Muscle-Strengthening Activities That Meet the 2008 Federal Physical Activity Guidelines, by Age Group, 1998–2010," in *Older Americans 2012: Key Indicators of Well-Being*, Federal Interagency Forum on Aging-Related Statistics, June 2012, http://www.agingstats.gov/Main_Site/Data/2012_Documents/docs/EntireChartbook.pdf (accessed May 28, 2013)

FIGURE 7.15

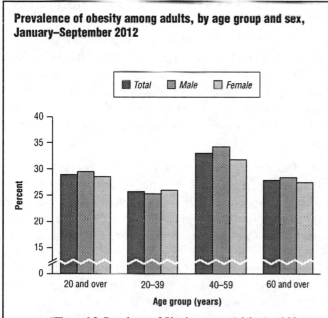

Prevalence of obesity among adults, by age group and sex, January–September 2012

SOURCE: "Figure 6.2. Prevalence of Obesity among Adults Aged 20 Years and over, by Age Group and Sex: United States, January–September 2012," in *Early Release of Selected Estimates Based on Data from the January–September 2012 National Health Interview Survey*, Centers for Disease Control and Prevention, National Center for Health Statistics, March 2013, http://www.cdc.gov/nchs/data/nhis/earlyrelease/earlyrelease201303_06.pdf (accessed June 14, 2013)

to date there are scant data about the levels of sexual activity among older adults. The data that are available are often limited to community-dwelling older adults, so there is nearly no information about the sexual behavior of institutionalized older adults.

After age 50 sexual responses slow; however, very rarely does this natural and gradual diminution cause older adults to end all sexual activity. More important, in terms of curtailing older adults' sexual activity is the lack of available partners, which limits opportunities for sexual expression, especially for older women. Another issue is the greater incidence of illness and progression of chronic diseases that occurs with advancing age. Medical problems with the potential to adversely affect sexual function include diabetes, hypothyroidism (a condition in which the thyroid is underactive—producing too little thyroid hormones), neuropathy (a disease or abnormality of the nervous system), cardiovascular disease, urinary tract infections, prostate cancer, incontinence, arthritis, depression, and dementia. Many pharmacological treatments for chronic illnesses have sexual side effects that range from diminished libido (sexual desire and drive) to erectile dysfunction. For example, some medications (e.g., antihypertensives, antidepressants, diuretics, steroids, anticonvulsants, and beta blockers) have high rates of sexual side effects.

FIGURE 7.16

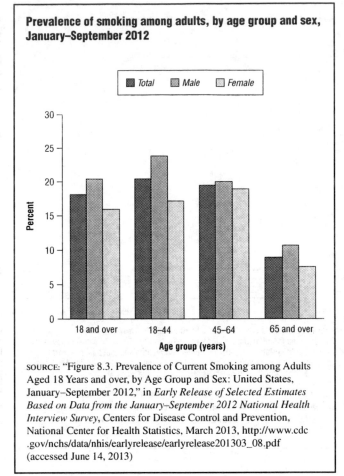

Prevalence of smoking among adults, by age group and sex, January–September 2012

SOURCE: "Figure 8.3. Prevalence of Current Smoking among Adults Aged 18 Years and over, by Age Group and Sex: United States, January–September 2012," in *Early Release of Selected Estimates Based on Data from the January–September 2012 National Health Interview Survey*, Centers for Disease Control and Prevention, National Center for Health Statistics, March 2013, http://www.cdc.gov/nchs/data/nhis/earlyrelease/earlyrelease201303_08.pdf (accessed June 14, 2013)

FIGURE 7.17

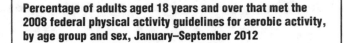

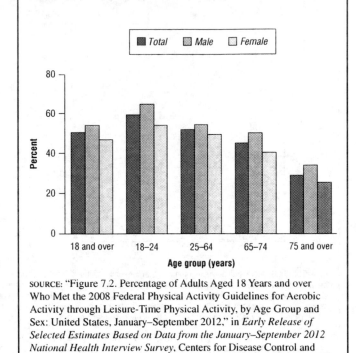

Percentage of adults aged 18 years and over that met the 2008 federal physical activity guidelines for aerobic activity, by age group and sex, January–September 2012

SOURCE: "Figure 7.2. Percentage of Adults Aged 18 Years and over Who Met the 2008 Federal Physical Activity Guidelines for Aerobic Activity through Leisure-Time Physical Activity, by Age Group and Sex: United States, January–September 2012," in *Early Release of Selected Estimates Based on Data from the January–September 2012 National Health Interview Survey*, Centers for Disease Control and Prevention, National Center for Health Statistics, March 2013, http://www.cdc.gov/nchs/data/nhis/earlyrelease/earlyrelease201303_07.pdf (accessed June 14, 2013)

One of the biggest recent changes in the sex lives of older adults is older men's use of potency drugs for erectile dysfunction (Viagra, Cialis, and Levitra) to enhance their performance. Since the 1998 debut of Viagra, these pharmaceutical solutions to erectile changes affecting older men have enjoyed tremendous popularity.

Sexuality Transmitted Infections

The article "Sex and the Older Woman" (*Harvard Women's Health Watch*, vol. 19, no. 5, January 2012) reports that more than 60% of women in their 50s, 45% of women in their 60s, and 28% of women in their 70s are sexually active. Because these women no longer require protection against pregnancy, many do not practice safe sex. In one study just 13% of older women used condoms. As a result, there has been an increase in sexually transmitted infections (STIs) among older women.

Data from the 2012 National Health Interview Survey reveal that adults aged 65 years and older were the least likely to have ever had an HIV test of any age group. Just 14.9% of men and 11.3% of women aged 65 years and older reported having had an HIV test. (See Figure 7.20.)

THE UNITED STATES LACKS SPECIALISTS IN GERIATRIC MEDICINE

In 1909 the American physician Ignatz L. Nascher (1863–1944) coined the term *geriatrics* from the Greek *geras* (old age) and *iatrikos* (physician). Geriatricians are physicians trained in internal medicine or family practice who obtain additional training and medical board certification in the diagnosis and treatment of older adults.

The American Geriatrics Society observes in "Who We Are" (http://www.americangeriatrics.org/about_us/who_we_are/) that in 2013 there were over 6,000 board-certified geriatricians—fewer than half of the estimated need. The shortage of specially trained physicians will intensify as the baby boom generation (people born between 1946 and 1964) joins the ranks of older adults. The American Geriatrics Society contends that financial disincentives pose the greatest barrier to new physicians entering geriatrics.

In "Even Fewer Geriatricians in Training" (NYTimes.com, January 9, 2013), Paula Span reports that the number of physicians training to become geriatricians decreased from 279 in 2012 to 251 in 2013. With fewer than 7,000 geriatricians and a projected need for at least

FIGURE 7.18

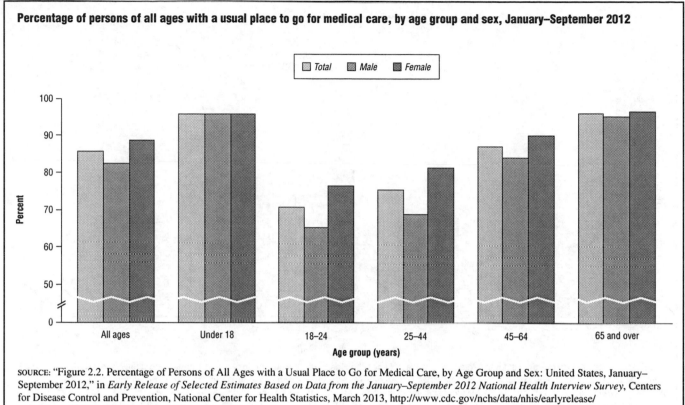

Percentage of persons of all ages with a usual place to go for medical care, by age group and sex, January–September 2012

Legend: Total | Male | Female

Percent (y-axis): 100, 90, 80, 70, 60, 50, 0

Age group (years): All ages, Under 18, 18–24, 25–44, 45–64, 65 and over

SOURCE: "Figure 2.2. Percentage of Persons of All Ages with a Usual Place to Go for Medical Care, by Age Group and Sex: United States, January–September 2012," in *Early Release of Selected Estimates Based on Data from the January–September 2012 National Health Interview Survey*, Centers for Disease Control and Prevention, National Center for Health Statistics, March 2013, http://www.cdc.gov/nchs/data/nhis/earlyrelease/earlyrelease201303_02.pdf (accessed June 14, 2013)

FIGURE 7.19

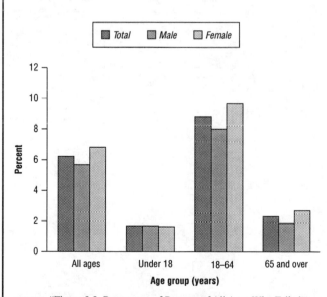

Percentage of persons of all ages who failed to obtain needed medical care due to cost, by age group and sex, January–September 2012

Legend: Total | Male | Female

Percent (y-axis): 12, 10, 8, 6, 4, 2, 0

Age group (years): All ages, Under 18, 18–64, 65 and over

SOURCE: "Figure 3.2. Percentage of Persons of All Ages Who Failed to Obtain Needed Medical Care Due to Cost at Some Time during the Past 12 Months, by Age Group and Sex: United States, January–September 2012," in *Early Release of Selected Estimates Based on Data from the January–September 2012 National Health Interview Survey*, Centers for Disease Control and Prevention, National Center for Health Statistics, March 2013, http://www.cdc.gov/nchs/data/nhis/earlyrelease/earlyrelease201303_03.pdf (accessed June 14, 2013)

five times as many, some medical educators advise using geriatricians as consultants to the primary care physicians who will be treating the United States' growing population of older adults.

FIGURE 7.20

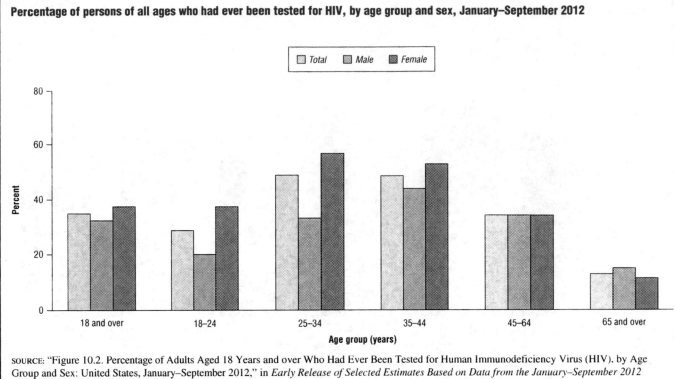

Percentage of persons of all ages who had ever been tested for HIV, by age group and sex, January–September 2012

SOURCE: "Figure 10.2. Percentage of Adults Aged 18 Years and over Who Had Ever Been Tested for Human Immunodeficiency Virus (HIV), by Age Group and Sex: United States, January–September 2012," in *Early Release of Selected Estimates Based on Data from the January–September 2012 National Health Interview Survey*, Centers for Disease Control and Prevention, National Center for Health Statistics, March 2013, http://www.cdc.gov/nchs/data/nhis/earlyrelease/earlyrelease201303_10.pdf (accessed June 14, 2013)

CHAPTER 8

MENTAL HEALTH AND MENTAL ILLNESS

Changes in mental capabilities are among the most feared aspects of aging. Mental health problems that impair functioning are among the most common age-related changes—and they are cause for concern because cognitive impairment (loss of intellectual functioning accompanied by memory loss and personality changes) is associated with increased risk for disability and progression to dementia (loss of intellectual functioning accompanied by memory loss and personality changes).

The aging population has spurred interest in age-related problems in cognition (the process of thinking, learning, and remembering). Cognitive difficulties much milder than those that are associated with organic brain diseases, such as Alzheimer's disease (a type of dementia), affect a significant proportion of older adults. Organic brain diseases, often referred to as organic brain syndromes, refer to physical disorders of the brain that produce mental health problems as opposed to psychiatric conditions, which may also cause mental health problems.

In "Mild Cognitive Impairment: Disparity of Incidence and Prevalence Estimates" (*Alzheimer's and Dementia*, vol. 8, no. 1, January 2012), Alex Ward et al. indicate that estimates of the prevalence (the total number of cases of a disorder in a given population at a specific time) of mild cognitive impairment among people of all ages vary, ranging from 3% to 29%. Brenda L. Plassman et al. estimate in "Incidence of Dementia and Cognitive Impairment, Not Dementia in the United States" (*Annals of Neurology*, vol. 70, no. 3, September 2011), an eight-year study of 456 adults aged 72 years and older, the national incidence rates (the rate of new cases of a disorder over a specified period) for cognitive impairment in the United States. The researchers find that the incidence of cognitive impairment without dementia is greater than the incidence of dementia and that people with cognitive impairment have an increased risk of progressing to dementia.

Because the number of people with cognitive impairments and dementia is anticipated to increase as the population ages, and older adults with cognitive impairment are at risk for institutionalization, the economic burden for society is expected to escalate. As such, the mental health and illness of older adults is an increasingly important public health issue.

MENTAL HEALTH

Mental health may be measured in terms of an individual's abilities to think and communicate clearly, learn and grow emotionally, deal productively and realistically with change and stress, and form and maintain fulfilling relationships with others. Mental health is a key component of wellness (self-esteem, resilience, and the ability to cope with adversity), which influences how people feel about themselves.

When mental health is defined and measured in terms of the absence of serious psychological distress, then older adults fare quite well compared with other age groups. The 2012 National Health Interview Survey, conducted by the Centers for Disease Control and Prevention, questioned whether respondents had experienced serious psychological distress within the 30 days preceding the interview. Adults aged 65 years and older were the least likely to have experienced serious psychological distress (1.9%) in 2012, compared with adults aged 45 to 64 years (3.9%) and adults aged 18 to 44 years (2.7%). (See Figure 8.1.)

Experience Shapes Mental Health in Old Age

One theory of aging, called continuity theory and explained by Robert C. Atchley in *The Social Forces in Later Life: An Introduction to Social Gerontology* (1985), posits that people who age most successfully are those who carry forward the habits, preferences, lifestyles, and relationships from midlife into late life. This theory has gained credence from research studies that find that traits

FIGURE 8.1

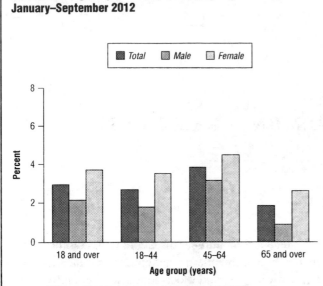

Percentage of adults who experienced serious psychological distress during the past 30 days, by age group and sex, January–September 2012

SOURCE: "Figure 13.2. Percentage of Adults Aged 18 Years and over Who Experienced Serious Psychological Distress during the Past 30 Days, by Age Group and Sex: United States, January–September 2012," in *Early Release of Selected Estimates Based on Data from the January–September 2012 National Health Interview Survey*, Centers for Disease Control and Prevention, National Center for Health Statistics, March 2013, http://www.cdc.gov/nchs/data/nhis/earlyrelease/earlyrelease201303_13.pdf (accessed June 14, 2013).

measured in midlife are strong predictors of outcomes in later life and that many psychological and social characteristics are stable across the life span. For most people, old age does not represent a radical departure from the past; changes often occur gradually and sometimes unnoticeably. Most older adults adapt to the challenges and changes associated with later life using well-practiced coping skills that were acquired earlier in life.

Adults who have struggled with mental health problems or mental disorders throughout their life often continue to suffer these same problems in old age. Few personal problems disappear with old age, and many progress and become more acute. Marital problems, which may have been kept at bay because one or both spouses were away at work, may intensify when a couple spends more time together in retirement. Reduced income, illness, and disability in retirement can aggravate an already troubled marriage and can strain even healthy interpersonal, marital, and other family relationships.

Older age can be a period of regrets, which can lead to mutual recriminations. With life expectancy rising, married couples can now expect to spend many years together in retirement. Most older couples manage the transition, but some have problems.

Coping with losses of friends, family, health, and independence may precipitate mental health problems. Hearing loss is common, and close correlations have been found between loss of hearing and depression. Visual impairment limits mobility and the ability to read and watch television. Loss of sight or hearing can cause perceptual disorientation, which in turn may lead to depression, paranoia, fear, and alienation.

A constant awareness of the imminence of death can also become a problem for older adults. Although most older adults resolve their anxieties and concerns about death, some live in denial and fear. How well older adults accept the inevitability of death is a key determinant of satisfaction and emotional well-being in old age.

Memory

Because memory is a key component of cognitive functioning, declining memory that substantially impairs older adults' functioning is a major risk factor for institutionalization. In "Self-Reported Increased Confusion or Memory Loss and Associated Functional Difficulties among Adults Aged ≥60 Years—21 States, 2011" (*Morbidity and Mortality Weekly Report*, vol. 62, no. 18, May 10, 2013), Mary L. Adams et al. report that an analysis of data from the 2011 Behavioral Risk Factor Surveillance System survey finds that 12.7% of older adults reported increased confusion or memory loss in the 12 months preceding the survey. Of those reporting increased confusion or memory loss, more than one-third (35.2%) described experiencing functional difficulties. The percentage reporting confusion or memory loss was significantly higher among people aged 85 years and older (15.6%), compared with those aged 60 to 64 years (12%) and 65 to 74 years (11.9%) and retirees (12.3%).

ORGANIC BRAIN DISEASES—DEMENTIAS

Dementia refers to a range of mental and behavioral changes caused by cerebrovascular or neurological diseases that permanently damage the brain, impairing the activity of brain cells. These changes can affect memory, speech, and the ability to perform the activities of daily living.

Occasional forgetfulness and memory lapses are not signs of dementia. Dementia is caused by disease and is not the inevitable result of growing older. Many disorders may cause or simulate dementia, which is not a single disorder—dementia refers to a condition that is caused by a variety of diseases and disorders, a small proportion of which are potentially reversible.

Furthermore, research suggests that although people with cognitive impairment have an increased risk for dementia, not all people with mild cognitive impairment will progress over time to dementia. Alex J. Mitchell and Mojtaba Shiri-Feshki conducted a large meta-analysis (a review that looks at the findings of many studies) and published their findings in "Rate of Progression of Mild Cognitive

Impairment to Dementia—Meta-analysis of 41 Robust Inception Cohort Studies" (*Acta Psychiatrica Scandinavica*, vol. 119, no. 4, April 2009). The researchers show that only a minority (20% to 40%) of people developed dementia even after long-term follow-up and that the risk appeared to decrease slightly with time. The analysis also suggests that mild cognitive impairment is not necessarily a transitional state between normal age-related changes and dementia. Mitchell and Shiri-Feshki find that some patients do not progress and others actually improve.

Multi-infarct Dementia

The National Institute of Neurological Disorders and Stroke indicates in "NINDS Multi-infarct Dementia Information Page" (June 6, 2013, http://www.ninds.nih.gov/disorders/multi_infarct_dementia/multi_infarct_dementia.htm) that multi-infarct dementia is a common cause of memory loss and progressive dementia. Multi-infarct dementia is caused by a series of small strokes that disrupt blood flow and damage or destroy brain tissue. Sometimes these small strokes are "silent"—meaning that they produce no obvious symptoms and are detected only on imaging studies, such as computed tomography (CT) or magnetic resonance imaging (MRI) scans of the brain. An older adult may have a number of small strokes before experiencing noticeable changes in memory, reasoning, or other signs of multi-infarct dementia.

Because strokes occur suddenly, the loss of cognitive skills and memory present quickly, although some affected individuals may appear to improve for short periods of time, then decline again after having more strokes. Establishing the diagnosis of multi-infarct dementia is challenging because its symptoms are difficult to distinguish from those of Alzheimer's disease. Treatment cannot reverse the damage already done to the brain. Instead, it focuses on preventing further damage by reducing the risk of additional strokes. This entails treating the underlying causes of stroke, such as hypertension (high blood pressure), diabetes, high cholesterol, and heart disease. Surgical procedures to improve blood flow to the brain, such as carotid endarterectomy (a surgical procedure that removes blockages from the carotid arteries, which supply blood to the brain), angioplasty (a procedure that opens narrowed or blocked blood vessels of the heart), or stenting (using wire scaffolds that hold arteries open), as well as medications to reduce the risk of stroke are used to treat this condition.

PEOPLE WITH DIABETES ARE AT INCREASED RISK. Kristine Yaffe et al. reveal in "Association between Hypoglycemia and Dementia in a Biracial Cohort of Older Adults with Diabetes Mellitus" (*Journal of the American Medical Association*, vol. 173, no. 14, July 22, 2013) that people with type 2 diabetes may be at an increased risk for developing dementia. The researchers find that people with dangerously low blood sugar levels, called hypoglycemia, which is caused by excess insulin, had a twofold increased risk of developing dementia than people with normal blood sugar levels. Yaffe et al. also find that people with dementia were at higher risk for hypoglycemia, possibly because their cognitive impairment hinders their efforts to effectively manage their diabetes.

Alzheimer's Disease

Alzheimer's disease (AD) is the most common form of dementia among older adults. It is characterized by severely compromised thinking, reasoning, behavior, and memory, and it may be among the most fearsome of age-related disorders because it challenges older adults' ability to live independently. The disease was named after Alois Alzheimer (1864–1915), the German neurologist who first described the anatomical changes in the brain—the plaques and tangles that are the characteristic markers of this progressive, degenerative disease.

According to the Alzheimer's Association, in *2013 Alzheimer's Disease Facts and Figures* (March 2013, http://www.alz.org/downloads/facts_figures_2013.pdf), an estimated 5.2 million Americans were afflicted with AD in 2013. The overwhelming majority (5 million) of AD sufferers were aged 65 years and older. An estimated 11% of people aged 65 years and older and nearly one-third (32%) of those aged 85 years and older had AD.

The Alzheimer's Association projects that the number of people aged 65 years and older with AD will reach 7.1 million in 2025 and that new AD cases each year will likely increase from 454,000 in 2010, to 615,000 in 2030, to 959,000 in 2050. The association asserts that if a cure or preventive measure is not found by 2050, then the number of Americans aged 65 years and older with AD will reach 13.8 million.

SYMPTOMS AND STAGES. In general, AD has a slow onset, with symptoms such as mild memory lapses and disorientation that may not be identified as problematical beginning between the ages of 55 and 80. As the disease progresses, memory loss increases and mood swings are frequent, accompanied by confusion, irritability, restlessness, and problems communicating. AD patients may experience trouble finding words, impaired judgment, difficulty performing familiar tasks, and changes in behavior and personality.

In "Seven Stages of Alzheimer's" (2013, http://www.alz.org/alzheimers_disease_stages_of_alzheimers.asp), the Alzheimer's Association describes the seven stages of how AD progresses. The stages range from the first and second, in which there is no and then little apparent cognitive decline, to stage 3, which is marked by mild lapses and is often discernible to family, friends, and coworkers. Stage 4 is called mild or early-stage

AD, and during this stage moderate cognitive decline is observed. For example, AD patients may have diminished recall of recent activities or current events and compromised ability to perform tasks such as paying bills or shopping for groceries. In stages 5 and 6 memory impairment continues along with personality changes, sleep disturbances, and, if left unsupervised, a dangerous tendency to wander off and become lost.

Ultimately, the disease progresses to stage 7, when patients are entirely unable to care for themselves. In their terminal stages, AD victims require round-the-clock care and supervision. They no longer recognize family members, other caregivers, or themselves, and they require assistance with daily activities such as eating, dressing, bathing, and using the toilet. Eventually, they may become incontinent, blind, completely unable to communicate, and have difficulty swallowing.

According to the Alzheimer's Association, in *2013 Alzheimer's Disease Facts and Figures*, in 2010 AD claimed 83,494 lives and was the sixth-leading cause of death in people of all ages and the fifth-leading cause of death among adults aged 65 years and older.

GENETIC ORIGINS OF AD. AD is not a normal consequence of growing older. It is a disease of the brain that develops in response to genetic predisposition and nongenetic causative factors. Scientists have identified some genetic components of the disease and have observed the different patterns of inheritance, ages of onset, genes, chromosomes, and proteins that are linked to the development of AD.

In "The *mec-4* Gene Is a Member of a Family of *Caenorhabditis elegans* Genes That Can Mutate to Induce Neuronal Degeneration" (*Nature*, vol. 349, no. no. 6310, February 14, 1991), Monica Driscoll and Martin Chalfie of Columbia University reported their discovery that a mutation in a single gene could cause AD. The defect was in the gene that directs cells to produce a substance called amyloid protein. The researchers also found that low levels of acetylcholine, a neurotransmitter that is involved in learning and memory, contribute to the formation of hard deposits of amyloid protein that accumulate in the brains of AD patients. In healthy people, the protein fragments are broken down and excreted by the body.

In 1995 three more genes linked to AD were identified. Two genes are involved with forms of early-onset AD, which can begin as early as age 30. The third gene, known as apolipoprotein E (apoE), regulates lipid metabolism and helps redistribute cholesterol. In the brain, apoE participates in repairing nerve tissue that has been injured. According to the National Institute on Aging (NIA), in the press release "Cortex Area Thinner in Youth with Alzheimer's-Related Gene" (April 24, 2007, http://www.nimh.nih.gov/science-news/2007/cortex-area-thinner-in-youth-with-alzheimers-related-gene.shtml), 40% of late-onset AD patients have at least one apoE-4 gene, whereas only 10% to 25% of the general population has an apoE-4 gene. The NIA notes in "Alzheimer's Disease Fact Sheet" (July 22, 2013, http://www.nia.nih.gov/Alzheimers/Publications/adfact.htm) that research confirms that the apoE-4 gene increases the risk of developing AD, but it is not yet known how it acts to increase this risk. The NIA observes that inheriting the apoE-4 gene does not necessarily mean that a person will develop AD and that the absence of the gene does not ensure that an individual will not develop AD.

In April 2011 two studies published in *Nature Genetics* (vol. 43, no. 5)—Adam C. Naj et al.'s "Common Variants at MS4A4/MS4A6E, CD2AP, CD33, and EPHA1 Are Associated with Late-Onset Alzheimer's Disease" and Paul Hollingworth et al.'s "Common Variants at ABCA7, MS4A6A/MS4A4E, EPHA1, CD33, and CD2AP Are Associated with Alzheimer's Disease"—identified five additional genes that are implicated in increasing the risk of developing the disease and the course of the disease. However, it should be noted that none of the recently identified genes play as important a role as apoE—the newly identified genes increase risk by just 10% to 15%, compared with apoE, which confers a 400-fold increase in risk of developing AD.

In January 2012 two groups of researchers—Harold Neumann and Mark J. Daly, in "Variant *TREM2* as Risk Factor for Alzheimer's Disease," and Rita Guerreiro et al., in "*TREM2* Variants in Alzheimer's Disease" (both published in *New England Journal of Medicine*, vol. 368, no. 2, January 10, 2013)—identified mutations in the TREM2 gene, which is thought to interfere with the brain's ability to prevent the buildup of plaque. This discovery is important because it identifies a potential way to alter the course of AD.

As of July 2013, there were two ongoing, long-term NIA initiatives: the Alzheimer's Disease Genetics Study, which began in 2003 and collects blood samples and deoxyribonucleic acid for researchers to use, and the Alzheimer's Disease Genetics Consortium, which began in 2007 and aims to compare genetic material from 10,000 people with AD to genetic material from 10,000 people without the disease. The NIA also participates in the Dominantly Inherited Alzheimer Network, an international research project that studies early-onset AD in adult children of a parent with a mutated gene.

DIAGNOSTIC TESTING. Historically, the only sure way to diagnose AD was to examine brain tissue under a microscope. The brain of a patient who has died of AD reveals a characteristic pattern that is the hallmark of the disease: tangles of fibers (neurofibrillary tangles) and clusters of degenerated nerve endings (neuritic plaques) in areas of the brain that are crucial for memory and intellect.

Evaluation of people with cognitive changes involves obtaining a thorough medical history and a physical examination to rule out cognitive changes that may result from an underlying illness such as diabetes, a psychiatric disorder such as depression, or a reaction to medication. Physicians ask patients a series of questions to assess their memory, thinking, reasoning, and problem-solving capabilities. Although a complete medical history, physical examination, and psychiatric and neurological assessment do not provide as definitive a diagnosis of AD as an examination of the brain, they can usually produce an accurate diagnosis by ruling out other potential causes of cognitive impairment. Diagnostic tests for AD may also include analysis of blood and spinal fluid as well as the use of brain scans (CT and MRI) to detect strokes or tumors and to measure the volume of brain tissue in the areas used for memory and cognition. Brain scans assist to accurately identify people with AD and predict who may develop AD in the future.

In "Alzheimer-Signature MRI Biomarker Predicts AD Dementia in Cognitively Normal Adults" (*Neurology*, vol. 76, no. 16, April 19, 2011), Brad C. Dickerson et al. used MRI to measure the thickness of the cerebral cortex (the outer portion of the brain that is responsible for higher-order functions such as information processing and language) to help predict which cognitively normal people would develop AD. The researchers hypothesized that the cortical thinning observed in patients with mild AD might be present in cognitively normal adults who will develop AD before they have any symptoms of the disease. Dickerson et al. find that cognitively normal adults who went on to develop AD had thinner cortical areas and those in the highest third of cortical thickness never developed AD. The researchers conclude that "this measure [is] a potentially important imaging biomarker of early neurodegeneration."

The NIA explains in "Alzheimer's Disease Fact Sheet" that apoE testing is used as a research tool to identify research subjects who may have an increased risk of developing AD. Investigators are then able to look for early brain changes in research subjects and compare the effectiveness of treatments for people with different apoE profiles. Because the apoE test does not accurately predict who will or will not develop AD, it is useful for studying AD risk in populations but not for determining any one individual's specific risk.

In "Identification of a Blood-Based Biomarker Panel for Classification of Alzheimer's Disease" (*International Journal of Neuropharmacology*, vol. 14, no. 9, October 2011), Christoph Laske et al. of the University of Tübingen recount their efforts to identify blood biomarkers for AD. The researchers collected 155 serum samples from people with early-stage AD and age-matched healthy controls and measured the levels of 24 biomarkers. They found that three specific biomarkers enabled them to distinguish the AD patients from the healthy controls more than 80% of the time. Laske et al. suggest that these and other blood-based biomarkers may be useful for distinguishing AD from other forms of dementia.

At the 28th International Conference of Alzheimer's Disease International (http://www.adi2013.org/docs/conference-documents/adi-2013-abstract-document.pdf?sfvrsn=2) in April 2013, Shieh-Yueh Yang et al. presented in "Risk Evaluation for Alzheimer's Disease by Assaying Biomarkers in Plasma Using Immunomagnetic Reduction" another new test that may determine the presence of AD using biomarkers for amyloid beta and tau proteins in plasma. The new test is described as able to detect AD more than 90% of the time and will cost as little as $50.

A simple and accurate test, such as the blood-based biomarkers, that distinguishes people with AD from those with cognitive problems or dementias arising from other causes will prove useful for scientists, physicians, and other clinical researchers. However, because advances in detection have outpaced treatment options, the availability of tests to predict who may develop AD raises ethical and practical questions: Do people really want to know their risks of developing AD? Is it helpful to predict a condition that is not yet considered preventable or curable?

DIAGNOSTIC GUIDELINES AND CRITERIA FOR AD. In 2011 the NIA and the Alzheimer's Association tasked a workgroup to establish new guidelines for diagnosing AD, and Guy M. McKhann et al. summarize the details in "The Diagnosis of Dementia Due to Alzheimer's Disease: Recommendations from the National Institute on Aging and the Alzheimer's Association Workgroup" (*Alzheimer's and Dementia*, vol. 7, no. 3, May 2011). The guidelines update diagnostic criteria that were developed in 1984 and aim to detect and treat the disease earlier than ever before. They also acknowledge that imaging and biomarkers should not "be used routinely in clinical diagnosis without further testing and validation."

The updated guidelines explain AD as a continuum of mental decline that may begin many years before the first symptoms arise. Furthermore, they describe the first of three phases: preclinical, which occurs absent symptoms; mild cognitive impairment, which involves noticeable memory problems without loss of ability to function independently; and Alzheimer's dementia, with its characteristic decline in reasoning and function.

The workgroup also created new criteria for determining cognitive impairment caused by AD, and Marilyn S. Albert et al. outline the details in "The Diagnosis of Mild Cognitive Impairment Due to Alzheimer's Disease: Recommendations from the National Institute on Aging and Alzheimer's Association Workgroup" (*Alzheimer's and Dementia*, vol. 7, no. 3, May 2011). The workgroup established two sets of criteria: one for use by health care providers without access to advanced imaging techniques or blood and cerebrospinal fluid analysis and one for use by clinical researchers. The second set of criteria describe the use of biomarkers that are based on imaging and blood and cerebrospinal fluid measures and establish four levels of confidence, depending on the presence and character of the biomarker findings.

TREATMENT. There is no cure or prevention for AD, and treatment focuses on managing symptoms. Medication may slow the appearance of some symptoms and can lessen others, such as agitation, anxiety, unpredictable behavior, and depression. Physical exercise and good nutrition are important, as is a calm and highly structured environment. The objective is to help the AD patient maintain as much comfort, normalcy, and dignity for as long as possible.

According to the Alzheimer's Association, in "Current Alzheimer's Treatments" (http://www.alz.org/research/science/alzheimers_disease_treatments.asp), in 2013 there were five prescription drugs—Aricept, Razadyne, Namenda, Exelon, and Cognex—for the treatment of AD that had been approved by the U.S. Food and Drug Administration, and National Institutes of Health (NIH) affiliates and pharmaceutical companies were involved in clinical trials of new drugs to treat AD. All the drugs being tested were intended to improve the symptoms of AD and slow its progression, but none was expected to cure AD. The investigational drugs aim to address three aspects of AD: to improve cognitive function in people with early-stage AD, to slow or postpone the progression of the disease, and to control behavioral problems such as wandering, aggression, and agitation of patients with AD.

In 2011 a new method of drug delivery, a transdermal patch that delivers the drug through the skin, compared favorably with oral drug administration. Pam Harrison reports in "Transdermal Patch for Alzheimer's Gets Caregiver Thumbs-Up: Delivery Method May Reduce Caregiver Stress, Enhance Patient Response" (Medscape.com, March 30, 2011) that Pablo Martinez-Lage et al. said that some patient caregivers felt the patch slowed, or even stopped, the deterioration that is the hallmark of AD. They opined that the continuous drug delivery offered by the patch might account for the reported improvement in the patients' behavior. Martinez-Lage et al. also observed that AD caregivers found administering the patch easier and less stressful than administering oral medication to potentially combative or uncooperative patients.

ADVANCES IN RESEARCH AND TREATMENT. In "Toll-Like Receptor 4 Stimulation with the Detoxified Ligand Monophosphoryl Lipid A Improves Alzheimer's Disease-Related Pathology" (*Proceedings of the National Academy of Sciences*, vol. 110, no. 5, January 29, 2013), Jean-Philippe Michaud et al. report on their progress developing a way to stimulate the brain's natural defense mechanisms in people with AD. The researchers identified a molecule called monophosphoryl lipid A (MPL) that stimulates the activity of the brain's immune cells. Weekly injections of MPL eliminated about 80% of plaques in mice, and the mice's ability to learn new tasks improved significantly. Michaud et al. think that ADL may be able to slow the progression of AD and may be useful as a vaccine intended to stimulate the production of antibodies against amyloid beta.

CARING FOR THE AD PATIENT. AD affects members of the patient's family. Although medication may suppress some symptoms and occasionally slow the progression of the disease, eventually most AD patients require constant care and supervision. In the past, nursing homes and residential care facilities were not equipped to provide this kind of care, and if they accepted AD patients at all, they admitted only those in the earliest stages of the disease. Since 2000 a growing number of nursing homes have welcomed AD patients, even though they are more difficult and costly to care for than older adults without AD. This change is primarily financially motivated, because nursing home occupancy rates have been dropping in response to the growth of alternative housing for older adults.

The Alzheimer's Association indicates in *2013 Alzheimer's Disease Facts and Figures* that in 2012, 15.4 million caregivers provided about 17.5 billion hours of unpaid care valued at $216.4 billion. Except for prescription medication, the average cost of care of Medicare beneficiaries with AD is higher than that of beneficiaries without AD. For example, in 2008, the most recent year for which these data were available, Medicare paid $10,293 for inpatient hospitalization and $18,353 for nursing homes for beneficiaries with AD and $4,138 and $816, respectively, for those without AD.

Many relatives of AD patients care for the affected family member at home as long as possible because they cannot afford institutional care or they feel an obligation to do so. No matter how devoted the caregiver, the time, patience, and resources required to provide care are immense, and the task is often overwhelming. As the patient's condition progresses, caregivers often find themselves socially isolated. Caregiving has been linked to increased rates of depression, compromised immune function, and a greater use of medication, particularly medications that are used to relieve symptoms of mental distress.

Caregivers who participate in support groups and make use of home health aides, adult day care, and respite care (facilities where patients stay for a limited number of days) not only feel healthier but also are better able to care for AD patients and maintain them at home longer than those who do not.

In *2013 Alzheimer's Disease Facts and Figures*, the Alzheimer's Association describes the growing burden that AD imposes on families, caregivers, and the U.S. health care system. The total cost of health and long-term care for people with AD was an estimated $203 billion in 2013 and is expected to reach $1.2 trillion per year by 2050.

MENTAL ILLNESS

Older people with mental illnesses were once considered senile—that is, mentally debilitated as a result of old age. Serious forgetfulness, emotional disturbances, and other behavioral changes do not, however, occur as a normal part of aging. They may be caused by chronic illnesses such as heart disease, thyroid disorders, or anemia; infections, poor diet, or lack of sleep; or prescription drugs, such as narcotic painkillers, sedatives, and antihistamines. Social isolation, loneliness, boredom, or depression may also cause memory lapses. When accurately diagnosed and treated, these types of problems can frequently be reversed.

Mental illness refers to all identifiable mental health disorders and mental health problems. In the landmark study *Mental Health: A Report of the Surgeon General, 1999* (1999, http://www.surgeongeneral.gov/library/mental health/home.html), the U.S. surgeon general defines mental disorders as "health conditions that are characterized by alterations in thinking, mood, or behavior (or some combination thereof) associated with distress and/or impaired functioning." The surgeon general distinguishes mental health problems from mental health disorders, describing the signs and symptoms of mental health problems as less intense and of shorter duration than those of mental health disorders, but acknowledges that both mental health problems and disorders may be distressing and disabling.

The surgeon general observes that nearly 20% of people aged 55 years and older experience mental disorders that are not part of normal aging. The most common disorders, in order of estimated prevalence rates, are anxiety (11.4%), severe cognitive impairment (6.6%), and mood disorders (4.4%) such as depression. The surgeon general also points out that mental disorders in older adults are frequently unrecognized, underreported, and undertreated.

Diagnosing mental disorders in older adults is challenging because their symptoms may be different from that of other adults. For example, many older adults complain about physical as opposed to emotional or psychological problems, and they present symptoms that are not typical of depression or anxiety disorders. Accurately identifying, detecting, and diagnosing mental disorders in older adults is also complicated by the following:

- Mental disorders often coexist with other medical problems.

- The symptoms of some chronic diseases may imitate or conceal psychological disorders.

- Older adults are more likely to report physical symptoms than psychological ones because there is less stigma associated with physical health or medical problems than with mental health problems.

The Growing Mental Health Needs of Older Adults

Stephen J. Bartels and John A. Naslund of the Dartmouth Institute for Health Policy and Clinical Practice in Lebanon, New Hampshire, report in "The Underside of the Silver Tsunami—Older Adults and Mental Health Care" (*New England Journal of Medicine*, vol. 368, no. 6, February 7, 2013) that between 5.6 million and 8 million adults aged 65 years and older have mental health or substance-use disorders and that by 2030 their ranks will grow to between 10.1 million and 14.4 million. Older adults with mental health disorders are more disabled than those with physical illness alone, and they make more hospital and emergency department visits, resulting in costs that are between 47% and 200% higher than their age peers without mental illness.

Depression

Symptoms of depression are an important indicator of physical and mental health in older adults, because people who experience symptoms of depression are also more likely to report higher rates of physical illness, disability, and health service utilization.

The prevalence of clinically relevant depressive symptoms (as distinguished from brief periods of sadness or depressed mood) increases with advancing age. According to the Federal Interagency Forum on Aging-Related Statistics, in *Older Americans 2012: Key Indicators of Well-Being* (June 2012, http://www.agingstats.gov/Main_Site/Data/2012_Documents/docs/EntireChartbook.pdf), in 2008, 18% of adults aged 85 years and older experienced these symptoms, compared with 12% of those aged 65 to 69 years. (See Figure 8.2.) Older women aged 65 to 84 years reported depressive symptoms more than older men. For example, 14% of women aged 70 to 74 years reported depressive symptoms, compared with 10% of men the same age.

Often, illness itself can trigger depression by altering the chemicals in the brain. Examples of illnesses that can touch off depression are diabetes, hypothyroidism (a condition in which the thyroid is underactive—producing too little thyroid hormones), kidney or liver dysfunction, heart disease, and infection. In patients with these ailments, treating the underlying disease usually eliminates the depression. David M. Clarke and Kay C. Currie find in "Depression, Anxiety, and Their Relationship with Chronic Diseases: A Review of the Epidemiology, Risk, and Treatment Evidence" (*Medical Journal of Australia*, vol. 190, no. 7, April 6, 2009) not only strong evidence for

FIGURE 8.2

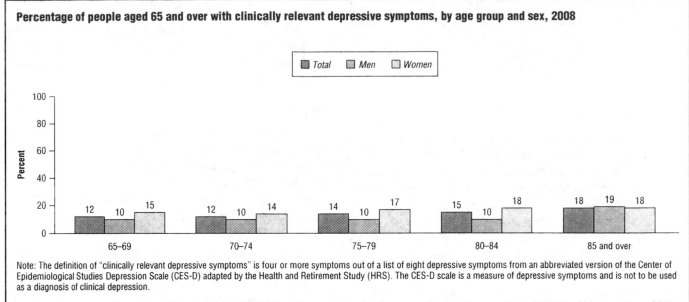

Percentage of people aged 65 and over with clinically relevant depressive symptoms, by age group and sex, 2008

Note: The definition of "clinically relevant depressive symptoms" is four or more symptoms out of a list of eight depressive symptoms from an abbreviated version of the Center of Epidemiological Studies Depression Scale (CES-D) adapted by the Health and Retirement Study (HRS). The CES-D scale is a measure of depressive symptoms and is not to be used as a diagnosis of clinical depression.

SOURCE: "Percentage of People Age 65 and over with Clinically Relevant Depressive Symptoms, by Age Group and Sex, 2008," in *Older Americans 2012: Key Indicators of Well-Being*, Federal Interagency Forum on Aging-Related Statistics, June 2012, http://www.agingstats.gov/Main_Site/Data/2012_Documents/docs/EntireChartbook.pdf (accessed May 28, 2013)

the association of physical illness, depression, and anxiety but also their effects on outcomes (how well patients fare). The researchers indicate that people with disabling chronic illnesses such as arthritis, stroke, and pulmonary diseases are likely to become depressed. Furthermore, Clarke and Currie note that some prescription medications, as well as over-the-counter (nonprescription) drugs, may also cause depression.

Depression causes some older adults to deliberately neglect or disregard their medical needs by eating poorly and failing to take prescribed medication or taking it incorrectly. These may be covert acts of suicide. Actual suicide, which is frequently a consequence of serious depression, is highest among older adults relative to all other age groups. In 2010 the death rate for suicide among people aged 75 to 84 years was 15.7% and among adults aged 85 years and older was 17.6%. (See Table 8.1.) Older men had the highest rates—32.3% for those aged 75 to 84 years and 47.3% for those aged 85 years and older.

TREATMENT OF DEPRESSION. According to the surgeon general, in *Mental Health*, despite the availability of effective treatments for depression, a substantial fraction of affected older adults do not receive treatment, largely because they either do not seek it or their depression is not identified or accurately diagnosed. For example, although many older patients respond well to antidepressants, some physicians do not prescribe them to older patients already taking many drugs for chronic medical conditions because they do not want to risk drug-drug interactions or add another drug to an already compli-

cated regimen. As a result, only a minority of older adults diagnosed with depression receives the appropriate drug dose and duration of treatment.

Treatment for depression includes psychotherapy, with or without the use of antidepressant medications, and electroconvulsive therapy (ECT). Psychotherapy is most often used to treat mild to moderate depression and is prescribed for a limited, defined period, generally ranging from 10 to 20 weeks. ECT is used for life-threatening depression that does not respond to treatment with antidepressant drugs.

In "Long Term Effect of Depression Care Management on Mortality in Older Adults: Follow-up of Cluster Randomized Clinical Trial in Primary Care" (*BMJ*, vol. 3, no. 10, June 2013), a five-year study of 1,226 older patients, Joseph J. Gallo et al. not only find that depression is independently associated with mortality risk in older adults but also confirm that treatment for depression reduces this risk. Of the total number of subjects, about 600 were determined to be suffering from major or minor depression. During the five-year follow-up, subjects who received treatment for depression were 24% less likely to die than those who were not treated.

In "Depressive Symptoms in Old Age: Relations among Sociodemographic and Self-Reported Health Variables" (*International Psychogeriatrics*, April 13, 2011), Gloria Teixeira Nicolosi et al. collected data from 303 adults aged 65 years and older to determine the circumstances and factors that are associated with

TABLE 8.1

Death rates for suicide, selected characteristics, selected years 1950–2010

[Data are based on death certificates]

Sex, race, Hispanic origin, and age	1950[a]	1960[a]	1970	1980	1990	2000	2009	2010
All persons				Deaths per 100,000 resident population				
All ages, age-adjusted[b]	13.2	12.5	13.1	12.2	12.5	10.4	11.8	12.1
All ages, crude	11.4	10.6	11.6	11.9	12.4	10.4	12.0	12.4
Under 1 year	—	—	—	—	—	—	—	—
1–4 years	—	—	—	—	—	—	—	—
5–14 years	0.2	0.3	0.3	0.4	0.8	0.7	0.6	0.7
15–24 years	4.5	5.2	8.8	12.3	13.2	10.2	10.0	10.5
15–19 years	2.7	3.6	5.9	8.5	11.1	8.0	7.5	7.5
20–24 years	6.2	7.1	12.2	16.1	15.1	12.5	12.6	13.6
25–44 years	11.6	12.2	15.4	15.6	15.2	13.4	14.6	15.0
25–34 years	9.1	10.0	14.1	16.0	15.2	12.0	13.1	14.0
35–44 years	14.3	14.2	16.9	15.4	15.3	14.5	16.1	16.0
45–64 years	23.5	22.0	20.6	15.9	15.3	13.5	17.9	18.6
45–54 years	20.9	20.7	20.0	15.9	14.8	14.4	19.2	19.6
55–64 years	26.8	23.7	21.4	15.9	16.0	12.1	16.4	17.5
65 years and over	30.0	24.5	20.8	17.6	20.5	15.2	14.8	14.9
65–74 years	29.6	23.0	20.8	16.9	17.9	12.5	13.7	13.7
75–84 years	31.1	27.9	21.2	19.1	24.9	17.6	15.8	15.7
85 years and over	28.8	26.0	19.0	19.2	22.2	19.6	16.4	17.6
Male								
All ages, age-adjusted[b]	21.2	20.0	19.8	19.9	21.5	17.7	19.2	19.8
All ages, crude	17.8	16.5	16.8	18.6	20.4	17.1	19.3	19.9
Under 1 year	—	—	—	—	—	—	—	—
1–4 years	—	—	—	—	—	—	—	—
5–14 years	0.3	0.4	0.5	0.6	1.1	1.2	0.8	0.9
15–24 years	6.5	8.2	13.5	20.2	22.0	17.1	16.1	16.9
15–19 years	3.5	5.6	8.8	13.8	18.1	13.0	11.6	11.7
20–24 years	9.3	11.5	19.3	26.8	25.7	21.4	20.8	22.2
25–44 years	17.2	17.9	20.9	24.0	24.4	21.3	23.0	23.6
25–34 years	13.4	14.7	19.8	25.0	24.8	19.6	21.0	22.5
35–44 years	21.3	21.0	22.1	22.5	23.9	22.8	24.9	24.6
45–64 years	37.1	34.4	30.0	23.7	24.3	21.3	27.9	29.2
45–54 years	32.0	31.6	27.9	22.9	23.2	22.4	29.3	30.4
55–64 years	43.6	38.1	32.7	24.5	25.7	19.4	26.1	27.7
65 years and over	52.8	44.0	38.4	35.0	41.6	31.1	29.1	29.0
65–74 years	50.5	39.6	36.0	30.4	32.2	22.7	24.0	23.9
75–84 years	50.0	53.6	42.0	42.3	56.1	38.6	32.9	32.3
85 years and over	58.3	57.4	42.4	50.6	65.9	57.5	44.0	47.3
Female								
All ages, age-adjusted[b]	5.6	5.6	7.4	5.7	4.8	4.0	4.9	5.0
All ages, crude	5.1	4.9	6.6	5.5	4.8	4.0	5.0	5.2
Under 1 year	—	—	—	—	—	—	—	—
1–4 years	—	—	—	—	—	—	—	—
5–14 years	0.1	0.1	0.2	0.2	0.4	0.3	0.5	0.4
15–24 years	2.6	2.2	4.2	4.3	3.9	3.0	3.6	3.9
15–19 years	1.8	1.6	2.9	3.0	3.7	2.7	3.2	3.1
20–24 years	3.3	2.9	5.7	5.5	4.1	3.2	4.1	4.7
25–44 years	6.2	6.6	10.2	7.7	6.2	5.4	6.2	6.4
25–34 years	4.9	5.5	8.6	7.1	5.6	4.3	5.1	5.3
35–44 years	7.5	7.7	11.9	8.5	6.8	6.4	7.4	7.5
45–64 years	9.9	10.2	12.0	8.9	7.1	6.2	8.5	8.6
45–54 years	9.9	10.2	12.6	9.4	6.9	6.7	9.3	9.0
55–64 years	9.9	10.2	11.4	8.4	7.3	5.4	7.4	8.0
65 years and over	9.4	8.4	8.1	6.1	6.4	4.0	4.0	4.2
65–74 years	10.1	8.4	9.0	6.5	6.7	4.0	4.6	4.8
75–84 years	8.1	8.9	7.0	5.5	6.3	4.0	3.6	3.7
85 years and over	8.2	6.0	5.9	5.5	5.4	4.2	3.2	3.3

depression. The researchers find that symptoms of depression are associated with a higher number of self-reported health problems, poor perceived health assessment, and lower levels of academic attainment. Among older women, health and financial problems are most closely associated with symptoms of depression.

Anxiety Disorders

Anxiety disorders (extreme nervousness and apprehension or sudden attacks of fear without apparent external causes) can be debilitating. Symptoms may include a "knot" in the stomach, sweating, or elevated blood pressure. If the anxiety is severe and long lasting, more serious

TABLE 8.1

Death rates for suicide, selected characteristics, selected years 1950–2010 [CONTINUED]

[Data are based on death certificates]

Sex, race, Hispanic origin, and age	1950[a]	1960[a]	1970	1980	1990	2000	2009	2010
White male[c]				Deaths per 100,000 resident population				
All ages, age-adjusted[b]	22.3	21.1	20.8	20.9	22.8	19.1	21.4	22.0
All ages, crude	19.0	17.6	18.0	19.9	22.0	18.8	21.9	22.6
15–24 years	6.6	8.6	13.9	21.4	23.2	17.9	17.6	18.3
25–44 years	17.9	18.5	21.5	24.6	25.4	22.9	25.7	26.2
45–64 years	39.3	36.5	31.9	25.0	26.0	23.2	31.4	33.0
65 years and over	55.8	46.7	41.1	37.2	44.2	33.3	31.5	31.7
65–74 years	53.2	42.0	38.7	32.5	34.2	24.3	26.6	26.3
75–84 years	61.9	55.7	45.5	45.5	60.2	41.1	35.3	34.9
85 years and over	61.9	61.3	45.8	52.8	70.3	61.6	46.9	50.8

—Category not applicable.

[a]Includes deaths of persons who were not residents of the 50 states and the District of Columbia (D.C.).

[b]Age-adjusted rates are calculated using the year 2000 standard population. Prior to 2001, age-adjusted rates were calculated using standard million proportions based on rounded population numbers. Starting with 2001 data, unrounded population numbers are used to calculate age-adjusted rates.

[c]The race groups, white, black, Asian or Pacific Islander, and American Indian or Alaska Native, include persons of Hispanic and non-Hispanic origin. Persons of Hispanic origin may be of any race. Death rates for the American Indian or Alaska Native, Asian or Pacific Islander, and Hispanic populations are known to be underestimated.

Notes: Starting with Health, United States, 2003, rates for 1991–1999 were revised using intercensal population estimates based on the 1990 and 2000 censuses. For 2000, population estimates are bridged-race April 1 census counts. Starting with Health, United States, 2012, rates for 2001–2009 were revised using intercensal population estimates based on the 2000 and 2010 censuses. For 2010, population estimates are bridged-race April 1 census counts. Figures for 2001 include September 11-related deaths for which death certificates were filed as of October 24, 2002. Age groups were selected to minimize the presentation of unstable age-specific death rates based on small numbers of deaths and for consistency among comparison groups. Starting with 2003 data, some states allowed the reporting of more than one race on the death certificate. The multiple-race data for these states were bridged to the single-race categories of the 1977 Office of Management and Budget standards, for comparability with other states.

SOURCE: Adapted from "Table 35. Death Rates for Suicide, by Sex, Race, Hispanic Origin, and Age: United States, Selected Years 1950–2010," in *Health, United States, 2012: With Special Feature on Emergency Care*, 2013, National Center for Health Statistics, http://www.cdc.gov/nchs/data/hus/2012/035.pdf (accessed June 1, 2013)

problems may develop. People suffering from anxiety over extended periods may have headaches, ulcers, irritable bowel syndrome, insomnia, or depression. Because anxiety tends to create various other emotional and physical symptoms, a cascade effect can occur in which these new problems produce even more anxiety.

Unrelenting anxiety that appears unrelated to specific environments or situations is called generalized anxiety disorder. People suffering from this disorder worry excessively about the events of daily life and the future. They are also more likely to experience physical symptoms such as shortness of breath, dizziness, rapid heart rate, nausea, stomach pains, and muscle tension than people who are afflicted with other panic disorders, social phobias, or agoraphobia (fear of being in an open space or a place where escape is difficult).

The surgeon general estimates in *Mental Health* the prevalence of anxiety disorder as about 11.4% of adults aged 55 years and older. Phobic anxiety disorders such as social phobia, which causes extreme discomfort in social settings, are among the most common mental disturbances in late life. In contrast, some disorders have low rates of prevalence among older adults, such as panic disorder (0.5%) and obsessive-compulsive disorder (1.5%). Generalized anxiety disorder, rather than specific anxiety syndromes, may be more prevalent in older people.

Effective treatment for anxiety involves medication, primarily benzodiazepines, such as Valium, Librium, and Xanax, as well as psychotherapy. Like other medications, the effects of benzodiazepines may last longer in older adults, and their side effects may include drowsiness, fatigue, physical impairment, memory or other cognitive impairment, confusion, depression, respiratory problems, abuse or dependence problems, and withdrawal reactions.

Nondrug treatment may also be effective for older adults suffering from debilitating anxiety. In "Antidepressant Medication Augmented with Cognitive-Behavioral Therapy for Generalized Anxiety Disorder in Older Adults" (*American Journal of Psychiatry*, vol. 170, no. 7, July 1, 2013), Julie L. Wetherell et al. compare cognitive behavioral therapy (CBT; goal-oriented treatment that focuses on changing thoughts to solve psychological problems), drug treatment alone, a combination of the two, and a placebo (a pill that contains no active drug) as treatment for generalized anxiety disorder in older adults. The researchers find that although both drug treatment and CBT relieved anxiety and prevented relapse when compared with placebo, CBT alone provided long-term relief from anxiety. Wetherell et al. conclude that although medication prevents relapse, CBT is able to prevent recurrences without the need for long-term drug treatment.

Schizophrenia

Schizophrenia is an extremely disabling form of mental illness. Its symptoms include hallucinations, paranoia, delusions, and social isolation. People suffering from schizophrenia "hear voices," and over time the voices take over in the schizophrenic's mind, obliterating reality and directing all kinds of erratic behaviors. Suicide attempts and violent attacks are common in the lives of schizophrenics. In an attempt to escape the torment inflicted by their brains, many schizophrenics turn to drugs. The National Institute of Mental Health indicates in *Schizophrenia* (2009, http://www.nimh.nih.gov/health/publications/schizophrenia/schizophrenia-booket-2009.pdf) that most symptoms of schizophrenia emerge early in life—the late teens or 20s and rarely begin after age 45.

In *Mental Health*, the surgeon general notes that the prevalence of schizophrenia among adults aged 65 years and older is estimated to be 0.6%, less than half of the 1.3% that is estimated for the population aged 18 to 54 years. However, the economic burden of late-life schizophrenia is high.

Drug treatment of schizophrenia in older adults is complicated. The medications that are used to treat schizophrenia, such as Haldol, effectively reduce symptoms (e.g., delusions and hallucinations) in many older patients, but they also have a high risk of disabling side effects, such as tardive dyskinesias (involuntary, rhythmic movements of the face, jaw, mouth, tongue, and trunk). Even newer atypical antipsychotic medications that are used to treat the symptoms of schizophrenia, such as Abilify, can produce troubling side effects, including tremors, restlessness, shakes, muscle stiffness, or other involuntary movements.

MISUSE OF ALCOHOL AND PRESCRIPTION DRUGS

The surgeon general observes in *Mental Health* that older adults are more likely to misuse, as opposed to abuse, alcohol and prescription drugs. The surgeon general estimates that the prevalence of heavy drinking (12 to 21 drinks per week) in the cohort (a group of individuals that shares a common characteristic such as birth years and is studied over time) of older adults is 3% to 9%. The prevalence rates are expected to rise as the baby boomer (people born between 1946 and 1964) cohort, with its history of alcohol and illegal drug use, joins the ranks of older adults. In "Substance Use Disorder among Older Adults in the United States in 2020" (*Addiction*, vol. 104, no. 1, January 2009), Beth Han et al. forecast that the number of adults aged 50 years and older with substance use disorder (alcohol/illicit drug dependence or abuse) is projected to double from an average of 2.8 million per year in 2006 to 5.7 million in 2020. The current group of older adults is more likely to suffer substance misuse problems, such as drug dependence,

FIGURE 8.3

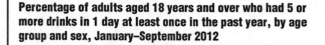

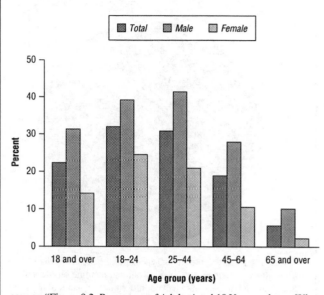

Percentage of adults aged 18 years and over who had 5 or more drinks in 1 day at least once in the past year, by age group and sex, January–September 2012

SOURCE: "Figure 9.2. Percentage of Adults Aged 18 Years and over Who Had 5 or More Drinks in 1 Day at Least Once in the Past Year, by Age Group and Sex: United States, January–September 2012," in *Early Release of Selected Estimates Based on Data from the January–September 2012 National Health Interview Survey*, Centers for Disease Control and Prevention, National Center for Health Statistics, March 2013, http://www.cdc.gov/nchs/data/nhis/earlyrelease/earlyrelease 201303_09.pdf (accessed June 14, 2013)

arising from underuse, overuse, or erratic use of prescription and over-the-counter medications.

Figure 8.3 shows that adults aged 65 years and older had the lowest rate of excessive alcohol consumption—just 5.6%—of all age groups. Older men (10%) were much more likely than older women (2.2%) to have met the National Health Interview Survey criteria for excessive alcohol consumption (five or more drinks in one day at least once in the past year).

Prevalence of Types of Older Problem Drinkers

In *Module 10C: Older Adults and Alcohol Problems* (March 2005, http://pubs.niaaa.nih.gov/publications/social/Module10COlderAdults/Module10C.html), the National Institute on Alcohol Abuse and Alcoholism (NIAAA) describes the prevalence of three types of problem drinkers: at-risk drinkers, problem drinkers, and alcohol-dependent drinkers.

- At-risk drinking is alcohol use that increases the risk of developing alcohol-related problems and complications. People over the age of 65 years who drink more than seven drinks per week (one per day) are

FIGURE 8.4

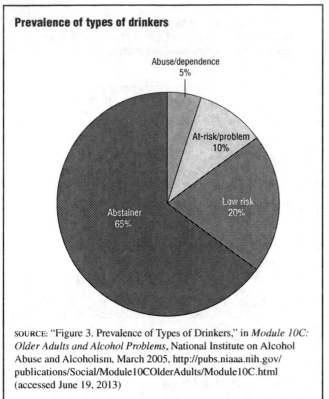

Prevalence of types of drinkers

Abuse/dependence 5%

At-risk/problem 10%

Low risk 20%

Abstainer 65%

SOURCE: "Figure 3. Prevalence of Types of Drinkers," in *Module 10C: Older Adults and Alcohol Problems*, National Institute on Alcohol Abuse and Alcoholism, March 2005, http://pubs.niaaa.nih.gov/publications/Social/Module10COlderAdults/Module10C.html (accessed June 19, 2013)

considered at risk of developing health, social, or emotional problems caused by alcohol.

• Problem drinkers have already suffered medical, psychological, family, financial, self-care, legal, or social consequences of alcohol abuse.

• Alcohol-dependent drinkers suffer from a medical disorder that is characterized by a loss of control over consumption, preoccupation with alcohol, and continued use despite adverse health, social, legal, and financial consequences.

Figure 8.4 shows the estimated prevalence rates of these different types of drinkers as well as the majority (65%) of older adults that abstains from alcohol consumption.

Types of Older Problem Drinkers

Another way to characterize older problem drinkers is by the duration and patterns of their drinking histories. The first group consists of those over the age of 60 years who have been drinking for most of their life. Members of this group are called survivors or early-onset problem drinkers. They have beaten the statistical odds by living to old age despite heavy drinking, but they are most likely to suffer from cirrhosis of the liver (a chronic degenerative disease of the liver marked by scarring of liver tissue and eventually liver failure) and mental health disorders such as depression.

The second group, intermittents, has historically engaged in binge drinking interspersed with periods of relative sobriety. These drinkers are at risk for alcohol abuse because they are more likely than others to self-medicate with alcohol to relieve physical pain and emotional distress or to assuage loneliness and social isolation.

Reactors or late-onset problem drinkers make up the third group. The stresses of later life, particularly the loss of work or a spouse, may precipitate heavy drinking. These people show few of the physical consequences of prolonged drinking and fewer disruptions in their life.

Alcohol-Related Issues Unique to Older Adults

Older adults generally have a decreased tolerance to alcohol. Consumption of a given amount of alcohol by older adults usually produces higher blood-alcohol levels than it would in a younger population. Chronic medical problems such as cirrhosis may be present, but older adults are less likely to require detoxification and treatment of alcohol-withdrawal problems. One possible explanation is that few lifelong alcohol abusers survive to old age.

Because older adults usually take more medication than people in other age groups, they are more susceptible to drug-alcohol interactions. Alcohol reduces the safety and effectiveness of many medications and, in combination with some drugs, may produce coma or death. Adverse consequences of alcohol consumption in older adults are not limited to problem drinkers. Older adults with medical problems, including diabetes, heart disease, liver disease, and central nervous system degeneration, may also suffer adverse reactions from alcohol consumption.

SCREENING, DIAGNOSIS, AND TREATMENT. The NIAAA advocates screening to identify at-risk drinkers, problem drinkers, and dependent drinkers to determine the need for further diagnostic evaluation and treatment. Furthermore, in *Module 10C* it provides a screening protocol that recommends:

• All adults aged 60 years and older should be screened for alcohol and prescription drug use/abuse as part of any medical examination or application for health or social services.

• Annual rescreening should be performed if certain physical symptoms emerge or if the individual is undergoing major life changes, stresses, or transitions.

• These screening criteria apply to any health, social, work, or recreation setting that serves older adults and are not limited to medical care and substance treatment settings.

Diagnosis of problem drinking in the older population is complicated by the fact that many psychological, behavioral, and physical symptoms of problem drinking also occur in people who do not have drinking problems.

For example, brain damage, heart disease, and gastrointestinal disorders often develop in older adults independent of alcohol use, but may also occur with drinking. In addition, mood disorders, depression, and changes in employment, economic, or marital status often accompany aging but can also be symptoms of alcoholism. Alcohol-induced organic brain syndrome is characterized by cognitive impairment (memory lapses, confusion, and disorientation). As a result, some older alcoholics may be incorrectly diagnosed as suffering from dementia or other mental illness.

Older problem drinkers make up a relatively small proportion of the total number of clients seen by most agencies for treatment of alcohol abuse. Little data about the effectiveness of intervention and treatment, which usually consists of some combination of counseling and education, in the older population exist. Nonetheless, the chances for recovery among older drinkers are considered good because older clients tend to complete the full course of therapy more often than younger clients.

There are indications that the number of older adults with alcohol and substance abuse problems will increase in the coming years. For example, in "A Rising Tide of Substance Abuse" (NYTimes.com, April 29, 2013), Richard A. Friedman observes that baby boomers are more likely to use alcohol and drugs than previous generations of older adults. He notes that during the first decade of the 21st century illicit drug use among adults aged 50 to 59 years more than doubled and asserts that

along with problem drinking prescription drug abuse is a growing problem. Friedman also notes that older adults' alcohol and drug use is different from teens' and young adults'. Rather than using these substances to "get high," Friedman explains, "the elderly turn to alcohol and drugs to alleviate the physical and psychological pain from the onslaught of medical and psychiatric illness, the loss of loved ones or social isolation."

WHO WILL TREAT THIS GROWING PROBLEM? Just as there is a serious shortage of geriatricians (physicians who are specially trained to care for older adults), Bartels and Naslund assert that there is a comparable shortfall of geriatric mental health providers. More than half of the available training slots for geriatric psychiatrists go unfilled each year, and a scant 4.2% of psychologists focus on treating older adults. Bartels and Naslund suggest growing the geriatric mental health workforce by cultivating "health coaches and lay community health workers trained to provide screening and brief interventions for geriatric mental health and substance-use disorders." Other potential solutions might be Internet-based technologies, which may provide opportunities for screening and treatment for older adults who are unable to seek or access care because they lack transportation or have limited mobility. The relative anonymity and privacy of seeking and receiving care online might also reduce some of the stigma that is associated with mental health treatment.

CHAPTER 9
CARING FOR OLDER ADULTS: CAREGIVERS

In the United States most long-term care of older adults continues to be provided by families as opposed to nursing homes, assisted living facilities, social service agencies, or government programs. This continuing commitment to family care of older adults in the community is remarkable in view of relatively recent changes in the fabric of American society. American family life has undergone significant changes in the past three decades. Most households require two incomes, and greater numbers of women have entered the workforce. Delayed marriage and childbearing has produced a so-called sandwich generation of family caregivers that is simultaneously caring for two generations: their children and their parents. For the first time in U.S. history, adults may spend more years caring for a parent than for a child. Increased geographic separation of families further compounds the difficulties of family caregiving.

Another challenge is that the supply of caregivers is not keeping pace with the growth in the older population. The number of older adults for every 100 adults of working age (aged 20 to 64 years) is called the dependency ratio. Laura B. Shrestha of the Congressional Research Service notes in *Age Dependency Ratios and Social Security Solvency* (October 27, 2006, http://aging.senate.gov/crs/ss4.pdf) that in 2015 there will be an estimated 23.5 older adults for every 100 working-age adults. (See Table 9.1.) When the youngest members of the baby boomer generation (those born between 1946 and 1964) begin approaching retirement age in 2025, there will be 31.2 older adults for every 100 people of working age.

In "Employment Projections—2010–20" (February 1, 2012, http://www.bls.gov/news.release/pdf/ecopro.pdf), the U.S. Bureau of Labor Statistics predicts growth in employment that far exceeds the average rate of 14.3% for home health aides (69.4%) and personal care aides (70.5%) between 2010 and 2020. Catherine Rampell

reports in "United States of Health Care" (NYTimes.com, February 1, 2012) that home health care services are booming. She notes that based on Bureau of Labor Statistics projections for 2010 to 2020 an additional 706,000 home health aides and 607,000 personal care aides will be employed.

Furthermore, the Institute of Medicine's Committee on the Future Health Care Workforce for Older Americans observes in *Retooling for an Aging America: Building the Health Care Workforce* (2008, http://www.nap.edu/openbook.php?record_id=12089&page=R1) that about 80% of older adults rely exclusively on unpaid help from family and friends for assistance at home and that less than 10% receive all their care from paid workers. The committee also notes that an estimated 29 million to 52 million Americans—as many as 31% of all U.S. adults—provide some kind of unpaid help or care.

The U.S. Senate bill S. 1028, Older Americans Act Amendments of 2013, which reauthorizes the Older Americans Act of 1965, contains provisions to help build a health care workforce with the necessary skills and training to meet the health and long-term care services needs of older adults. Assigned to a congressional committee in May 2013, the bill was endorsed by the American Geriatrics Society (May 23, 2013, http://www.americangeriatrics.org/files/documents/Adv_Resources/Older.Americans.Act.Reauthorization.Bill.pdf), a national nonprofit organization that consists of over 6,000 health professionals dedicated to meeting the health care needs of older adults. The society said it was "pleased" the bill "address[es] workforce shortages and support[s] family caregivers" and establishes "grants to states to conduct assessments of family or informal caregiver needs as well as the testing of models that provide direct care workers with further training for new roles."

TABLE 9.1

Age dependency ratios, 2010–30

| | Population (in thousands) | | | | Dependency ratio (number of dependents per 100 persons of working age) | | | |
Year	Total	Children (0–19)	Working age (20–64)	Older persons (65–65+)	All dependents	Children (0–19)	Older persons (65–65+)
2014	324,710	85,525	194,629	44,556	66.8	43.9	22.9
2015	327,202	85,796	195,496	45,910	67.4	43.9	23.5
2016	329,662	86,106	196,245	47,311	68.0	43.9	24.1
2017	332,086	86,466	196,874	48,746	68.7	43.9	24.8
2018	334,497	86,859	197,405	50,233	69.4	44.0	25.4
2019	336,892	87,247	197,826	51,819	70.3	44.1	26.2
2020	339,270	87,547	198,213	53,510	71.2	44.2	27.0
2021	341,626	87,736	198,642	55,248	72.0	44.2	27.8
2022	343,958	87,883	199,059	57,016	72.8	44.1	28.6
2023	346,255	88,003	199,475	58,777	73.6	44.1	29.5
2024	348,514	88,233	199,736	60,545	74.5	44.2	30.3
2025	350,729	88,597	199,789	62,343	75.5	44.3	31.2
2026	352,871	88,942	199,847	64,082	76.6	44.5	32.1
2027	354,936	89,266	199,965	65,705	77.5	44.6	32.9
2028	356,946	89,574	200,139	67,233	78.3	44.8	33.6
2029	358,898	89,863	200,347	68,688	79.1	44.9	34.3
2030	360,794	90,133	200,644	70,017	79.8	44.9	34.9

SOURCE: Adapted from Laura B. Shrestha, "Appendix Table 1. Age Dependency Ratios, United States, 1950–2080," in *Age Dependency Ratios and Social Security Solvency*, Congressional Research Service, The Library of Congress, October 27, 2006, http://aging.senate.gov/crs/ss4.pdf (accessed August 3, 2013)

FAMILY CAREGIVERS

According to the Family Caregiver Alliance, in "Fact Sheet: Selected Caregiver Statistics" (2013, http://www.caregiver.org/caregiver/jsp/content_node.jsp?nodeid=439), the majority of adults who received long-term care at home in 2013 relied exclusively on informal caregivers—family and friends. Every year, approximately 66 million Americans devote billions of hours providing this care, which includes help with tasks such as bathing, meal preparation, and managing medications, for adult family members aged 20 years and older. Forty-four million caregivers provide care for adults aged 50 years and older, and of this group 14.9 million care for an older adult suffering from dementia (loss of intellectual functioning accompanied by memory loss and personality changes). Millions of others provide care for adults aged 65 years and older, enabling them to remain in the community and age in place (remain in their own home rather than relocating to assisted living facilities or other supportive housing).

Caregiving in the United States

In "Selected Caregiver Statistics," the Family Caregiver Alliance describes the average caregiver as a 48-year-old working woman who spends three or more years caring for a parent who does not live with her. Caregivers provide an average of 20.4 hours of care per week. According to the alliance, over 30% have provided care for five years or longer and 15% for more than 10 years. Caregivers shop, prepare food, clean house, do laundry, provide transportation, and administer medication. They also assist with personal care, such as feeding, dressing, bathing, and toileting. In addition, caregivers spend an average of 13 hours per month researching disease care and treatment as well as coordinating physician visits and managing finances.

Caregiving can take a toll on physical and mental health and well-being. Research reveals that caregivers may suffer a range of health problems including:

- Elevated blood pressure and insulin levels, which in turn increase the risk of developing cardiovascular disease

- High levels of physical and emotional stress and impaired immune function, which renders them less able to defend against illness

- Depression, anxiety, anger, and other emotional problems

The Economics of Caregiving

Most of the costs and responsibility for long-term care for older adults rest with family caregivers. The shift toward increasing reliance on this informal system of care was spurred by changes in the health care financing system that resulted in shorter hospital stays, rising costs of nursing home care, older adults preferring home care over institutional care, and a shortage of long-term care workers. Taken together, these factors continue to increase the likelihood that frail, disabled, and ill older adults will be cared for by relatives.

In *The MetLife Study of Caregiving Costs to Working Caregivers: New Insights and Innovations for Reducing Health Care Costs for Employers* (February 2010, https://www.metlife.com/assets/cao/mmi/publications/studies/2011/mmi-caregiving-costs-working-caregivers.pdf), the

MetLife Mature Market Institute finds that caregivers cost U.S. employers $13.4 billion annually. These costs result from absenteeism, workers' moving from full-time to part-time work, replacing workers who leave, and interruptions to the workday. Furthermore, the MetLife Mature Market Institute notes in "The MetLife Study of Caregiving Costs to Working Caregivers: Double Jeopardy for Baby Boomers Caring for Their Parents" (2013, https://www.metlife.com/mmi/research/caregiving-cost-working-caregivers.html#key findings) that the cost impact of caregiving in terms of leaving the workforce prematurely and the lost wages, pension, and Social Security benefits is $303,880 for women and $283,715 for men.

A Slow and Uncertain Economy Affects Informal Caregiving

According to Susannah Fox, Maeve Duggan, and Kristen Purcell of the Pew Research Center, in *Family Caregivers Are Wired for Health* (June 20, 2013, http://www.pewinternet.org/~/media//Files/Reports/2013/Pew Research_FamilyCaregivers.pdf), 39% of adults provided care for a loved one in 2012. More than one-third (36%) of U.S. adults served as a caregiver for one or more adults, and 47% of the adults being cared for were either a parent or parent-in-law. Interviewed by Yasmeen Abutaleb, in "Two-fifths of U.S. adults care for sick, elderly relatives" (Reuters.com, June 20, 2013), Susannah Fox, the study's lead author, explained that the number of family caregivers grew 10% between 2010 to 2012 and that the slow U.S. economy spurred this growth—families no longer have the resources to pay for professional caregivers.

The Effects of the Patient Protection and Affordable Care Act on Informal Caregivers

In March 2010 President Barack Obama (1961–) signed the Patient Protection and Affordable Care Act (PPACA; also known as the Affordable Care Act or Obamacare) into law. The law, which reformed health care delivery to improve access to care, will be fully implemented in 2014. The Family Caregiver Alliance explains in "Health Care Reform and Family Caregivers" (2010, http://www.caregiver.org/content/pdfs/HCR%20provisions%20for%20caregivers-2010.pdf) that the law acknowledges the need for home care services and offers incentives for the states to provide these services through Medicaid (a federal and state health care program for people below the poverty level) for older adults with low incomes—up to 300% of the maximum Supplemental Security Income payment. Beginning in 2010 the law allocated $10 million per year for five years to support Aging and Disability Resource Center initiatives, which serve as entry points for older adults in need of long-term care services. It also requires federally funded geriatric education centers to offer free or low-cost training to family caregivers.

Although the PPACA will affect every American, industry observers anticipate that older adults and their caregivers will benefit the most from it. For example, in *Averting the Caregiving Crisis: Why We Must Act Now* (October 2010, http://www.rosalynncarter.org/UserFiles/File/RCI_Position_Paper100310_Final.pdf), the Rosalynn Carter Institute for Caregiving notes that the PPACA calls for coordination between family and formal caregivers as a way to improve access to care. It requires programs to engage in shared decision-making between all stakeholders—patients, health care providers, and family caregivers. It also calls for caregiver education and training about subjects ranging from medication management to communication techniques for working with people who have dementia.

The Effects of the PPACA on Paid Caregivers

The PPACA redirects reimbursement to incentivize health professionals to care for people with chronic conditions in the community rather than in hospitals. It created the Community-Based Care Transitions Program to assist Medicare beneficiaries to return to their home following hospital discharge. It also created the Independence at Home Medical Practice Pilot Program that began in January 2012 to provide coordinated, primary care services to Medicare beneficiaries with multiple chronic conditions in their home. The Centers for Medicare and Medicaid Services indicates in the fact sheet "Independence at Home Demonstration" (March 2013, http://www.cms.gov/Medicare/Demonstration-Projects/DemoProjectsEvalRpts/Downloads/IAH_FactSheet.pdf) that as of April 2013 there were 15 practices participating in the pilot program.

The PPACA also aims to increase the numbers of health care workers by:

- Offering grant funding and other incentives to encourage students and health professionals to train in primary care, geriatrics, chronic care, and long-term care

- Providing funding to train health care workers who are direct-service providers such as home health aides and other providers of long-term and community-based services

- Establishing the Personal Care Attendants Workforce Advisory Panel to assess and advise on issues involving direct-care workers including salaries, wages, and benefits

- Instituting the National Health Care Workforce Commission to advise on ways to better meet the growing need for health care workers

In *National Association for Home Care and Hospice: 2013 Legislative Priorities* (February 2013, http://www

the National Association for Home Care and Hospice (NAHC) calls for state certification of home care workers to ensure that they are properly trained and supervised and for payment to the agencies that employ them that is sufficient to provide basic employee benefits including health insurance.

THE CONTINUUM OF FORMAL SERVICES

As the older population increases, the segment of the population that is available to provide unpaid care, generally consisting of family members, has decreased. Because the availability of caregivers has diminished, increasing numbers of older adults in need of assistance will rely on a combination of family caregiving and paid professional services or on professional services alone.

Home Health Care

Home health care agencies provide a wide variety of services. Services range from helping with activities of daily living, such as bathing, housekeeping, and meals, to skilled nursing care. Home health care agencies employ registered nurses, licensed practical nurses, and home health aides to deliver the bulk of these services. Other personnel involved in home health care include physical therapists, social workers, and speech-language pathologists.

Home health care grew faster during the early 1990s than any other segment of health services. Its growth is attributable to the fact that in many cases caring for patients at home is preferable to and more cost effective than care that is provided in a hospital, nursing home, or other residential facility.

Before 2000 Medicare coverage for home health care was limited to patients immediately following discharge from the hospital. By 2000 Medicare covered beneficiaries' home health care services with no requirement for prior hospitalization. There were also no limits to the number of professional visits or to the length of coverage. As long as the patient's condition warranted it, the following services were provided:

- Part-time or intermittent skilled nursing and home health aide services

- Speech-language pathology services

- Physical and occupational therapy

- Medical social services

- Medical supplies

- Durable medical equipment (with a 20% co-payment)

Since 2000 the population receiving home care services has changed. Although the PPACA contains provisions to increase community-based chronic and long-term care, as of July 2013 much of home health care was associated with rehabilitation from critical illnesses, and fewer users were long-term patients with long-term conditions. This changing pattern of use reflects a shift from longer-term care for chronic conditions to short-term postacute care. Compared with postacute care users, the long-term patients are older, more functionally disabled, more likely to be incontinent, and more expensive to serve.

In *Basic Statistics about Home Care* (2010, http://www.nahc.org/assets/1/7/10HC_Stats.pdf), the most recent information available on this topic as of July 2013, the NAHC notes that approximately 12 million people received home care services from more than 33,000 providers of home care services in 2009 and that annual expenditures for home health care services were an estimated $72.2 billion.

Respite Care and Adult Day Care

Respite care enables caregivers to take much-needed breaks from the demands of caregiving. It offers relief for families who may be overwhelmed and exhausted by the demands of caregiving and may be neglecting their own needs for rest and relaxation.

Respite care takes many forms. In some cases the respite worker comes to the home to take care of the older adult so that the caregiver can take a few hours off for personal needs, relaxation, or rest. Inpatient respite care, which is offered by some nursing homes and board-and-care facilities, provides an alternative to in-home care. Respite care is also available for longer periods, so that caregivers can recuperate from their own illnesses or even take vacations.

Adult day care programs, which are freestanding or based in hospitals, provide structured programs where older adults may receive the social, health, and recreational services they need to restore or maintain optimal functioning. Although they are not specifically intended to provide respite for caregivers, adult day care programs temporarily relieve families of the physical and emotional stress of caregiving.

Community Services

Besides home health care services, many communities offer a variety of services to help older adults and their caregivers:

- Home care aides assist with chores such as housecleaning, grocery shopping, or laundry, as well as with the activities of daily living

- Repair services help with basic home maintenance, as well as minor changes to make homes secure and safe, such as the installation of grab bars in bathrooms, special seats in the shower, or ramps for wheelchairs

- Home-delivered meal programs deliver nutritious meals to those who can no longer cook or shop for groceries

- Companion and telephone reassurance services keep in touch with older adults living alone (volunteers make regular visits or phone calls to check on and maintain contact with isolated older adults)

- Trained postal or utility workers spot signs of trouble at the homes of older people

- Emergency Response Systems devices allow older adults to summon help in emergencies (when the user pushes the button on the wearable device, it sends a message to a response center or police station)

- Senior centers offer recreation programs, social activities, educational programs, health screenings, and meals

- Communities provide transportation to help older adults run errands and attend medical appointments (these services are often subsidized or free of charge)

- Adult day care centers care for older adults who need supervised assistance (services may include health care, recreation, meals, rehabilitative therapy, and respite care)

Home and Community-Based Services

Home and community-based services refer to the entire array of supportive services that help older people live independently in their homes and communities. In 1981 federal law implemented the Medicaid Home and Community-Based Services (HCBS) waiver program. Before the passage of this legislation, Medicaid long-term care benefits were primarily limited to nursing homes. The HCBS legislation provided a vehicle for states to offer services not otherwise available through their Medicaid programs to serve people in their own homes, thereby preserving their independence and ties to family and friends at a cost no higher than that of institutional care. States have the flexibility to design HCBS waiver programs to meet the specific needs of defined groups.

Seven specific services may be provided under HCBS waivers:

- Case management services

- Homemaker services

- Home health aide services

- Personal care services

- Adult day care/health care services

- Respite care services

- Rehabilitation services

Other services may be provided at the request of the state if approved by the federal government. Services must be cost effective and necessary for the prevention of institutionalization. States have flexibility in designing their waiver programs; this allows them to tailor their programs to the specific needs of the populations they want to serve.

The HCBS waiver program has grown since its enactment in 1981. According to Catherine Ogle Perrin, in *Home and Community-Based 1915(c) Medicaid Waivers That Pay for Respite Support: State-by-State Tables of Medicaid Waiver Information* (August 2012, http://archrespite.org/images/Books/HCBS_Waivers_Respite_FInal_8-31-2012.pdf), in 2007, the most recent year for which data were available, 1.2 million people received care through HCBS waivers—813,848 through the home health benefit and 826,251 through the personal care services benefit. Besides enhancing HCBS funding, the PPACA authorized a new Medicaid plan, Community First Choice, which provides home care services.

The National Aging Network

The National Aging Network (September 20, 2010, http://www.eldercare.gov/ELDERCARE.NET/Public/About/Aging_Network/Index.aspx), which is funded by the Older Americans Act (OAA), provides funds for supportive home and community-based services to 629 area agencies on aging, 246 Native American organizations, 56 state units on aging, and over 29,000 service providers. It also awards funds for disease prevention/health promotion services, elder rights programs, the National Family Caregiver Support Program, and the Native American Caregiver Support Program. All older Americans may receive services through the OAA, but it specifically targets vulnerable older populations—those older adults who are disadvantaged by social or health disparities.

Eldercare Locator

The U.S. Administration on Aging sponsors the Eldercare Locator Directory (http://www.eldercare.gov/Eldercare.NET/Public/Index.aspx), a nationwide toll-free service that helps older adults and their caregivers find local services. The Eldercare Locator program connects those who contact it to an information specialist who has access to multiple databases, including the National Aging Network.

BenefitsCheckUp

The National Council on Aging offers the online BenefitsCheckUp program (http://www.benefitscheckup.org), which examines a database of more than 2,000 programs to determine older adults' eligibility for federal, state, and local private and public benefits and programs. Users respond to a few questions and then the program lists which federal, state, and local programs they might be eligible for and how to apply. It is the first Internet-based service that is designed to help older Americans, their families, and caregivers determine quickly and easily which benefits they qualify for and how to claim them.

In each state, there are approximately 70 programs available to individuals. Among the programs included are those that help older adults find income support, prescription drug savings, government health programs, energy assistance, property tax relief, nutrition programs, in-home services, veteran's programs, and volunteer, educational, and training programs. As of July 2013, the BenefitsCheckUp program had helped over 3.6 million people find benefits worth $13.3 billion to which they were entitled.

Women's Institute for a Secure Retirement

Founded in 1996 with a grant from the Heinz Family Philanthropies, the Women's Institute for a Secure Retirement (WISER; http://www.wiserwomen.org/) works to help women understand and plan for retirement income. WISER publications help women navigate the complexities of Social Security, divorce, pensions, savings and investments, banking, homeownership, long-term care, and disability insurance. WISER also conducts research and workshops to identify opportunities for women to secure adequate retirement income.

Volunteer Caregivers

In "A Volunteer Army of Caregivers" (NYTimes.com, March 28, 2013), Paula Span describes the efforts of Janice Lynch Schuster of the Altarum Institute, a nonprofit public health research and consulting group, to generate interest in the creation of a volunteer service corps of caregivers, like the Peace Corps. The volunteer caregivers could be high school students, recent college graduates, or older adults. The volunteers would help older adults in the community who are unable to pay for caregiver services to obtain needed care. Schuster also believes such a program has the potential to strengthen the connections between the generations and reduce age segregation and ageism.

Geriatric Care Managers Help Older Adults Age in Place

The increasing complexity of arranging care for older adults, especially when families live at a distance from the older adults in need of care, has given rise to a new service profession: geriatric care management. Geriatric care managers have varied educational backgrounds and professional credentials. They may be gerontologists (professionals who study the social, psychological, and biological aspects of aging), nurses, or social workers who specialize in issues that are related to aging and services for older adults. Geriatric care managers work with a formal or informal network of social workers, nurses, psychologists, elder law attorneys, advocates, and agencies that serve older adults.

Geriatric care managers work with families and increasingly with corporations wishing to assist employees to create flexible plans of care to meet the needs of older adults. They oversee home health staffing needs, monitor the quality of in-home services and equipment, and serve as liaisons for families at a distance from their older relatives. In "Geriatric Care Managers—Could One Help You with Your Elderly Loved One?" (HuffingtonPost.com, May 31, 2012), Marie Marley reports that fees for geriatric care management vary widely, but usually range from $75 to $150 per hour.

Hired homemakers/caregivers, transportation services, home modifications, and other services are also available. The total monthly cost of services varies. An older adult who needs light housekeeping or companionship for three hours twice a week might spend around $300 per month, whereas someone who needs 24-hour-per-day supervision might pay $5,000 per month or more—much more if care from a certified home health aide or licensed vocational nurse is required.

Geriatric care management is especially important for older adults with dementia. Amy Benson et al. find in "Change in Burden and Distress among Caregivers of Community-Dwelling Older Adults with Dementia Enrolled in Care Management" (*American Journal of Geriatric Psychiatry*, vol. 21, no. 3, March 2013) that care managers help ease caregivers' distress, especially during particularly trying periods such as when medication is used to control troubling behavioral symptoms. The researchers suggest that caregiver access to education, support, and care management "may help improve caregiver well-being and ability to cope with patient symptoms, enabling caregivers to provide at-home care for longer periods prior to nursing home placement."

CHAPTER 10
HEALTH CARE USE, EXPENDITURES, AND FINANCING

Health care use and expenditures tend to be concentrated among older adults. Because older adults often suffer multiple chronic conditions, they are hospitalized more frequently, use the most prescription and over-the-counter (nonprescription) drugs, make the highest number of physician visits, and require care from more physician-specialists and other health care providers—such as podiatrists and physical therapists—than any other age group.

Nearly all older Americans have health insurance through Medicare, which covers inpatient hospitalization, outpatient care, physician services, home health care, short-term skilled nursing facility care, hospice (end-of-life care) services, and prescription drugs. Historically, older adults' use of health care services has changed in response to physician practice patterns, advances in medical technology, and Medicare reimbursement for services. For example, advances in medical technology and physician practice patterns have shifted many medical procedures once performed in hospitals to outpatient settings such as ambulatory surgery centers.

Another example of changes in usage occurred during the 1980s, when the average lengths of stay (ALOS) in hospitals for Medicare patients declined in response to the introduction of prospective payment and diagnostic-related groups—methods used to reimburse various providers for services performed. Although the ALOS decreased between 1992 and 2009, from 8.4 days to 5.4 days, the hospitalization rate increased from 306 to 320 hospital stays per 1,000 Medicare enrollees. (See Figure 10.1.)

Older adults are responsible for disproportionate health care expenditures. For example, the Centers for Medicare and Medicaid Services (CMS) notes in "NHE Fact Sheet" (January 9, 2013, http://www.cms.gov/) that in 2004 older adults consisted of just 12% of the U.S. population, yet they accounted for 34% of health care expenditures. That same year personal health care spending for people aged 65 years and older was $14,797,

which was 5.6 times higher than health care spending for children and 3.3 times higher than spending for working-aged adults. In "Healthy Aging: Helping People to Live Long and Productive Lives and Enjoy a Good Quality of Life—At a Glance 2011" (May 11, 2011, http://www.cdc .gov/chronicdisease/resources/publications/AAG/aging .htm), the Centers for Disease Control and Prevention explains that these disproportionate expenses are in part attributable to the fact that 80% of older adults have one chronic health condition and 50% have at least two chronic conditions. The CMS projects that the national health expenditure will grow to $4.5 trillion by 2021. (See Table 10.1; note that because these numbers are projections, they differ from numbers presented in other tables and figures.) Medicare is projected to reach $1 billion by 2021, accounting for 22.2% of all health care expenditures.

FINANCING HEALTH CARE FOR OLDER ADULTS

The Patient Protection and Affordable Care Act (PPACA) of 2010 contains about 165 provisions that affect Medicare. By reducing costs, increasing revenues, strengthening certain benefits, combating fraud and abuse, and conducting research to identify and strengthen provider payment mechanisms and health care delivery systems, these provisions are intended to improve the quality of health care for beneficiaries and reduce its costs.

The PPACA aims to ensure that all Americans have access to health care. Besides access to care, it addresses aspects of health care reform, including:

- Improving the quality and efficiency of health care— there is special emphasis placed on improving clinical outcomes (how patients fare as a result of treatment) for people receiving care through government entitlement programs

FIGURE 10.1

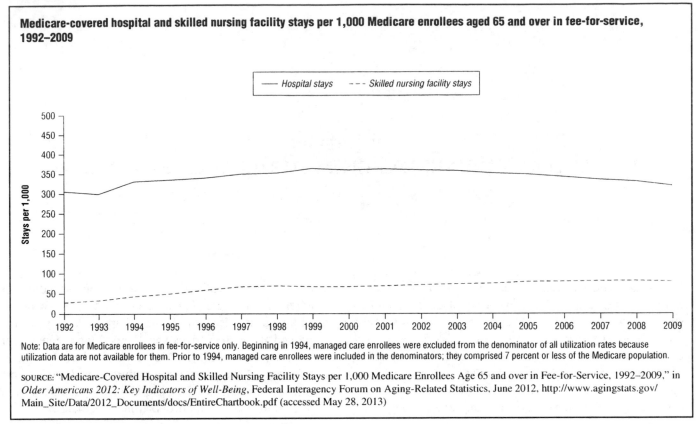

Medicare-covered hospital and skilled nursing facility stays per 1,000 Medicare enrollees aged 65 and over in fee-for-service, 1992–2009

Note: Data are for Medicare enrollees in fee-for-service only. Beginning in 1994, managed care enrollees were excluded from the denominator of all utilization rates because utilization data are not available for them. Prior to 1994, managed care enrollees were included in the denominators; they comprised 7 percent or less of the Medicare population.

SOURCE: "Medicare-Covered Hospital and Skilled Nursing Facility Stays per 1,000 Medicare Enrollees Age 65 and over in Fee-for-Service, 1992–2009," in *Older Americans 2012: Key Indicators of Well-Being*, Federal Interagency Forum on Aging-Related Statistics, June 2012, http://www.agingstats.gov/Main_Site/Data/2012_Documents/docs/EntireChartbook.pdf (accessed May 28, 2013)

- Prevention of chronic disease and improving public health—the PPACA created a new interagency council to promote healthy policies and to establish a national prevention and health promotion strategy; it also established the Prevention and Public Health Investment Fund to expand and support national investment in prevention and public health

- Health care workforce—increasing the supply, training, and quality of health care workers

- Transparency and program integrity—providing public information and combatting fraud and abuse

- Community living assistance services and supports—the PPACA instituted the Community Living Assistance Services and Supports Independence Benefit Plan, a voluntary, self-funded long-term care (LTC) insurance program, to help older adults pay for community living assistance services

Of the many changes resulting from enactment of this health care reform legislation, several are particularly relevant to older adults. For example, the PPACA eliminates lifetime and unreasonable limits on benefits, prohibits cancellation of health insurance policies, and enables people with preexisting conditions to acquire insurance coverage. The act increases Medicare provider fees in rural areas and extends Medicare bonus payments for ground and air ambulance services in rural areas. It also created an independent Medicare Advisory Board to present Congress with proposals to reduce costs and improve quality for Medicare beneficiaries.

The Health Care and Education Affordability Reconciliation Act of 2010 amends the PPACA. It contains a number of provisions that are important for older adults, including closing the Medicare prescription drug benefit known as the "donut hole." Jonathan Blum of the CMS explains in "What Is the Donut Hole?" (2013, http://blog.medicare.gov/2010/08/09/what-is-the-donut%C2%A0hole/) that the donut hole is a coverage gap in the Medicare Part D program that requires Medicare beneficiaries to pay 100% of their prescription drug costs from the time when their total annual drug costs reach $2,800 until their total prescription costs reach $4,550. The PPACA, as amended by the Health Care and Education Affordability Reconciliation Act, retroactively provides a $250 rebate to each Medicare beneficiary who reached the donut hole by January 1, 2010. After January 1, 2011, the PPACA began decreasing the donut hole by reducing beneficiaries' co-payments, with the intention of completely closing the hole by 2020.

The PPACA governs the maximum out-of-pocket drug expenses for Medicare beneficiaries. In "Medicare Drug Costs to Fall in 2014, but Donut Hole Widens" (Reuters.com, February 21, 2013), Mark Miller explains that because Medicare's drug costs decreased 4% in 2012, the standard annual plan deductible will be lower

TABLE 10.1

National health expenditures by source of funds, 2006–21

Year	Total	Out-of-pocket payments	Health insurance[a] Total	Private health insurance	Medicare	Medicaid	Other health insurance programs[b]	Other third party payers[c]
Historical estimates			Amount in billions					
2006	$2,031.5	$271.9	$1,520.2	$740.2	$403.1	$306.8	$70.1	$239.3
2007	2,153.4	287.3	1,610.2	776.2	432.3	326.4	75.4	255.9
2008	2,250.1	294.0	1,700.7	807.6	466.9	343.8	82.4	255.4
2009	2,349.5	294.4	1,793.3	828.8	499.8	374.4	90.3	261.8
2010	2,444.6	299.7	1,870.8	848.7	524.6	401.4	96.1	274.1
Projected								
2011	2,543.2	304.4	1,953.4	864.4	557.8	428.7	102.5	285.3
2012	2,655.3	312.1	2,046.1	888.6	590.8	458.9	107.7	297.0
2013	2,757.8	322.7	2,127.5	925.2	598.4	491.0	113.0	307.6
2014	2,964.9	317.7	2,331.6	997.8	635.0	579.2	119.5	315.5
2015	3,132.7	328.9	2,474.6	1,060.4	666.5	621.0	126.8	329.2
2016	3,329.2	340.0	2,642.7	1,130.5	707.0	672.4	132.7	346.5
2017	3,526.5	359.4	2,799.3	1,191.0	754.8	719.4	134.1	367.8
2018	3,743.0	381.6	2,971.8	1,252.5	809.1	769.9	140.3	389.5
2019	3,985.3	402.9	3,172.1	1,329.2	867.9	825.8	149.1	410.3
2020	4,252.4	426.0	3,394.3	1,412.0	934.9	888.6	158.8	432.1
2021	4,532.7	449.2	3,628.5	1,495.4	1,006.9	957.4	168.9	455.0
Historical estimates			Per capita amount					
2006	$6,812	$912	d	d	d	d	d	d
2007	7,151	954	d	d	d	d	d	d
2008	7,405	967	d	d	d	d	d	d
2009	7,671	961	d	d	d	d	d	d
2010	7,919	971	d	d	d	d	d	d
Projected								
2011	8,172	978	d	d	d	d	d	d
2012	8,463	995	d	d	d	d	d	d
2013	8,716	1,020	d	d	d	d	d	d
2014	9,290	996	d	d	d	d	d	d
2015	9,729	1,022	d	d	d	d	d	d
2016	10,248	1,046	d	d	d	d	d	d
2017	10,760	1,097	d	d	d	d	d	d
2018	11,322	1,154	d	d	d	d	d	d
2019	11,953	1,209	d	d	d	d	d	d
2020	12,647	1,267	d	d	d	d	d	d
2021	13,370	1,325	d	d	d	d	d	d
Historical estimates			Percent distribution					
2006	100.0	13.4	74.8	36.4	19.8	15.1	3.4	11.8
2007	100.0	13.3	74.8	36.0	20.1	15.2	3.5	11.9
2008	100.0	13.1	75.6	35.9	20.8	15.3	3.7	11.4
2009	100.0	12.5	76.3	35.3	21.3	15.9	3.8	11.1
2010	100.0	12.3	76.5	34.7	21.5	16.4	3.9	11.2
Projected								
2011	100.0	12.0	76.8	34.0	21.9	16.9	4.0	11.2
2012	100.0	11.8	77.1	33.5	22.3	17.3	4.1	11.2
2013	100.0	11.7	77.1	33.5	21.7	17.8	4.1	11.2
2014	100.0	10.7	78.6	33.7	21.4	19.5	4.0	10.6
2015	100.0	10.5	79.0	33.8	21.3	19.8	4.0	10.5
2016	100.0	10.2	79.4	34.0	21.2	20.2	4.0	10.4
2017	100.0	10.2	79.4	33.8	21.4	20.4	3.8	10.4
2018	100.0	10.2	79.4	33.5	21.6	20.6	3.7	10.4
2019	100.0	10.1	79.6	33.4	21.8	20.7	3.7	10.3
2020	100.0	10.0	79.8	33.2	22.0	20.9	3.7	10.2
2021	100.0	9.9	80.1	33.0	22.2	21.1	3.7	10.0

and prescription drug plan premiums may also be reduced. However, the speed with which Medicare beneficiaries enter the donut hole is not governed by the PPACA; it is tied to per capita (per head) total Medicare Part D drug expenses. So, somewhat ironically, nearly one out of five (19%) Medicare beneficiaries will enter the donut hole sooner. In 2013 the threshold was $2,970; beyond that amount beneficiaries pay 50% of the cost of brand-name drugs until they have spent $4,750.

The major government health care entitlement programs are Medicare and Medicaid. They provide financial assistance for people aged 65 years and older, the poor, and people with disabilities. Before the existence of

Year	Total	Out-of-pocket payments	Health insurance[a]				Other health insurance programs[b]	Other third party payers[c]
			Total	Private health insurance	Medicare	Medicaid		
Historical estimates			Annual percent change from previous year shown					
2006	—	—	—	—	—	—	—	—
2007	6.0	5.6	5.9	4.9	7.2	6.4	7.6	6.9
2008	4.5	2.3	5.6	4.0	8.0	5.3	9.3	−0.2
2009	4.4	0.2	5.4	2.6	7.0	8.9	9.6	2.5
2010	4.0	1.8	4.3	2.4	5.0	7.2	6.5	4.7
Projected								
2011	4.0	1.6	4.4	1.8	6.3	6.8	6.6	4.1
2012	4.4	2.5	4.7	2.8	5.9	7.0	5.1	4.1
2013	3.9	3.4	4.0	4.1	1.3	7.0	4.9	3.5
2014	7.5	-1.5	9.6	7.9	6.1	18.0	5.8	2.6
2015	5.7	3.5	6.1	6.3	4.9	7.2	6.1	4.3
2016	6.3	3.4	6.8	6.6	6.1	8.3	4.7	5.3
2017	5.9	5.7	5.9	5.4	6.8	7.0	1.0	6.1
2018	6.1	6.2	6.2	5.2	7.2	7.0	4.6	5.9
2019	6.5	5.6	6.7	6.1	7.3	7.3	6.3	5.3
2020	6.7	5.7	7.0	6.2	7.7	7.6	6.4	5.3
2021	6.6	5.5	6.9	5.9	7.7	7.7	6.4	5.3

[a]Includes private health insurance (employer sponsored insurance, state health insurance exchanges, and other private insurance), Medicare, Medicaid, Children's Health Insurance Program (Titles XIX and XXI), Department of Defense, and Department of Veterans' Affairs.
[b]Children's Health Insurance Program (Titles XIX and XXI), Department of Defense, and Department of Veterans' Affairs.
[c]Includes worksite health care, other private revenues, Indian Health Service, workers' compensation, general assistance, maternal and child health, vocational rehabilitation, other federal programs, Substance Abuse and Mental Health Services Administration, other state and local programs, and school health.
[d]Calculation of per capita estimates is not applicable.
Notes: The health spending projections were based on the National Health Expenditures (NHE) released in January 2012. The projections include impacts from the Affordable Care Act. Per capita amounts based on July 1 Census resident based population estimates. Numbers and percents may not add to totals because of rounding.

SOURCE: "Table 4. Health Consumption Expenditures; Aggregate and per Capita Amounts, Percent Distribution and Annual Percent Change by Source of Funds: Calendar Years 2006–2021," in *National Health Expenditures Projections 2011–2021*, Centers for Medicare and Medicaid Services, Office of the Actuary, 2012, http://www.cms.gov/Research-Statistics-Data-and-Systems/Statistics-Trends-and-Reports/NationalHealthExpendData/Downloads/Proj2011PDF.pdf (accessed August 3, 2013)

these programs, many older Americans could not afford adequate medical care. For older adult beneficiaries, the Medicare program provides reimbursement for hospital and physician care, whereas Medicaid pays for the cost of nursing home care.

MEDICARE

The spirit in which this law is written draws deeply upon the ancient dreams of all mankind. In Leviticus, it is written, "Thou shall rise up before the hoary head, and honor the face of an old man."

—Senator Russell B. Long (D-LA) at the original vote for Medicare in 1965

The Medicare program, which was enacted under Title XVIII ("Health Insurance for the Aged") of the Social Security Act, was signed into law by President Lyndon B. Johnson (1908–1973) and went into effect on July 1, 1966. That year 19 million older adults entered the program. Michelle M. Megellas of Novartis Pharmaceuticals in Colleyville, Texas, forecasts in "Medicare Modernization: The New Prescription Drug Benefit and Redesigned Part B and Part C" (*Proceedings Baylor University Medical Center*, vol. 19, no. 1, January 2006) that by 2030 the number of Americans insured by Medicare will exceed 78 million.

The establishment of the Medicare program in 1966 served to improve equity in health care. Before the creation of Medicare about half of the older population was uninsured, and the insured population was often limited to benefits of just $10 per day. Furthermore, because poverty rates among older adults hovered at about 30%, some of the older population could not be expected to pay for private health insurance. The Medicare program extended health care coverage to a population with growing health needs and little income.

In 2008 the Medicare program covered 60% of the health care costs of older Americans. (See Figure 10.2.) Medicaid covered 7% and other payers, primarily private health insurers, covered 15%. Older adults paid 18% of their health care costs out of pocket. Historically, Medicare has focused almost exclusively on acute (short-term) care services such as hospitals, physicians, and short-term rehabilitation and home health care, but in 2006 Medicare offered its first prescription drug benefits. Other public and private payers finance LTC.

The Medicare program consists of several parts:

- Part A provides hospital insurance. Coverage includes physicians' fees, nursing services, meals, semiprivate rooms, special care units, operating room costs,

FIGURE 10.2

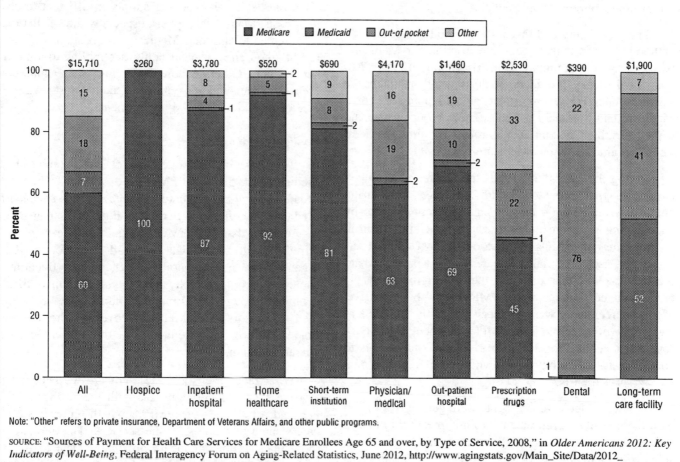

Sources of payment for health care services for Medicare enrollees age 65 and over, by type of service, 2008

Average cost per enrollee

Legend: ■ Medicare ■ Medicaid ▨ Out-of pocket □ Other

Note: "Other" refers to private insurance, Department of Veterans Affairs, and other public programs.

SOURCE: "Sources of Payment for Health Care Services for Medicare Enrollees Age 65 and over, by Type of Service, 2008," in *Older Americans 2012: Key Indicators of Well-Being*, Federal Interagency Forum on Aging-Related Statistics, June 2012, http://www.agingstats.gov/Main_Site/Data/2012_Documents/docs/EntireChartbook.pdf (accessed May 28, 2013)

laboratory tests, and some drugs and supplies. Part A also covers rehabilitation services, limited posthospital skilled nursing facility care, home health care, and hospice care for the terminally ill.

- Part B (Supplemental Medical Insurance) is elective medical insurance; enrollees must pay premiums to get coverage. It covers private physicians' services, diagnostic tests, outpatient hospital services, outpatient physical therapy, speech pathology services, home health services, and medical equipment and supplies.

- The third part of Medicare, sometimes known as Part C, is the Medicare Advantage program, which was established by the Balanced Budget Act of 1997 to expand beneficiaries' options and allow them to participate in private-sector health plans. The PPACA restructured payments to the Medicare Advantage plans in response to geographic differences in fees and rewards plans that demonstrate quality with bonuses.

- Part D, the Medicare prescription drug benefit, was enacted after Congress passed the Prescription Drug, Improvement, and Modernization Act of 2003.

According to the Boards of Trustees of the Federal Hospital Insurance and Federal Supplementary Medical Insurance Trust Funds, in *2013 Annual Report of the Boards of Trustees of the Federal Hospital Insurance and Federal Supplementary Medical Insurance Trust Funds* (May 31, 2013, http://www.cms.gov/Research-Statistics-Data-and-Systems/Statistics-Trends-and-Reports/ReportsTrustFunds/Downloads/TR2013.pdf), in 2012, $574.2 billion was spent to provide coverage for the 50.7 million people who were enrolled in Medicare. The majority of Medicare recipients were aged 65 years and older.

Reimbursement under Medicare

Historically, Medicare reimbursed physicians on a fee-for-service basis (paid for each visit, procedure, or treatment delivered), as opposed to per capita or per member per month (PMPM). In response to the increasing administrative burden of paperwork, reduced compensation, and delays in reimbursements, some physicians opt out of Medicare participation—they do not provide services under the Medicare program and choose not to accept Medicare patients into their practice. Others continue to provide services to Medicare beneficiaries, but they do not "accept assignment"—that is, their patients must pay out of pocket for services and then seek reimbursement from Medicare.

The Tax Equity and Fiscal Responsibility Act of 1982 authorized a "risk managed care" option for Medicare, based on agreed-on prepayments. Beginning in 1985 CMS contracted to pay providers, such as health maintenance organizations (HMOs) or other prepaid plans, to serve Medicare and Medicaid patients. These groups were paid a predetermined amount per enrollee for their services. These became known as Medicare-risk HMOs.

During the 1980s and 1990s the federal government, employers that provided health coverage for retiring employees, and many states sought to control costs by encouraging Medicare and Medicaid beneficiaries to enroll in Medicare-risk HMOs. Medicare-risk HMOs kept costs down because, essentially, the federal government paid the health plans that operated them with fixed fees—a predetermined dollar amount PMPM. For this fixed fee, Medicare recipients were to receive a fairly comprehensive array of benefits. The PMPM payment provided a financial incentive for Medicare-risk HMO physicians to control costs, unlike physicians who were reimbursed on a fee-for-service basis.

Although Medicare recipients were generally satisfied with these HMOs (even when enrolling meant they had to change physicians and thereby end long-standing relationships with their family doctors), many of the health plans did not fare well. The health plans suffered for a variety of reasons: some plans had underestimated the service utilization rates of older adults, and some were unable to provide the stipulated range of services as effectively as they were intended. For other plans, the PMPM payment was simply not sufficient to enable them to cover all the clinical services and administrative overhead.

Regardless, the health plans providing these "senior HMOs" competed fiercely to enroll older adults. Some health plans feared that closing their Medicare-risk programs would be viewed negatively by employer groups, which, when faced with the choice of plans that offered coverage for both younger workers and retirees or one that only covered the younger workers, would choose the plans that covered both. Despite losing money, most health plans maintained their Medicare-risk programs to avoid alienating the employers they depended on to enroll workers who were younger, healthier, and less expensive to serve than the older adults.

Approximately 10 years into operations, some Medicare-risk programs faced a challenge that proved insurmountable. Their enrollees had aged and required more health care services than they had previously. For example, a senior HMO member who had joined as a healthy 65-year-old could now be a frail 75-year-old with multiple chronic health conditions requiring costly health care services. The PMPM had increased over the years, but for some health plans it was simply insufficient to cover their costs. Many health plans, especially the smaller ones, were forced to end their Medicare-risk programs abruptly, leaving thousands of older adults scrambling to join other health plans. Others endured, offering older adults comprehensive care and generating substantial cost savings for employers and the federal government.

Medicare Advantage

The Balanced Budget Act of 1997 replaced the Medicare-risk plans with Medicare+Choice, which later became known as Medicare Advantage. These plans offer Medicare beneficiaries a wider range of managed care plan options than just HMOs—older adults can join preferred provider organizations and provider-sponsored organizations that generally offer greater freedom of choice of providers (physicians and hospitals) than is available through HMO membership. Figure 10.3 shows the two ways to obtain Medicare coverage: through traditional, or original, Medicare or through a Medicare Advantage plan.

When older adults join the Medicare Advantage plans that have entered into contracts with the CMS, the plans are paid a fixed amount PMPM, which represents Medicare's share of the cost of the services. The attraction of these plans is that members no longer have to pay the regular Medicare deductibles and co-payments for covered services. Some plans charge modest monthly premiums, and/or nominal co-payments as services are used, but there are no other charges by the plan for physician visits, hospitalization, or use of other covered services. However, members of the Medicare Advantage plans must continue to pay the Medicare Part B monthly premium. According to the CMS, in "Will Premiums for Medicare Advantage Plans Go up in 2013?" (2013, http://www.medicare.com/advantage-plans/will-premiums-for-medicare-advantage-plans-increase-in-2013.html), an estimated 14.5 million Medicare beneficiaries were enrolled in the Medicare Advantage plans in 2013.

In *Medicare Advantage Plan Star Ratings and Bonus Payments in 2012* (November 2011, http://kaiserfamily foundation.files.wordpress.com/2013/01/8257.pdf), the Kaiser Family Foundation examines all the Medicare Advantage plans' quality ratings, which range from one to five stars (one star indicates poor performance and five stars denote excellent performance), for 2011. These ratings were used to calculate payments in 2012. Plans with four-star ratings or better received bonus payments. In 2012 more than a quarter (26%) of all Medicare Advantage members were in plans that received ratings

FIGURE 10.3

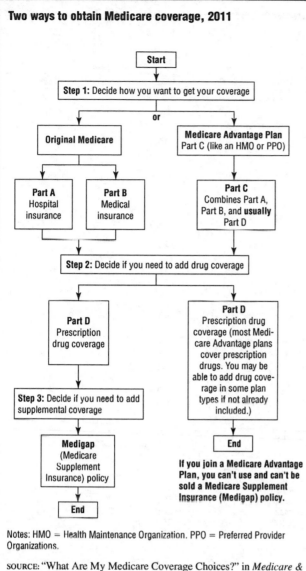

Two ways to obtain Medicare coverage, 2011

Start

Step 1: Decide how you want to get your coverage

or

Original Medicare

Medicare Advantage Plan
Part C (like an HMO or PPO)

Part A
Hospital
insurance

Part B
Medical
insurance

Part C
Combines Part A,
Part B, and **usually**
Part D

Step 2: Decide if you need to add drug coverage

Part D
Prescription
drug coverage

Part D
Prescription drug
coverage (most Medi-
care Advantage plans
cover prescription
drugs. You may be
able to add drug cove-
rage in some plan
types if not already
included.)

Step 3: Decide if you need to add
supplemental coverage

Medigap
(Medicare
Supplement
Insurance) policy

End

End

If you join a Medicare Advantage
Plan, you can't use and can't be
sold a Medicare Supplement
Insurance (Medigap) policy.

Notes: HMO = Health Maintenance Organization. PPO = Preferred Provider Organizations.

SOURCE: "What Are My Medicare Coverage Choices?" in *Medicare & You 2013*, Centers for Medicare and Medicaid Services, November 2012, http://www.medicare.gov/publications/pubs/pdf/10050.pdf (accessed June 20, 2013)

of four or more stars. Nonetheless, 59% of Medicare Advantage members were in plans that received 3 to 3.5 stars, which the CMS defines as average performance, and 9% were in plans that earned fewer than 3 stars.

Insurance to Supplement Medicare Benefits

In 2010, 11.9 million (30.6%) older adults had private insurance obtained through the workplace to supplement their Medicare coverage. (See Table 10.2.) The most popular private insurance is supplemental insurance known as Medigap insurance. Federal regulations mandate that all Medigap policies sold offer a standard minimum set of benefits, but there are variations that offer additional coverage and benefits. As Table 10.2 shows, the percentage of older adults with Medigap insurance declined from 33.9% in 1992 to 19.6% in 2010, whereas the percentage with only Medicare or another public plan rose from 9.9% to 14.6% over the same period.

Besides Medigap policies, older adults may also purchase Medicare supplement health insurance called Medicare SELECT, which offers essentially the same coverage as Medigap policies, but requires use of preferred providers (specific hospitals and in some cases plan physicians) to receive full benefits. Although Medicare SELECT policies restrict older adults' choices, they are generally less expensive than Medigap policies.

A less popular option is hospital indemnity coverage—insurance that pays a fixed cash amount for each day of hospitalization up to a designated number of days. Some coverage may have added benefits such as surgical benefits or skilled nursing home benefits. Most policies have a maximum annual number of days or a lifetime maximum payment amount.

The Prescription Drug, Improvement, and Modernization Act

Congress passed the Prescription Drug, Improvement, and Modernization Act of 2003, which represents the largest expansion of Medicare since its creation in 1965. The legislation established a Medicare prescription drug benefit. The benefit took full effect in January 2006. Among other things, it provides help for low-income beneficiaries and those with the highest drug costs.

Medicare Prescription Drug Coverage

Enrollees in the Medicare prescription drug program, called Part D, pay a monthly premium, which varies by plan, and a yearly deductible that in 2013 was no more than $325. They also pay part of the cost of their prescriptions, including a co-payment or coinsurance. Table 10.3 shows how the prescription drug plan works for Ms. Smith, a hypothetical Medicare drug plan member in 2013. Costs vary among the different drug plans—some plans offer more coverage and access to a wider range of drugs for a higher monthly premium. According to the Kaiser Family Foundation, in "The Medicare Prescription Drug Benefit Fact Sheet" (November 19, 2012, http://kff.org/medicare/fact-sheet/the-medicare-prescription-drug-benefit-fact-sheet/), in 2013 the monthly Part D premiums ranged from $15 to $165.40, with an average premium of $40.18, a 7% increase from 2012. Older adults with limited incomes may not have to pay premiums or deductibles for the drug coverage.

Medicare Faces Challenges

Like Social Security, the Medicare program's continuing financial viability is in jeopardy. The Social Security and Medicare trust funds are examined annually by the Social Security and Medicare Boards of Trustees, which publish an annual report on the current and

TABLE 10.2

Health insurance coverage for persons aged 65 and older, by type of coverage and selected characteristics, selected years 1992–2010

[Data are based on household interviews of a sample of noninstitutionalized Medicare beneficiaries]

Characteristic	Medicare Risk Health Maintenance Organization[a]					Medicaid[b]				
	1992	1995	2000	2009	2010	1992	1995	2000	2009	2010
Age					Number, in millions					
65 years and over	1.1	2.6	5.9	9.8	10.3	2.7	2.8	2.7	3.0	3.2
					Percent distribution					
65 years and over	3.9	8.9	19.3	26.1	26.7	9.4	9.6	9.0	8.0	8.4
65–74 years	4 2	9.5	20.6	25.8	26.9	7.9	8.8	8.5	7.7	7.7
75–84 years	3.7	8.3	18.5	27.7	27.6	10.6	9.6	8.9	8.3	9.1
85 years and over	*	7.3	16.3	23.2	23.7	16.6	13.6	11.2	8.8	9.5
Sex										
Male	4 6	9.2	19.3	25.4	25.4	6.3	6.2	6.3	5.8	6.3
Female	3.4	8.6	19.3	26.7	27.8	11.6	12.0	10.9	9.8	10.1
Race and Hispanic origin										
White, not Hispanic or Latino	3.6	8.4	18.4	23.7	23.9	5.6	5.4	5.1	5.1	5.4
Black, not Hispanic or Latino	*	7.9	20.7	33.1	34.3	28.5	30.3	23.6	17.4	16.8
Hispanic	*	15.5	27.5	46.2	47.2	39.0	40.5	28.7	18.3	18.8
Percent of poverty level[c]										
Below 100%	3.6	7.7	18.4	—	—	22.3	17.2	15.9	—	—
100%–less than 200%	3.7	9.5	23.4	—	—	6.7	6.3	8.4	—	—
200% or more	4.2	10.1	18.0	—	—	*	*	*	—	—
Marital status										
Married	4.6	9.5	18.7	26.1	27.1	4.0	4.3	4.3	3.6	3.6
Widowed	2.3	7.7	19.4	24.7	25.4	14.9	15.0	13.6	12.2	12.6
Divorced	*	9.7	24.4	30.4	29.1	23.4	24.5	20.2	16.5	16.9
Never married	*	*	15.8	23.4	23.1	19.2	19.0	17.0	18.5	19.8

Characteristic	Employer-sponsored plan[d]					Medigap[e]				
	1992	1995	2000	2009	2010	1992	1995	2000	2009	2010
Age					Number, in millions					
65 years and over	12.5	11.3	10.7	11.9	11.9	9.9	9.5	7.6	7.7	7.6
					Percent distribution					
65 years and over	42.8	38.6	35.2	31.5	30.6	33.9	32.5	25.0	20.3	19.6
65–74 years	46.9	41.1	36.6	33.2	32.5	31.4	29.9	21.7	18.4	17.4
75–84 years	38.2	37.1	35.0	29.7	28.4	37.5	35.2	27.8	21.4	21.3
85 years and over	31.6	30.2	29.4	29.5	28.5	38.3	37.6	31.1	25.4	24.7
Sex										
Male	46.3	42.1	37.7	34.5	32.9	30.6	30.0	23.4	18.2	18.2
Female	40.4	36.0	33.4	29.2	28.9	36.2	34.4	26.2	21.9	20.8
Race and Hispanic origin										
White, not Hispanic or Latino	45.9	41.3	38.6	34.1	33.5	37.2	36.2	28.3	23.4	23.0
Black, not Hispanic or Latino	25.9	26.7	22.0	25.6	23.7	13.6	10.2	7.5	5.3	6.7
Hispanic	20.7	16.9	15.8	17.8	14.8	15.8	10.1	11.3	6.7	6.4
Percent of poverty level[c]										
Below 100%	29.0	32.1	28.1	—	—	30.8	29.8	22.6	—	—
100%–less than 200%	37.5	32.0	27.0	—	—	39.3	39.1	28.4	—	—
200% or more	58.4	52.8	49.0	—	—	32.8	32.2	26.2	—	—
Marital status										
Married	49.9	44.6	41.0	37.3	35.9	33.0	32.6	25.6	20.4	19.6
Widowed	34.1	30.3	28.7	26.2	26.3	37.5	35.2	26.7	22.8	22.0
Divorced	27.3	26.6	22.4	18.1	18.9	27.9	24.1	16.9	14.9	15.3
Never married	38.0	35.1	28.5	27.8	25.2	29.1	26.2	21.9	16.4	17.5

projected financial status of the programs. This section reviews the origins of the challenges Medicare faces and the trustees' findings in *The 2013 Annual Report of the Board of Trustees of the Federal Old-Age and Survivors Insurance and Federal Disability Insurance Trust Funds* (May 31, 2013, http://www.socialsecurity.gov/oact/tr/2013/tr2013.pdf).

A NATIONAL BIPARTISAN COMMISSION CONSIDERS THE FUTURE OF MEDICARE. The National Bipartisan Commission on the Future of Medicare was created by Congress in the Balanced Budget Act of 1997. The commission was charged with examining the Medicare program and drafting recommendations to avert a future financial crisis and reinforce the program in anticipation

TABLE 10.2

Health insurance coverage for persons aged 65 and older, by type of coverage and selected characteristics, selected years 1992–2010
[CONTINUED]

[Data are based on household interviews of a sample of noninstitutionalized Medicare beneficiaries]

*Estimates are considered unreliable if the sample cell size is 50 or fewer.
—Data not available.
ªEnrollee has Medicare risk Health Maintenance Organization (HMO) regardless of other insurance.
ᵇEnrolled in Medicaid and not enrolled in a Medicare risk HMO.
ᶜPercent of poverty level is based on family income and family size and composition using U.S. Census Bureau poverty thresholds.
ᵈPrivate insurance plans purchased through employers (own, current, or former employer, family business, union, or former employer or union of spouse) and not enrolled in a Medicare risk HMO or Medicaid.
ᵉSupplemental insurance purchased privately or through organizations such as American Association of Retired Persons or professional organizations, and not enrolled in a Medicare risk HMO, Medicaid, or employer-sponsored plan.
Notes: Data for noninstitutionalized Medicare beneficiaries. Insurance categories are mutually exclusive. Persons with more than one type of coverage are categorized according to the order in which the health insurance categories appear in the table.

SOURCE: "Table 125. Health Insurance Coverage of Noninstitutionalized Medicare Beneficiaries Aged 65 Years and over, by Type of Coverage and Selected Characteristics: United States, Selected Years 1992–2010," in *Health, United States, 2012: With Special Feature on Emergency Care*, 2013, National Center for Health Statistics, http://www.cdc.gov/nchs/data/hus/2012/125.pdf (accessed June 1, 2013)

TABLE 10.3

How Medicare Part D provides prescription drug benefits, 2013

Monthly premium—Ms. Smith pays a monthly premium throughout the year.

1. Yearly deductible	2. Copayment or coinsurance (what you pay at the pharmacy)	3. Coverage gap	4. Catastrophic coverage
Ms. Smith pays the first $325 of her drug costs before her plan starts to pay its share.	Ms. Smith pays a copayment, and her plan pays its share for each covered drug until their combined amount (plus the deductible) reaches $2,970.	Once Ms. Smith and her plan have spent $2,970 for covered drugs, she's in the coverage gap. In 2013, she pays 47.5% of the plan's cost for her covered brand-name prescription drugs and 79% of the plan's cost for covered generic drugs. What she pays (and the discount paid by the drug company) counts as out-of-pocket spending, and helps her get out of the coverage gap.	Once Ms. Smith has spent $4,750 out-of-pocket for the year, her coverage gap ends. Now she only pays a small coinsurance or copayment for each covered drug until the end of the year.

SOURCE: "Monthly Premium—Ms. Smith Pays a Monthly Premium throughout the Year," in *Medicare & You 2013*, Centers for Medicare and Medicaid Services, November 2012, http://www.medicare.gov/publications/pubs/pdf/10050.pdf (accessed June 20, 2013)

---

of the retirement of the baby boomers (people born between 1946 and 1964).

The commission observed that like Social Security, Medicare would suffer because there would be fewer workers per retiree to fund it. (See Figure 10.4.) It predicted that beneficiaries' out-of-pocket costs would rise and forecasted soaring Medicare enrollment. (See Figure 10.5.) Perhaps the commission's direst prediction was the determination that, without reform, the Medicare Part A fund would become bankrupt by 2008.

When the commission disbanded in March 1999, it was unable to forward an official recommendation to Congress because the plan it proposed fell one vote short of the required majority needed to authorize an official recommendation. The plan would have changed Medicare into a premium system, where instead of Medicare directly covering beneficiaries, the beneficiaries would be given a fixed amount of money to purchase private health insurance. The plan would have also raised the age of eligibility from 65 to

FIGURE 10.4

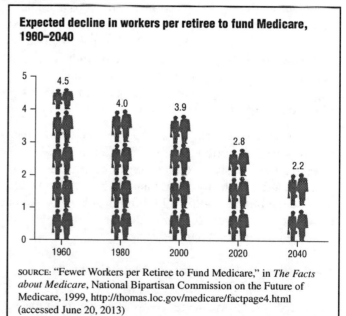

Expected decline in workers per retiree to fund Medicare, 1960–2040

SOURCE: "Fewer Workers per Retiree to Fund Medicare," in *The Facts about Medicare*, National Bipartisan Commission on the Future of Medicare, 1999, http://thomas.loc.gov/medicare/factpage4.html (accessed June 20, 2013)

FIGURE 10.5

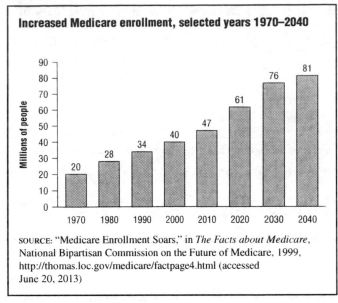

Increased Medicare enrollment, selected years 1970–2040

SOURCE: "Medicare Enrollment Soars," in *The Facts about Medicare*, National Bipartisan Commission on the Future of Medicare, 1999, http://thomas.loc.gov/medicare/factpage4.html (accessed June 20, 2013)

67, as has already been done with Social Security, and provided prescription drug coverage for low-income beneficiaries, much like the Medicare Prescription Drug, Improvement, and Modernization Act of 2003.

THE MEDICARE PRESCRIPTION DRUG, IMPROVEMENT, AND MODERNIZATION ACT AIMS TO REFORM MEDICARE. The Medicare Prescription Drug, Improvement, and Modernization Act of 2003 was intended to introduce private-sector enterprise into a Medicare model in urgent need of reform. Under the act, premiums and deductibles may rise quickly because they are indexed to the growth in per capita Medicare expenditures.

Older adults with substantial incomes face increasing premium costs. According to the CMS, in "Medicare 2013 Costs at a Glance" (2013, http://www.medicare .gov/your-medicare-costs/costs-at-a-glance/costs-at-glance .html), in 2013 older adults with annual incomes of $85,000 or less or couples earning $170,000 or less paid the standard premium, $104.90, for Medicare Part B. Individuals and couples with higher incomes paid additional income-adjusted amounts monthly, ranging from $209.80 to $335.70 per month.

The act also expanded coverage of preventive medical services. According to the CMS, new beneficiaries receive a free physical examination along with laboratory tests to screen for heart disease and diabetes. The act also provided employers with $89 billion in subsidies and tax breaks to help offset the costs that are associated with maintaining retiree health benefits.

Medicare's Problems May Be More Urgent Than Those of Social Security

Forecasts of Medicare costs show them outpacing Social Security costs because it is anticipated that per

capita health care costs will continue to grow faster than the per capita gross domestic product (GDP; the total value of goods and services that are produced by the United States) in the future. In *Status of the Social Security and Medicare Programs: A Summary of the 2013 Annual Reports* (May 2013, http://www.ssa.gov/ oact/TRSUM/tr13summary.pdf), the Social Security and Medicare Boards of Trustees project that Medicare expenditures will increase from 3.6% of the GDP in 2010, to 5.6% in 2035, to 6.5% by 2087. (See Figure 10.6.) According to the trustees, Medicare paid out more in benefits than it collected in 2012 and by 2026 it will be insolvent (incapable of meeting financial obligations).

The trustees observe that the 2010 health care reform legislation improved the financial outlook for Medicare. The 2013 projections for Medicare consider the cost reductions that were mandated by the health care reform legislation. Nonetheless, the trustees caution that "in the interests of those who depend on these programs as beneficiaries, as well as those who contribute to them as taxpayers, we urge lawmakers to correct the financial imbalances of Social Security and Medicare soon."

MEDICAID

Congress enacted Medicaid in 1965 under Title XIX ("Grants to States for Medical Assistance Programs") of the Social Security Act. It is a joint federal-state program that provides medical assistance to selected categories of low-income Americans: the aged, people who are blind and/or disabled, and families with dependent children. Medicaid covers hospitalization, physicians' fees, laboratory and radiology fees, and LTC in nursing homes. It is the largest source of funds for medical and health-related services for the United States' poorest people and the second-largest public payer of health care costs, after Medicare. In 2008 Medicaid provided coverage for 7% of adults aged 65 years and older. (See Figure 10.2.)

Katherine Young et al. report in *Enrollment-Driven Expenditure Growth: Medicaid Spending during the Economic Downturn, FY 2007–2011* (April 2013, http:// kaiserfamilyfoundation.files.wordpress.com/2013/05/ 8309-02.pdf) that Medicaid LTC expenditures in fiscal year 2011 totaled $123 billion, with 45% of Medicaid being spent on home and community-based services. The increase in home and community-based services signals a substitution of these services for institutionalization. As a result of this growth in community services and the slower growth in institutional services—an average of 1.4%—the difference in spending for both categories of service narrowed. This trend is expected to persist as Medicaid programs continue to invest more resources in alternatives to institutional services.

Young et al. observe that the 2010 health care reform legislation offers states the opportunity to expand access to

FIGURE 10.6

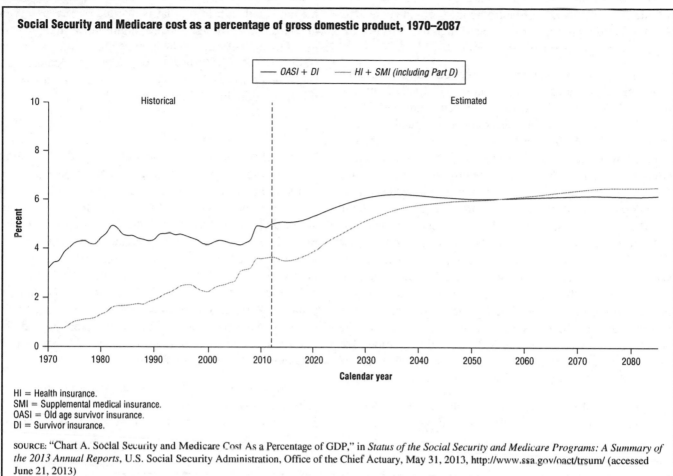

Social Security and Medicare cost as a percentage of gross domestic product, 1970–2087

HI = Health insurance.
SMI = Supplemental medical insurance.
OASI = Old age survivor insurance.
DI = Survivor insurance.

SOURCE: "Chart A. Social Security and Medicare Cost As a Percentage of GDP," in *Status of the Social Security and Medicare Programs: A Summary of the 2013 Annual Reports*, U.S. Social Security Administration, Office of the Chief Actuary, May 31, 2013, http://www.ssa.gov/oact/trsum/ (accessed June 21, 2013)

Medicaid Home and Community-Based Services programs. The PPACA supports and extends the duration of a demonstration project that gives the states financial incentives to transition Medicaid beneficiaries from institutional to community-based care. It instituted the Community First Choice Option, which provides home and community-based services to people with incomes up to 300% of the maximum Supplemental Security Income payment who require the level and intensity of care provided in an institutional setting. The PPACA strengthens and expands state home and community-based services programs by broadening the range of covered services and permitting the states to offer full Medicaid benefits to people receiving home and community-based services.

In *The Cost and Coverage Implications of the ACA Medicaid Expansion: National and State-by-State Analysis* (November 2012, http://kaiserfamilyfoundation.files.wordpress.com/2013/01/8384_es.pdf), John Holahan et al. of the Urban Institute analyze the impact of Medicaid expansion and conclude that if all the states choose to expand their Medicaid programs:

- The federal government will fund the majority of the increased Medicaid costs.

- The number of uninsured Americans will be reduced by 48%.

- The incremental cost to the states will be a scant 0.3% increase over their projected expenditures without the PPACA expansion.

- Overall, states will likely realize a net savings when other cost-savings, such as less uncompensated care, are considered.

VETERANS' BENEFITS

People who served in the U.S. military are entitled to medical treatment at any veterans' facility in the nation. The U.S. Department of Veterans Affairs (VA) reports in "Trends in the Utilization of VA Programs and Services" (January 2012, http://www.va.gov/vetdata/docs/Quick Facts/Utilization_trends_FINALv5.pdf) that in fiscal year 2010 approximately 5.7 million veterans received nearly $44 billion in health services.

The Veterans Millennium Health Care and Benefits Act of 1999 extended benefits and services for veterans. It enhanced access to and availability of an expanded range of health care programs and improved housing programs. Among the health care programs that were stipulated by the act, the requirement to provide extended and LTC and a pilot program related to assisted living are especially relevant for older veterans.

The number of veterans aged 65 years and older who received health care from the Veterans Health Administration (VHA) increased steadily between 1990 and 2011. (See Figure 10.7.) This increase may be attributable in part to the fact that VHA benefits cover services that are not covered by Medicare, such as prescription drugs (Medicare coverage began in 2006), mental health care, LTC (nursing home and community-based care), and specialized services for people with disabilities. Figure 10.8 shows the total growth in people served by the VHA and the growing utilization of outpatient services. In *Older Americans 2012: Key Indicators of Well-Being* (June 2012, http://www.agingstats.gov/Main_Site/Data/2012_Documents/docs/EntireChartbook.pdf), the Federal Interagency Forum on Aging-Related Statistics indicates that among veterans aged 65 years and older, about 2.6 million sought health care services from the VHA in 2011. Another 1.2 million "older veterans were enrolled to receive health care from the VHA but did not use its services in 2011."

The VA offers a number of health services that are designed to meet older veterans' unique health care needs, such as posttraumatic stress disorder (PTSD; a mental health condition that is marked by severe anxiety, uncontrollable thoughts, and nightmares that are triggered by a terrifying event such as violence). Its National Center for PTSD (http://www.ptsd.va.gov/professional/) trains practitioners how to diagnose and effectively treat this condition in older veterans who may have PTSD as well as other cognitive, emotional, and physical problems.

Benefits for older veterans also include job training and allowances to pursue higher education, vocational skills training, or apprenticeships. For example, monthly allowances help veterans to attend college—the allowances increase for veterans who have dependents, enabling them to care for their dependents while they attend school. A 2010 national survey found that many veterans do not make use of their benefits. Figure 10.9 shows that only 36.9% of veterans ever used VA education and training services and 28.4% ever used VA health care services. Significant percentages of veterans said their main reason for not applying or using VA benefits was that they were unaware of them.

Veterans and their families can receive respite care to relieve family caregivers of veterans, nursing home services through three national programs (VA-owned and

FIGURE 10.7

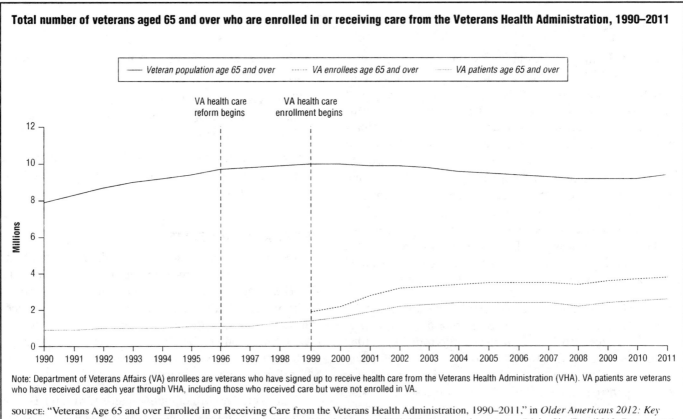

Total number of veterans aged 65 and over who are enrolled in or receiving care from the Veterans Health Administration, 1990–2011

Note: Department of Veterans Affairs (VA) enrollees are veterans who have signed up to receive health care from the Veterans Health Administration (VHA). VA patients are veterans who have received care each year through VHA, including those who received care but were not enrolled in VA.

SOURCE: "Veterans Age 65 and over Enrolled in or Receiving Care from the Veterans Health Administration, 1990–2011," in *Older Americans 2012: Key Indicators of Well-Being*, Federal Interagency Forum on Aging-Related Statistics, June 2012, http://www.agingstats.gov/Main_Site/Data/2012_Documents/docs/EntireChartbook.pdf (accessed May 28, 2013)

FIGURE 10.8

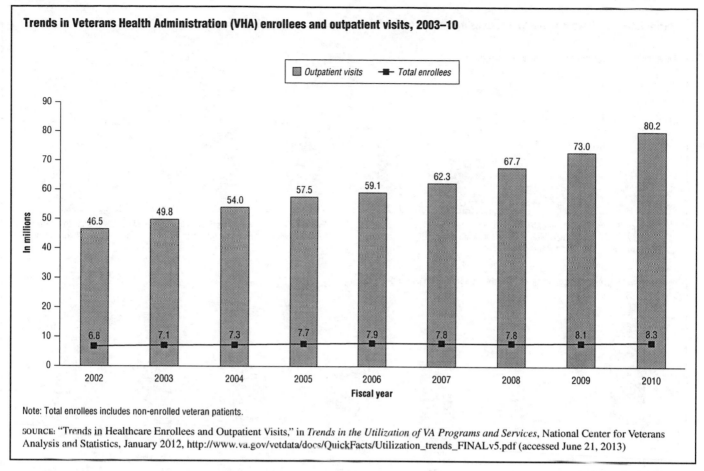

Trends in Veterans Health Administration (VHA) enrollees and outpatient visits, 2003–10

Note: Total enrollees includes non-enrolled veteran patients.

SOURCE: "Trends in Healthcare Enrollees and Outpatient Visits," in *Trends in the Utilization of VA Programs and Services*, National Center for Veterans Analysis and Statistics, January 2012, http://www.va.gov/vetdata/docs/QuickFacts/Utilization_trends_FINALv5.pdf (accessed June 21, 2013)

-operated community living centers, state veterans' homes owned and operated by the states, and the contract community nursing home program), home care services for veterans who require regular aid and assistance, home loan assistance, disability compensation for those with service-related disabilities, and nonservice-connected pensions for low-income, war-era veterans. Veterans and their dependents may qualify for education and training programs and there is a college fee waiver for eligible dependents. In addition, surviving families of veterans who served during times of war may be helped by burial cost reimbursement and death pensions.

LONG-TERM HEALTH CARE

The options for quality, affordable LTC in the United States are limited but improving. Nursing home costs range from $50,000 to more than $200,000 per year, depending on services and location. In *Market Survey of Long-Term Care Costs: The 2012 MetLife Market Survey of Nursing Home, Assisted Living, Adult Day Services, and Home Care Costs* (November 2012, https://www.metlife.com/assets/cao/mmi/publications/studies/2012/studies/mmi-2012-market-survey-long-term-care-costs.pdf), the MetLife Mature Market Institute notes that in 2012 nursing home care cost an average of $90,520 per year

for a private room. Many nursing home residents rely on Medicaid to pay these fees. In 2008 Medicaid covered 52% of LTC facility costs for older Americans. (See Figure 10.2.) The second-most-common source of payment at admission was private insurance, followed by the prospective resident's own income, family support, and Medicare (which only pays for short-term stays after hospitalization). The primary source of payment changes as a stay lengthens. After their funds are "spent down," nursing home residents on Medicare shift to Medicaid.

Although nursing home care may seem cost prohibitive, an untrained caregiver who makes home visits can cost more than $25,000 per year, and skilled care costs much more. According to the U.S. Bureau of Labor Statistics (March 29, 2013, http://www.bls.gov/oes/current/oes311011.htm), in 2012 the mean (average) hourly rate for home care aides was $10.49 per hour. In home and community-based services settings, the Bureau of Labor Statistics indicates that licensed practical nurses and licensed vocational nurses (March 29, 2013, http://www.bls.gov/oes/current/oes292061.htm) earned a mean hourly rate of $21.11 per hour and registered nurses (March 29, 2013, http://www.bls.gov/oes/current/oes291141.htm) earned $31.51 per hour.

FIGURE 10.9

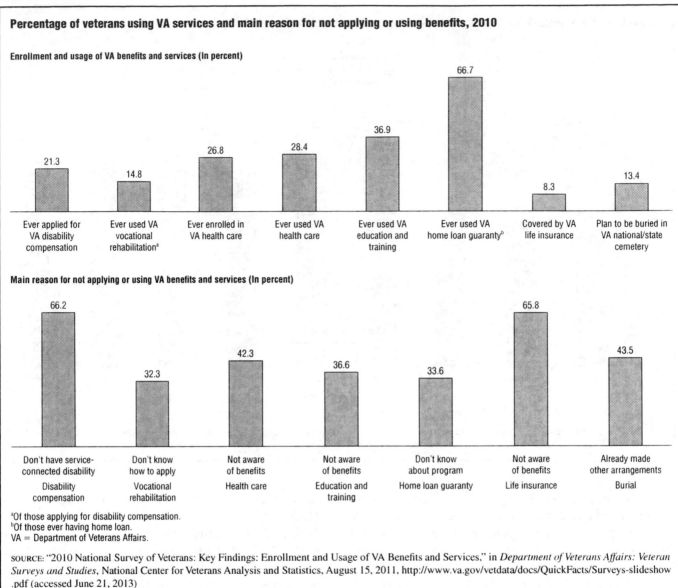

Percentage of veterans using VA services and main reason for not applying or using benefits, 2010

Enrollment and usage of VA benefits and services (In percent)

Value	Category
21.3	Ever applied for VA disability compensation
14.8	Ever used VA vocational rehabilitation[a]
26.8	Ever enrolled in VA health care
28.4	Ever used VA health care
36.9	Ever used VA education and training
66.7	Ever used VA home loan guaranty[b]
8.3	Covered by VA life insurance
13.4	Plan to be buried in VA national/state cemetery

Main reason for not applying or using VA benefits and services (In percent)

Value	Reason	Category
66.2	Don't have service-connected disability	Disability compensation
32.3	Don't know how to apply	Vocational rehabilitation
42.3	Not aware of benefits	Health care
36.6	Not aware of benefits	Education and training
33.6	Don't know about program	Home loan guaranty
65.8	Not aware of benefits	Life insurance
43.5	Already made other arrangements	Burial

[a]Of those applying for disability compensation.
[b]Of those ever having home loan.
VA = Department of Veterans Affairs.

SOURCE: "2010 National Survey of Veterans: Key Findings: Enrollment and Usage of VA Benefits and Services," in *Department of Veterans Affairs: Veteran Surveys and Studies*, National Center for Veterans Analysis and Statistics, August 15, 2011, http://www.va.gov/vetdata/docs/QuickFacts/Surveys-slideshow .pdf (accessed June 21, 2013)

The MetLife Mature Market Institute reports an even higher average cost for home health aide services: $21 per hour in 2012. Hourly rates for home health aides varied widely, from $13 per hour in Shreveport, Louisiana, to $32 per hour in Rochester, Minnesota. As a result, many older adults cannot afford this expense and may exhaust their lifetime savings long before the need for care ends.

Who Pays for Long-Term Care?

Payment for LTC is derived from three major sources: Medicaid, private insurance (LTC insurance), and out-of-pocket spending. In "Medicaid and Long-Term Care Services and Supports" (June 2012, http://kaiser familyfoundation.files.wordpress.com/2013/01/2186-09.pdf), the Kaiser Family Foundation notes that Medicaid is the primary payer for LTC services.

Medicare, Medicaid, and Long-Term Care

Medicare does not cover custodial or long-term nursing home care but, under specific conditions, it pays for short-term rehabilitative stays in nursing homes and for some home health care. (Custodial care is nonmedical care that helps individuals with their activities of daily living.) Medicaid is the only public program with LTC coverage.

Medicaid, however, does not work like private insurance, which offers protection from catastrophic expense. Medicaid is a means-tested program, so middle-income people needing nursing home care become eligible for Medicaid only after they spend down their own personal income and assets.

Even then, Medicaid will not necessarily pay the entire nursing home bill. Nursing home residents must also meet income eligibility standards. In some states older adults with incomes too high for regular Medicaid eligibility, but with substantial medical bills, are allowed to spend down to become income-eligible for Medicaid. They must incur medical bills until their income for a given period, minus the medical expenses, falls below the Medicaid threshold.

Although every state's Medicaid program covers LTC, each makes different choices about the parameters of its program. Eligibility rules and protection for the finances of spouses of nursing home residents vary, but federal law requires states to allow the community spouse to retain enough of the institutionalized spouse's income to maintain a monthly allowance for minimum living costs. The CMS indicates in "2013 SSI and Spousal Impoverishment Standards" (November 2012, http://www.medicaidannuity.com/LinkClick.aspx?fileticket=MdJBoJktdeQ%3D&tabid=76) that the allowance is set by each state according to federal guidelines—in 2013 the allowance was no less than $1,891.25 and no more than $2,365 per month. The community spouse is also allowed to retain joint assets—an amount equal to half of the couple's resources at the time the spouse enters the institution, up to a federally specified maximum ($115,920 in 2013).

Figure 10.2 shows the breakdown of LTC expenditures for older adults by the source of payment. In 2008 Medicaid paid the largest proportion (52%) of institutional expenses, but a considerable proportion (41%) was paid out of pocket. Medicare made the largest contribution (92%) toward home care services, whereas 1% of services were covered by Medicaid and 5% were paid out of pocket.

Private Long-Term Care Insurance

Another source of financing is LTC insurance. Private LTC insurance policies typically cover some portion of the cost of nursing home care and home health care services. The U.S. Department of Health and Human Services explains in "What Is Long-Term Care Insurance?" (2013, http://longtermcare.gov/costs-how-to-pay/what-is-long-term-care-insurance/) that the cost of a policy is based on the age of the purchaser, the maximum dollar amount the policy pays per day, the maximum number of days per year that the policy will pay for, and optional features such as benefits that increase to adjust for inflation.

According to the Department of Health and Human Services, in "Long-Term Care Insurance Costs" (2013, http://longtermcare.gov/costs-how-to-pay/what-is-long-term-care-insurance/long-term-care-insurance-costs/), in 2007, the most recent year for which data were available, the average LTC policy cost about $2,207 per year, covered 4.8 years of benefits, provided a daily benefit

of $160, and covered LTC at home and in a facility. The average policy also included some provision to protect against the erosion of benefits by inflation.

The premiums for private LTC insurance are tax deductible. The American Association for Long Term Care Insurance notes in "Long-Term Care Insurance Tax-Deductibility Rules—LTC Tax Rules" (2013, http://www.aaltci.org/long-term-care-insurance/learning-center/tax-for-business.php/) that in 2011 the Internal Revenue Service increased deductibility levels to encourage the purchase of LTC insurance. The amount that may be deducted increases with advancing age. For example, in 2013 people up to age 40 could deduct $360, whereas older adults aged 60 to 70 years could deduct up to $3,640 and adults aged 70 years and older could deduct $4,550. Many states offer tax incentives to promote the purchase of LTC insurance.

In "Long-Term-Care Insurance: Insurers Are Forced to Boost Premiums or Stop Selling Policies" (August 2012, http://www.consumerreports.org/cro/2012/08/long-term-care-insurance/index.htm), Consumer Reports states that between 2007 and 2012 half of the 20-leading insurance companies, including major companies such as MetLife, Unum, and Prudential, stopped selling new LTC policies. Insurance companies are abandoning the LTC market "because they overestimated how many people would stop paying for their policies over time and underestimated the costs of long-term care. And low interest rates have made it difficult to grow the reserves they need on hand to pay claims."

In addition, some companies that continue to offer policies have instituted steep rate hikes. For example, Consumer Reports notes that in 2012 some John Hancock policyholders' premiums increased 40% and Genworth Financial increased its rates 18% for a quarter of its policyholders. For policyholders who are hard pressed to pay higher premiums, some companies offer the option of paying a lower premium for a policy with reduced benefits.

To determine if a person needs LTC insurance, Consumer Reports cites the advice of the financial planner Ken Weingarten. Weingarten indicates that retired couples with $2.5 million or more in liquid assets probably do not need LTC insurance because they can afford to pay for care. Retired couples with less than $500,000 will probably not be able to afford the premiums. The retirees with assets between $500,000 and $2.5 million will probably be best served by LTC insurance.

HEALTH CARE REFORM LEGISLATION MAY INCREASE ACCESS TO LONG-TERM CARE INSURANCE. The PPACA contained the Community Living Assistance Services and Supports (CLASS) Act, which aimed to help people remain in their home rather than enter an

LTC facility. It would have established a federally administered, public and voluntary LTC insurance option for workers. The act went into effect on January 1, 2011, but was repealed on January 1, 2013. According to Howard Gleckman, in "Fiscal Cliff Deal Repeals CLASS Act, Creates Long-Term Care Commission" (Forbes.com, January 1, 2013), an analysis revealed that the act would have created premiums that were not widely affordable.

Although the CLASS Act was repealed as part of the fiscal year 2013 budget, the budget agreement called for a 15-member national commission—nine Democrats and six Republicans—to devise a plan to improve the delivery and financing of LTC services. Writing about the commission in "SCAN Foundation CEO Envisions Opportunity for Long-Term Care Solutions in New Commission" (HealthAffairs.org, January 24, 2013), Bruce Chernof, the chief executive officer of the SCAN Foundation, a nonprofit charitable organization that seeks to transform health care for older adults in ways that encourage independence and preserve dignity, asserts, "There must be approaches for working Americans to address their future long-term care needs in order to decrease the mounting pressures on individuals and families, Medicaid, and to a lesser degree Medicare. Whether the ultimate solutions lie in the private sector, public sector, or through a hybrid approach, national public policy must drive the solution set that creates reasonable guardrails for these tools and their associated markets to thrive."

HOME HEALTH CARE

In *National Home and Hospice Care Survey: Home Health—Data Highlights* (February 13, 2012, http://www.cdc.gov/nchs/nhhcs/nhhcs_home_highlights.htm), the National Center for Health Statistics describes home health care as "provided to individuals and families in their places of residence for the purpose of promoting, maintaining, or restoring health or for maximizing the level of independence while minimizing the effects of disability and illness, including terminal illness."

Andrea Sisko et al. observe in "Health Spending Projections through 2018: Recession Effects Add Uncertainty to the Outlook" (*Health Affairs*, vol. 28, no. 2, March–April 2009) that between 2013 and 2018 home health care spending growth is expected to remain steady, averaging 7.9% per year and reaching $134.9 billion in the next decade. Although Medicare has been the principal payer for home health care, Medicaid became the largest payer for these services in 2010, as care continued to be redirected from institutions to home and community-based services settings.

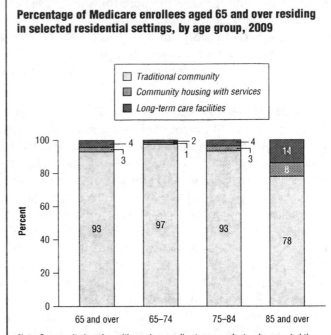

FIGURE 10.10

Percentage of Medicare enrollees aged 65 and over residing in selected residential settings, by age group, 2009

Legend:
- Traditional community
- Community housing with services
- Long-term care facilities

Note: Community housing with services applies to respondents who reported they lived in retirement communities or apartments, senior citizen housing, continuing care retirement facilities, assisted living facilities, staged living communities, board and care facilities/homes, and similar situations, and who reported they had access to one or more of the following services through their place of residence: meal preparation; cleaning or housekeeping services; laundry services; help with medications. Respondents were asked about access to these services, but not whether they actually used the services. A residence (or unit) is considered a long-term care facility if it is certified by Medicare or Medicaid; or has 3 or more beds, is licensed as a nursing home or other long-term care facility, and provides at least one personal care service; or provides 24-hour, 7-day-a-week supervision by a non-family, paid caregiver.

SOURCE: "Percentage of Medicare Enrollees Age 65 and over in Selected Residential Settings, by Age Group, 2009," in *Older Americans 2012: Key Indicators of Well-Being*, Federal Interagency Forum on Aging-Related Statistics, June 2012, http://www.agingstats.gov/Main_Site/Data/2012_Documents/docs/EntireChartbook.pdf (accessed May 28, 2013)

Community Housing with Home Care Services

Some older adults access home care services through their place of residence. Assisted living facilities, retirement communities, and continuing care retirement communities are community housing alternatives that often provide services such as meal preparation, laundry and cleaning services, transportation, and assistance adhering to prescribed medication regimens.

In 2009 just 3% of Medicare recipients aged 65 years and older lived in community housing that offered at least one home care service, and an additional 4% lived in LTC facilities. (See Figure 10.10.) The percentage of people residing in community housing that offered home care services was higher in the older age groups. Among people aged 85 years and older, 8% lived in community housing with services and 14% lived in LTC facilities.

Older adults living in community housing with support services had more functional limitations than those

FIGURE 10.11

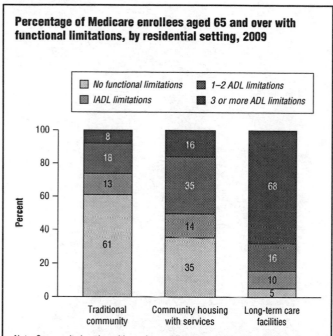

Percentage of Medicare enrollees aged 65 and over with functional limitations, by residential setting, 2009

Note: Community housing with services applies to respondents who reported they lived in retirement communities or apartments, senior citizen housing, continuing care retirement facilities, assisted living facilities, staged living communities, board and care facilities/homes, and similar situations, and who reported they had access to one or more of the following services through their place of residence: meal preparation; cleaning or housekeeping services; laundry services; help with medications. Respondents were asked about access to these services, but not whether they actually used the services. A residence (or unit) is considered a long-term care facility if it is certified by Medicare or Medicaid; or has 3 or more beds, is licensed as a nursing home or other long-term care facility, and provides at least one personal care service; or provides 24-hour, 7-day-a-week supervision by a non-family, paid caregiver. Instrumental activities of daily living (IADL) limitations refer to difficulty performing (or inability to perform, for a health reason) one or more of the following tasks: using the telephone, light housework, heavy housework, meal preparation, shopping, managing money. Only the questions on telephone use, shopping, and managing money are asked of long-term care facility residents. Activities of Daily Living (ADL) limitations refer to difficulty performing (or inability to perform, for a health reason) the following tasks: bathing, dressing, eating, getting in/out of chairs, toileting. Long-term care facility residents with no limitations may include individuals with limitations in certain IADLs such as doing light or heavy housework or meal preparation. These questions were not asked of facility residents.

SOURCE: "Table 36b. Percentage of Medicare Enrollees Age 65 and over with Functional Limitations, by Residential Setting, 2009," in *Older Americans 2012: Key Indicators of Well-Being*, Federal Interagency Forum on Aging-Related Statistics, June 2012, http://www.agingstats .gov/Main_Site/Data/2012_Documents/docs/EntireChartbook.pdf (accessed May 28, 2013)

living in the community but fewer than residents of LTC facilities. Sixteen percent of older adults living in community housing with services had three or more activities of daily living limitations, compared with 8% of older adults living in the community and 68% of older adults in LTC facilities. (See Figure 10.11.)

CHAPTER 11

CRIME AND ABUSE OF OLDER ADULTS

My Administration is a determined advocate for older Americans. Through the Elder Justice Act, which was enacted as part of the Affordable Care Act, we are working to prevent elder abuse, neglect, and exploitation. States and tribes are investigating risk factors for abuse and neglect and identifying strategies to stop it. We convened the Elder Justice Coordinating Council to better focus prevention efforts across the Federal Government. We are committed to combatting exploitation by empowering seniors to meet financial challenges and helping them avoid scams. And we continue to pursue a rigorous criminal justice response to elder abuse, neglect, and exploitation—one that holds offenders accountable, gives professionals meaningful training, and ensures victims get the help they need.

—President Barack Obama, "Presidential Proclamation—World Elder Abuse Awareness Day" (June 14, 2013)

In "What Is Elder Abuse?" (2013, http://www.preventelderabuse.org/elderabuse/), the National Committee for the Prevention of Elder Abuse (NCPEA), a nonprofit organization that is dedicated to the prevention of abuse and neglect of older people and adults with disabilities, defines elder abuse as "any form of mistreatment that results in harm or loss to an older person" and explains that elder abuse encompasses physical and sexual abuse, domestic violence, psychological abuse, financial abuse, and neglect. The NCPEA (2013, http://www.preventelderabuse.org) asserts that financial exploitation of older adults is often associated with other forms of abuse and neglect and that it "threatens the health, dignity, and economic security of millions of older Americans."

CRIME AGAINST OLDER ADULTS

Older adults have lower rates of violent crime than other age groups, and their rate of serious violent crime (rape or sexual assault, robbery, and aggravated assault) stayed relatively constant during the first decade of the 21st century. In 2010 adults aged 65 years and older had the lowest rate of violent victimization of any age group—2.4 per 1,000 people, compared with 33.9 per 1,000 people among adults aged 18 to 20 years. (See Figure 11.1.)

Jennifer L. Truman and Michael Planty of the Bureau of Justice Statistics indicate in *Criminal Victimization, 2011* (October 2012, http://www.bjs.gov/content/pub/pdf/cv11.pdf) that in 2011 victimization rates for violent crime declined with the advancing age of the victim, consistent with data that were reported in previous years. In 2011 the rate of violent victimizations of people aged 65 years and older was 4.4 per 1,000 people and the rate of serious violent crime was 1.7 per 1,000 people. (See Table 11.1.)

The Physical and Emotional Impact of Crime

According to the Bureau of Justice Statistics, most older Americans who are the victims of violent crime are not physically injured. Physical injuries, however, do not tell the whole story. Victimization and fear of victimization can have far more serious effects on the quality of older adults' lives than they might for younger people.

Older adults are often less resilient than younger people. Even so-called nonviolent crimes, such as purse snatching, vandalism, or burglary, can be devastating. Stolen or damaged articles and property are often irreplaceable because of their sentimental value. Furthermore, nonviolent crimes leave victims with a sense of violation and heightened vulnerability.

Older People Are Considered Easy Prey

Because of their physical limitations, older adults are often considered easy prey. They are less likely than younger victims to resist criminal attacks. Their reluctance to resist may be based on awareness that they lack the strength to repel a younger aggressor and that they are physically frail and at risk of injuries that could permanently disable them. The U.S. Bureau of Justice Statistics reports that crime victims over the age of 65 years who try to protect themselves most often use nonphysical

FIGURE 11.1

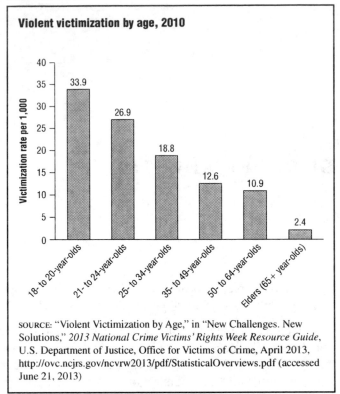

Violent victimization by age, 2010

SOURCE: "Violent Victimization by Age," in "New Challenges. New Solutions," *2013 National Crime Victims' Rights Week Resource Guide*, U.S. Department of Justice, Office for Victims of Crime, April 2013, http://ovc.ncjrs.gov/ncvrw2013/pdf/StatisticalOverviews.pdf (accessed June 21, 2013)

actions, such as arguing, reasoning, or screaming. Younger victims are more likely to use physical action, such as attacking, resisting, or running from or chasing offenders.

Besides physical limitations, there may be other factors that place older adults at increased risk of mistreatment or victimization. These risks include retirement or unemployment (80.9%), a prior traumatic event (62%), low household income (45.7%), low levels of social support (43.6%), use of social services (40.8%), requiring assistance with the activities of daily living (37.8%), and poor health (22.3%). (See Figure 11.2.)

FRAUD

Older adults are considered easy prey for fraud, deception, and exploitation. They are more readily accessible to con artists than other age groups because they are likely to be at home to receive visits from door-to-door salespeople or calls from telemarketers. Older adults who are homebound or otherwise isolated may not have regular contact with others who might help them to identify possible schemes or frauds. Law enforcement officials and consumer advocates assert that older people are targeted because:

- They are more likely than younger people to have substantial financial savings, home equity, or credit, all of which are tempting to fraud perpetrators.

- They are often reluctant to be rude to others, so they may be more likely to hear out a con's story. They may also be overly trusting.

- They are less likely to report fraud because they are embarrassed, they do not know how or to whom to report the crime, or they fear appearing incapable of handling their personal finances.

- Older adults who do report fraud may not make good witnesses. Their memories may fade over the span of time between the crime and the trial, and on the witness stand they may be unable to provide detailed enough information to lead to a conviction.

In "Is Psychological Vulnerability Related to the Experience of Fraud in Older Adults?" (*Clinical Gerontologist*, vol. 36, no. 2, April 25, 2013), Peter A. Lichtenberg, Laurie Stickney, and Daniel Paulson estimate that the prevalence of fraud among older adults is 4.5%. In a population study of 4,400 older adults, the researchers find that the most psychologically vulnerable older adults with the highest levels of depression and the lowest levels of socialization experienced more fraud than those who were not psychologically vulnerable.

The Federal Trade Commission (FTC) is the government's lead consumer protection agency. FTC authority extends over practically the entire economy, including business and consumer transactions via telephone and the Internet. The FTC's consumer mission includes prohibiting unfair or deceptive acts or practices.

The U.S. Food and Drug Administration (FDA) and the FTC actively work to prevent health fraud and scams. These agencies identify products with substandard or entirely useless ingredients as well as those with fraudulent or misleading advertising to prevent the dissemination of unsubstantiated or deceptive claims about the benefits of particular products or services.

The FTC acts not only to prevent consumer fraud but also to monitor its occurrence. In *Consumer Fraud in the United States, 2011: The Third FTC Survey* (April 2013, http://www.ftc.gov/os/2013/04/130419fraudsurvey.pdf), Keith B. Anderson of the FTC reports the results of a 2011 survey. Anderson indicates that older consumers were significantly less likely to be the victims of specific kinds of fraud such as weight-loss products, prize promotions, debt-related fraud, or income-related fraud. Whereas 14.3% of adults aged 45 to 54 years were the victims of fraud in 2011, just 9.1% of adults aged 55 to 64 years, 7.3% of those aged 65 to 74 years, and 6.5% of those aged 75 years and older were the victims of fraud. (See Table 11.2.)

Health Fraud

Older adults may be particularly susceptible to false or misleading claims about the safety and/or efficacy (the

TABLE 11.1

Violent crime rates, by sex, race, Hispanic origin, and age of victim, 2002, 2010, and 2011

Demographic characteristic of victim	Violent crime					Serious violent crime[a]				
	Rates[b]			Percent change[c]		Rates[b]			Percent change[c]	
	2002	2010	2011	2002–2011	2010–2011	2002	2010	2011	2002–2011	2010–2011
Total	32.1	19.3	22.5	−30%	17%	10.0	6.6	7.2	−28%	9%
Sex										
Male	33.5	20.1	25.4	−24%	27%	10.4	6.4	7.7	−26%	20%
Female	30.7	18.5	19.8	−36	7	9.5	6.8	6.7	−30	−2
Race/Hispanic origin[d]										
White[e]	32.6	18.3	21.5	−34%	18%	8.6	5.8	6.5	−24%	13%
Black[e]	36.1	25.9	26.4	−27	2	17.8	10.4	10.8	−39	4
Hispanic	29.9	16.8	23.8	−20	42	12.3	6.7	7.2	−42	7
American Indian/Alaska Native[e]	62.9	77.6	45.4	−28	−42	14.3	47.3	12.6	−12	−73
Asian/Native Hawaiian/other Pacific Islander[e]	11.7	10.3	11.2	−4	9	3.4	2.3	2.5	−25	12
Two or more races[e]	—	52.6	64.6	—	23	—	17.7	26.2	—	48
Age										
12–17	62.7	28.1	37.7	−40%	34%	17.0	11.7	8.8	−48%	−25%
18–24	68.5	33.9	49.0	−28	45	24.7	17.0	16.3	−34	−4
25–34	39.9	29.7	26.5	−34	−11	12.3	7.1	9.5	−22	34
35–49	26.7	18.2	21.9	−18	21	7.6	5.6	7.0	−8	24
50–64	14.6	12.7	13.0	−11	3	4.4	3.7	4.3	−4	15
65 or older	3.8	3.0	4.4	17	48	1.8	0.9	1.7	−9	91
Marital status										
Never married	56.3	31.8	35.5	−37%	11%	16.1	11.9	11.7	−27%	−2%
Married	16.0	7.8	11.0	−31	40	5.7	2.2	3.7	−34	70
Widowed	7.1	6.7	3.8	−46	−43	4.4	3.0	0.7	−85	−78
Divorced	44.5	35.2	37.8	−15	7	10.9	11.2	9.2	−15	−18
Separated	76.0	60.2	72.9	−4	21	34.8	18.8	26.4	−24	40

—Less than 0.5.
[a]Includes rape or sexual assault, robbery, and aggravated assault.
[b]Per 1,000 persons age 12 or older.
[c]Calculated based on unrounded estimates.
[d]The collection of racial and ethnic categories changed in 2003 to allow respondents to choose more than one racial category.
[e]Excludes persons of Hispanic or Latino origin.

SOURCE: Jennifer L. Truman and Michael Planty, "Table 5. Rate and Percent Change of Violent Victimization, by Demographic Characteristics of Victim, 2002, 2010, and 2011," in *Criminal Victimization, 2011*, U.S. Department of Justice, Bureau of Justice Statistics, October 2012, http://www.bjs.gov/content/pub/pdf/cv11.pdf (accessed May 28, 2013)

FIGURE 11.2

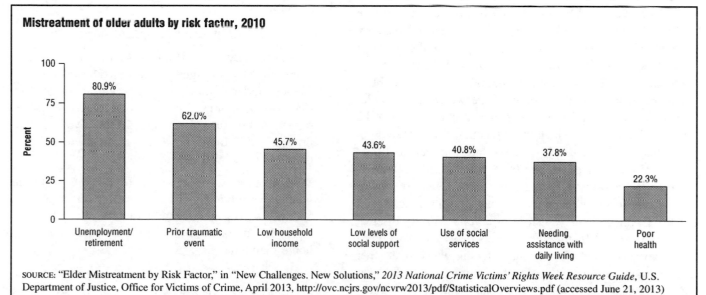

Mistreatment of older adults by risk factor, 2010

SOURCE: "Elder Mistreatment by Risk Factor," in "New Challenges. New Solutions," *2013 National Crime Victims' Rights Week Resource Guide*, U.S. Department of Justice, Office for Victims of Crime, April 2013, http://ovc.ncjrs.gov/ncvrw2013/pdf/StatisticalOverviews.pdf (accessed June 21, 2013)

TABLE 11.2

Fraud victimization rates by age, 2011

Type of fraud	Overall	Age						
		18–24	25–34	35–44	45–54	55–64	65–74	75 and older
Any surveyed fraud	10.8%	11.7%	11.1%	12.1%	14.3%	9.1%	7.3%	6.5%
Any specific surveyed fraud	7.9%	8.7%	8.6%	8.6%	10.1%	7.6%	5.6%	3.7%
Weight-loss products	2.1%	1.8%	3.0%	1.9%	2.7%	2.8%	0.8%	1.2%
Prize promotions	1.0%	1.3%	0.7%	0.3%	0.5%	1.8%	2.8%	0.4%
Unauthorized billing-related fraud[a]	2.9%	2.4%	2.0%	4.9%	3.7%	3.1%	1.2%	1.8%
Debt-related fraud[b]	1.9%	1.0%	3.0%	2.8%	2.5%	1.2%	0.6%	0.3%
Income-related fraud[c]	1.7%	4.3%	1.6%	2.1%	1.9%	0.7%	1.1%	0.1%
Other frauds included in survey[d]	2.6%	3.4%	2.1%	1.4%	4.7%	1.9%	1.7%	3.5%
Number of observations[e]	3,638	196	338	520	702	776	580	412

Notes: Figures are based on simple cross-tabulations, not taking into account other characteristics.
[a]Unauthorized billing-related fraud includes unauthorized billing—buyers' guides, unauthorized billing—internet services, and unauthorized billing—other products (one of the more general types of fraud included in the survey).
[b]Debt-related fraud includes credit repair, debt relief, mortgage relief, and advance fee loans.
[c]Income-related fraud includes work-at-home programs, business opportunities, pyramid schemes, and government job offers.
[d]Other frauds included in survey include credit card insurance, counterfeit checks, and paid for something never received.
[e]The sum of the number of observations in the subgroups will not sum to the total. Some people did not answer the questions necessary to assign them to a subgroup.

SOURCE: Keith B. Anderson, "Table 13. Fraud Victimization Rates, 2011, by Age," in *Consumer Fraud in the United States, 2011: The Third FTC Survey*, Federal Trade Commission, April 2013, http://www.ftc.gov/os/2013/04/130419fraudsurvey.pdf (accessed June 21, 2013)

ability of an intervention to produce the intended diagnostic or therapeutic effect in optimal circumstances) of over-the-counter (nonprescription) drugs, devices, foods, and dietary supplements because the marketing of such products often relates to conditions that are associated with aging. Also, many of these unproven treatments promise false hope and offer immediate cures for chronic (long-term) diseases or complete relief from pain. It is understandable that older adults who are frightened or in pain might be seduced by false promises of quick cures.

Working together, the FDA and the FTC combat deceptive advertising for health products such as false and unsubstantiated claims for dietary supplements. One example of an FDA action is described in the press release "Bethel Nutritional Consulting, Inc. Issues a Voluntary Recall of Weight-Loss Pills 'Bethel 30' Found to Contain an Undeclared Drug Ingredient" (June 11, 2013, http://www.fda.gov/Safety/Recalls/ucm356233.htm). The FDA explains that it tested a sample of the weight-loss supplement Bethel 30 and found that the sample contained the drugs sibutramine, which was taken off the market in October 2010 because it posed a safety threat, and phenolphthalein, a laxative. The FDA warns, "Sibutramine is known to substantially increase blood pressure and/or pulse rate in some patients and may present a significant risk for patients with a history of coronary artery disease, congestive heart failure, arrhythmias or stroke. This product may also interact, in life-threatening ways, with other medications a consumer may be taking." Bethel Nutritional Consulting, Inc., the company that manufactured the weight-loss product, responded to this finding by voluntarily recalling the product.

Financial Fraud, Abuse, and Exploitation

Financial crimes against older adults are largely underreported but are estimated to total losses of at least $2.9 billion each year. This section describes findings from *The MetLife Study of Elder Financial Abuse: Crimes of Occasion, Desperation, and Predation against America's Elders* (June 2011, https://www.metlife.com/assets/cao/mmi/publications/studies/2011/mmi-elder-financial-abuse.pdf), a study about reported instances of elder financial abuse in the news and other relevant media that was conducted by the MetLife Mature Market Institute, the NCPEA, and the Center for Gerontology at the Virginia Polytechnic Institute and State University.

The study's principal findings include:

- Approximately half (51%) of the reported fraud was committed by strangers. Financial abuse by family, friends, and neighbors was reported about one-third (34%) of the time, and 12% of reported fraud was perpetrated by businesses. Just 4% involved Medicare or Medicaid fraud; however, these represented the greatest financial losses to victims.

- Most victims were aged 80 to 89 years old, and women were twice as likely to suffer financial abuse. Victims were generally vulnerable as a result of having to rely on others to assist them with health care or home maintenance.

- Well over half (60%) of the perpetrators were male, aged 30 to 59 years, and were strangers who sought out vulnerable older adults—those with limited mobility, lived alone, or were visibly confused.

- News stories about elder abuse surged during the holiday season—between November 2010 and January 2011. Financial losses during this period attributable to family, friends, or neighbors were higher than losses sustained other times.

- Financial abuse of older adults is more common than previously estimated and may be as high as 41 victims per 1,000 people.

- News stories cited deceit, threats, and emotional manipulation as well physical and sexual violence as the means that were used to perpetrate financial abuse.

The study concludes that in addition to financial ruin, elder financial abuse "engenders health care inequities, fractures families, reduces available health care options, and increases rates of mental health issues among elders. Elder financial abuse invariably results in losses of human rights and dignity. Despite growing public awareness from a parade of high-profile financial abuse victims, it remains underreported, under-recognized, and under-prosecuted."

Medicare Fraud

Every year Medicare loses millions of dollars due to fraud and abuse. The *MetLife Study of Elder Financial Abuse* reports that Medicare and Medicaid fraud totaled $306.1 million in a three-month period (April to June 2010), during which researchers monitored newsfeeds.

The Health Insurance Portability and Accountability Act of 1996 allocated funds to protect Medicare's integrity and prevent fraud. In one of the largest efforts in the history of Medicare, the program has undertaken a major campaign to help eliminate Medicare fraud, waste, and abuse.

To combat Medicare fraud at the beneficiary level, the Administration on Aging (AoA) provides grants to local organizations to help older Americans become more vigilant health care consumers so that they can identify and prevent fraudulent health care practices. The Senior Medicare Patrol (SMP) program trains community volunteers, many of whom are retired professionals, such as doctors, nurses, accountants, investigators, law enforcement personnel, attorneys, and teachers, to help Medicare beneficiaries become better health care consumers. In "Performance Data for the Senior Medicare Patrol Projects: June 2012 Performance Report" (June 21, 2012, http://oig.hhs.gov/oei/reports/oei-02-12-00190.pdf), Stuart Wright of the U.S. Department of Health and Human Services indicates that in 2011 the SMP's 5,700 volunteers conducted 66,300 one-on-one counseling sessions and 11,100 group education sessions. Over 431,100 beneficiaries attended group education sessions, up from 298,000 in 2010, and there were 592,700 media airings and 8,800 community outreach education events. The SMP reported cost avoidance "on behalf of the Medicare program, the Medicaid program, beneficiaries, and others" of over $247,800 in 2011. Since its inception in 1997, the program's volunteers have recovered nearly $4.6 million in Medicare funds and saved Medicare beneficiaries and taxpayers approximately $106 million.

ABUSE AND MISTREATMENT OF OLDER ADULTS

Domestic violence against older adults first gained publicity during the late 1970s, when Representative Claude Denson Pepper (1900–1989; D-FL) held widely publicized hearings about the mistreatment of older adults. In the three decades since those hearings, policy makers, health professionals, social service personnel, and advocates for older Americans have sought ways to protect the older population from physical, psychological, and financial abuse.

Magnitude of the Problem

It is difficult to determine exactly how many older adults are victims of abuse or mistreatment. As with child abuse and domestic violence among younger adults, the number of actual cases is larger than the number of reported cases. There is consensus among professionals and agencies that deal with issues of elder abuse that it is far less likely to be reported than child or spousal abuse. The challenge of estimating the incidence (the rate of new cases of a disorder over a specified period) and prevalence (the total number of cases of a disorder in a given population at a specific time) of this problem is further compounded by the varying definitions of abuse and reporting practices used by the voluntary, state, and federal agencies, as well as the fact that comprehensive national data are not collected. Furthermore, research suggests that abuse often occurs over long periods and that only when it reaches a critical juncture, such as instances of severe injury, will the neglect or abuse become evident to health, social service, or legal professionals.

Although the magnitude of the problem of abuse of older adults is unknown, its social and moral importance is obvious. Abuse and neglect of older individuals in society violate a sacred trust and moral commitment to protect vulnerable individuals and groups from harm and to ensure their well-being and security.

High-profile cases of elder abuse and the media's spotlight on the problem have helped increase Americans' awareness that it is a pervasive problem that occurs among people of all races, ethnicities, incomes, and educational attainment. For example, in 2009 the media chronicled the trial of Anthony D. Marshall (1924–), the son of the wealthy socialite and philanthropist Brooke Astor (1902–2007), who was charged with stealing millions of dollars from his mother's estate. In October 2009 the 85-year-old Marshall was found guilty of draining his mother's fortune as she suffered from Alzheimer's disease and was sentenced to up to three years in prison. In June 2013, after years of legal appeals, Marshall surrendered to begin his prison term.

Greater Efforts Are Needed to Combat Elder Abuse

In her testimony *Elder Justice: Stronger Federal Leadership Could Help Improve Response to Elder Abuse* (March 2, 2011, http://www.gao.gov/new.items/d11384t.pdf) before the U.S. Senate's Special Committee on Aging, Kay E. Brown of the U.S. Government Accountability Office (GAO) stated that in 2009 the prevalence of elder abuse was approximately 14.1% among noninstitutionalized older Americans (people who are not in the U.S. military, school, jail, or mental health facilities) and suggested that this was probably a low estimate of prevalence. During the same committee hearing Mark Lachs (March 2, 2011, http://aging.senate.gov/events/hr230ml.pdf) of Cornell University noted that a study conducted in New York state revealed that for every reported instance of elder abuse as many as 24 remain unreported. The committee was advised that although family members and staff are largely responsible for abuse and neglect of older adults in nursing homes and other facilities, older adults might also be victimized by fellow nursing home residents.

The committee also heard testimony from Mickey Rooney (1920–; http://aging.senate.gov/events/hr230mr.pdf), an American actor and World War II (1939–1945) veteran, who suffered from elder abuse. Rooney described the loss of control he experienced:

> In my case, I was eventually and completely stripped of the ability to make even the most basic decisions in my own life. Over the course of time, my daily life became unbearable. Worse, it seemed to happen out of nowhere. At first, it was something small, something I could control. But then it became something sinister that was completely out of control. I felt trapped, scared, used, and frustrated. But above all, I felt helpless. For years I suffered silently. I couldn't muster the courage to seek the help I knew I needed. Even when I tried to speak up, I was told to be quiet. It seemed like no one believed me.

His testimony underscored the observation that any older adult can fall victim to abuse and that this problem is not limited exclusively to older adults in nursing homes or those who suffer from cognitive impairments.

Brown concluded in her testimony that many state adult protective service programs charged with addressing elder abuse have struggled to keep pace with growing caseloads because they lack the funding and leadership to effectively fulfill their responsibilities. She called for stronger and more effective federal guidance for adult protective service programs. Among the many actions to combat such abuse, Brown recommended

that the Department of Health and Human Services develop an effective method for national surveillance of elder abuse and the collection of data as well as a system for compiling and disseminating these data nationwide.

A National Strategy to Combat Abuse

The GAO explains in *Elder Justice: National Strategy Needed to Effectively Combat Elder Financial Exploitation* (November 2012, http://www.gao.gov/assets/660/650074.pdf) that although combating financial abuse of older adults is primarily the responsibility of state and local social service, criminal justice, and consumer protection agencies, the federal government also has an important role. To identify the issues surrounding this problem, the GAO interviewed state and local social service, criminal justice, and consumer protection officials in California, Illinois, New York, and Pennsylvania (states with large populations of older adults); officials in seven federal agencies; and elder abuse experts. It also reviewed relevant research and legislation.

The GAO finds that although the states are largely responsible for combating elder financial abuse, the federal government could circulate information and assist to enhance public awareness of the problem. The Elder Justice Coordinating Council, which consists of officials from federal agencies that coordinate elder justice activities, was proposed as a group that could lead development and implementation of a coordinated national strategy. Coordination is important because even though countering elder abuse is the stated mission of just one federal agency—the Consumer Financial Protection Bureau—as Figure 11.3 shows many other agencies also work to prevent and identify elder abuse, to protect consumers, or to respond to consumer inquiries.

The GAO determines that the states need assistance to gain expertise, improve collaboration between law enforcement and adult protective services agencies, and obtain the necessary data for them to address elder abuse. For example, the GAO finds that law enforcement officials in four states were unclear about how they should obtain the federal support they need to respond to interstate and international cases. To help the states, the U.S. Department of Justice has developed a website that provides information, training, and other materials prosecutors can use to gain expertise in investigating and prosecuting elder abuse and financial exploitation.

Types of Mistreatment

Most documented instances of elder abuse involve maltreatment of an older person by someone who has a special relationship with the older adult, such as a spouse, sibling, child, friend, or caregiver. Until recently, most

FIGURE 11.3

Federal agencies involved in combatting elder abuse

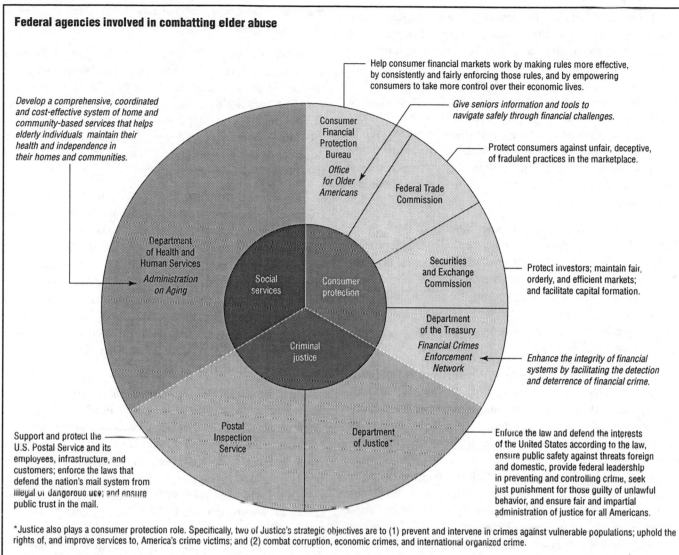

Develop a comprehensive, coordinated and cost-effective system of home and community-based services that helps elderly individuals maintain their health and independence in their homes and communities.

Help consumer financial markets work by making rules more effective, by consistently and fairly enforcing those rules, and by empowering consumers to take more control over their economic lives.

Give seniors information and tools to navigate safely through financial challenges.

Protect consumers against unfair, deceptive, of fradulent practices in the marketplace.

Protect investors; maintain fair, orderly, and efficient markets; and facilitate capital formation.

Enhance the integrity of financial systems by facilitating the detection and deterrence of financial crime.

Enforce the law and defend the interests of the United States according to the law, ensure public safety against threats foreign and domestic, provide federal leadership in preventing and controlling crime, seek just punishment for those guilty of unlawful behavior, and ensure fair and impartial administration of justice for all Americans.

Support and protect the U.S. Postal Service and its employees, infrastructure, and customers; enforce the laws that defend the nation's mail system from illegal or dangerous use; and ensure public trust in the mail.

*Justice also plays a consumer protection role. Specifically, two of Justice's strategic objectives are to (1) prevent and intervene in crimes against vulnerable populations; uphold the rights of, and improve services to, America's crime victims; and (2) combat corruption, economic crimes, and international organized crime.

SOURCE: "Figure 2. Federal Agencies with Missions That Involve Combating Elder Financial Exploitation," in *Elder Justice: National Strategy Needed to Effectively Combat Elder Financial Exploitation*, Government Accountability Office, November 2012, http://www.gao.gov/assets/660/650074.pdf (accessed June 24, 2013)

---

data indicated that adult children were the most common abusers of older family members, but Pamela B. Teaster of the University of Kentucky indicates in *A Response to the Abuse of Vulnerable Adults: The 2000 Survey of State Adult Protective Services* (June 2003, http://www.ncea.aoa.gov/Resources/Publication/docs/apsreport 030703.pdf) that the landmark 2000 National Center on Elder Abuse (NCEA) survey found that spouses are the most common perpetrators of abuse and mistreatment. The major types of elder abuse and mistreatment include:

- Physical abuse—inflicting physical pain or bodily injury

- Sexual abuse—nonconsensual sexual contact of any kind with an older person

- Emotional or psychological abuse—inflicting mental anguish by, for example, name calling, humiliation, threats, or isolation

- Neglect—willful or unintentional failure to provide basic necessities, such as food and medical care, as a result of caregiver indifference, inability, or ignorance

- Material or financial abuse—exploiting or misusing an older person's funds or assets

- Abandonment—the desertion of an older adult by an individual who has physical custody of the elder or who has assumed responsibility for providing care for the older person

- Self-neglect—behaviors of an older person that threaten his or her own health or safety

Reporting Abuse

Like child abuse and sexual assault crimes, many crimes against older adults are not reported because the victims are physically or mentally unable to summon help or because they are reluctant or afraid to publicly accuse relatives or caregivers. Loneliness or dependency prevents many victims from reporting the crimes, even when they are aware of them, because they are afraid to lose the companionship and care of the perpetrator. When financial abuse is reported, the source of the information is likely to be someone other than the victim: a police officer, ambulance attendant, bank teller, neighbor, or other family member.

The AoA estimates in "Protect Seniors in the Year of Elder Abuse Prevention" (2013, http://www.aoa.gov/AoA Root/AoA_Programs/Elder_Rights/YEAP/index.aspx) that 2.1 million older Americans suffer abuse, neglect, or exploitation each year. According to the agency, this number is "only part of the picture: Experts believe that for every case of elder abuse or neglect reported, as many as five cases go unreported."

In "Elder Abuse and Neglect: When Home Is Not Safe" (*Clinics in Geriatric Medicine*, vol. 25, no. 1, February 2009), Linda Abbey of the Virginia Commonwealth University reports that all 50 states require physicians and other social service professionals to report evidence of abuse, neglect, and exploitation when an older adult is in an institution and most also require reporting when abuse occurs in a private home. Abbey notes that according to a 2004 study of state programs funded by the AoA, the most common reporters for older adults were family members (17%), social services (10.6%), friends/neighbors (8%), the older adults themselves (6.3%), long-term care staff (5.5%), law enforcement (5.3%), and nurses/aides (3.8%). Physicians represented just 1.4% of reporters. Abbey asserts that low physician reporting may be attributable to lack of awareness of the problem, lack of training about how to identify abuse, denial that the family may be abusing a loved one, concern about compromising relationships with the family, reluctance to become involved with legal proceedings, and time pressures that prevent the identification of instances of abuse. She also opines that physician discomfort with the problem may impede case finding and observes that "family violence does not fit neatly within the traditional medical paradigm of symptoms, diagnoses and treatment."

Causes of Elder Abuse

According to the NCEA, no single theory can explain why older people are abused. The causes of abuse are diverse and complicated. Some relate to the personality of the abuser, some reflect the relationship between the abuser and the abused, and some are reactions to stressful situations. Although some children truly dislike their parents and the role of caregiver, many others want to care for their parents or feel it is the right thing to do but may be emotionally or financially unable to meet the challenges of caregiving.

STRESS. Meeting the daily needs of a frail and dependent older adult is demanding and may be overwhelming for some family caregivers. When the older person lives in the same household as the caregiver, crowding, differences of opinion, and constant demands often add to the strain of providing physical care. When the older person lives in a different house, the pressure of commuting and managing two households may be stressful.

FINANCIAL BURDEN. Caring for an older adult often places a financial strain on a family. Older parents may need financial assistance at the same time that their children are raising their own families. Instead of an occasional night out, a long-awaited vacation, or a badly needed newer car, families may find themselves paying for ever-increasing medical care, prescription drugs, special dietary supplements, extra food and clothing, or therapy. Saving for their children's college education, for their children's weddings, or for retirement may be difficult or impossible.

In "Financial Elder Abuse Increases in a Down Economy" (OrlandoSentinel.com, June 21, 2012), Jill Schlesinger observes that persistent economic uncertainty following the so-called Great Recession (which lasted from late 2007 to mid-2009) may be implicated in the uptick in elder abuse cases. The *MetLife Study of Elder Financial Abuse* finds a 12% increase in financial abuse of older adults between 2008 and 2010. Schlesinger opines, "While financial scams have long been in existence, the rate at which they occur increases when the economy falters."

CYCLE OF ABUSE. One theory of the causation of abuse of older adults posits that people who abuse an older parent or relative were themselves abused as children. The National Council on Child Abuse and Family Violence confirms this pattern of abuse in "Elder Abuse Information" (2013, http://www.nccafv.org/elder.htm), stating, "In a family where there is a tendency to physically harm members who are weak or dependent, the aging members of society, who are among the most vulnerable, become the next victims in the cycle of intergenerational family violence." The council cautions that "it is important to remember that violence and its related behaviors are learned and often passed from one generation to the next. A child who is abused by a parent may become an adult who uses violence toward a spouse or child then, as caretaker for an aging parent, extends the abuse to his/her parent or relative."

INVASION OF PRIVACY. Monique I. Sellas and Laurel H. Krouse indicate in "Elder Abuse" (June 8, 2011, http://emedicine.medscape.com/article/805727-overview) that a shared living arrangement is a major risk factor for mistreatment of older adults, with older people living alone at the lowest risk for abuse. A shared residence increases the opportunities for contact, conflict, and mistreatment. When the home must be shared, there is an inevitable loss of a certain amount of control and privacy. Movement may be restricted, habits may need to change, and rivalries between generations may follow. Frustration and anxiety may result as both older parent and supporting child try to suppress anger, with varying degrees of success.

SOCIAL ISOLATION. Sellas and Krouse note that social isolation is linked to abuse and the mistreatment of older adults. It may be that socially isolated families are better able to hide unacceptable behaviors from friends and neighbors who might report the abuse. Although there are no data to support the corollary to this finding, it is hypothesized that mistreatment is less likely in families that are rooted in strong social networks.

ALZHEIMER'S DISEASE OR OTHER DEMENTIA. According to Randy R. Gainey and Brian K. Payne, in "Caregiver Burden, Elder Abuse, and Alzheimer's Disease: Testing the Relationship" (*Journal of Health and Human Services Administration*, vol. 29, no. 2, Fall 2006), "caregiver burden" (the stress that is associated with caring for older adults with dementia with limited community support services) is the most frequently cited explanation for the observation that people suffering from dementia are at a greater risk for mistreatment. The researchers looked at instances of mistreatment of older adults with Alzheimer's and those who were not cognitively impaired and found almost no difference in caregiver burden among those caring for older adults with or without dementia. Research has not pinpointed the relationship between dementia and the risk for abuse; however, it may be that dementia itself is not the risk factor but instead the disruptive behaviors that result from dementia. This hypothesis is consistent with research that shows that the disruptive behavior of Alzheimer's patients is an especially strong predictor and cause of caregiver stress.

REVERSE DEPENDENCY. Some sources believe that abusers may be quite dependent, emotionally and financially, on their victims for housing, financial assistance, and transportation than are nonabusing caregivers. They appear to have fewer resources and are frequently unable to meet their own basic needs. Rather than having power in the relationship, they are relatively powerless. From these observations, some researchers speculate that abusing caregivers may not always be driven to violence by the physical and emotional burden of caring for a seriously disabled older person but may have mental health problems of their own that can lead to violent behavior. Several studies specifically point to depression as a characteristic of perpetrators of elder mistreatment.

Intimate Partner Violence: The Abusive Spouse

The U.S. Preventive Services Task Force indicates in "Screening for Intimate Partner Violence and Abuse of Elderly and Vulnerable Adults" (January 2013, http://www.uspreventiveservicestaskforce.org/uspstf12/ipvelder/ipvelderfinalrs.htm) that intimate partner violence (IPV) and abuse of older and vulnerable adults is common but often undetected. Nearly 31% of women and 26% of men report some form of IPV during their lifetime. Approximately 25% of women and 14% of men experience severe IPV during their lifetime.

The high rate of spousal abuse among the older population is possibly because many older adults live with their spouse, so the opportunity for spousal violence is great. Violence against an older spouse may be the continuation of an abusive relationship that began years earlier—abuse does not end simply because a couple ages. Sometimes, however, the abuse may not begin until later years, in which case it is often associated with mental illness, alcohol abuse, unemployment, postretirement depression, and/or loss of self-esteem.

The problem of spousal abuse among older adults may be underestimated and underreported. In "Perceptions of Intimate Partner Violence, Age, and Self-Enhancement Bias" (*Journal of Elder Abuse and Neglect*, vol. 23, no. 1, January 2011), Michael N. Kane, Diane Green, and Robin J. Jacobs find that students preparing for careers in human services such as social work, psychology, and criminal justice were less likely to take allegations of domestic violence between older adults seriously. The students mistakenly assumed that a 30-year-old couple was more likely to engage in conflict and violence than a 75-year-old couple. They also felt that the 30-year-old couple was more likely to change its circumstances than the older couple. Kane, Green, and Jacobs opine that these are ageist beliefs and call for increased awareness and sensitivity to the issue, stating that "raising awareness may help students to identify the possibility of intimate partner abuse when the bruises on the 70-year-old face of Aunt Rose are not attributable to being clumsy but are attributable to 72-year-old Uncle Frank."

Intervention and Prevention

All 50 states and the District of Columbia have laws addressing abuse of older adults, but like laws aiming to prevent and reduce child abuse and domestic violence among younger people, they are often ineffective. The effectiveness of these laws varies from state to state and even from county to county within a given state. No standard definition of abuse exists among enforcement agencies. In many cases authorities cannot legally intervene and terminate an abusive condition unless a report is filed, the abuse is verified, and the victim files a formal complaint. An older adult could understandably be reluctant, physically unable, or too fearful to accuse or prosecute an abuser.

Clearly, the best way to stop elder abuse is to prevent its occurrence. Older people who know that they will eventually need outside help should carefully analyze the potential challenges of living with their family and, if necessary and possible, make alternate arrangements. Furthermore, older adults should take action to protect their money and assets to ensure that their valuables cannot be easily taken from them.

Families or individuals who must serve as caregivers for older adults, voluntarily or otherwise, must be helped to realize that their frustration and despair do not have to result in abuse. Health and social service agencies offer interventions including group support programs and counseling to help caregivers and their families. Many communities allocate resources to assist families to offset the financial burden of elder care, for example, through tax deductions or subsidies for respite care.

Medical Professionals Can Help Identify Elder Abuse

Medical professionals (physicians, nurses, and others) can play a key role in preventing and combating elder abuse if they recognize which of their older adult patients might be vulnerable or victimized. The Investor Protection Trust conducted a survey of physicians and nurses in 2013 and published the results in *Elder Investment Fraud and Financial Exploitation: Do Doctors Know the Symptoms?* (June 12, 2013, http://www.investorprotection.org/downloads/IPT_EIFFE_Medical_Survey_06-12-13.pdf). In the press release "Survey: 1 in 5 Doctors, Nurses Aware They Are Often Dealing with Older Victims of Investment Swindles" (June 12, 2013, http://www.investorprotection.org/downloads/IPT_EIFFE_Medical_Survey_Release_06-12-13.pdf), the Investor Protection Trust lists some of the major findings from the survey, including:

- 92% of medical practitioners said "mild cognitive impairment often makes seniors more vulnerable to investment fraud/financial exploitation"

- 84% of medical practitioners "are willing to refer an elderly patient who may be the victim of investment fraud to those who may be able to help them with their financial affairs or to the proper authorities for help"

- 82% of medical practitioners said "investment fraud/financial exploitation targeting the elderly is a serious problem"

- 61% of medical practitioners expressed interest "in continuing medical education... credits to learn more about spotting the signs of investment fraud/financial exploitation of the elderly"

- 21% of medical practitioners said "they are aware that they often are dealing with the elderly victims of investment fraud/financial exploitation"

INSTITUTIONAL ABUSE: A FORGOTTEN POPULATION?

Abuse of the older population can and does occur in the institutions (nursing homes, board-and-care facilities, and retirement homes) that are charged with, and compensated for, caring for the nation's older population. The term *institutional abuse* generally refers to the same forms of abuse as domestic abuse crimes but is perpetrated by people who have legal or contractual obligations to provide older adults with care. Although the Omnibus Budget Reconciliation Act of 1987 states that nursing homes must take steps to attain or maintain the "highest practicable physical, mental, and psychosocial well-being of each resident," too many residents are victims of neglect or abuse by these facilities or their employees.

Older adult residents of long-term care facilities or supportive housing are thought to be at higher risk for abuse and neglect than community-dwelling older adults. They are particularly vulnerable because most suffer from one or more chronic diseases that impair their physical and cognitive functioning, rendering them dependent on others. Furthermore, many are either unable to report abuse or neglect or are fearful that reporting may generate reprisals from the facility staff or otherwise adversely affect their life. Others are unaware of the availability of help.

There are federal laws and regulations that govern nursing homes, but there is no federal oversight of residential care facilities, such as personal care homes, adult congregate living facilities, residential care homes, homes for the aged, domiciliary care homes, board-and-care homes, and assisted living facilities. As a result, it is more difficult than with nursing homes to estimate the prevalence or nature of abuse or neglect in these facilities. Despite reports in recent years that have raised the specter of widespread and serious abuse of institutionalized older people, as of July 2013 there had never been a systematic study of the prevalence of abuse in nursing homes or other residential facilities.

Several studies of elder abuse in long-term care facilities—such as Lawrence B. Schiamberg et al.'s "Physical Abuse of Older Adults in Nursing Homes: A Random Sample Survey of Adults with an Elderly Family Member in a Nursing Home" (*Journal of Elder Abuse and Neglect*, vol. 24, no. 1, 2012), Linda R. Phillips and Guifang Gao's "Mistreatment in Assisted Living Facilities: Complaints, Substantiations, and Risk Factors" (*Gerontologist*, vol. 51, no. 3, January 2011), and Radka Buzgová and Katerina Ivanová's "Violation of Ethical Principles in Institutional Care for Older People" (*Nursing Ethics*, vol. 18, no. 1, January 2011)—find that it is associated with high staff turnover, which in turn may reflect unsatisfactory working conditions or other organizational problems as well as the use of unlicensed or poorly trained personnel.

Types of Abuse and Neglect

Nursing home neglect and abuse can take many forms, including:

- Failure to provide proper diet and hydration
- Failure to assist with personal hygiene
- Over- or undermedication
- Failure to answer call lights promptly
- Failure to turn residents in their beds to promote circulation and prevent decubitus ulcers (bedsores)
- Slapping or other physical abuse
- Leaving residents in soiled garments or beds or failure to take them to the toilet
- Use of unwarranted restraints
- Emotional or verbal abuse
- Retaliation for making a complaint
- Failure to provide appropriate medical care
- Sexual assault, unwanted touching, indecent exposure, or rape
- Theft of the resident's property or money

In "Nurse Aides' Reports of Resident Abuse in Nursing Homes" (*Journal of Applied Gerontology*, vol. 31, no. 3, June 2012), Nicholas Castle of the University of Pittsburgh reports the results of a survey of 4,451 nurses' aides working in long-term care facilities. More than one-third (36%) of the nurses' aides had witnessed abuse, including incidents of physical and verbal or psychological abuse, such as:

- Argumentative behavior with residents
- Intimidation
- Threatening to stop caring for a resident
- Inappropriate delays in administering medication
- Punching, slapping, kicking, or hitting
- Sexual abuse

Resident Risk Factors

Although there has been scant research describing the factors that contribute to risk for abuse of institutionalized older adults, some studies indicate that the risk for abuse increases in direct relationship to the older resident's dependence on the facility's staff for safety, protection, and care. For example, Diana K. Harris and Michael L. Benson, in *Maltreatment of Patients in Nursing Homes: There Is No Safe Place* (2006), and Mark Miller, a New York state long-term care ombudsman, in "Ombudsmen on the Front Line: Improving Quality of Care and Preventing Abuse in Nursing Homes" (*Generations*, vol. 2, no. 4, July–August 2001), suggest that residents with Alzheimer's disease or another dementia are at greater risk for abuse in the average nursing home population. In "Elder Abuse and Neglect in Long-Term Care" (*Clinics in Geriatric Medicine*, vol. 21, no. 2, May 2005), Seema Joshi and Joseph H. Flaherty of the St. Louis Veterans Administration Medical Center indicate that residents with behavioral symptoms, such as physical aggressiveness, appear to be at higher risk for abuse by staff; this finding is supported by interviews with the certified nursing assistants.

Social isolation may also increase the risk for abuse. Residents who have no visitors are especially vulnerable because they lack family or friends who could oversee their care, bear witness to and report any abuses, and advocate on their behalf.

Efforts to Identify and Reduce Abuse

In an effort to improve the quality of care and eliminate abuse in nursing homes, government regulations and laws have been enacted that require greater supervision and scrutiny of nursing homes. President Ronald Reagan (1911–2004) signed the Omnibus Budget Reconciliation Act of 1987, which included protections for patient rights and treatment. The law went into effect in October 1990, but compliance with the law varies from state to state and from one nursing facility to another.

In 1987 the AoA established the Prevention of Elder Abuse, Neglect, and Exploitation program. This program trains law enforcement officers, health care workers, and other professionals about how to identify and respond to elder abuse and supports education campaigns to increase public awareness of elder abuse and how to prevent it.

Many states have adopted additional legislation to help stem instances of institutional abuse and neglect. For example, in 1998 the state of New York enacted Kathy's Law, which created the new felony-level crime of "abuse of a vulnerable elderly person." At the state level there are many agencies involved in identifying and investigating cases of abuse and neglect. These agencies differ across states but may include ombudsmen (offices that assist patients who have complaints), adult protective services, the state survey agency responsible for licensing nursing homes, the state agency responsible for the operation of the nurse aide registry, Medicaid fraud units in the attorney general's office, and professional licensing boards.

The NCEA asserts in "Raise Awareness" (2013, http://www.ncea.aoa.gov/Get_Involved/Awareness/index.aspx) that raising public awareness of the problem is vital for preventing it. It encourages adult children to discuss mistreatment, abuse, and exploitation with their parents and other older adults and to take specific steps to reduce the risk of abuse, such as by carefully screening prospective caregivers.

LONG-TERM CARE OMBUDSMAN PROGRAM. Long-term care ombudsmen are advocates for residents of nursing homes, board-and-care homes, assisted living facilities, and other adult care facilities. The Long-Term Care Ombudsman Program was established under the Older Americans Act of 1965, which is administered by the AoA.

In "Long-Term Care Ombudsman Program" (July 18, 2013, http://www.aoa.gov/AoARoot/AoA_Programs/Elder_Rights/Ombudsman/index.aspx), the AoA reports that 9,065 volunteers and 1,186 paid ombudsmen worked to resolve 204,044 complaints in fiscal year 2011. More than two-thirds (70%) of all nursing homes and one-third (33%) of all board-and-care, assisted living, and similar homes were visited regularly by state and local ombudsmen.

IMPORTANT NAMES
AND ADDRESSES

AARP (formerly American Association of Retired Persons)
601 E St. NW
Washington, DC 20049
1-888-687-2277
URL: http://www.aarp.org/

Administration on Aging
One Massachusetts Ave. NW
Washington, DC 20001
(202) 619-0724
FAX: (202) 357-3555
E-mail: aclinfo@acl.hhs.gov
URL: http://www.aoa.gov/

Alliance for Aging Research
750 17th St. NW, Ste. 1100
Washington, DC 20006
(202) 293-2856
FAX: (202) 955-8394
E-mail: info@agingresearch.org
URL: http://www.agingresearch.org/

Alzheimer's Association
225 N. Michigan Ave., 17th Floor
Chicago, IL 60601-7633
(312) 335-8700
1-800-272-3900
FAX: 1-866-699-1246
E-mail: info@alz.org
URL: http://www.alz.org/

American Association for Geriatric Psychiatry
7910 Woodmont Ave., Ste. 1050
Bethesda, MD 20814-3004
(301) 654-7850
FAX: (301) 654-4137
E-mail: main@aagponline.org
URL: http://www.aagponline.org/

American Geriatrics Society
40 Fulton St., 18th Floor
New York, NY 10038
(212) 308-1414
FAX: (212) 832-8646

E-mail: info.amger@americangeriatrics.org
URL: http://www.americangeriatrics.org/

American Heart Association
7272 Greenville Ave.
Dallas, TX 75231
1-800-242-8721
E-mail: review.personal.info@heart.org
URL: http://www.americanheart.org/

ARCH National Respite Network and Resource Center
4016 Oxford St.
Annandale, VA 22003
(703) 256-2084
FAX: (703) 256-0541
URL: http://archrespite.org/

Arthritis Foundation
1330 W. Peachtree St., Ste. 100
Atlanta, GA 30309
(404) 872-7100
1-800-283-7800
URL: http://www.arthritis.org/

Assisted Living Federation of America
1650 King St., Ste. 602
Alexandria, VA 22314
(703) 894-1805
FAX: (703) 894-1831
URL: http://www.alfa.org/

Boomer Project
2601 Floyd Ave.
Richmond, VA 23220
(804) 358-8981
FAX: (804) 342-1790
E-mail: matt@boomerproject.com
URL: http://www.boomerproject.com/

Caregiver Action Network (formerly the National Family Caregivers Association)
10400 Connecticut Ave., Ste. 500
Kensington, MD 20895-3944
(301) 942-6430
FAX: (301) 942-2302

E-mail: info@caregiveraction.org
URL: http://caregiveraction.org/

Centers for Disease Control and Prevention
1600 Clifton Rd.
Atlanta, GA 30333
1-800-232-4636
E-mail: cdcinfo@cdc.gov
URL: http://www.cdc.gov/

Centers for Medicare and Medicaid Services
7500 Security Blvd.
Baltimore, MD 21244
(410) 786-3000
1-877-267-2323
URL: http://www.cms.gov/

Children of Aging Parents
PO Box 167
Richboro, PA 18954
1-800-227-7294
URL: http://www.caps4caregivers.org/

CNY Mature Workers Employment Alliance
826 Euclid Ave.
Syracuse, NY 13210
(315) 446-3587
E-mail: mwea4cny@mwea-cny.com
URL: http://cnymwa.ning.com/

Eldercare Locator Directory
1-800-677-1116
URL: http://www.eldercare.gov/

Encore.org (formerly Civic Ventures)
PO Box 29542
San Francisco, CA 94129
(415) 430-0141
FAX: (415) 430-0144
URL: http://www.encore.org/

Family Caregiver Alliance
785 Market St., Ste. 750
San Francisco, CA 94103

(415) 434-3388
1-800-445-8106
E-mail: info@caregiver.org
URL: http://www.caregiver.org/

Gerontological Society of America
1220 L St. NW, Ste. 901
Washington, DC 20005
(202) 842-1275
FAX: (202) 842-1150
URL: http://www.geron.org/

Gray Panthers
10 G St. NE, Ste. 600
Washington, DC 20002
(202) 737-6637
1-800-280-5362
URL: http://www.graypanthers.org/

Insurance Institute for Highway Safety
1005 N. Glebe Rd., Ste. 800
Arlington, VA 22201
(703) 247-1500
FAX: (703) 247-1588
URL: http://www.highwaysafety.org/

LeadingAge
2519 Connecticut Ave. NW
Washington, DC 20008-1520
(202) 783-2242
FAX: (202) 783-2255
E-mail: info@leadingage.org
URL: http://leadingage.org/

Medicare Rights Center
1224 M St. NW, Ste. 100
Washington, DC 20005
(202) 637-0961
1-800-333-4114
FAX: (202) 637-0962
URL: http://www.medicarerights.org/

**National Academy of Elder Law
Attorneys**
1577 Spring Hill Rd., Ste. 220
Vienna, VA 22182
(703) 942-5711
FAX: (703) 563-9504
URL: http://www.naela.org/

National Alliance for Caregiving
4720 Montgomery Ln., Second Floor
Bethesda, MD 20814
URL: http://www.caregiving.org/

**National Association for Home Care and
Hospice**
228 Seventh St. SE
Washington, DC 20003
(202) 547-7424
FAX: (202) 547-3540
URL: http://www.nahc.org/

National Caregiving Foundation
801 N. Pitt St., Ste. 116
Alexandria, VA 22314
1-800-930-1357

E-mail: info@caregivingfoundation.org
URL: http://www.caregivingfoundation.org/

**National Caucus and Center on Black
Aged**
1220 L St. NW, Ste. 800
Washington, DC 20005
(202) 637-8400
FAX: (202) 347-0895
E-mail: support@ncba-aged.org
URL: http://www.ncba-aged.org/

**National Center for Health Statistics
Division of Data Services**
3311 Toledo Rd.
Hyattsville, MD 20782
1-800-232-4636
URL: http://www.cdc.gov/nchs

**National Center on Elder Abuse
University of California, Irvine
Program in Geriatric Medicine**
101 The City Drive South
200 Building
Orange, CA 92868
1-855-500-3537
FAX: (714) 456-7933
URL: http://www.ncea.aoa.gov/

**National Consumer Voice for Quality
Long-Term Care (formerly the National
Citizens' Coalition for Nursing Home
Reform)**
1001 Connecticut Ave. NW, Ste. 425
Washington, DC 20036
(202) 332-2275
FAX: 1-866-230-9789
E-mail: info@theconsumervoice.org
URL: http://www.theconsumervoice.org/

National Hispanic Council on Aging
Walker Bldg.
734 15th St. NW, Ste. 1050
Washington, DC 20005
(202) 347-9733
FAX: (202) 347-9735
URL: http://www.nhcoa.org/

**National Hospice and Palliative Care
Organization**
1731 King St., Ste. 100
Alexandria, VA 22314
(703) 837-1500
FAX: (703) 837-1233
E-mail: nhpco_info@nhpco.org
URL: http://www.nhpco.org/

**National Indian Council
on Aging**
10501 Montgomery Blvd. NE, Ste. 210
Albuquerque, NM 87111
(505) 292-2001
FAX: (505) 292-1922
E-mail: info@nicoa.org
URL: http://www.nicoa.org/

National Institute on Aging
Bldg. 31, Rm. 5C27
31 Center Dr., MSC 2292
Bethesda, MD 20892
(301) 496-1752
FAX: (301) 496-1072
URL: http://www.nih.gov/nia

National Osteoporosis Foundation
1150 17th St. NW, Ste. 850
Washington, DC 20036
(202) 223-2226
1-800-231-4222
FAX: (202) 223-2237
URL: http://www.nof.org/

National PACE Association
801 N. Fairfax St., Ste. 309
Alexandria, VA 22314
(703) 535-1565
FAX: (703) 535-1566
E-mail: info@npaonline.org
URL: http://www.npaonline.org/

National Senior Citizens Law Center
1444 Eye St. NW, Ste. 1100
Washington, DC 20005
(202) 289-6976
FAX: (202) 289-7224
URL: http://www.nsclc.org/

**National Society for American Indian
Elderly**
200 E. Fillmore St., Ste. 151
Phoenix, AZ 85004
(602) 424-0542
E-mail: info@nsaie.org
URL: http://www.nsaie.org/

National Urban League
120 Wall St.
New York, NY 10005
(212) 558-5300
FAX: (212) 344-5332
URL: http://nul.iamempowered.com/

Older Women's League
1625 K St. NW, Ste. 1275
Washington, DC 20006
(202) 567-2606
E-mail: info@owl-national.org
URL: http://www.owl-national.org/

**Pension Benefit Guaranty
Corporation**
1200 K St. NW
Washington, DC 20005-4026
(202) 326-4242
1-800-736-2444
URL: http://www.pbgc.gov/

Pension Rights Center
1350 Connecticut Ave. NW, Ste. 206
Washington, DC 20036
(202) 296-3776
1-888-420-6550
URL: http://www.pensionrights.org/

SeniorNet
12801 Worldgate Dr., Ste. 500
Herndon, VA 20170
(571) 203-7100
FAX: (703) 871-3901
URL: http://www.seniornet.org/

Service Corps of Retired Executives
409 Third St. SW, Sixth Floor
Washington, DC 20024

1-800-634-0245
URL: http://www.score.org/

U.S. Census Bureau
4600 Silver Hill Rd.
Washington, DC 20233
URL: http://www.census.gov/

U.S. Department of Veterans Affairs
810 Vermont Ave. NW
Washington, DC 20011

1-800-827-1000
URL: http://www.va.gov/

U.S. Social Security Administration
Office of Public Inquiries
Windsor Park Bldg.
6401 Security Blvd.
Baltimore, MD 21235
1-800-772-1213
URL: http://www.ssa.gov/

RESOURCES

Many of the demographic data cited in this text were drawn from U.S. Census Bureau and U.S. Bureau of Labor Statistics publications, including "Older Americans Month: May 2013" (March 2013), *The Next Four Decades—The Older Population in the United States: 2010 to 2050* (Grayson K. Vincent and Victoria A. Velkoff, May 2010), and the 2009 American Community Survey. The Guinness World Records and the National Centenarian Awareness Project provided information about the growing number of centenarians in the United States.

The reports *A Profile of Older Americans: 2012* (April 2013) by the Administration on Aging and *Older Americans 2012: Key Indicators of Well-Being* (June 2012) by the Federal Interagency Forum on Aging-Related Statistics provided useful data about older adults. Additional population data were drawn from *The World Factbook* (2013) by the Central Intelligence Agency.

The *The 2013 Retirement Confidence Survey: Perceived Savings Needs Outpace Reality for Many* (Ruth Helman et al., March 2013) by the Employee Benefit Research Institute and Matthew Greenwald & Associates provided information about pension plans and other employee benefits. The U.S. Department of Labor and the National Economic Council Interagency Working Group on Social Security described trends in labor force participation. The Urban Institute and Milliman 2013 Pension Funding Study provided information about pensions. The Equal Employment Opportunity Commission offered information about age discrimination issues and claims. Peter Shapiro's *A History of National Service in America* (1994) detailed the establishment of a national senior service during the administration of President John F. Kennedy.

The Boomer Report, a quarterly survey of 1,400 consumers by the Boomer Project/Survey Sampling International, describes the thoughts and behaviors of members of the baby boomer generation. *Encore Career Choices: Purpose, Passion and a Paycheck in a Tough Economy* (November 2011) by the MetLife Foundation and Civic Ventures reported that two out of five Americans aged 44 to 70 years are interested in so-called encore careers.

The National Highway Traffic Safety Administration, in *Older Driver Program: Five-Year Strategic Plan 2012–2017* (December 2010), documented the increasing numbers of older drivers. In *Transportation-Disadvantaged Populations: Federal Coordination Efforts Could Be Further Strengthened* (June 2012), the U.S. Government Accountability Office explored ways to improve transportation options for older adults. The Insurance Institute for Highway Safety reported in "Fatality Facts 2011: Older People" (2013) that although the oldest and youngest drivers have the highest fatality rates on a per mile driven basis, older drivers involved in crashes are less likely than younger drivers to hurt others. In "New Data on Older Adult Drivers" (April 2011), the Centers for Disease Control and Prevention reports that older drivers take fewer risks than younger drivers. The American Medical Association and the National Highway Traffic Safety Administration developed the *Physician's Guide to Assessing and Counseling Older Drivers* (February 2010), which details medical conditions and their potential effects on driving skills.

The U.S. Department of Housing and Urban Development's Office of Community Planning and Development described in *The 2011 Annual Homeless Assessment Report to Congress* (November 2012) the plight of homeless older Americans. The National Low Income Housing Coalition report *Out of Reach 2013* (Elina Bravve, Megan Bolton, and Sheila Crowley, March 2013) documented rental housing cost data. In *Changing Attitudes, Changing Motives: The MetLife Study of How Aging Homeowners Use Reverse Mortgages* (March 2012), the National Council on Aging and the MetLife Mature Market Institute described how older adults are using reverse mortgages. The National Center for Health Statistics 2010 National Survey of Residential Care Facilities described characteristics of facilities and residents.

The U.S. Social Security Administration provided information about the history and future of Social Security as well as benefits and eligibility in publications such as *Fast Facts and Figures about Social Security, 2012* (August 2012), "Social Security Basic Facts" (June 2013), and *The 2013 Annual Report of the Board of Trustees of the Federal Old-Age and Survivors Insurance and Federal Disability Insurance Trust Funds* (May 2012).

The Centers for Medicare and Medicaid Services (CMS) coordinates Medicare and Medicaid. The CMS provided information about the history, the beneficiaries, and the future of these entitlement programs. The Centers for Disease Control and Prevention (CDC) provided vital health statistics in publications such as *Health, United States, 2012* (May 2013) and the 2012 National Health Interview Survey. The Kaiser Family Foundation reports on Medicare, Medicaid, and long-term care expenditures in many reports, including "Enrollment-Driven Expenditure Growth: Medicaid Spending during the Economic Downturn, FY 2007–2011" (Katherine Young et al., April 2013) and *The Cost and Coverage Implications of the ACA Medicaid Expansion: National and State-by-State Analysis* (John Holahan et al., November 2012). The U.S. Department of Veterans Affairs reported in "Trends in the Utilization of VA Programs and Services" (January 2012) on the services that are used by U.S. veterans.

In *Market Survey of Long-Term Care Costs: The 2012 MetLife Market Survey of Nursing Home, Assisted Living, Adult Day Services, and Home Care Costs* (November 2012) the MetLife Mature Market Institute reported on the costs that are associated with nursing homes and assisted living.

The AARP underwrites research about older Americans. One example of its research cited in this text is the AARP Public Policy Institute report *Nightmare on Main Street: Older Americans and the Mortgage Market Crisis* (Lori A. Trawinski, July 2012), which offered insight into older homeowners' experiences with home values, mortgages, and foreclosure.

Many organizations and publications provide information on specific health and medical problems of older adults. Among the many publications cited in this text are the American Heart Association's "Older Americans and Cardiovascular Diseases" (March 2013), the American Cancer Society's *Cancer Facts and Figures, 2013* (2013), the CDC's "Falls among Older Adults: An Overview" (September 2012), and the Alzheimer's Association's *2013 Alzheimer's Disease Facts and Figures* (March 2013). The Department of Veterans Affairs provided demographic projections of the health and other needs of older veterans.

Similarly, many agencies, organizations, and professional organizations, notably LeadingAge, the National Center for Education Statistics, the Mature Workers Employment Alliance, and the American Geriatrics Society, offered data and analyses of myriad issues of importance to older Americans.

Professional medical journals offered research findings and information about health and disease among older adults as well as health service utilization and financing. Articles from the following journals were cited in this text: *Acta Psychiatrica Scandinavica, Addiction, Aging, Neuropsychology, and Cognition, Alzheimer's and Dementia, American Journal of Geriatric Psychiatry, American Journal of Psychiatry, Annals of Neurology, Annual Review of Public Health, Archives of Neurology, Archives of Ophthalmology, BMJ, Clinical Gerontologist, Clinics in Geriatric Medicine, Current Directions in Psychological Science, Gerontologist, Harvard Women's Health Watch, Health Affairs, Health Psychology, Home Healthcare Nurse, International Psychogeriatrics, Journal of the American Medical Association, Journal of the American Medical Association Internal Medicine, Journal of Elder Abuse and Neglect, Journal of Health and Human Services Administration, Journal of Personality and Social Psychology, Nature Genetics, New England Journal of Medicine, Neurology, Nursing Older People, Proceedings of the National Academy of Sciences, Psychological Science,* and *Psychology and Aging.*

Because the aging population affects nearly every aspect of society, from employment and housing to health care and politics, consumer publications frequently feature articles about and of interest to older adults. Articles cited in this volume were drawn from Forbes.com, *Monthly Labor Review, Nature,* NYTimes.com, Time .com, USNews.com, and WSJ.com.

Information about abuse and mistreatment of older adults was found in *The MetLife Study of Elder Financial Abuse: Crimes of Occasion, Desperation, and Predation against America's Elders* (June 2011) by the MetLife Mature Market Institute, the National Committee for the Prevention of Elder Abuse, and the Center for Gerontology at the Virginia Polytechnic Institute and State University; *Elder Justice: National Strategy Needed to Effectively Combat Elder Financial Exploitation* (November 2012) by the Government Accountability Office; and *Consumer Fraud in the United States, 2011: The Third FTC Survey* (Keith B. Anderson, April 2013) by the Federal Trade Commission. The Bureau of Justice Statistics' *Criminal Victimization, 2011* (Jennifer L. Truman and Michael Planty, October 2012) and the *Journal of Elder Abuse and Neglect* provided data about fraud, abuse, and violent victimization of older adults.

We are very grateful to the Gallup Organization for permitting us to present the results of its renowned opinion polls and graphics.

INDEX

Page references in italics refer to photographs. References with the letter t following them indicate the presence of a table. The letter f indicates a figure. If more than one table or figure appears on a particular page, the exact item number for the table or figure being referenced is provided.

A

AAA (American Automobile Association), 98–99

AARP
  on cataracts, 115–116
  contact information, 181
  on continuing care communities, 57
  Create the Good organization, 77
  on driving classes for older adults, 98–99
  lobbying efforts of, 89
  membership in, 5
  on older workers, 69, 71

"AARP Driver Safety: History and Facts" (AARP), 98–99

AARP Public Policy Institute, 28

"AARP Statement on 2013 Social Security Trustees Report" (AARP), 89

Abbey, Linda, 176

Abrahms, Sally, 46

Absenteeism
  absences from work, by age/sex, 72t
  of older workers, 69

Abuse/mistreatment of older adults
  causes of, 176–177
  elder abuse, definition of, 169
  federal agencies involved in combating elder abuse, 175f
  institutional abuse, 178–180
  intervention/prevention, 177–178
  intimate partner violence, 177
  magnitude of problem, 173–174
  medical professionals for identification of elder abuse, 178

  national strategy to combat, 174
  reporting abuse, 176
  testimony on efforts to combat, 174
  types of mistreatment, 174–175

Abutaleb, Yasmeen, 147

Accessory apartments, 57–58

Accidents
  motor vehicle, 93–94, 96
  vehicular, leading causes of nonfatal injuries, ages 65–85, 96(t6.4)

Activities of daily living (ADLs)
  difficulties with basic/complex actions, by age, sex, 107f
  Medicare enrollees aged 65/older unable to perform activities of daily living, 105f
  Medicare enrollees aged 65/older unable to perform certain physical functions, by sex, 106f
  rates of chronic conditions that limit, 101–103

ADA (Americans with Disabilities Act), 99

Adams, Mary L., 132

ADEA. *See* Age Discrimination in Employment Act

ADEA Amendments of 1978, 66

"Adecco Staffing Mature Worker Survey" (Adecco Staffing), 69

Adherence, to prescription drugs, 121

ADLs. *See* Activities of daily living

Administration for Children and Families, 34

Administration on Aging (AoA)
  on alternative transportation for older adults, 99–100
  contact information, 181
  on elder abuse, 176
  Eldercare Locator Directory, 149
  on housing costs, 58–59
  on increase in number of older adults, 1
  on living arrangements of older people, 45
  Long-Term Care Ombudsman Program, 180

  Medicare fraud and, 173
  Prevention of Elder Abuse, Neglect, and Exploitation program, 179
  A Profile of Older Americans: 2012, 3, 7, 9, 11, 20

Adult congregate living facilities, 49

Adult day care programs, 148

Adults, older. *See* Older adults

Affluence, 31

Affordable Care Act. *See* Patient Protection and Affordable Care Act

"Affordable Prescription Drugs" (American Federation of State, County, and Municipal Employees), 120

African Americans
  general health of older Americans, 101
  income of, 20
  living arrangements of older people, 46
  racial/ethnic diversity of older population, 9

Agan, Tom, 72–73

Age
  absences from work by, 72t
  age discrimination, 73, 75–76
  aging labor force, 66–67, 69
  Americans living in nursing homes by, 45
  birth rates, by age of mother, 65t
  death, leading causes of, 121–122
  death, leading causes of/numbers of deaths by, 113t
  difficulties with basic/complex actions by, 107f
  fraud victimization rates by, 172t
  health, percentage of people aged 65/over who reported having good to excellent health by, 104(f7.1)
  health ratings by, 101
  homeownership rates by, 58, 59t
  hospital utilization by, 103
  households by age of householder, size of household, 46t
  labor force, median age of, 66t, 67t

labor force participation rates by, 68t, 70t

licensed drivers by, 92t

living arrangements by, 48(t3.2)

mandatory retirement, 65

obese, adults aged 65/older who are, by sex/age group, 119f

obesity among adults, prevalence of, by age group/sex, 127(f7.15)

Parkinson's disease and, 117

of people in residential care, 54

population aged 65 and over living alone, by age group/sex, 48(t3.3)

retirement and, 64, 76

sheltered homeless people, by age, geography, 50t

sheltered people and U.S. population, age distribution of, 50f

smoking among adults, prevalence of, by age group/sex, 128(f7.16)

speeding drivers in fatal crashes by, 94t

tenure with current employer for employed workers, median years of, by age, sex, 73t

unemployment rates by, 67t

violent crime rates, by sex, race, Hispanic origin, and age of victim, 171t

violent victimization by, 170f

violent victimization rate by, 169

visits to physician offices, hospital outpatient departments, emergency departments, by age, sex, race, 110t–111t

visits to primary care physicians by, 112t

volunteerism and, 77

Age dependency ratios, 145, 146t

Age Dependency Ratios and Social Security Solvency (Shresthra), 145

Age discrimination

ADEA claims, filing, 75

Age Discrimination in Employment Act, 66, 73

mandatory retirement as, 65

retire, pressure to, 73, 75

U.S. Supreme Court decisions augment ADEA, 75–76

Age Discrimination in Employment Act (ADEA)

charges, 74t

provisions of, 66, 73

U.S. Supreme Court decisions that augment, 75–76

Ageism, 16

Agency for Healthcare Research and Quality (AHRQ), 53, 55

Age-related macular degeneration (AMD), 115, 116

Age-sex pyramid. *See* Population pyramid

Aging

attitudes about, 16–17

driving skills, age-related impairment of, 96–99

effects of positive perception of, 14–16

fears of health problems with, 101

healthy, 122–126

sexuality in, 126–128

of U.S. politicians, 89

See also Health and medical problems; Healthy aging

"Aging America and the Boomer Wars" (Moody), 17

"Aging and Stereotype Suppression" (Radvansky, Lynchard, & Hippel), 16

Aging in place

geriatric care managers aid in, 150

housing challenges for older adults and, 60

public housing and, 60–61

Agricultural economy, 65–66

AHRQ (Agency for Healthcare Research and Quality), 53, 55

Albert, Marilyn S., 135–136

Alboher, Marci, 76

Albright, Madeleine, 63

Alcohol

adults who had 5+ drinks in 1 day, by age group/sex, 141f

issues unique to older adults, 142–143

misuse of, 141–143

older problem drinkers, prevalence of types of, 141–142

older problem drinkers, types of, 142

prevalence of types of drinkers, 142f

Allaire, Jason C., 86

Alliance for Aging Research, 181

ALOS. *See* Average lengths of stay

"Alternative Transportation—It Could Work for You" (NHTSA), 91

Alzheimer, Alois, 136–137

Alzheimer's Association

on care for AD patients, 136–137

contact information, 181

on deaths, numbers of caused by Alzheimer's, 134

on numbers afflicted with Alzheimer's, 133

on nursing homes and Alzheimer's disease, 52

"Seven Stages of Alzheimer's," 133

on treatments, 136

Alzheimer's disease

diagnostic guidelines/criteria for, 135–136

diagnostic testing for, 134–135

elder abuse and, 177

genetic origins of, 134

hearing loss linked to, 115

incidence of, 101

institutional abuse and, 179

nursing homes and, 52

overview of, 133

patients, caring for, 136–137

research/treatment, advances in, 136

symptoms/stages, 133–134

treatment of, 136

"Alzheimer's Disease Fact Sheet" (NIA), 134, 135

Alzheimer's Disease Genetics Consortium (NIA), 134

Alzheimer's Disease Genetics Study (NIA), 134

"Alzheimer-Signature MRI Biomarker Predicts AD Dementia in Cognitively Normal Adults" (Dickerson et al.), 134

AMA (American Medical Association), 97–98

"Amazon Goes after Older Adults & Seniors with New Store" (Perez), 35

Amazon.com, 35

AMD (age-related macular degeneration), 115, 116

American Association for Geriatric Psychiatry, 181

American Association for Long Term Care Insurance, 165

American Association of Community Colleges, 81

American Automobile Association (AAA), 98–99

American Cancer Society, 111, 122

American Community Survey, 46

American Council on Education, 65

American Federation of State, County, and Municipal Employees, 120

American Geriatrics Society, 128, 145, 181

American Heart Association, 121, 181

American Medical Association (AMA), 97–98

Americans with Disabilities Act (ADA), 99

Amyloid protein, 134

Anderson, Keith B., 170

Annual Statistical Supplement to the Social Security Bulletin (SSA), 37

"Antidepressant Medication Augmented with Cognitive-Behavioral Therapy for Generalized Anxiety Disorder in Older Adults" (Wetherell et al.), 140

Anxiety disorders, 139–140

AoA. *See* Administration on Aging

Apolipoprotein E (apoE), 134

ARCH National Respite Network and Resource Center, 181

"Are You Ready? What You Need to Know about Ageing" (WHO), 7

Arizona, Sun City communities in, 58

Arthritis

overview of, 105

prevalence of, 106, 114f

types of, 105–106

Arthritis Foundation, 105–106, 181

Asian Americans

income of, 20

living arrangements of, 46

racial/ethnic diversity of older population, 9

Assessing the Impact of Severe Economic Recession on the Elderly: Summary of a Workshop (Majmundar), 31

Assisted living
board-and-care facilities, 55–56
costs of, 56–57
description of, 55
supportive housing, classes of, 48–50
"Assisted Living" (Assisted Living Federation of America), 55
"Assisted Living Defined" (AHRQ), 55
Assisted Living Federation of America, 55, 181
Associated Press, 76
"Association between Hypoglycemia and Dementia in a Biracial Cohort of Older Adults with Diabetes Mellitus" (Yaffe et al.), 133
"Association between Positive Age Stereotypes and Recovery from Disability in Older Persons" (Levy et al.), 17
"Association of Hearing Loss with Hospitalization and Burden of Disease in Older Adults" (Genther et al.), 115
Astor, Brooke, 173–174
Atchley, Robert C., 131–132
Attitudes, about aging, 16–17
Automobiles, for older drivers, 99
Average lengths of stay (ALOS)
by age, 103
decrease of, 103–104, 151
"Average US Household Far from Regaining Its Wealth" (Rugaber), 27–28
Averting the Caregiving Crisis: Why We Must Act Now (Rosalynn Carter Institute for Caregiving), 147

B

Baby boomers
aging labor force, 66
contribution to U.S. population, 4*f*
dependency ratio and, 145
retirement and, 64, 76
society/culture, effects on, 17
use of alcohol/drugs, 143
"Back on Campus to Experience Road Not Taken" (Strauss), 81–82
"Back to School: 2012–2013" (U.S. Census Bureau), 64
Balanced Budget Act of 1997, 156
Banerjee, Sudipto, 36
Bartels, Stephen J., 137
Basic Statistics about Home Care (NAHC), 148
Because We Care: A Guide for People Who Care (AoA), 99–100
Behavior, 137
Benefits
amount for worker with maximum-taxable earnings, 37*t*
number/average, by type of benefit/sex, 38*t*

retirement plan, private sector workers with, 27*t*
Social Security, older adults receiving, by benefits to total income, 23(*f*2.4)
See also Health insurance; Social Security; Veterans' benefits
BenefitsCheckUp program, 149–150
Benson, Amy, 150
Benson, Michael L., 179
Berger, Andrea K., 16
Bernard, Tara Siegel, 39
"Best New-Cars (and Features) for Senior Drivers" (Gorzelany), 99
"Best Nursing Homes 2012: Behind the Rankings" (Comarow), 50–51
Bethel Nutritional Consulting, Inc., 172
"Bethel Nutritional Consulting, Inc. Issues a Voluntary Recall of Weight-Loss Pills 'Bethel 30' Found to Contain an Undeclared Drug Ingredient" (FDA), 172
Biomarkers, 135
Birth rates
by age of mother, 65*t*
effect on population, 3
of women aged 40 to 44 years, 64
Block Grant Programs, 99
Blogging, 86
Blood glucose, 107, 110–111
BLS. *See* U.S. Bureau of Labor Statistics
Blum, Jonathan, 152
Board-and-care facilities
description of, 48, 55–56
institutional abuse, 178–180
Boards of Trustees of the Federal Hospital Insurance and Federal Supplementary Medical Insurance Trust Funds, 155
Bolton, Megan, 59–60
Bones, 107
Boomer Project, 35, 181
Boomer Report, 35
Boomers. *See* Baby boomers
"Boomers Aren't Working Forever, after All" (Miller), 64
Brain diseases. *See* Dementia
Bravve, Elina, 59–60
Brown, Kay E., 174
"Budget Negotiating Chip Has Big Downside for Old and Poor" (Bernard), 39
"Building Blocks of Successful Aging: A Focus Group Study of Older Adults' Perceived Contributors to Successful Aging" (Reichstadt et al.), 15
Butrica, Barbara A., 19–20
Buzgová, Radka, 178

C

Caffrey, Christine, 54–55
Cahill, Kevin E., 69
California, pension fraud in, 25
Camph, Donald H., 91

Cancer
death rates for malignant neoplasms, 123*t*–124*t*
deaths from, 122
as leading cause of death, 105
prostate cancer, 111
"Cancer and the Elderly" (National Comprehensive Cancer Network), 122
Cancer Facts and Figures, 2013 (American Cancer Society), 111, 122
Career
changes, increase in, 64–65
encore careers, 76
Caregiver Action Network, 181
"Caregiver Burden, Elder Abuse, and Alzheimer's Disease: Testing the Relationship" (Gainey & Payne), 177
Caregivers
age dependency ratios, 146*t*
BenefitsCheckUp program, 149–150
community services, 148–149
cost of, 163
elder abuse, causes of, 176–177
Eldercare Locator Directory, 149
family caregivers, 146–148
geriatric care managers, 150
home and community-based services, 149
home health care, 148
National Aging Network, 149
overview of, 145
respite care/adult day care, 148
respite care for veterans, 162–163
volunteer caregivers, 150
Women's Institute for a Secure Retirement, 150
Castle, Nicholas, 179
Cataracts, 115–116
CBT (cognitive behavioral therapy), 140
CCRCs (continuing care retirement communities), 50, 57
Centenarians, 7–8
Centers for Disease Control and Prevention (CDC)
on chronic diseases, 105
contact information, 181
on health care expenditures for older adults, 151
on infectious diseases, 118–119
"New Data on Older Adult Drivers," 94, 97
"Older Adult Drivers: Get the Facts," 91
on older adults who stop driving, 97
on oral health problems, 117
on osteoarthritis, 105–106
2012 National Health Interview Survey, 131
Centers for Medicare and Medicaid Services (CMS)
contact information, 181
on health care expenditures for older adults, 151

immunizations against flu/pneumonia in nursing homes and, 119

"Independence at Home Demonstration," 147

on LTC coverage, 165

"Medicare 2013 Costs at a Glance," 160

Medicare reimbursement, 156

Central Intelligence Agency (CIA)

on global life expectancy, 6

on U.S. fertility rate, 3

on U.S. life expectancy, 5

Cerebrovascular disease

death rates for, 125t–126t

deaths from, 122

as leading cause of death, 105

Chalfie, Martin, 134

"Change in Burden and Distress among Caregivers of Community-Dwelling Older Adults with Dementia Enrolled in Care Management" (Benson et al.), 150

Changing Attitudes, Changing Motives: The MetLife Study of How Aging Homeowners Use Reverse Mortgages (National Council on Aging and the MetLife Mature Market Institute), 59

Chernof, Bruce, 166

Childbearing, 64

Children

decline in percentage of population, 1

grandparents living with grandchildren, 46–47, 49t

See also Family

Children of Aging Parents, 181

"Chronic Diseases and Health Promotion" (CDC), 105

Chronic diseases/conditions

arthritis, 105–106

arthritis, prevalence of, 114f

diabetes, 107, 110–111

diagnosed diabetes among adults aged 18 and over, prevalence of, 116(f7.8)

difficulties with basic/complex actions, by age, sex, 107f

eye diseases, 115–117

health care expenditures and, 151

hearing loss, 114–115

hearing/seeing, trouble with, or no natural teeth, people aged 65 and over who reported having, by selected characteristics, 117t

hearing/seeing, trouble with, or no natural teeth, people aged 65 and over who reported having, by sex, 116(f7.9)

incidence of, 101

malnutrition, 113

Medicare enrollees aged 65/older unable to perform activities of daily living, 105f

Medicare enrollees aged 65/older unable to perform certain physical functions, by sex, 106f

most frequently occurring, 101

oral health problems, 117

osteoporosis, 107

osteoporosis pyramid for prevention and treatment, 115f

overview of, 105

Parkinson's disease, 117

percentage of people aged 65/over who reported having, 104(f7.2), 114(t7.7)

percentage of people aged 65/over who reported having, by sex, race/Hispanic origin, 114(t7.6)

prevalence of, 105

prostate problems, 111

rates of chronic conditions that limit ADLs, 101–102

urinary incontinence, 111–113

vision changes, 115

Chronic lower respiratory diseases, 105

CIA. *See* Central Intelligence Agency

Cigarettes. *See* Smoking

City of Jackson, Smith v., 75

Civic Ventures, 76

Clark, Robert F., 55–56

Clarke, David M., 137–138

CLASS (Community Living Assistance Services and Supports) Act, 165–166

Clinton, Hillary Rodham, 63

CMS. *See* Centers for Medicare and Medicaid Services

CNY Mature Workers Employment Alliance, 181

Cognitive behavioral therapy (CBT), 140

Cognitive function

Alzheimer's disease and, 134

cognitive impairment, 131

cognitive impairment, dementia and, 132–133

declining in older adults, 131

hearing loss and, 114–115

memory, 132

Cohousing, 57

Cohousing Association of the United States, 57

COLAs (cost-of-living adjustments), 37

Colby, Jennifer, 89

College, 64

Comarow, Avery, 50–51

"Common Variants at ABCA7, MS4A6A/ MS4A4E, EPHA1, CD33, and CD2AP Are Associated with Alzheimer's Disease" (Hollingworth et al.), 134

"Common Variants at MS4A4/MS4A6E, CD2AP, CD33, and EPHA1 Are Associated with Late-Onset Alzheimer's Disease" (Naj et al.), 134

Community First Choice Medicaid plan, 161

Community housing with home care services, 166–167

Community living assistance services, 152

Community Living Assistance Services and Supports (CLASS) Act, 165–166

Community Living Assistance Services and Supports Independence Benefit Plan, 152

Community services, 148–149

Community-Based Care Transitions Program, 147

Consumer Financial Protection Bureau, 174

Consumer Fraud in the United States, 2011: The Third FTC Survey (Federal Trade Commission), 170

Consumer Reports, 165

Consumers

aging, market growth of, 35

baby boomers, 35–36

expenses, effects of household size on, 31, 33–34

expenses, overview of, 31

unit expenditures, by expenditure types, 93t

Contact information, 181–183

"Continuing Care Communities: A Big Investment with Catches" (Ebeling), 57

Continuing care retirement communities (CCRCs), 50, 57

Continuity theory, 131–132

Corporation for National and Community Service, 77

"Cortex Area Thinner in Youth with Alzheimer's-Related Gene" (NIA), 134

The Cost and Coverage Implications of the ACA Medicaid Expansion: National and State-by-State Analysis (Holahan et al.), 161

Cost-of-living adjustments (COLAs), 37

Costs

of assisted living, 56–57

of continuing care retirement communities, 57

economics of caregiving, 146–147

of hiring older workers, 69, 71

of long-term health care, 163–164

medical care, percentage of persons of all ages with usual place to go for, by age group/sex, 129(f7.18)

of prescription drugs, 120, 120f

of private long-term care insurance, 165

of rental housing, 59–60

See also Expenditures

Council of Large Public Housing Authorities, 60

Court cases

Gross v. FBL Financial Services, Inc., 75

Meacham et al. v. Knolls Atomic Power Laboratory, 75

Smith v. City of Jackson, 75

Create the Good organization, 77

"Creation of Households Program in Nursing Home Improves Residents' Health Status, Reduces Staff Turnover, and Boosts Demand for Services" (AHRQ), 53

Crime

fraud, 170, 172–173

fraud victimization rates by age, 172t

mistreatment of older adults by risk factor, 171*f*

older people as easy prey, 169–170

physical/emotional impact of, 169

rates of violent victimizations, 169

violent crime rates, by sex, race, Hispanic origin, age of victim, 171*t*

violent victimization by age, 170*f*

Criminal Victimization, 2011 (Truman & Planty), 169

Crowley, Sheila, 59–60

"Current Alzheimer's Treatments" (Alzheimer's Association), 136

Currie, Kay C., 137–138

Cycle of abuse, 176

D

Daly, Mark J., 134

Davies, Emily, 8

Death

acceptance of, effects on mental health, 132

chronic diseases as leading causes of, 105

leading causes of, 121–122

leading causes of/numbers of deaths, by age, 113*t*

from prostate cancer, 111

"Death in the United States, 2011" (Miniño), 3

Death rates

for cerebrovascular disease, 125*t*–126*t*

for malignant neoplasms, 123*t*–124*t*

for motor vehicle-related injuries, 95*t*–96*t*

for suicide, 138, 139*t*–140*t*

See also Mortality rates

"Declining Car Risk for Older Drivers" (Parker-Pope), 98

Defined benefit/contribution plans, 23

Del Webb, 58

Demand response transportation, 100

Dementia

Alzheimer's disease, 133–137

elder abuse and, 177

geriatric care management for people with, 150

institutional abuse and, 179

multi-infarct dementia, 133

overview of, 132–133

Demographic transition, 3

The Demography of Population Aging (Mirkin & Weinberger), 7

Dependency ratio, 145

Depression

aging, perceptions of, 13

malnutrition and, 113

in older adults, 137–138

people aged 65+ with, by age group/sex, 138*f*

treatment of, 138–139

"Depression, Anxiety, and Their Relationship with Chronic Diseases: A Review of the Epidemiology, Risk, and Treatment Evidence" (Clarke & Currie), 137–138

"Depressive Symptoms in Old Age: Relations among Sociodemographic and Self-Reported Health Variables" (Nicolosi et al.), 138–139

"De-risking Efforts by Plan Sponsors Reduce Pension Obligations, but Continued Discount Rate Declines Produce Record-High Pension Plan Deficits in 2012" (Ehrhardt, Wadia, & Perry), 24

Diabetes

dementia and, 133

diagnosed diabetes among adults aged 18/over, prevalence of, 116(*f*7.8)

overview of, 107, 110–111

prevalence of, 105

Diabetic retinopathy

as cause of blindness, 115

overview of, 116–117

"The Diagnosis of Dementia Due to Alzheimer's Disease: Recommendations from the National Institute on Aging and the Alzheimer's Association Workgroup" (McKhann et al.), 135

"The Diagnosis of Mild Cognitive Impairment Due to Alzheimer's Disease: Recommendations from the National Institute on Aging and Alzheimer's Association Workgroup" (Albert), 135–136

Diagnosis-related groups, 103–104

Dickerson, Brad C., 134

Disability

arthritis as leading cause of, 106

chronic conditions that limit ADLs, 101–103

Medicare enrollees aged 65/older unable to perform certain ADLs, 105*f*

in older population, 119–120

Discrimination. *See* Age discrimination

Disease

depression resulting from, 137

organic brain diseases, 132–137

See also Chronic diseases/conditions; Health

Domestic violence. *See* Abuse/mistreatment of older adults

"Don't Be the Office Tech Dinosaur" (Shellenbarger), 72

"Donut hole," 152–153

Dopamine, 117

DOT (U.S. Department of Transportation), 93

Drinking. *See* Alcohol

Driscoll, Monica, 134

Drivers, older adult

consumer unit expenditures, by expenditure types, 93*t*

death rates for motor vehicle-related injuries, 95*t*–96*t*

driving skills, age-related impairment of, 96–99

leading causes of nonfatal injuries, ages 65–85, 96(*t*6.4)

licensed drivers, by sex/age group, 92*t*

motor vehicle accidents, 93–94, 96

older drivers who avoid driving under specific conditions by sex, 96*f*

overview of, 91–92

speeding drivers in fatal crashes, by age/sex, 94*t*

transportation alternatives, providing, 99–100

transportation initiatives for, 92–93

Drug therapy

alcohol-drug interactions, 142

for Alzheimer's, 136

for anxiety disorder, 140

for depression, 138

Drug-drug interactions, 121

Drugs

drug use among older adults, 120–121

effects on driving, 97–98

for heart disease, 121–122

Medicare drug costs/coverage, 152–153

Medicare prescription drug program, 157

misuse of, 141

for osteoporosis treatment, 107

prescription drug costs/sources of payment for noninstitutionalized Medicare enrollees aged 65+, average annual, 120*f*

sexual side effects of, 127

for treatment of Parkinson's disease, 117

Duggan, Maeve, 147

Dyskinesias, 117

E

Early Release of Selected Estimates Based on Data from the January–March 2012 National Health Interview Survey (NCHS), 111

Earnings test, 38

Ebeling, Ashlea, 57

ECHO (elder cottage housing opportunity) units, 57–58

Economic Opportunity Act of 1964, 77

Economic recession. *See* Great Recession

Economics, of caregiving, 146–147

Economics, older Americans

aggregate income by source, 24*f*

aging consumers, growth of, 35–36

annual retirement earnings test exempt amounts, 39(*t*2.10)

average annual expenditures/characteristics by age, 32*t*–34*t*

benefit amount for worker with maximum-taxable earnings, 37*t*

consumer expenses, 31, 33–34

duration of unemployment, 21t

family households/persons aged 65+ reporting income, 23(f2.3)

financial outlook of, 86–87

income distribution of population aged 65+, 22(f2.2)

income from specified sources, by age group, 26t

life expectancy at birth/age 65, 43t

median household net worth by race, aged 65+, 28f

net worth of older adults, 26–28

number/average monthly benefit, by type of benefit/sex, 38t

older adults, economic well-being of, 20, 23–26

older adults receiving income by source, 27f

older adults receiving Social Security benefits, by relative importance of benefits to total income, 23(f2.4)

overview of, 19–20

people in poverty, by selected characteristics, 29t–30t

poverty among older adults, 28–31

poverty rate by age group, 22(f2.1)

poverty rates by age, 30f

poverty thresholds, by size of family/ number of children, 31t

private sector workers with retirement plan benefits, 27t

Social Security, 36–38

Social Security, future of, 38–40

Social Security as source of retirement funds, by age, 43(t2.14)

Social Security as source of retirement funds, by income, 43(t2.15)

Social Security Income federal payment amounts, 39(t2.9)

sources of income for population aged 65+, 25f

SSI payments by eligibility category/ age/source of payment, 41t

SSI recipients by eligibility category/ age, 40t

Supplemental Security Income, 38

well-off older adults, 31

Economy, worker roles and, 65

Economy food plan, 28–30

ECT (electroconvulsive therapy), 138

Eden Alternative, 53–54

Edison, Thomas Alva, 63

Education

age of college students, 64

educational attainment of population aged 65+, 82(f5.1)

educational attainment of population aged 65+, by race/Hispanic origin, 82(f5.2)

enrollment in degree-granting institutions, by sex/age, 83t–84t

learning, lifelong, 81–82, 85–86

of older adults, 81

personal financial situation, self-assessment of, 87(t5.2)

EEOC (Equal Employment Opportunity Commission), 73

"The Effect of Birth Cohort on Well-Being: The Legacy of Economic Hard Times" (Sutin et al.), 13

"Effect of Obesity on Falls, Injury, and Disability" (Himes & Reynolds), 6

Ehrhardt, John W., 24

80-plus population, 7

Einstein, Albert, 63

Elder abuse. See Abuse/mistreatment of older adults

"Elder Abuse" (Sellas & Krouse), 176–177

"Elder Abuse and Neglect in Long-Term Care" (Joshi & Flaherty), 179

"Elder Abuse and Neglect: When Home Is Not Safe" (Abbey), 176

"Elder Abuse Information" (National Council on Child Abuse and Family Violence), 176

Elder cottage housing opportunity (ECHO) units, 57–58

Elder Investment Fraud and Financial Exploitation: Do Doctors Know the Symptoms? (Investor Protection Trust), 178

Elder Justice Act, 169

Elder Justice Coordinating Council, 169, 174

Elder Justice: National Strategy Needed to Effectively Combat Elder Financial Exploitation (GAO), 174

Elder Justice: Stronger Federal Leadership Could Help Improve Response to Elder Abuse (Brown), 174

Eldercare Locator Directory, 149, 181

Elderhostel. See Road Scholar

Electroconvulsive therapy (ECT), 138

Emergency departments. See Hospitals

"Emotion Regulation in Older Age" (Urry & Gross), 14

Employee Retirement Income Security Act (ERISA), 20, 24

Employers

age discrimination by, 73, 75–76

cost of caregivers for, 147

favor older workers, 69

Employment

duration of unemployment, 21t

private sector workers with retirement plan benefits, 27t

projections for home health care, 145

unemployment rates by age, 67t

See also Work

"Employment Outlook: 2010–2020 Labor Force Projections to 2020: A More Slowly Growing Workforce" (Toossi), 69

"Employment Projections—2010-20" (BLS), 145

Encore Career Choices: Purpose, Passion and a Paycheck in a Tough Economy (MetLife Foundation & Civic Ventures), 76

The Encore Career Handbook: How to Make a Living and a Difference in the Second Half of Life (Alboher), 76

Encore careers, 76

Encore.org, 181

"Enhancing Older Adult Mobility through Person-Centered Mobility Management" (NCST), 92–93

Enrollment-Driven Expenditure Growth: Medicaid Spending during the Economic Downturn, FY 2007–2011 (Young), 160–161

Equal Employment Opportunity Commission (EEOC), 73

ERISA (Employee Retirement Income Security Act), 20, 24

Erosheva, Elena A., 120

Ethnicity, 9

"Even Fewer Geriatricians in Training" (Span), 128–129

"Every Cloud Has a Silver Lining: Could It Be Affordable Senior Housing?" (Sanders), 61

Exercise

adults aged 18 years + that met 2008 federal physical activity guidelines for aerobic activity, 128(f7.17)

for healthy aging, 124–125

for osteoporosis treatment, 107

population aged 45/older who engage in regular physical activity, 127(f7.14)

for treatment of Parkinson's disease, 117

"Expectations about Memory Change across the Life Span Are Impacted by Aging Stereotypes" (Lineweaver, Berger, & Hertzog), 16

Expenditures

annual expenditures/characteristics by age, 32t–34t

consumer unit expenditures, by expenditure types, 93t

on health care for older adults, trends in, 151

on home health care, 166

on long-term health care, 163–164

on Medicaid, 160

on Medicare, 154, 155, 160

Medicare enrollees age 65/over, sources of payment for health care services for, by type of service, 155f

national health expenditures by source of funds, 153t–154t

Patient Protection and Affordable Care Act and, 151–153

Social Security/Medicare cost as percentage of GDP, 161f

See also Costs

"Eye Diseases of the Aging—Symptoms, Causes and Treatments" (AARP), 115–116

Eyes
  major eye diseases, 115–117
  people aged 65/over who reported having hearing/seeing, trouble with, or no natural teeth, by selected characteristics, 117t
  people aged 65/over who reported having hearing/seeing, trouble with, or no natural teeth, by sex, 116(f7.9)
  vision changes with age, 115

F
"Fact Sheet: Selected Caregiver Statistics" (Family Caregiver Alliance), 146
Fair market rent (FMR), 59–60
Families
  caring for AD patients, 136–137
  effects of household size on consumer expenses, 31, 33–34
  family households/persons aged 65+ reporting income, 23(f2.3)
  median household net worth by race of head of household aged 65+, 28f
  poverty thresholds, by size of family/number of children, 31t
Family
  elder abuse, causes of, 176–177
  elder abuse, prevention of, 178
  elder abuse/mistreatment, types of, 174–175
  financial abuse by, 172, 173
  intimate partner violence, 177
  older people living with, 46
Family Caregiver Alliance
  contact information, 181–182
  "Fact Sheet: Selected Caregiver Statistics," 146
  "Health Care Reform and Family Caregivers," 147
Family caregivers
  caregiving in U.S., 146
  challenges for, 145
  economics of caregiving, 146–147
  PPACA, effects on informal caregivers, 147
  PPACA, effects on paid caregivers, 147–148
  statistics on, 146
  veterans' benefits and, 162–163
Family Caregivers Are Wired for Health (Fox, Duggan, & Purcell), 147
Fast Facts and Figures about Social Security, 2012, (SAS), 24
Fastenberg, Dan, 75–76
"Fatality Facts 2011: Older People" (IIHS), 93–94, 98, 185
FBL Financial Services, Inc., Gross v., 75

FDA. *See* U.S. Food and Drug Administration
Federal Insurance Contributions Act (FICA), 36
Federal Interagency Coordinating Council on Access and Mobility, 92
Federal Interagency Forum on Aging-Related Statistics
  on depression in older adults, 137
  on measures of disability, 102
  on net worth of older Americans, 26–28
  Older Americans 2012: Key Indicators of Well-Being, 1–3, 7, 20, 101
  on tobacco consumption, 124
  on veterans' benefits from VHA, 162
Federal Old-Age and Survivors Insurance & Federal Disability Insurance Trust Funds, 39
Federal Trade Commission (FTC), 170, 172
Females
  labor force participation rates for older women, 67, 69
  living arrangements of older people, 45–46
  older, marital status among, 9
  older adults in labor force by gender, 66
  oldest-old, numbers of, 7
  Women's Institute for a Secure Retirement, 150
  See also Gender
Fertility, 3
Fever, 118
Fibromyalgia, 106
"Fibromyalgia Fact Sheet" (National Fibromyalgia Association), 106
FICA (Federal Insurance Contributions Act), 36
50+ Active and Healthy Living Store, 35
Financial abuse
  causes of, 176
  identification of by medical professionals, 178
  national strategy to combat, 174
  against older adults, 172–173
  reporting of, 176
Financial burden, 176
"Financial Elder Abuse Increases in a Down Economy" (Schlesinger), 176
Financing, health care for older adults, 151–154
  See also Expenditures
"Fiscal Cliff Deal Repeals CLASS Act, Creates Long-Term Care Commission" (Gleckman), 166
Fixed route/scheduled services transportation, 100
Flaherty, Joseph H., 179
Fleck, Carole, 19–20
Flinders, Abigail, 121
Florida, Sun City communities in, 58
FMR (fair market rent), 59–60

"For Nursing Homes, 'It's Diversify or Die'" (Sedensky), 52
"Forecasting Age-Related Macular Degeneration through the Year 2050: The Potential Impact of New Treatments" (Rein et al.), 116
The Foreign-Born Population in the United States: 2010 (Grieco et al.), 9
Foster Grandparent Program, 77
401(k) plan, 23
Fox, Susannah, 147
Fractures, 107
Franklin, Benjamin, 63
Fraud
  financial, 172–173
  health, 170, 172
  identification of by medical professionals, 178
  Medicare, 173
  pension, 25
  targeting of older people, 170
  victimization rates by age, 172t
Friedman, Richard A., 143
FTC (Federal Trade Commission), 170, 172
Full-time work, 69
Funding. *See* Expenditures

G
Gainey, Randy R., 177
Gallo, Joseph J., 138
Gandhi, Mohandas, 81
GAO. *See* U.S. Government Accountability Office
Gao, Guifang, 178
GDP. *See* Gross domestic product
Gender
  absences from work by, 72t
  chronic conditions, percentage of people aged 65/over who reported having, 114(t7.6)
  deaths from heart disease and, 121
  difficulties with basic/complex actions by, 107f
  disability measures and, 102, 103
  financial fraud and, 172
  hearing/seeing, trouble with, or no natural teeth, people aged 65 and over who reported having, 116(f7.9)
  intimate partner violence and, 177
  labor force participation rates by, 66, 68t, 70t
  labor force participation rates for older women, 67, 69
  licensed drivers by, 92t
  living arrangements of older people and, 45–46, 49f
  Medicare enrollees aged 65/older unable to perform certain physical functions by, 106f
  obesity rates by, 119f, 124, 127(f7.15)
  osteoporosis and, 107

of people in residential care, 54

population aged 65/over living alone, by age group/sex, 48(*t*3.3)

prostate problems and, 111

smoking by, 126*f*, 128(*f*7.16)

speeding drivers in fatal crashes by, 94*t*

stroke risk and, 122

tenure with current employer for employed workers by, 73*t*

urinary incontinence and, 111–112

violent crime rates by, 171*t*

visits to physician offices, hospital outpatient departments, emergency departments by, 110*t*–111*t*

visits to primary care physicians by, 112*t*

Generalized anxiety disorder, 140

Genetics, 134

Genther, Dane J., 115

Genworth Financial, 165

Geriatric care managers, 150

"Geriatric Care Managers—Could One Help You with Your Elderly Loved One?" (Marley), 150

Geriatricians, lack of, 128–129

Gerontological Society of America, 182

Gerontology, 5

Gerontology Research Group (GRG), 7

Giandrea, Michael D., 69

Ginzler, Elinor, 52

Glaucoma, 116

Gleckman, Howard, 166

Glenn, John, 63

Gorzelany, Jim, 99

Gould, Doug, 72

Gout, 106

Grandchildren

Foster Grandparent Program, 77

grandparents living with, 46–47

grandparents living with grandchildren, by race, sex, 49*t*

Grandparents

Foster Grandparent Program, 77

grandparents living with grandchildren, by race, sex, 49*t*

"Grandparents Day 2012: Sept. 9" (U.S. Census Bureau), 46

"Granny units," 57–58

Gray Panthers, 182

"Gray Power," 89

"The Grayest Congress" (Colby), 89

Great Recession

effects on older adults, 19

elder abuse and, 176

layoffs/reductions in response to, 75

multigenerational households and, 46

Green, Diane, 177

Green House Project, 54

Greenberg, James A., 5–6

GRG (Gerontology Research Group), 7

Grieco, Elizabeth M., 9

Gross, James J., 14

Gross domestic product (GDP)

Medicare costs and, 160

Social Security/Medicare cost as percentage of GDP, 161*f*

Gross v. FBL Financial Services, Inc., 75

"Growing Old in America: Expectations vs. Reality" (Pew Research Center), 12–13

Guerreiro, Rita, 134

Guinness World Records, 7

H

Han, Beth, 141

Hansen, James E., 63

Happiness

among older adults, 13–14

perceptions of aging and, 14–16

Harris, Diana K., 179

Harris, Meghan K., 117

HCBS waiver program, 149

Health

of baby boomers, 17

driving and age-related changes, 96–99

as limiting factor in use of automobiles, 91

mental, shortage of providers for, 143

obesity and, 6

See also Mental health/mental illness

Health, United States, 2012 (NCHS)

on deaths from strokes, 122

on life expectancy, 5

on nursing home residents, 50

on people limited in ADLs, 101–102

Health and medical problems

arthritis, 105–106

arthritis, prevalence of, 114*f*

chronic conditions, percentage of people aged 65 and over who reported having, 104(*f*7.2), 114(*t*7.7)

chronic conditions, percentage of people aged 65 and over who reported having, by sex, race/Hispanic origin, 114(*t*7.6)

chronic diseases/conditions, prevalence of, 105

death, leading causes of, 121–122

death, leading causes of/numbers of deaths, by age, 113*t*

death rates for cerebrovascular disease, 125*t*–126*t*

death rates for malignant neoplasms, 123*t*–124*t*

diabetes, 107, 110–111

diagnosed diabetes among adults aged 18 and over, prevalence of, 116(*f*7.8)

difficulties with basic/complex actions, by age, sex, 107*f*

disability in older population, 119–120

driving, effects on, 97–98

drug use among older adults, 120–121

eye diseases, 115–117

geriatric medicine, U.S. lack of specialists in, 128–129

health, percentage of adults who reported their health as fair or poor, 102*t*–103*t*

health, percentage of people aged 65 and over who reported having good to excellent health, by age, race/ethnicity, 104(*f*7.1)

health of older Americans, general, 101–105

healthy aging, 122–126

hearing loss, 114–115

hearing/seeing, trouble with, or no natural teeth, people aged 65 and over who reported having, by selected characteristics, 117*t*

hearing/seeing, trouble with, or no natural teeth, people aged 65 and over who reported having, by sex, 116(*f*7.9)

HIV, percentage of persons of all ages who had ever been tested for, by age group/sex, 130*f*

hospital discharges, days of care, average length of stay, 108*t*–109*t*

infectious diseases, 118–119

malnutrition, 113

medical care, percentage of persons of all ages who failed to obtain needed care due to cost, by age group/sex, 129(*f*7.19)

medical care, percentage of persons of all ages with usual place to go for, by age group/sex, 129(*f*7.18)

Medicare enrollees aged 65 and older unable to perform activities of daily living, 105*f*

Medicare enrollees aged 65 and older unable to perform certain physical functions, by sex, 106*f*

obese, adults aged 65 and older who are, by sex/age group, 119*f*

obesity among adults, prevalence of, by age group/sex, 127(*f*7.15)

oral health problems, 117

osteoporosis, 107

osteoporosis pyramid for prevention and treatment, 115*f*

Parkinson's disease, 117

physical activity, adults aged 18 years and over that met 2008 federal physical activity guidelines for aerobic activity, 128(*f*7.17)

physical activity, population aged 45 and older who engage in regular, 127(*f*7.14)

prescription drug costs and sources of payment for noninstitutionalized Medicare enrollees aged 65 and older, average annual, 120*f*

prostate problems, 111

sexuality in aging, 126–128

smoking, adults aged 65 and older who smoke cigarettes, by sex, 126*f* smoking among adults, prevalence of, by age group/sex, 128(f7.16)

urinary incontinence, 111–113

vaccinated against influenza and pneumococcal disease, adults aged 65 and older who reported having been, by race/Hispanic origin, 118f

vision changes, 115

visits to physician offices, hospital outpatient departments, emergency departments, by age, sex, race, 110t–111t

visits to primary care physicians, by age, sex, race, 112t

Health care

financing health care for older adults, 151–154

health insurance coverage for persons aged 65 and older, by type of coverage, 158t–159t

home health care, 166–167

for homeless people, 47

long-term health care, 163–166

Medicaid, 160–161

medical care, percentage of persons of all ages who failed to obtain needed care due to cost, by age group/sex, 129(f7.19)

medical care, percentage of persons of all ages with usual place to go for, by age group/sex, 129(f7.18)

Medicare, 154–160

Medicare, expected decline in workers per retiree to fund, 159f

Medicare coverage, two ways to obtain, 157f

Medicare enrollees age 65/over, sources of payment for health care services for, by type of service, 155f

Medicare enrollees aged 65 and over residing in selected residential settings, by age group, 166f

Medicare enrollees aged 65/over with functional limitations, by residential setting, 167f

Medicare enrollment, increased, 160f

Medicare Part D, how it provides prescription drug benefits, 159(t10.3)

Medicare-covered hospital/skilled nursing facility stays per 1,000 Medicare enrollees aged 65 and over in fee-for-service, 152f

national health expenditures by source of funds, 153t–154t

overview of, 151

PPACA, effects on caregivers, 147–148

Social Security/Medicare cost as percentage of GDP, 161f

veterans aged 65/over who are enrolled in or receiving care from VHA, total number of, 162f

veterans' benefits, 161–163

veterans using VA services/main reason for not applying or using benefits, percentage of, 164f

VHA enrollees/outpatient visits, trends in, 163f

Health Care and Education Affordability Reconciliation Act of 2010, 152

"Health Care Reform and Family Caregivers" (Family Caregiver Alliance), 147

Health care workers, 147

Health fraud, 170, 172

Health insurance

financing health care for older adults, 151–154

health insurance coverage for persons aged 65 and older, by type of coverage, 158t–159t

Medicaid, 160–161

Medicare, 154–160

Medicare, expected decline in workers per retiree to fund, 159f

Medicare coverage, two ways to obtain, 157f

Medicare enrollees age 65 and over, sources of payment for health care services for, by type of service, 155f

Medicare enrollees aged 65 and over residing in selected residential settings, by age group, 166f

Medicare enrollees aged 65 and over with functional limitations, by residential setting, 167f

Medicare enrollment, increased, 160f

Medicare Part D, how it provides prescription drug benefits, 159(t10.3)

Medicare-covered hospital/skilled nursing facility stays per 1,000 Medicare enrollees aged 65 and over in fee-for-service, 152f

national health expenditures by source of funds, 153t–154t

for older adults, trends in, 151

Social Security/Medicare cost as percentage of GDP, 161f

veterans aged 65 and over who are enrolled in or receiving care from VHA, total number of, 162f

veterans' benefits, 161–163

veterans using VA services/main reason for not applying or using benefits, 164f

VHA enrollees and outpatient visits, trends in, 163f

Health Insurance Portability and Accountability Act of 1996, 173

Health issues

of caregivers, 146

of homelessness, 47

See also Health and medical problems

Health maintenance organizations (HMOs), 156

"Health Spending Projections through 2018: Recession Effects Add Uncertainty to the Outlook" (Sisko et al.), 166

Healthy aging

adults aged 18 years/over that met 2008 federal physical activity guidelines for aerobic activity, 128(f7.17)

health practices for, 122–124

obesity among adults, prevalence of, by age group/sex, 127(f7.15)

physical activity, 124–125

population aged 45/older who engage in regular physical activity, 127(f7.14)

preventive health services, use of, 125–126

smoking, adults aged 65/older who smoke cigarettes, by sex, 126f

smoking among adults, prevalence of, by age group/sex, 128(f7.16)

smoking, quitting, 124

weight, maintaining healthy, 124

"Healthy Aging: Helping People to Live Long and Productive Lives and Enjoy a Good Quality of Life—At a Glance 2011" (CDC), 151

Hearing

loss, 114–115

people aged 65/over who reported having trouble with hearing/seeing, or no natural teeth, 117t

people aged 65/over who reported having trouble with hearing/seeing, or no natural teeth, by sex, 116(f7.9)

"Hearing Loss and Incident Dementia" (Lin et al.), 114–115

"Hearing Loss Prevalence and Risk Factors among Older Adults in the United States" (Lin et al.), 114

Heart disease, 105, 121–122

Helman, Ruth, 25–26

Hertzog, Christopher, 16

HHS (U.S. Department of Health and Human Services), 99, 165

Himelfarb, Igor, 86–87

Himes, Christine L., 6

Hippel, William von, 16

Hispanics

general health of older Americans, 101

income of, 20

living arrangements of older people, 46

racial/ethnic diversity of older population, 9

A History of National Service in America (Shapiro), 77

HIV. See Human immunodeficiency virus

HMOs (health maintenance organizations), 156

Holahan, John, 161

Hollingworth, Paul, 134

Home and Community-Based 1915(c) Medicaid Waivers That Pay for Respite Support: State-by-State Tables of Medicaid Waiver Information (Perrin), 149

Home and community-based services, 149

Home equity, 59

Home health aides, 163–164
Home health care
　agencies, services of, 148
　community housing with home care
　　services, 166–167
　cost of home health aides, 163–164
　description of, 166
　industry, growth of, 48
　PPACA, effects on caregivers, 147–148
　projections for, 145
Homelessness
　overview of, 47
　sheltered homeless people, by age,
　　geography, 50t
　sheltered people and U.S. population,
　　age distribution of, 50f
Homeownership
　housing slump, effects of, 58
　rates, 58t
　rates, by age of householder, 59t
　rates of for older people, 58
　renting vs., 59–60
　reverse mortgages, 59
　sale/leaseback with life tenancy, 59
　strategic defaults, 59
Hopper, Grace Murray, 63
Hospital indemnity coverage, 157
Hospitals
　hearing loss and hospitalization, 115
　hospital discharges, days of care,
　　average length of stay, 108t–109t
　hospital utilization statistics, 103–104
　hospitalizations of older adults,
　　frequency of, 151
　Medicare-covered hospital/skilled
　　nursing facility stays per 1,000
　　Medicare enrollees aged 65 and over in
　　fee-for-service, 152f
　visits to physician offices, hospital
　　outpatient departments, emergency
　　departments, by age, sex, race, 110t–111t
Hosseinpoor, Ahmad Reza, 6
Households
　by age of householder, size of
　　household, 46t
　living arrangements by age/selected
　　characteristics, 48(t3.2)
　living arrangements of persons aged 65/
　　older, 47f
　net worth of, 26–28
　older people living with spouse, other
　　relatives, or alone, 45–47
　operating costs of, 31, 33–34
　shared household, elder abuse and, 176–177
　See also Living arrangements
Housing
　costs of, 58–59
　housing challenges for older adults, 60
　public housing, 60–61
　renting, affordability of, 59–60
Housing market, 58

"How Is the Financial Crisis Affecting
　Retirement Savings?" (Soto), 31
HUD (U.S. Department of Housing and
　Urban Development), 47, 61
"HUD's Public Housing Program"
　(Department of Housing and Urban
　Development), 61
Hugo, Victor, 5
Human immunodeficiency virus (HIV)
　percentage of persons of all ages who
　　had ever been tested for, by age group/
　　sex, 130f
　tests for older adults, 128
Hypertension (high blood pressure), 105

I
IADLs (instrumental activities of daily
　living), 102–103
ICF (intermediate care facility), 50
"Identification of a Blood-Based Biomarker
　Panel for Classification of Alzheimer's
　Disease" (Laske et al.), 135
IIHS. See Insurance Institute for Highway
　Safety
Illinois, pension fraud in, 25
"Illinois Is Accused of Fraud by S.E.C."
　(Walsh), 25
"Incidence of Dementia and Cognitive
　Impairment, Not Dementia in the United
　States" (Plassman et al.), 131
Income
　aggregate, by source, 24f
　annual retirement earnings test exempt
　　amounts, 39(t2.10)
　distribution, 20
　distribution of population aged 65+,
　　22(f2.2)
　encore careers and, 76
　family households/persons aged 65+,
　　23(f2.3)
　housing costs, percentage spent on,
　　58–59
　as limiting factor in use of automobiles,
　　91
　Medicare premiums and, 160
　older adults, by source, 27f
　pension funds, 20, 23–25
　personal savings, 25–26
　Social Security, as source of retirement
　　funds, by age, 43(t2.14)
　Social Security, as source of retirement
　　funds, by income, 43(t2.15)
　Social Security, relative to total income,
　　23(f2.4)
　Social Security benefit amount for
　　worker with maximum-taxable
　　earnings, 37t
　Social Security Income federal payment
　　amounts, 39(t2.9)
　sources of, 20
　sources of for population aged 65+, 25f

from specified sources, by age group, 26t
Supplemental Security Income,
　payments by eligibility category/age/
　source of payment, 41t
Supplemental Security Income,
　recipients by eligibility category/age,
　40t
"Independence at Home Demonstration"
　(Centers for Medicare and Medicaid
　Services), 147
Independence at Home Medical Practice
　Pilot Program, 147
Industrial Revolution, 65–66
Infectious diseases
　adults aged 65+ who reported having
　　been vaccinated against influenza/
　　pneumococcal disease, by race/
　　Hispanic origin, 118f
　influenza, 118–119
　pneumonia, 119
Influenza (flu)
　adults aged 65+ who reported having
　　been vaccinated against influenza/
　　pneumococcal disease, by race/
　　Hispanic origin, 118f
　overview of, 118–119
Information industry, workers in, 66
Innovation, 72–73
Innovations Exchange program, 53
Institute of Medicine's Committee on the
　Future Health Care Workforce for Older
　Americans, 145
Institutional abuse, 178–180
Instrumental activities of daily living
　(IADLs), 102–103
Insulin, 110–111
Insurance Institute for Highway Safety
　(IIHS)
　contact information, 182
　on fatal crashes among older drivers,
　　93–94, 98
　on public transportation, 99
Interest rates, 28
Intermediate care facility (ICF), 50
Internal Revenue Service, 165
"International Shortfall Inequality in Life
　Expectancy in Women and in Men,
　1950–2010" (Hosseinpoor et al), 6
Internet, use by older adults, 85
Intimate partner violence (IPV), 177
Investor Protection Trust, 178
"Is Psychological Vulnerability Related to
　the Experience of Fraud in Older
　Adults?" (Lichtenberg, Stickney, &
　Paulson), 170
Ivanová, Katerina, 178

J
Jacobs, Robin J., 177
Job tenure
　of older workers, 69, 71

tenure with current employer for employed workers, median years of, by age, sex, 73*t*

Jobs. *See* Employment; Work

John Hancock insurance, 165

Johnson, Lyndon B., 154

Joints, 105–106

Joshi, Seema, 179

Justification of Estimates for Appropriations Committees: Fiscal Year 2013 (Administration on Aging), 45

K

Kaiser Family Foundation, 156–157

Kane, Michael N., 177

Kathy's Law, 179

Kennedy, John F., 77

Keys Amendment, 56

Kimura, Jiroemon, 7–8

King, Dana E., 17

Knolls Atomic Power Laboratory, Meacham et al. v., 75

Krouse, Laurel H., 176–177

L

Labor force
aging, 66–67, 69
changes in, 64–65
median age of, 66*t*
participation rates, by age, gender, 68*t*
participation rates, by age, gender, race/ethnicity, 70*t*
retirement from, 63–64
unemployment rates by age, 67*t*

Lachs, Mark, 174

LaHood, Ray H., 93

Laske, Christoph, 135

Laws, 24–25

See also Legislation and international treaties

Lawsuits, ADEA claims, 75

Layoffs, 75–76

LeadingAge, 182

"Learn about Osteoporosis" (National Osteoporosis Foundation), 107

Legislation and international treaties
ADEA Amendments of 1978, 66
Age Discrimination in Employment Act, 66, 73
Americans with Disabilities Act, 99
Balanced Budget Act of 1997, 156
Community Living Assistance Services and Supports (CLASS) Act, 165–166
Economic Opportunity Act of 1964, 77
Elder Justice Act, 169
Employee Retirement Income Security Act, 20, 24
Federal Insurance Contributions Act, 36
Health Care and Education Affordability Reconciliation Act of 2010, 152

Health Insurance Portability and Accountability Act of 1996, 173
Keys Amendment, 56
Medicare Prescription Drug, Improvement, and Modernization Act of 2003, 160
Older Americans Act Amendments of 2013, 145
Older Americans Act of 1965, 56, 149
Older Workers Benefit Protection Act, 73
Omnibus Budget Reconciliation Act of 1987, 178, 179
Patient Protection and Affordable Care Act, 147–148, 151–153, 165–166
Pension Protection Act, 24
Prescription Drug, Improvement, and Modernization Act of 2003, 155, 157
Retirement Equity Act, 24
Section 202 Supportive Housing for the Elderly Act, 61
Social Security Act, 36, 154, 160
Social Security Amendments of 1977, 37–38
Tax Equity and Fiscal Responsibility Act of 1982, 156
Transportation Equity Act for the 21st Century, 99
U.S. Housing Act of 1937, 60
Veterans Millennium Health Care and Benefits Act of 1999, 161–162

Leonhardt, David, 86

Levo-dopa (L-dopa), 117

Levy, Becca R., 14–15, 17

Lewis, Kern, 36

Licensed Board and Care Homes: Preliminary Findings from the 1991 National Health Provider Inventory (Clark et al.), 55–56

Lichtenberg, Peter A., 170

Life care communities, 50

Life expectancy
at birth/age 65, 43*t*
countries with lowest, 7*t*
by country, 6*f*
global, 6
trends in, 5–6
work/retirement changes and, 64

Life Expectancy in the United States (Shrestha), 64

Life experience, 131–132

LIHEAP (Low Income Home Energy Assistance Program), 34

Lin, Frank R., 114–115

Lineweaver, Tara T., 16

Living arrangements
by age/selected characteristics, 48(*t*3.2)
assisted living, 55–57
continuing care retirement communities, 57
elder abuse and, 176–177

elder cottage housing opportunity units, 57–58
grandparents living with grandchildren, by race, sex, 49*t*
home, owning/renting, 58–60
homelessness, 47
homeownership rates, 58*t*
homeownership rates, by age of householder, 59*t*
households by age of householder, size of household, 46*t*
housing challenges for older adults, 60
housing slump and, 58
living with spouse, other relatives, or alone, 45–47
long-term care/supportive housing, classes of, 47–50
Medicare-certified providers, 52*t*
nursing homes, 50–54
nursing homes, residents/occupancy rates of, by state, 51*t*
of persons aged 65 and older, 47*f*
of population aged 65 and over, by sex, race, Hispanic origin, 49*f*
population aged 65 and over living alone, by age group/sex, 48(*t*3.3)
public housing, 60–61
residential care, characteristics of people in, 54–55, 54(*f*3.4)
residential care, most common chronic conditions of persons in, 56*f*
residential care, persons in, receiving assistance with activities of daily living, 55*f*
residential care with Medicaid, persons in, by age, 54(*f*3.5)
retirement communities, 58
shared housing/cohousing, 57
sheltered homeless people, by age, geography, 50*t*
sheltered people and U.S. population, age distribution of, 50*f*

Loneliness
aging, perceptions of, 13, 14
Eden Alternative and, 53–54
malnutrition and, 113
mental illness and, 137
problem drinking and, 142
reporting of elder abuse and, 176

Long, Russell B., 154

Long-term care (LTC)
assisted living, 55–57
institutional abuse, 178–180
long-term care/supportive housing, classes of, 47–50
number of older people living in, 47–48
nursing homes, 50–54
residential care, 54–55

"Long-Term Care Insurance Costs" (U.S. Department of Health and Human Services), 165

"Long-Term-Care Insurance: Insurers Are Forced to Boost Premiums or Stop Selling Policies" (Consumer Reports), 165

"Long-Term Care Insurance Tax-Deductibility Rules—LTC Tax Rules" (American Association for Long Term Care Insurance), 165

Long-Term Care Ombudsman Program, 180

"Long-Term Care Ombudsman Program" (Administration on Aging), 180

"Long Term Effect of Depression Care Management on Mortality in Older Adults: Follow-up of Cluster Randomized Clinical Trial in Primary Care" (Gallo et al.), 138

Long-term health care
    costs of, 163–164
    Medicare, Medicaid and, 164–165
    payment for, 164
    private long-term care insurance, 165–166

Longevity, 14–16

"Longevity Increased by Positive Self-Perceptions of Aging" (Levy et al.), 14–15

Low Income Home Energy Assistance Program (LIHEAP), 34

LTC. See Long-term care

Lungs, 118, 119

Lynchard, Nicholas A., 16

M

"'Magic Carpet' Could Help Prevent Falls" (University of Manchester), 60

Majmundar, Malay, 31

Males
    living arrangements of older people, 45–46
    older, marital status among, 9
    older adults in labor force by gender, 66
    oldest-old, numbers of, 7
    prostate problems among, 111
    See also Gender

Malignant neoplasms. See Cancer

Malnutrition, 113

"Malnutrition and Older Americans" (National Resource Center on Nutrition, Physical Activity, and Aging), 113

Maltreatment of Patients in Nursing Homes: There Is No Safe Place (Harris & Benson), 179

Mandatory retirement, 65, 66

Manton, Kenneth G., 119–120

Manufacturing, 65–66

Market Survey of Long-Term Care Costs: The 2012 MetLife Market Survey of Nursing Home, Assisted Living, Adult Day Services, and Home Care Costs (MetLife Mature Market Institute), 56–57, 163

Marketing to Baby Boomers—US—December 2012 (Mintel International Group Ltd.), 36

Marley, Marie, 150

Marriage
    intimate partner violence, 177
    marital problems in old age, 132
    marital status among older population, 9
    older adults living with spouse, 45
    postponement of, 64

Marshall, Anthony D., 173–174

Martin, John W., 35

Martinez-Lage, Pablo, 136

Mayo Clinic, 122

McCain, John, 63

McDermott, Kerry, 8

McKhann, Guy M., 135

Meacham et al. v. Knolls Atomic Power Laboratory, 75

Mead, Margaret, 63

"The mec-4 Gene Is a Member of a Family of Caenorhabditis elegans Genes That Can Mutate to Induce Neuronal Degeneration" (Driscoll & Chalfie), 134

Medicaid
    coverage of nursing home costs, 163
    expansion of, 160–161
    fraud, 172–173
    function of, 153–154
    health insurance coverage for persons aged 65/older, by type of coverage, 158t–159t
    Home and Community-Based Services (HCBS) waiver program, 149
    home health care expenditures, 166
    immunizations against flu/pneumonia in nursing homes and, 119
    long-term care coverage, 164–165
    overview of, 160
    payment for residential care, 54
    PPACA, effects on caregivers, 147

Medical care. See Health care

Medical problems. See Health and medical problems

Medical professionals, 178
    See also Physicians

Medicare
    challenges of, 157–158
    coverage, two ways to obtain, 157f
    coverage for older adults, 151
    coverage of nursing home costs, 163
    enrollees age 65+, sources of payment for health care services for, by type of service, 155f
    enrollees aged 65+ unable to perform activities of daily living, 105f
    enrollees aged 65+ unable to perform certain physical functions, by sex, 106f
    enrollment, increased, 160f
    establishment of, 154
    expansion of, 157

expected decline in workers per retiree to fund, 159f

fraud, 172–173

future of, 158–159

health insurance coverage for persons aged 65/older, by type of coverage, 158t–159t

home health care coverage, 148

home health care expenditures, 166

immunizations against flu/pneumonia in nursing homes and, 119

insurance to supplement Medicare benefits, 157

long-term care and, 164

Medicare Advantage, 156–157

Medicare Part D, how it provides prescription drug benefits, 159(t10.3)

Medicare-certified providers, 52t

Medicare-covered hospital/skilled nursing facility stays per 1,000 Medicare enrollees aged 65 and over in fee-for-service, 152f

parts of, 154–155

PPACA, effects on caregivers, 147

PPACA reform of, 151–154

prescription drug costs/sources of payment for noninstitutionalized Medicare enrollees aged 65+, average annual, 120f

prescription drug coverage, 157

preventive services/screenings covered by, 126

reform of, 159

reimbursement under, 155–156

Social Security/Medicare cost as percentage of GDP, 161f

"Medicare 2013 Costs at a Glance" (CMS), 160

Medicare Advantage, 155, 156–157

Medicare Advantage Plan Star Ratings and Bonus Payments in 2012 (Kaiser Family Foundation), 156–157

"Medicare Drug Costs to Fall in 2014, but Donut Hole Widens" (Miller), 152–153

"Medicare Modernization: The New Prescription Drug Benefit and Redesigned Part B and Part C" (Megellas), 154

Medicare Prescription Drug, Improvement, and Modernization Act of 2003, 160

"The Medicare Prescription Drug Benefit Fact Sheet" (Kaiser Family Foundation), 157

Medicare Rights Center, 182

Medicare-risk HMOs, 156

Medication. See Drugs

Medigap insurance
    health insurance coverage for persons aged 65+, by type of coverage, 158t–159t
    overview of, 157

Megellas, Michelle M., 154

Memory
    aging and, 16
    Alzheimer's disease and, 133
    causes of changes in, 137
    decline of in older adults, 132
Men. *See* Gender; Males
Mental Health: A Report of the Surgeon General (U.S. surgeon general)
    on alcohol/prescription drug misuse in older adults, 141
    on anxiety disorder, 140
    on mental disorders, 137–138
    on schizophrenia in older adults, 141
Mental health/mental illness
    adults who experienced serious psychological distress, by age group/sex, 132*f*
    adults who had 5+ drinks in 1 day, by age group/sex, 141*f*
    alcohol/prescription drugs, misuse of, 141–143
    death rates for suicide, 139*t*–140*t*
    dementias, 132–137
    depressive symptoms, people aged 65+ with, by age group/sex, 138*f*
    experiences, influence on mental health in old age, 131–132
    growing mental health needs of older adults, 137–141
    homeless people and, 47
    memory, 132
    mental illness in older adults, 137
    overview of, 131
    prevalence of types of drinkers, 142*f*
Mental health providers, 143
MetLife Foundation, 76
MetLife Mature Market Institute
    on cost of home health aides, 164
    on costs of assisted living, 56–57
    on costs of caregiving, 146–147
    on costs of nursing homes, 163
    financial fraud study, 172–173
    MetLife Study of Elder Financial Abuse, 176
    on retirement of baby boomers, 64
    on reverse mortgages, 59
"The MetLife Study of Caregiving Costs to Working Caregivers: Double Jeopardy for Baby Boomers Caring for Their Parents" (MetLife Mature Market Institute), 147
The MetLife Study of Caregiving Costs to Working Caregivers: New Insights and Innovations for Reducing Health Care Costs for Employers (MetLife Mature Market), 146–147
The MetLife Study of Elder Financial Abuse: Crimes of Occasion, Desperation, and Predation against America's Elders (MetLife Mature Market Institute), 172–173, 176
Michaud, Jean-Philippe, 136

Middle-old adults, 5, 6–7
Migration, 3
Milbank Memorial Fund, 60
"Mild Cognitive Impairment: Disparity of Incidence and Prevalence Estimates" (Ward et al.), 131
Millennials, 69
Miller, Mark
    on housing slump, 58
    on institutional abuse, 179
    on Medicare drug costs, 152–153
Miniño, Arialdi M., 3
Mintel International Group Ltd., 36
Mirkin, Barry, 7
"Mission, Vision and Values" (Pioneer Network), 52
"Mistreatment in Assisted Living Facilities: Complaints, Substantiations, and Risk Factors" (Phillips & Gao), 178
Mistreatment of older adults. *See* Abuse/mistreatment of older adults
Mitchell, Alex J., 132–133
Module 10C: Older Adults and Alcohol Problems (NIAAA), 141–142
Moeller, Philip, 28
Monophosphoryl lipid A (MPL), 136
Moody, Harry R., 17
Moreno, Debra, 75–76
Morris, Frank C., Jr., 75
Mortality rates, 3
    See also Death rates
Mortgages
    mortgage crisis, effect on older Americans, 28
    strategic defaults, reverse mortgages, 59
Motor vehicle accidents, 93–94, 96
"Movement Disorders" (Harris et al.), 117
MPL (monophosphoryl lipid A), 136
Multigenerational households
    grandparents living with grandchildren, by race, sex, 49*t*
    rise in, 46–47
Multi-infarct dementia, 133
Myths, about older workers, 69, 71–73
"Myths about Older Workers" (North Carolina Collaboration on Lifelong Learning and Engagement), 71

N
Naj, Adam C., 134
Nascher, Ignatz L., 128
Naslund, John A., 137
National Academy of Elder Law Attorneys, 182
National Aging Network, 149
National Alliance for Caregiving, 182
National Association for Home Care and Hospice, 148, 182
National Association for Home Care and Hospice: 2013 Legislative Priorities (NAHC), 147–148

National Bipartisan Commission on the Future of Medicare, 158–159
National Caregiving Foundation, 182
National Caucus and Center on Black Aged, 182
National Center for Health Statistics (NCHS)
    on characteristics of people in residential care, 54–55
    contact information, 182
    "Death in the United States, 2011," 3
    on deaths from strokes, 122
    on diabetes, 111
    "Health, United States, 2012," 5
    on home health care, 166
    on nursing home residents, 50
    on people limited in ADLs, 101–102
National Center for Injury Prevention and Control, 94
National Center for PTSD, 162
National Center on Elder Abuse (NCEA)
    on causes of elder abuse, 176
    on institutional abuse awareness, 179–180
    survey on elder abuse, 175
National Center on Elder Abuse, University of California, Irvine, Program in Geriatric Medicine, 182
National Center on Senior Transportation (NCST), 92–93
National Committee for the Prevention of Elder Abuse (NCPEA), 169
National Comprehensive Cancer Network, 122
National Consumer Voice for Quality Long-Term Care, 182
National Council on Aging, 59, 149–150
National Council on Child Abuse and Family Violence, 176
National Fibromyalgia Association, 106
National Health Interview Survey, 141
National Highway Traffic Safety Administration (NHTSA)
    Older Driver Program: Five-Year Strategic Plan 2012–2017, 91, 99
    Physician's Guide to Assessing and Counseling Older Drivers, 97–98
    on safety of older drivers, 98
National Hispanic Council on Aging, 182
National Home and Hospice Care Survey: Home Health—Data Highlights (National Center for Health Statistics), 166
National Hospice and Palliative Care Organization, 182
National Indian Council on Aging, 182
National Institute of Neurological Disorders and Stroke, 133
National Institute on Aging (NIA)
    on apoE-4 gene, 134
    contact information, 182
    "Cortex Area Thinner in Youth with Alzheimer's-Related Gene," 134
    on testing for Alzheimer's, 135

National Institute on Alcohol Abuse and Alcoholism (NIAAA), 141–142

National Institute on Drug Abuse, 120

National Institutes of Health, 111–112

National Kidney and Urologic Diseases Information Clearinghouse, 111

National Low Income Housing Coalition, 59–60

National Nursing Home Survey, 51–52

National Osteoporosis Foundation, 107, 182

National PACE Association, 182

A National Public Health Agenda for Osteoarthritis 2010 (Arthritis Foundation & CDC), 105–106

National Resource Center on Nutrition, Physical Activity, and Aging, 113

National Senior Citizens Law Center, 182

National Service Corps (NSC), 77

National service organizations, 77

National Society for American Indian Elderly, 182

National Urban League, 182

NCEA. *See* National Center on Elder Abuse

NCHS. *See* National Center for Health Statistics

NCPEA (National Committee for the Prevention of Elder Abuse), 169

NCST (National Center on Senior Transportation), 92–93

"Need Extra Income? Put a Cottage in Your Backyard" (Newcomb), 58

Net worth
median household, by race, aged 65+, 28*f*
mortgage crisis/low interest rates, 28
overview of, 26–28

Neumann, Harold, 134

"New Data on Older Adult Drivers" (CDC), 94, 96, 97

New Jersey, pension fraud in, 25

A New Vision of America's Highways: Long-Distance Travel, Recreation, Tourism, and Rural Travel (Camph), 91

New York
Kathy's Law, 179
pension fraud in, 25

Newcomb, Tim, 58

Newport, Frank, 11, 86–87

The Next Four Decades—The Older Population in the United States: 2010 to 2050 (Vincent & Velkoff), 1

"NHE Fact Sheet" (CMS), 151

"NHIS Arthritis Surveillance" (CDC), 106

NHTSA. *See* National Highway Traffic Safety Administration

NIA. *See* National Institute on Aging

NIAAA (National Institute on Alcohol Abuse and Alcoholism), 141–142

Nicolosi, Gloria Teixeira, 138–139

Nightmare on Main Street: Older Americans and the Mortgage Market Crisis (Trawinski), 28

"NINDS Multi-infarct Dementia Information Page" (National Institute of Neurological Disorders and Stroke), 133

North Carolina Collaboration on Lifelong Learning and Engagement, 69, 71

NSC (National Service Corps), 77

"Nurse Aides' Reports of Resident Abuse in Nursing Homes" (Castle), 179

Nurses
elder abuse and, 178
as geriatric care managers, 150
for home health care, 148
wages of, 163

Nursing homes
categories of, 50
costs of long-term health care, 163–164
diversification of, 51–52
Eden Alternative, 53–54
immunizations against flu/pneumonia in, 119
institutional abuse, 178–180
Medicare-certified providers, 52*t*
Medicare/Medicaid coverage of LTC, 164–165
number of older people living in, 47–48
nursing homes, residents/occupancy rates of, by state, 51*t*
percentage of population living in, 45
Pioneer Network, 52
quality of life for residents, improvements to, 53
residents of, 50–51

"Nursing Homes Create Home-Like, Resident-Focused Environment and Culture, Leading to Better Quality and Financial Performance, Higher Resident Satisfaction, and Lower Staff Turnover" (AHRQ), 53

Nutrition, 113

O

Obama, Barack
in multigenerational household, 47
on prevention of elder abuse, 169
on social security benefits, 39

Obama, Malia, 47

Obama, Michelle, 47

Obama, Sasha, 47

Obamacare. *See* Patient Protection and Affordable Care Act

Obesity
adults aged 65+ who are obese, by sex/age group, 119*f*
arthritis and, 106
diabetes and, 111
disability trends and, 119–120
effects on life expectancy/health, 5–6
obesity among adults, prevalence of, by age group/sex, 127(*f*7.15)
rates of, 124
rates of hypertension/diabetes and, 105

"Obesity and Early Mortality in the United States" (Greenberg), 5–6

O'Keeffe, Georgia, 63

Old age
defining, 5
enjoyment of, 12–14
longevity/happiness, perceptions of aging influence on, 14–16

"Old vs. Young" (Leonhardt), 86

Old-Age, Survivors, and Disability Insurance (OASDI), 36
See also Social Security

"Older Adult Drivers: Get the Facts" (CDC), 91

Older adults
aged 65 and older, by age group, 5*f*
aged 80 and older, 3*f*
aging consumers, growth of, 35–36
alcohol-related issues unique to, 142–143
baby boomers, contribution to population of, 4*f*
centenarians, 7–8
consumer expenses of, 31, 33–34
definition of, 5
economic well-being of, 20, 23–26
foreign-born, 9
happiness among, 13–14
income distribution among, 20
income sources, 20
increase of percentage of population, 1
in labor force, 66–67, 69
marital status of, 8
mental health needs of, 137–141
net worth of, 26–28
numbers living in U.S., 6–7
oldest-old, 7
overview of, 6–7
pension funds, 20, 23–25
place in industrialized/nonindustrialized cultures, 16
poverty among, 28–31
racial/ethnic diversity, 8
reliance on Social Security, 36
three groups of, 5
well-off, 31
where they live, 9, 11

Older Americans
adults, older in U.S., 6–9
aging, attitudes about, 16–17
contributions of, 63
life expectancy of, 5–6
locations of, 9, 11
old age, defining, 5
old age, enjoyment of, 12–16
overview of, 1–3
populations, aging of, 3–4

Older Americans 2012: Key Indicators of Well-Being (Federal Interagency Forum on Aging-Related Statistics)
on depression, 137
findings of, 1–3

on health of older Americans, 101
on income distribution, 20
on net worth of older Americans, 26–28
on oldest-old, 7
on tobacco consumption, 124
on veterans' benefits from VHA, 162
Older Americans Act Amendments of 2013, 145
Older Americans Act of 1965
Long-Term Care Ombudsman Program established under, 180
long-term care ombudsman programs with, 56
National Aging Network funded by, 149
"Older Americans and Cardiovascular Diseases" (American Heart Association), 121, 122
"Older Americans Month: May 2013" (U.S. Census Bureau), 1, 7
Older Americans' Moral Attitudes Changing (Wilke & Saad), 87
Older Driver Program: Five-Year Strategic Plan 2012-2017 (NHTSA), 91, 99
Older Driver Safety: Knowledge Sharing Should Help States Prepare for Increase in Older Driver Population (GAO), 99
Older Women's League, 182
Older workers
aging labor force, 66–67, 69
myths/stereotypes about, 69, 71–73
recasting work/retirement, 64–65
Older Workers (BLS), 66–67
"Older Workers and Short-Term Jobs: Patterns and Determinants" (Cahill, Giandrea, & Quinn), 69
Older Workers Benefit Protection Act, 73
"Older Workers See Gains in Jobs Report" (Fleck), 19–20
The Oldest Boomers: Healthy, Retiring Rapidly and Collecting Social Security (MetLife Mature Market Institute), 64
Oldest-old adults
definition of, 5
life expectancy of, 7
numbers living in U.S., 6–7
racial/ethnic diversity of, 9
"Ombudsmen on the Front Line: Improving Quality of Care and Preventing Abuse in Nursing Homes" (Miller), 179
Omnibus Budget Reconciliation Act of 1987, 178, 179
"Oral Health—Preventing Cavities, Gum Disease, Tooth Loss, and Oral Cancers: At a Glance 2011" (CDC), 117
Oral health problems
hearing/seeing, trouble with, or no natural teeth, people aged 65 and over who reported having, by selected characteristics, 117t
hearing/seeing, trouble with, or no natural teeth, people aged 65 and over who reported having, by sex, 116(f7.9)
of older adults, 117

Organic brain diseases. *See* Dementia
Osteoarthritis, 105–106
Osteoporosis
overview of, 107
physical activity to delay, 124
pyramid for prevention and treatment, 115f
Out of Reach 2013 (Bravve, Bolton, & Crowley), 59–60

P

Parker-Pope, Tara, 98
Parkinson's disease, 117
Parkinson's Disease Foundation, 117
Part A, Medicare program, 154–155
Part B (Supplemental Medical Insurance), 155, 156
Part C (Medicare Advantage program), 155
Part D, Medicare prescription drug benefit, 152, 155, 157
Part-time work, 69
Patient Protection and Affordable Care Act (PPACA)
access to long-term care insurance and, 165–166
Community First Choice Medicaid plan, 149
effects on informal caregivers, 147
effects on paid caregivers, 147–148
financial health care reform with, 151–153
Paulson, Daniel, 170
Payne, Brian K., 177
Pelosi, Nancy, 63
Pension Benefit Guaranty Corporation, 182
Pension funds
decline in, 24–25
defined benefit/contribution plans, 23
federal pension laws, 24
overview of, 20
private/public pensions, 24
Pension Protection Act (PPA), 24
Pension Rights Center, 182
Pepper, Claude Denson. *See* Abuse/mistreatment of older adults
Per member per month (PMPM), 155, 156
"Perceptions of Intimate Partner Violence, Age, and Self-Enhancement Bias" (Kane, Green, & Jacobs), 177
Perez, Sarah, 35
"Performance Data for the Senior Medicare Patrol Projects: June 2012 Performance Report" (Wright), 173
Performance, of older workers, 69
Perrin, Catherine Ogle, 149
Perry, Alan, 24
Pew Forum on Religion and Public Life, 11
Pew Research Center, 12–13
Phenolphthalein, 172
Phillips, Linda R., 178

Phobic anxiety disorders, 140
"Physical Abuse of Older Adults in Nursing Homes: A Random Sample Survey of Adults with an Elderly Family Member in a Nursing Home" (Schiamberg), 178
Physical activity. *See* Exercise
Physical hazards, 60
Physicians
elder abuse, identification of, 178
Medicare reimbursement and, 155–156
reporting of elder abuse, 176
visit rates for older adults, 104
visits to physician offices, hospital outpatient departments, emergency departments, by age, sex, race, 110t–111t
visits to primary care physicians, by age, sex, race, 112t
Physician's Guide to Assessing and Counseling Older Drivers (AMA & NHTSA), 97–98
"Pick Baby Boomers as Your Target Market for the Holidays" (Lewis), 36
Pickens, T. Boone, 63
Pioneer Network, 52
Planty, Michael, 169
Plassman, Brenda L., 131
Plus 50 Encore Completion Program, 81
Plus 50 Initiative, 81
The Plus 50 Initiative Evaluation: Initiative Impact (American Association of Community Colleges), 81
PMPM (per member per month), 155, 156
Pneumonia
adults aged 65+ who reported having been vaccinated against influenza/pneumococcal disease, by race/Hispanic origin, 118f
from influenza, 118
overview of, 119
Politics
aging politicians, 89
Americans' attitudes on gay relations, by age group, 88(f5.3)
Americans' attitudes on stem cell research, by age group, 88(f5.4)
financial outlook and, 86–87
moral acceptability of social issues, 87(t5.3)
of older adults, 86
views on social issues, 87–89
"Polls Suggest Congress Might Have Waited Too Long on Gun Control" (Steinhauser), 88–89
Polypharmacy, 121
"Polypharmacy in Older Adults at Home: What It Is and What to Do about It—Implications for Home Healthcare and Hospice" (Riker & Setter), 121
Population
aged 65/over as percent of total, 14f
aged 65/over by race/Hispanic origin, 11f, 11t

aged 65/over, marital status of by age/sex, 12*f*

aged 65/over, percent increase in, 15*f*

aged 80-plus, 7

aged 85/over by race, 12*t*

aging of, 3–4

children/older adults as percent of global, 2*f*

foreign-born by age, 13*f*

projections by age/sex, 2010/2030/2060, 10*f*

projections by age/sex, 2015–60, 8*t*–9*t*

U.S. by age, projected, 2*t*

Population pyramid, 7

"Positive Affect Measured Using Ecological Momentary Assessment and Survival in Older Men and Women" (Steptoe & Wardle), 16

Posttraumatic stress disorder (PTSD), 162

Potency drugs, 128

Poverty

    Medicaid for people living in, 160–161

    Medicare program and, 154

    overview of, 28–30

    people in, by selected characteristics, 29*t*–30*t*

    rate by age group, 22(*f*2.1)

    rates by age, 30*f*

    thresholds, by size of family/number of children, 31*t*

    thresholds, older adult, 30–31

"The Power of Positive Emotions: It's a Matter of Life or Death—Subjective Well-Being and Longevity over 28 Years in a General Population" (Xu & Roberts), 15–16

PPA (Pension Protection Act), 24

PPACA. *See* Patient Protection and Affordable Care Act

Presbyopia (tired eyes), 115

"Prescribing for Older People" (Flinders), 121

Prescription Drug, Improvement, and Modernization Act of 2003, 155, 157

Prescription drugs. *See* Drugs

Prescription Drugs: Abuse and Addiction (National Institute on Drug Abuse), 120

"Presidential Proclamation—World Elder Abuse Awareness Day" (Obama), 143

Prevent Blindness America

    on diabetic retinopathy, 117

    on glaucoma, 116

Prevention and Public Health Investment Fund, 152

Prevention of Elder Abuse, Neglect, and Exploitation program, 179

Preventive health services

    of Medicare, 160

    use of, 125–126

Privacy, invasion of, 176–177

Private health insurance

    coverage of nursing home costs, 163

    for long-term care, 165–166

A Profile of Older Americans: 2012 (Administration on Aging)

    data from, 3

    on distribution of population, 9, 11

    on housing costs, 58–59

    on income distribution, 20

    on living arrangements of older people, 45

    on number of older adults, 1

    on oldest-old, 7

Prostate cancer, 111

"Prostate Enlargement: Benign Prostatic Hyperplasia" (National Kidney and Urologic Diseases Information Clearinghouse), 111

Prostate problems, 111

Prostatitis, 111

"Protect Seniors in the Year of Elder Abuse Prevention" (Administration on Aging), 176

Psychological distress, adults who experienced, 132*f*

Psychotherapy, 138

PTSD (posttraumatic stress disorder), 162

Public housing, 60–61

Public Housing and Supportive Services for the Frail Elderly: A Guide for Housing Authorities and Their Collaborators (Milbank Memorial Fund & Council of Large Public Housing Authorities), 60

Purcell, Kristen, 147

Q

"Q&A: Older Drivers" (IIHS), 97–98, 99

Quality of life

    access to transportation and, 91, 92

    chronic diseases/conditions and, 105

    educational attainment and, 81

    exercise for, 124

    hearing loss and, 114

    of nursing home residents, 52, 53–54

"Quick Stats on Arthritis" (CDC), 106

Quinn, Joseph F., 69

R

Race/ethnicity

    adults aged 65+ who reported having been vaccinated against influenza/pneumococcal disease by, 118*f*

    among older population, 9

    chronic conditions, percentage of people aged 65+ who reported having, 114(*t*7.6)

    educational attainment and, 81

    health, percentage of people aged 65+ who reported having good to excellent health by, 104(*f*7.1)

    health of older Americans by, 101

    income distribution by, 20

    influenza vaccinations by, 118–119

    labor force participation rates by, 70*t*

living arrangements of population aged 65+ by, 46, 49*f*

of people in residential care, 54

variations of net worth among, 27–28

violent crime rates, by sex, race, Hispanic origin, age of victim, 171*t*

visits to physician offices, hospital outpatient departments, emergency departments by, 110*t*–111*t*

visits to primary care physicians by, 112*t*

Radvansky, Gabriel A., 16

"Raise Awareness" (NCEA), 179–180

Rampell, Catherine, 145

"A Randomized Controlled Trial of Cognitive Training Using a Visual Speed of Processing Intervention in Middle Aged and Older Adults" (Wolinsky et al.), 86

"Rate of Progression of Mild Cognitive Impairment to Dementia—Meta-analysis of 41 Robust Inception Cohort Studies" (Mitchell & Shiri-Feshki), 132–133

RCF. *See* Residential care facility

RCS (Retirement Confidence Survey), 25–26

Reagan, Ronald, 179

Real estate market, 58

"Recent Declines in Chronic Disability in the Elderly U.S. Population: Risk Factors and Future Dynamics" (Manton), 119–120

"Record Unemployment among Older Workers Does Not Keep Them out of the Job Market" (BLS), 67

Redford, Robert, 63

"Reductions in Force: The Supreme Court Escalates the Legal Risks" (Morris), 75

Regret, 132

Reichstadt, Jennifer, 15

Reimbursement, under Medicare, 155–156

Rein, David B., 116

Relatives. *See* Family

Religion, 11

Religion among the Millennials (Pew Forum on Religion and Public Life), 11

Renting

    affordability of, 59–60

    housing costs, percentage of income spent on, 58–59

    sale/leaseback with life tenancy, 59

"Report Card on the Boomers" (Martin), 35

Reporting

    of elder abuse, 173, 176

    of fraud, 170

    of institutional abuse, 178

Research, Alzheimer's, 136

Residential care

    characteristics of people in, 54–55, 54(*f*3.4)

    most common chronic conditions of persons in, 56*f*

    persons in, receiving assistance with activities of daily living, 55*f*

    persons in residential care with Medicaid, by age, 54(*f*3.5)

Residential care facility (RCF)
  definition of, 50
  description of, 49
  institutional abuse, 178–180
"Residential Vacancies and
  Homeownership in the First Quarter
  2013" (U.S. Census Bureau), 58
"Residents Living in Residential Care
  Facilities: United States, 2010" (Caffrey
  et al.), 54–55
Respite care
  description of, 148
  for veterans/their families, 162–163
A Response to the Abuse of Vulnerable
  Adults: The 2000 Survey of State Adult
  Protective Services (Teaster), 175
Retirement
  baby boomers and, 76
  defining/redefining, 63–64
  earnings, test exempt amounts, 39(t2.10)
  older adults in labor force and, 66
  older women in workforce and, 67, 69
  pressure to retire as age discrimination,
    73, 75
  private sector workers with retirement
    plan benefits, 27t
  recasting, 64–65
  volunteerism in, 76–77
  volunteers by age groups, 78t
  volunteers by annual hours volunteered,
    79t
  volunteers by type of organization, 80t
  worker roles and, 65, 66
Retirement communities
  development of, 58
  institutional abuse, 178–180
Retirement Confidence Survey (RCS),
  25–26
Retirement Equity Act, 24
"Retirement Plan Assets" (Butrica), 19–20
Retooling for an Aging America: Building
  the Health Care Workforce (Institute of
  Medicine's Committee on the Future
  Health Care Workforce for Older
  Americans), 145
Reverse dependency, 177
Reverse mortgages, 59
Reynolds, Sandra L., 6
Rheumatoid arthritis, 106
Ride sharing programs, 100
Riker, Gretchen I., 121
"A Rising Tide of Substance Abuse"
  (Friedman), 143
"Risk Evaluation for Alzheimer's Disease
  by Assaying Biomarkers in Plasma
  Using Immunomagnetic Reduction"
  (Yang et al.), 135
Road Scholar, 85
Robert Wood Johnson Foundation, 54
Roberts, Robert E., 15–16
Robinson, Marian, 47

Rooney, Mickey, 174
Roosevelt, Franklin D., 19, 36
Rosalynn Carter Institute for Caregiving, 147
Rugaber, Christopher S., 27–28

S
Saad, Lydia, 87
Safe Driving for Mature Operators, 98–99
Safety, of older drivers, 98–99
Sale/leaseback with life tenancy, 59
Same-sex relationships, 87
Sanders, Alisha, 61
Sandwich generation, 145
Savage, David G., 75
Savings, personal, 25–26
SBA (Small Business Administration), 77
"SCAN Foundation CEO Envisions
  Opportunity for Long-Term Care
  Solutions in New Commission"
  (Chernof), 166
Schiamberg, Lawrence B., 178
Schizophrenia, 141
Schlesinger, Jill, 176
Schuster, Janice Lynch, 150
SCORE, 77
Screening
  for early detection of diseases, 122
  of older drivers, 99
  use of preventive services, 125–126
"Screening for Intimate Partner Violence
  and Abuse of Elderly and Vulnerable
  Adults" (U.S. Preventive Services Task
  Force), 177
"Seasonal Flu Shot: Questions & Answers"
  (CDC), 118–119
Section 202 Supportive Housing for the
  Elderly Act, 61
Sedensky, Matt, 52
Selective attention, 98
"Self-Reported Increased Confusion or
  Memory Loss and Associated Functional
  Difficulties among Adults Aged 60+
  Years—21 States, 2011" (Adams), 132
Sellas, Monique I., 176–177
Senior Corps, 77
"Senior Corps Fact Sheet" (Corporation for
  National and Community Service), 77
Senior Medicare Patrol (SMP) program, 173
Senior Transportation program, 92
SeniorNet, 183
Service Corps of Retired Executives, 77, 183
Service industry, 66
Setter, Stephen M., 121
Seven in 10 Americans Are Very or
  Moderately Religious (Newport), 11
"Seven Stages of Alzheimer's"
  (Alzheimer's Association), 133
"Sex and the Older Woman" (Women's
  Health Watch), 128
Sexuality, in aging, 126–128

Sexually transmitted infections
  HIV, percentage of persons of all ages
    who had ever been tested for, by age
    group/sex, 130f
  in older adults, 128
Shapiro, Peter, 77
Shared housing, 57
Shellenbarger, Sue, 72
Shelters
  increase in sheltered people, 47
  sheltered homeless people, by age,
    geography, 50t
  sheltered people/U.S. population, age
    distribution of, 50f
Sherr, Ian, 86
Shiri-Feshki, Mojtaba, 132–133
Shrestha, Laura B., 64, 145
Sibutramine, 172
Sisko, Andrea, 166
Skilled nursing facility (SNF)
  definition of, 50
  Medicare-covered hospital/skilled
    nursing facility stays per 1,000
    Medicare enrollees aged 65/over in fee-
    for-service, 152f
Small Business Administration (SBA), 77
Smart homes, 60
Smith v. City of Jackson, 75
Smoking
  adults aged 65+ who smoke cigarettes,
    by sex, 126f
  among adults, prevalence of, by age
    group/sex, 128(f7.16)
  decline in, 124
SMP (Senior Medicare Patrol) program, 173
SNF. See Skilled nursing facility
The Social Forces in Later Life: An
  Introduction to Social Gerontology
  (Atchley), 131–132
Social isolation
  as elder abuse cause, 177
  mental illness and, 137
  problem drinking and, 142
  as risk for abuse, 179
Social networks, 85–86
Social programs, 47
Social Security
  Amendments of 1977, 37–38
  benefit amount for worker with
    maximum-taxable earnings, 37t
  benefits, collection of with retirement, 64
  benefits, older adults in labor force
    and, 66
  benefits/beneficiaries, 37
  challenges of, 157–158, 159
  future of, 38–39
  income federal payment amounts,
    39(t2.9)
  long-term solvency, ensuring, 40
  number/average monthly benefit, by type
    of benefit/sex, 38t

older adults receiving, by benefits to total income, 23(f2.4)

overview of, 36

preserving, 39–40

Social Security/Medicare cost as percentage of GDP, 161f

as source of retirement funds, by age, 43(t2.14)

as source of retirement funds, by income, 43(t2.15)

SSI, 38

Social Security Act, 154, 160

Social Security Amendments of 1977, 37–38

Social Security and Medicare Boards of Trustees, 157–158, 160

"Social Security Basic Facts" (SSA), 36–37

Social Services Block Grants, 99

Society

Americans' attitudes on gay relations, by age group, 88(f5.3)

Americans' attitudes on stem cell research, by age group, 88(f5.4)

moral acceptability of social issues, 87(t5.3)

perceptions of old age by, 16–17

social issues, older adults' views on, 87–89

Society for Human Resource Management, 69

Soto, Mauricio, 31

Span, Paula, 128–129, 150

Spouses

intimate partner violence, 177

older adults living with, 45

as perpetrators of elder abuse, 175

See also Marriage

SSA. See U.S. Social Security Administration

SSI. See Supplemental Security Income

"SSI Federally Administered Payments" (SSA), 38

States

assisted living facilities, regulation of, 55

efforts to improve driver safety for older adults, 99

elder financial abuse, combating, 174

institutional abuse, legislation to prevent, 179

nursing home occupancy rates by, 50

nursing homes, residents/occupancy rates of, by state, 51t

populations of older Americans in, 9, 11

Statin drugs, 121–122

"Statins: Are These Cholesterol-Lowering Drugs Right for You?" (Mayo Clinic), 122

Statistical information

absences from work, by age/sex, 72t

adults who had 5+ drinks in 1 day, by age group/sex, 141f

age dependency ratios, 146t

Age Discrimination in Employment Act charges, 74t

aggregate income by source, 24f

Americans' attitudes on gay relations, by age group, 88(f5.3)

Americans' attitudes on stem cell research, by age group, 88(f5.4)

annual retirement earnings test exempt amounts, 39(t2.10)

arthritis, prevalence of, 114f

average annual expenditures/characteristics by age, 32t–34t

baby boomers, contribution to population, 4f

benefit amount for worker with maximum-taxable earnings, 37t

birth rates, by age of mother, 65t

children/older adults as percent of global population, 2f

chronic conditions, percentage of people aged 65+ who reported having, 104(f7.2), 114(t7.7)

chronic conditions, percentage of people aged 65+ who reported having, by sex, race/Hispanic origin, 114(t7.6)

consumer unit expenditures, by expenditure types, 93t

death, leading causes of/numbers of deaths, by age, 113t

death rates for cerebrovascular disease, 125t–126t

death rates for malignant neoplasms, 123t–124t

death rates for motor vehicle-related injuries, 95t–96t

death rates for suicide, 139t–140t

depressive symptoms, people aged 65+ with, by age group/sex, 138f

diagnosed diabetes among adults aged 18/over, prevalence of, 116(f7.8)

difficulties with basic/complex actions, by age, sex, 107f

drinkers, prevalence of types of, 142f

educational attainment of population aged 65+, 82(f5.1)

educational attainment of population aged 65+, by race/Hispanic origin, 82(f5.2)

enrollment in degree-granting institutions, by sex/age, 83t–84t

family households/persons aged 65+ reporting income, 23(f2.3)

foreign-born population by age, 13f

fraud victimization rates by age, 172t

grandparents living with grandchildren, by race, sex, 49t

health, percentage of adults who reported their health as fair or poor, 102t–103t

health, percentage of people aged 65+ who reported having good to excellent health, by age, race/ethnicity, 104(f7.1)

health insurance coverage for persons aged 65+, by type of coverage, 158t–159t

hearing/seeing, trouble with, or no natural teeth, people aged 65/over who reported having, 117t

hearing/seeing, trouble with, or no natural teeth, people aged 65/over who reported having, by sex, 116(f7.9)

HIV, percentage of persons of all ages who had ever been tested for, by age group/sex, 130f

homeownership rates, 58t

homeownership rates, by age of householder, 59t

hospital discharges, days of care, average length of stay, 108t–109t

households by age of householder, size of household, 46t

income, sources of, for population aged 65+, 25f

income distribution of population aged 65+, 22(f2.2)

income from specified sources, by age group, 26t

labor force, median age of, 66t, 67t

labor force participation rates, by age, gender, 68t

labor force participation rates, by age, gender, race/ethnicity, 70t

leading causes of nonfatal injuries, ages 65–85, 96(t6.4)

licensed drivers, by sex/age group, 92t

life expectancy, countries with lowest, 7t

life expectancy at birth/age 65, 43t

life expectancy by country, 6f

living arrangements by age/selected characteristics, 48(t3.2)

living arrangements of persons aged 65/older, 47f

living arrangements of population aged 65/over, by sex, race, Hispanic origin, 49f

median household net worth by race, aged 65+, 28f

medical care, percentage of persons of all ages who failed to obtain needed care due to cost, by age group/sex, 129(f7.19)

medical care, percentage of persons of all ages with usual place to go for, by age group/sex, 129(f7.18)

Medicare, expected decline in workers per retiree to fund, 159f

Medicare enrollees age 65/over, sources of payment for health care services for, by type of service, 155f

Medicare enrollees aged 65/older unable to perform activities of daily living, 105f

Medicare enrollees aged 65/older unable to perform certain physical functions, by sex, 106f

Medicare enrollees aged 65/over residing in selected residential settings, by age group, 166f

Medicare enrollees aged 65/over with functional limitations, by residential setting, 167f

Medicare enrollment, increased, 160f

Medicare-certified providers, 52t

Medicare-covered hospital/skilled nursing facility stays per 1,000 Medicare enrollees aged 65 and over in fee-for-service, 152f

mistreatment of older adults by risk factor, 171f

moral acceptability of social issues, 87(t5.3)

national health expenditures by source of funds, 153t–154t

number/average monthly benefit, by type of benefit/sex, 38t

nursing homes, residents/occupancy rates of, by state, 51t

obese, adults aged 65/older who are, by sex/age group, 119f

obesity among adults, prevalence of, by age group/sex, 127(f7.15)

older adults receiving income by source, 27f

older adults receiving Social Security benefits, by relative importance of benefits to total income, 23(f2.4)

older adults working part time by full-time career job status, percentage of, 71f

older drivers who avoid driving under specific conditions by sex, 96f

osteoporosis pyramid for prevention and treatment, 115f

people aged 65/older, by age group, 5f

people in poverty, by selected characteristics, 29t–30t

personal financial situation, self-assessment of, 87(t5.2)

persons aged 80/older, percentage of, 3f

physical activity, adults aged 18 years/over that met 2008 federal physical activity guidelines for aerobic activity, 128(f7.17)

physical activity, population aged 45/older who engage in regular, 127(f7.14)

population 65/over as percent of total, 14f

population 65/over by race/Hispanic origin, 11t

population 65/over, marital status of by age/sex, 12f

population 65/over, percent increase in, 15f

population 85/over, 12t

population aged 65/over by race/Hispanic origin, 11f

population aged 65/over living alone, by age group/sex, 48(t3.3)

population projections by age/sex, 2010/2030/2060, 10f

population projections by age/sex, 2015–60, 8t–9t

poverty rate by age group, 22(f2.1)

poverty rates by age, 30f

poverty thresholds, by size of family/number of children, 31t

prescription drug costs/sources of payment for noninstitutionalized Medicare enrollees aged 65/older, average annual, 120f

psychological distress, adults who experienced serious, by age group/sex, 132f

residential care, characteristics of people in, 54(f3.4)

residential care, most common chronic conditions of persons in, 56f

residential care, persons in, receiving assistance with activities of daily living, 55f

residential care with Medicaid, persons in, by age, 54(f3.5)

retirement plan benefits, private sector workers with, 27t

sheltered homeless people, by age, geography, 50t

sheltered people/U.S. population, age distribution of, 50f

smoking, adults aged 65/older who smoke cigarettes, by sex, 126f

smoking among adults, prevalence of, by age group/sex, 128(f7.16)

Social Security as source of retirement funds, by age, 43(t2.14)

Social Security as source of retirement funds, by income, 43(t2.15)

Social Security Income federal payment amounts, 39(t2.9)

Social Security/Medicare cost as percentage of GDP, 161f

speeding drivers in fatal crashes, by age/sex, 94t

SSI payments by eligibility category/age/source of payment, 41t

SSI recipients by eligibility category/age, 40t

tenure with current employer for employed workers, median years of, by age, sex, 73t

unemployment, duration of, 21t

unemployment rates by age, 67t

U.S. population by age, projected, 2t

vaccinations against influenza/pneumococcal disease, 118f

veterans aged 65/over who are enrolled in or receiving care from VHA, total number of, 162f

veterans using VA services/main reason for not applying or using benefits, percentage of, 164f

VHA enrollees/outpatient visits, trends in, 163f

violent crime rates, by sex, race, Hispanic origin, and age of victim, 171t

violent victimization by age, 170f

visits to physician offices, hospital outpatient departments, emergency departments, by age, sex, race, 110t–111t

visits to primary care physicians, by age, sex, race, 112t

volunteers by age groups, 78t

volunteers by annual hours volunteered, 79t

volunteers by type of organization, 80t

"Statistics on Parkinson's" (Parkinson's Disease Foundation), 117

"The Status of Baby Boomers' Health in the United States: The Healthiest Generation?" (King et al.), 17

Status of the Social Security and Medicare Programs: A Summary of the 2013 Annual Reports (Social Security and Medicare Boards of Trustees), 160

Steinhauser, Paul, 88–89

Stem cell research, 87

Steptoe, Andrew, 16

Stereotypes
about baby boomers, 17
about older workers, 69, 71–73
older adult, 16–17

Stickney, Laurie, 170

Strategic defaults, 59

Strauss, Robert, 81–82

Stress
alcohol and, 142
of caregivers, 146, 148
as cause of elder abuse, 176
mental health and, 131

Stroke
contribution to dementia, 133
deaths from, 122

"Stroke: Definition" (Mayo Clinic), 122

"Stroke Recovery: Regaining Arm Use" (WebMD), 122

"Study Points to Videogame Popularity among Boomer Women" (Sherr), 86

"Substance Use Disorder among Older Adults in the United States in 2020" (Han et al.), 141

"Successful Aging through Digital Games: Socioemotional Differences between Older Adult Gamers and Non-gamers" (Allaire et al.), 86

Suicide
death rates for, 139t–140t
from depression, 138

Sun City communities, 58

Supercentenarians, 7

Supplemental Security Income (SSI)
overview of, 38
payments by eligibility category/age/source of payment, 41t
PPACA, effects on caregivers, 147

recipients by eligibility category/age, 40*t*
rental housing costs and, 60
Supportive housing, 48–50
"Supreme Court Makes Age Bias Suits Harder to Win" (Savage), 75
"Survey: 1 in 5 Doctors, Nurses Aware They Are Often Dealing with Older Victims of Investment Swindles" (Investor Protection Trust), 178
Sutin, Angelina R., 13
Szalavitz, Maia, 13

T

Tax deductions, 165
Tax Equity and Fiscal Responsibility Act of 1982, 156
Taylor, Chris, 59
Teaster, Pamela B., 175
Technology
aids for older drivers, 99
myth of older workers as technophobes, 72
video games played by older adults, 86
Teeth
oral health problems of older adults, 117
people aged 65/over who reported having no natural teeth, 117*t*, 116(*f7.9*)
Tenure
with current employer for employed workers, median years of, by age, sex, 73*t*
job tenure of older workers, 69, 71
Terkel, Studs, 63
Texas, Sun City communities in, 58
Texting, 86
"That's a Lot of Candles! World's Oldest Person Celebrates His 116th Birthday and Becomes Longest Living Man EVER" (McDermott & Davies), 7–8
Thomas, William, 53–54
"3 Generations under One Roof" (Abrahms), 46
"3 Ways Low Interest Rates Hurt Seniors" (Moeller), 28
3M Co., 76
"3M Settles Age-Discrimination Suit for up to $12M" (Associated Press), 76
"Time not on the Side of Older Americans in Housing Slump" (Miller), 58
Time Trends in Poverty for Older Americans between 2001–2009 (Banerjee), 36
Tobacco. *See* Smoking
"Toll-Like Receptor 4 Stimulation with the Detoxified Ligand Monophosphoryl Lipid A Improves Alzheimer's Disease-Related Pathology" (Michaud et al.), 136
Toossi, Mitra, 69
"Transdermal Patch for Alzheimer's Gets Caregiver Thumbs-Up: Delivery Method May Reduce Caregiver Stress, Enhance Patient Response" (Martinez-Lage et al.), 136

Transportation
alternatives to driving, 99
needs of older adults, meeting, 100
types of for nondrivers, 99–100
See also Drivers, older adult
Transportation Equity Act for the 21st Century, 99
Transportation initiatives, 92–93
Transportation-Disadvantaged Populations: Federal Coordination Efforts Could Be Further Strengthened (GAO), 92, 99
Transportation-Disadvantaged Seniors: Efforts to Enhance Senior Mobility Could Benefit from Additional Guidance and Information (GAO), 100
Trawinski, Lori A., 28
Treatment
of alcohol misuse, 142–143
for Alzheimer's, 136
for anxiety disorder, 140
of cancer, 122
for depression, 138
of Parkinson's disease, 117
"*TREM2* Variants in Alzheimer's Disease" (Guerreiro et al.), 134
"Trends in the Utilization of VA Programs and Services" (U.S. Department of Veterans Affairs), 161
Trotsky, Leon, 1
Truman, Jennifer L., 169
Tweeting, 86
"Two-fifths of U.S. adults care for sick, elderly relatives" (Fox), 147
The 2011 Annual Homeless Assessment Report to Congress (HUD's Office of Community Planning and Development), 47
2011 Behavioral Risk Factor Surveillance System, 132
2012 Annual Report (Road Scholar), 85
2012 National Health Interview Survey (CDC), 126, 128, 131
2013 Alzheimer's Disease Facts and Figures (Alzheimer's Association), 133, 134, 136–137
The 2013 Annual Report of the Board of Trustees of the Federal Old-Age and Survivors Insurance and Federal Disability Insurance Trust Funds (Federal Old-Age and Survivors Insurance & Federal Disability Insurance Trust Funds), 39, 158
2013 Annual Report of the Boards of Trustees of the Federal Hospital Insurance and Federal Supplementary Medical Insurance Trust Funds (Boards of Trustees of the Federal Hospital Insurance and Federal Supplementary Medical Insurance Trust Funds), 155
"2013 Best Employers for Workers over 50 Announced" (AARP), 69
"2013 Community College Fast Facts" (American Association of Community Colleges), 81

The 2013 Retirement Confidence Survey: Perceived Savings Needs Outpace Reality for Many (Helman et al.), 25
"2013 SSI and Spousal Impoverishment Standards" (CMS), 165
Type 2 diabetes, 111

U

"The Underside of the Silver Tsunami— Older Adults and Mental Health Care" (Bartels & Naslund), 137
Unemployment
among older adults, 67
duration of, 21*t*
rates by age, 67*t*
United Methodist Senior Services of Mississippi, 54
United Nations' Department of Economic and Social Affairs, 6
United States, 1–3
See also Population
"United States of Health Care" (Rampell), 145
United We Ride, 92
University of Manchester, 60
Urban Institute, 31
Urinary incontinence, 111–113
Urological Diseases in America 2012 (National Institutes of Health), 111–112
Urry, Heather L., 14
U.S. Bureau of Justice Statistics, 169–170
U.S. Bureau of Labor Statistics (BLS)
on age of U.S. labor force, 66–67
"Employment Projections—2010–20," 145
on older workers, 69
on rates for home care, 163
on unemployment among older adults, 19
on volunteerism, 77
"Who Has Benefits in Private Industry in 2012?," 23
U.S. Census Bureau
on age of college students, 64
contact information, 183
on fertility rates during baby boom, 3
on grandparents living with grandchildren, 46
on homeownership rates, 58
on increase in number of older adults, 1
on living arrangements of older people, 45
on numbers of centenarians in U.S., 7
U.S. Department of Agriculture (USDA), 28–30
U.S. Department of Health and Human Services (HHS), 99, 165
U.S. Department of Housing and Urban Development (HUD), 47, 61
U.S. Department of Transportation (DOT), 93
U.S. Department of Veterans Affairs (VA)
contact information, 183
veterans' benefits, 161–163

U.S. Food and Drug Administration (FDA)
  prevention of fraud, 170
  prevention of health fraud, 172
U.S. Government Accountability Office (GAO)
  on alternative transportation for older adults, 100
  elder abuse, national strategy to combat, 174
  on states' efforts to improve safety for older drivers, 99
  Transportation-Disadvantaged Populations, 92, 99
U.S. Housing Act of 1937, 60
"U.S. Inquiry Said to Focus on California Pension Fund" (Walsh), 25
U.S. military. *See* Veterans' benefits
U.S. Preventive Services Task Force, 177
U.S. Securities and Exchange Commission, 25
U.S. Social Security Administration (SSA)
  Annual Statistical Supplement to the Social Security Bulletin, 37
  contact information, 183
  description of, 19
  on growth of pensions among older adults, 24
  "Social Security Basic Facts," 36–37
  "SSI Federally Administered Payments," 38
U.S. Supreme Court, 75–76
U.S. Surgeon General
  on alcohol/prescription drug misuse in older adults, 141
  on anxiety disorder, 140
  on mental disorders, 137–138
  on schizophrenia in older adults, 141
USDA (U.S. Department of Agriculture), 28–30
"Using Group-Based Latent Class Transition Models to Analyze Chronic Disability Data from the National Long-Term Care Survey 1984–2004" (White & Erosheva), 120

V

VA. *See* U.S. Department of Veterans Affairs
Vaccinations
  adults aged 65/older who reported having been vaccinated against influenza and pneumococcal disease, by race/Hispanic origin, 118*f*
  for influenza, 118–119
  for pneumonia, 119
"Variant TREM2 as Risk Factor for Alzheimer's Disease" (Neumann & Daly), 134
Velkoff, Victoria A., 1
Veterans' benefits
  overview of, 161–163

veterans aged 65/over who are enrolled in or receiving care from VHA, total number of, 162*f*
veterans using VA services/main reason for not applying or using benefits, percentage of, 164*f*
VHA enrollees and outpatient visits, trends in, 163*f*
Veterans Health Administration (VHA)
  enrollees and outpatient visits, trends in, 163*f*
  veterans aged 65/over who are enrolled in or receiving care from VHA, total number of, 162*f*
  veterans receiving health care from, 162
  veterans using VA services/main reason for not applying or using benefits, percentage of, 164*f*
Veterans Millennium Health Care and Benefits Act of 1999, 161–162
VHA. *See* Veterans Health Administration
Viagra, 128
Victimization
  fraud victimization rates by age, 172*t*
  rates of violent victimizations, 169
  violent crime rates, by sex, race, Hispanic origin, and age of victim, 171*t*
  violent victimization by age, 170*f*
Video games, 86
Vincent, Grayson K., 1
"Violation of Ethical Principles in Institutional Care for Older People" (Buzgová & Ivanová), 178
Vision
  changes with aging, 115
  hearing/seeing, trouble with, or no natural teeth, people aged 65 and over who reported having, by selected characteristics, 117*t*
  hearing/seeing, trouble with, or no natural teeth, people aged 65 and over who reported having, by sex, 116(*f*7.9)
  major eye diseases, 115–117
"Vision Problems in the U.S." (Prevent Blindness America), 116, 117
VISTA (Volunteers in Service to America), 77
"A Volunteer Army of Caregivers" (Span), 150
Volunteering in the United States—2012 (BLS), 77
Volunteerism
  in retirement, 76–77
  volunteer caregivers, 150
  volunteers by age groups/other characteristics, 78*t*
  volunteers by annual hours volunteered/other characteristics, 79*t*
  volunteers by type of organization/other selected characteristics, 80*t*
Volunteers in Service to America (VISTA), 77
Voting, 89

W

Wadia, Zorast, 24
Walsh, Mary Williams, 25
Ward, Alex, 131
Wardle, Jane, 16
Wealth, 31
WebMD, 122
Weight, 124
  See also Obesity
Weinberger, Mary Beth, 7
Weingarten, Ken, 165
Wetherell, Julie L., 140
"What Happens When You Walk Away from Your Home?" (Taylor), 59
"What Is Elder Abuse?" (NCPEA), 169
"What Is Long-Term Care Insurance?" (U.S. Department of Health and Human Services), 165
"What Is Osteoporosis?" (National Osteoporosis Foundation), 107
"What Is Rheumatoid Arthritis?" (Arthritis Foundation), 106
"What Is the Donut Hole?" (Blum), 152
"What We Do" (AARP), 89
White, Toby A., 120
Whites
  general health of older Americans, 101
  income of, 20
  living arrangements of older people, 46
  racial/ethnic diversity of older population, 9
"Who Has Benefits in Private Industry in 2012?" (BLS), 23
"Who We Are" (American Geriatrics Society), 128
WHO (World Health Organization), 7
"Why Innovators Get Better with Age" (Agan), 72–73
Wilke, Joy, 87
"Will Premiums for Medicare Advantage Plans Go up in 2013?" (CMS), 156
WISER (Women's Institute for a Secure Retirement), 150
"With Age Comes Happiness" (Szalavitz), 13
Wolinsky, Fredric D., 86
Women. *See* Females; Gender
Women in the Labor Force: A Databook (BLS), 67, 69
Women's Health Watch, 128
Women's Institute for a Secure Retirement (WISER), 150
Work
  absences from work, by age/sex, 72*t*
  age discrimination, 73, 75–76
  Age Discrimination in Employment Act charges, 74*t*
  aging labor force, 66–67, 69
  birth rates, by age of mother, 65*t*
  changing roles, 65–66

contributions of older Americans, 63

labor force, median age of, 66*t*, 67*t*

labor force participation rates, by age, gender, 68*t*

labor force participation rates, by age, gender, race/ethnicity, 70*t*

older adults working part time by full-time career job status, percentage of, 71*f*

older workers, myths/stereotypes about, 69, 71–73

recasting, 64–65

retirement, baby boomers and, 76

retirement, defining/redefining, 63–64

retirement, volunteerism in, 76–77

tenure with current employer for employed workers, median years of, by age, sex, 73*t*

unemployment rates by age, 67*t*

volunteers by age groups/other characteristics, 78*t*

volunteers by annual hours volunteered/ other characteristics, 79*t*

volunteers by type of organization/other selected characteristics, 80*t*

"Worker Debra Moreno Wins $193,000 in Age Discrimination Lawsuit" (Fastenberg), 75–76

Workers. *See* Older workers

Working: People Talk about What They Do All Day and How They Feel about What They Do (Terkel), 63

The World Factbook: United States (CIA)

on fertility rate, 3

on global life expectancy, 6

on U.S. life expectancy, 5

World Health Organization (WHO), 7

World Population Prospects: The 2012 Revision—Key Findings and Advance Tables (United Nations' Department of Economic and Social Affairs), 6

Wright, Stuart, 173

X

Xu, Jingping, 15–16

Y

Yaffe, Kristine, 133

Yang, Shieh-Yueh, 135

Young Americans Most Positive about Direction of Finances (Newport & Himelfarb), 86–87

Young, Katherine, 160–161

Young-old adults

definition of, 5

numbers living in U.S., 6–7